Praise for

THE DUCHESS COUNTESS

"Terrifically entertaining: if you liked *Bridgerton*, you'll love this."
—*The Week* (UK), "Book of the Week"

"A rollicking read. [Ostler] tells Elizabeth's story with admirable style and gusto, and clearly finds her heroine irresistible."
—*The Sunday Times* (London)

"This is a scintillating story superbly told. . . . [Ostler] has a remarkable ability to demonstrate her deep knowledge of the period without being boring or a show-off. She packs every paragraph with eye-opening detail, making you feel as though you're living in the eighteenth century, but never veers from the central story of a woman trying to hold herself together in that vicious society while the men did as they pleased."
—*The Times* (London)

"In this sparkling galivant through the eighteenth century . . . Ostler has her finger firmly on the pulse of the Georgian aristocracy, and has bracingly revived its extravagance and absurdity. . . . The book also does an excellent job of shining a light on issues with thought-provoking modern relevance, highlighting the troubling power of the press and the glaring double standards that ground women to a halt while barely slowing down their brothers."
—*BBC History Magazine*

"The book's spritely, wry tone is a pleasure to read throughout. In the early chapters, it felt cinematic almost to a fault: a quantity of costume and other visual detail that would make a historical adviser redundant on any screen adaptation."

—*TLS*

"Ably capturing [Chudleigh's] singular character, Ostler displays her deep knowledge of the era, smoothly melding history and biography. An indomitable subject finds a biographer worthy of her."

—*Kirkus Reviews*

"Elizabeth Chudleigh was a glamorous celebrity in eighteenth-century Europe. . . . Her life bordered on the surreal, and this scrupulously documented biography packs in period details, historical context, and lots of juicy gossip. Determined *Bridgerton* fans will not be disappointed."

—*Library Journal*

"What a superb, gripping, decadent, colorful biography that brings an extraordinary woman and a whole world blazingly to life. Filled new research, written so elegantly with empathy, passion, and cool analysis, *The Duchess Countess* is an unforgettable, unputdownable read that seems both modern and historical, utterly relevant today—featuring a cast of characters from Marie Antoinette to Catherine the Great, but also the life of a woman who is both adventuress and victim, who achieved vast wealth and great notoriety, becoming one of Europe's most famous women and the star of the most scandalous court case of the century."

—Simon Sebag Montefiore, author of *New York Times* bestseller *The Romanovs*

"Before there was Becky Sharp, there was Elizabeth Chudleigh, Duchess of Kingston and the greatest social grifter of them all. She lives once again, thanks to Catherine Ostler's captivating biography. Definitely dangerous to know, pretty bad, and quite possibly mad, there's no better fun to be had than a ringside seat at the tragi-comic circus that was her life."

—Amanda Foreman, author of *Georgiana: Duchess of Devonshire*

"Although this book is a beautifully written and deeply researched life of one of the most remarkable women of the eighteenth century, it is also a scintillating portrait of an age. Since Elizabeth Chudleigh knew so many of Europe's most talented, fascinating and important people—as well as its most dissipated rakes—the book is populated by as wide a galère of personalities as one is ever likely to meet in a biography. The author has ransacked every archive and visited every place connected with her subject from London to Saint Petersburg, and the result is the first ever fair-minded estimation of one of the great adventuresses of history. Funny, intelligent, witty, profound, and on occasion moving, this book sets a new standard for eighteenth-century biography writing."

—Andrew Roberts, author of *Churchill: Walking with Destiny*

"Fascinating. Magnificent. Sensitively told. Complex, capricious, beautiful, and boldly ambitious, Elizabeth Chudleigh was also one of the most reviled women in Georgian England. In resurrecting her tale, Catherine Ostler allows the Duchess of Kingston to emerge from the prejudices of the past like a resplendent phoenix."

—Hallie Rubenhold, author of *The Scandalous Lady W* and *Mistress of My Fate*

THE
DUCHESS COUNTESS

THE DUCHESS
COUNTESS

The Woman Who Scandalized
Eighteenth-Century London

CATHERINE OSTLER

ATRIA PAPERBACK
New York   London   Toronto   Sydney   New Delhi

ATRIA
PAPERBACK

An Imprint of Simon & Schuster, Inc.
1230 Avenue of the Americas
New York, NY 10020

Copyright © 2021 by Catherine Ostler
Originally published in Great Britain in 2021 by Simon & Schuster UK Ltd.

First Atria Paperback edition November 2022

ATRIA PAPERBACK and colophon are trademarks of Simon & Schuster, Inc.

For information about special discounts for bulk purchases,
please contact Simon & Schuster Special Sales at 1-866-506-1949 or
business@simonandschuster.com.

The Simon & Schuster Speakers Bureau can bring authors to your
live event. For more information or to book an event, contact the
Simon & Schuster Speakers Bureau at 1-866-248-3049 or visit our website at
www.simonspeakers.com.

Manufactured in the United States of America

1 3 5 7 9 10 8 6 4 2

Library of Congress Cataloging-in-Publication Data has been applied for.

ISBN 978-1-9821-7973-1
ISBN 978-1-9821-7974-8 (pbk)
ISBN 978-1-9821-7975-5 (ebook)

To Clemmie, Nathaniel, and Angelica

Contents

NOTES ON THE TEXT

DATES

In the middle of Elizabeth's story—on September 2, 1752—the calendar changed from the Old Style (Julian) to the New Style (Gregorian), an act introduced by the 4th Earl of Chesterfield to bring Britain into line with most of Western Europe. The act dictated that the new year began on January 1 rather than on March 25 (Lady Day), and meant that eleven days were lost.

Dates before September 2, 1752, are given in the Old Style (not adjusted for the eleven days), but for simplicity's sake I have adapted them to the years that we recognize, that is, January–March is made part of the subsequent, rather than the original, year. Dates in Russia—the only country that adhered to the Julian Calendar (until 1918)—are sometimes given in both.

In the process of the calendar shift, some people stuck to their old-style birthdays, and others added eleven days. Elizabeth minimized the problem of an altered birthdate by subtracting five years from her age, rather than quibbling over a few days.

MONEY

If we take an easy-to-multiply figure for the conversion of £1 in 1744 to today's value,* we could use 200, since according to the Bank of England, £1 in 1744 was equivalent to £250.72 in 2019; and the

---

* I have chosen the year Elizabeth first drew a salary as maid of honour as the year of comparison.

Economic History Association found £1 in 1744 to be equivalent
to £167.20 in 2018.[1] There was minimal inflation for most of the
century, so as an approximate measurement this works for the whole
of Elizabeth's lifespan. There were 12 pence in a shilling, 20 shillings
in a pound, and 21 shillings in a guinea. A crown was five shillings.

Britain was more financially divided than it is now. Only 3 percent of families had an annual income of £300 or more in the
mid-century; the average income in 1759–60 has been assessed as
around £45 a year.[2] Twenty pounds a year—an upper servant's
wage—was considered necessary for survival, although many servants had bed and board included.[3] Housing and servant labor came
cheap; consumables, including food, were high-cost. London, as
ever, was more expensive than the rest of the country.

It has been estimated that to "live like a gentleman" in 1734—to
be able to afford theater tickets, books, a carriage—would require
£500 a year.[4] A baronet might have an income of £1,500–£4,000; a
peer £2,500–£40,000.[5] Elizabeth's salary of £200, therefore, was an
enormous amount compared to the average wage, but restrictive for
someone of no independent means trying to live an upper-class life.

CONTEMPORARY QUOTES

I have generally modernized old spelling, capitalization, and punc-
tuation for ease of reading.

THE
DUCHESS COUNTESS

Hanover

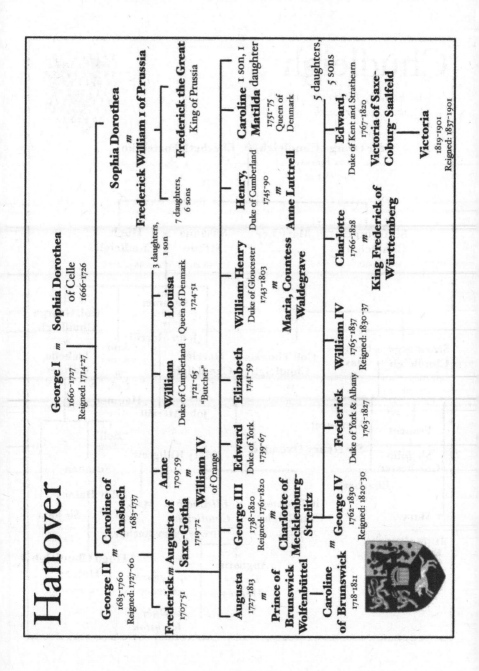

George I *m* **Sophia Dorothea**
1660-1727   of Celle
Reigned: 1714-27   1666-1726

George II *m* **Caroline of Ansbach**
1683-1760   1683-1737
Reigned: 1727-60

Sophia Dorothea *m* **Frederick William I of Prussia**

Frederick *m* **Augusta of Saxe-Gotha**
1707-51   1719-72

Anne *m* **William IV**
1709-59   of Orange

William
Duke of Cumberland
1721-65
"Butcher"

Louisa
Queen of Denmark
1724-51

3 daughters,
1 son

Frederick the Great
King of Prussia

Augusta *m* **Prince of Brunswick Wolfenbüttel**
1727-1813

George III *m* **Charlotte of Mecklenburg-Strelitz**
1738-1820
Reigned: 1761-1820

Edward
Duke of York
1739-67

Elizabeth
1741-59

William Henry
Duke of Gloucester
1743-1803
m
Maria, Countess Waldegrave

Henry,
Duke of Cumberland
1745-90
m
Anne Luttrell

Caroline 1 son, 1 **Matilda daughter**
1751-75
Queen of
Denmark

Caroline of Brunswick *m* **George IV**
1718-1821   1762-1830
Reigned: 1820-30

Frederick
Duke of York & Albany
1763-1827

William IV
1765-1837
Reigned: 1830-37

Charlotte
1766-1828
m
King Frederick of Württemberg

Edward,
Duke of Kent and Strathearn
1767-1820
m
Victoria of Saxe-Coburg-Saalfeld

5 daughters, 5 sons

Victoria
1819-1901
Reigned: 1837-1901

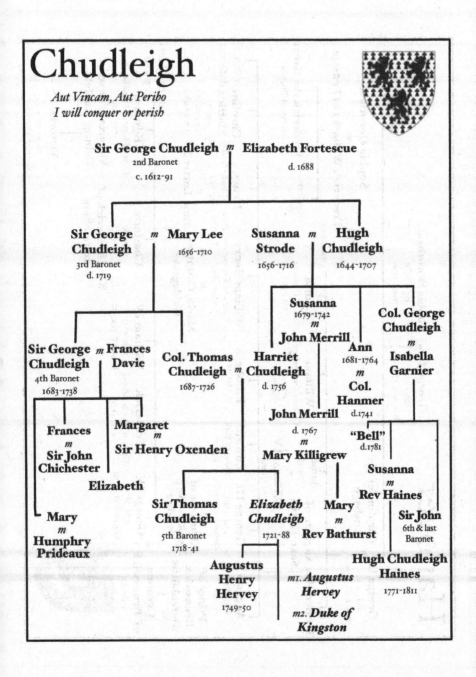

Chudleigh

Aut Vincam, Aut Peribo
I will conquer or perish

Sir George Chudleigh *m* **Elizabeth Fortescue**
2nd Baronet
c. 1612-91
d. 1688

Sir George Chudleigh *m* **Mary Lee**
3rd Baronet
d. 1719
1656-1710

Susanna Strode *m* **Hugh Chudleigh**
1656-1716
1644-1707

Susanna
1679-1742
m
John Merrill

Col. George Chudleigh
m
Isabella Garnier

Sir George Chudleigh *m* **Frances Davie**
4th Baronet
1683-1738

Col. Thomas Chudleigh
1687-1726

Harriet Chudleigh *m*
d. 1756

Ann
1681-1764
m
Col. Hanmer
d.1741

Frances
m
Sir John Chichester

Margaret
m
Sir Henry Oxenden

John Merrill
d. 1767
m
Mary Killigrew

"Bell"
d.1781

Elizabeth

Susanna
m
Rev Haines

Mary
m
Humphry Prideaux

Sir Thomas Chudleigh
5th Baronet
1718-41

Elizabeth Chudleigh
1721-88

Mary
m
Rev Bathurst

Sir John
6th & last
Baronet

Augustus Henry Hervey
1749-50

m1. Augustus Hervey

m2. Duke of Kingston

Hugh Chudleigh Haines
1771-1811

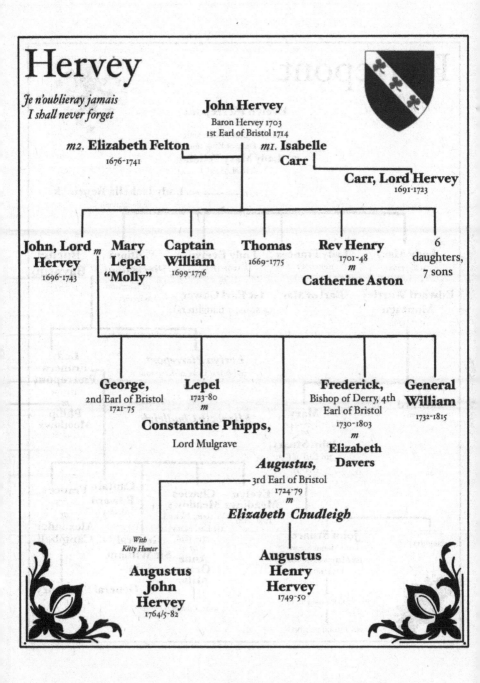

Hervey

Je n'oublieray jamais
I shall never forget

John Hervey
Baron Hervey 1703
1st Earl of Bristol 1714

m2. Elizabeth Felton
1676-1741

m1. Isabelle Carr

Carr, Lord Hervey
1691-1723

John, Lord Hervey *m* **Mary Lepel "Molly"**
1696-1743

Captain William
1699-1776

Thomas
1669-1775

Rev Henry
1701-48
m
Catherine Aston

6 daughters, 7 sons

George,
2nd Earl of Bristol
1721-75

Lepel
1723-80
m
Constantine Phipps,
Lord Mulgrave

Frederick,
Bishop of Derry, 4th
Earl of Bristol
1730-1803
m
Elizabeth Davers

General William
1732-1815

Augustus,
3rd Earl of Bristol
1724-79
m
Elizabeth Chudleigh

With Kitty Hunter

Augustus John Hervey
1764/5-82

Augustus Henry Hervey
1749-50

Pierrepont

Pie Repone te
Trust in providence

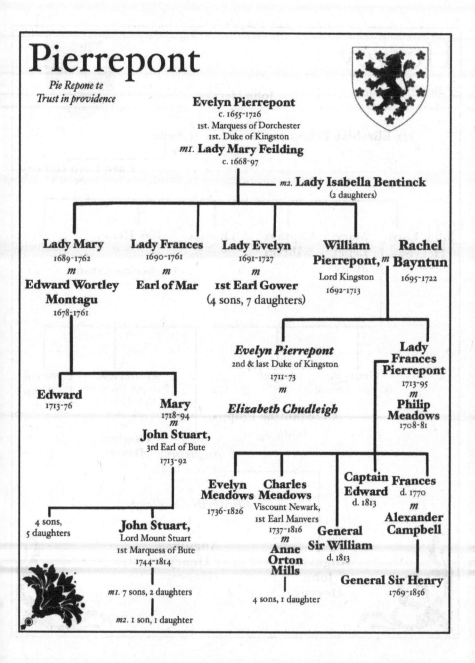

Evelyn Pierrepont
c. 1655-1726
1st. Marquess of Dorchester
1st. Duke of Kingston

m1. **Lady Mary Feilding**
c. 1668-97

m2. **Lady Isabella Bentinck**
(2 daughters)

Lady Mary	**Lady Frances**	**Lady Evelyn**	**William**	**Rachel**
1689-1762	1690-1761	1691-1727	**Pierrepont,** *m*	**Bayntun**
m	*m*	*m*	Lord Kingston	1695-1722
Edward Wortley Montagu	**Earl of Mar**	**1st Earl Gower**	1692-1713	
1678-1761		(4 sons, 7 daughters)		

Evelyn Pierrepont
2nd & last Duke of Kingston
1711-73
m

Elizabeth Chudleigh

Lady Frances Pierrepont
1713-95
m
Philip Meadows
1708-81

Edward
1713-76

Mary
1718-94
m
John Stuart,
3rd Earl of Bute
1713-92

Evelyn Meadows
1736-1826

Charles Meadows
Viscount Newark,
1st Earl Manvers
1737-1816
m
Anne Orton Mills

Captain Edward
d. 1813

Frances
d. 1770
m
Alexander Campbell

4 sons,
5 daughters

John Stuart,
Lord Mount Stuart
1st Marquess of Bute
1744-1814

General Sir William
d. 1813

General Sir Henry
1769-1856

m1. 7 sons, 2 daughters

m2. 1 son, 1 daughter

4 sons, 1 daughter

INTRODUCTION

In April 1776, the world held its breath.

The determination of George Washington's band of American revolutionaries was being tested as they prepared for battle to defend New York: would they cede to the British yoke or strike out for independence and unleash the dominance, for the coming centuries, of what was to become the United States of America?

These decisive days were the last time that George III, the Hanoverian British king, could have conceivably held on to his American empire. The British peace commissioner, Admiral Howe, still hoped "words rather than bullets"[1] might solve the crisis when he arrived on Long Island.

Yet in London, the drama was—incredibly—elsewhere. Among the House of Lords, the judiciary, the press, and the literati, all eyes were on a woman in black, charged with bigamy.

The trial saw the queen, two future kings, Queen Victoria's father, Georgiana, Duchess of Devonshire, James Boswell, Horace Walpole, and most of the bishops, peers, and peeresses in the land in Westminster Hall, either as jury or spectator. Half of the Cabinet was there, the secretary of war a witness.

The woman accused was christened Elizabeth Chudleigh, but when she was talked about in the coffeehouses, written about in the penny papers, gossiped about by diarists, and sketched by cartoonists, they more often nicknamed her the Duchess-Countess.

Now we see it more clearly: the distracted incompetence of a tired colonial power engaged in the displacement activity of persecuting an errant, aristocratic woman. But the story of the Duchess-Countess casts other, more human, shafts of light onto this period of history, in which the seeds of so much of our culture were sown: the struggle of a forward-thinking woman in a society undergoing the birth pangs of modernity; the rise of journalism, an incipient always-on form of social media, and its occasionally willing collaborator, the celebrity; the way in which Elizabeth used soft power and the art of public relations, before either had those names.

The Georgian patriarchy had law, land, money, and church on their side: alternative forms of influence had to be found for a woman who wanted to travel, build, and mix as if she were man or monarch.

Duchess, countess, courtier, socialite, hostess, mariner, property developer, celebrity, vodka distiller, press manipulator, arts patron, bigamist: Elizabeth Chudleigh was the great antiheroine of the Georgian era. Her story reads like a dark fairy tale, Cinderella gone hideously, publicly wrong with all the force of a Hogarthian twist, with too many princes and glass slippers left smashed in her wake.

The Hon. Elizabeth Chudleigh, Elizabeth Hervey, Duchess of Kingston, Countess of Bristol—by the time she went on trial, no one knew what to call her—started her life in the public sphere as a maid of honour to the Princess of Wales at the Georgian court, married one man in secret and denied it, only to wed another. She was convicted of bigamy and then pursued across the world by her second husband's relations, the newspapers, and the ill-wishes of her enemies. After her court humiliation, rather than choosing to live out the rest of her days in hermetic retirement or atonement, she went on a floating odyssey from Rome to St. Petersburg, befriending popes, princes, and tsarinas. She became one of the three most talked-about women in Europe, alongside Marie Antoinette and Catherine the Great. The Hermitage in St. Petersburg still possesses the paintings and the giant but delicate musical chandelier she took there to persuade the court to embrace her, taking advantage of the vibrant Anglomania that gripped Imperial Russia at the time.

Tracing the story from her childhood at the Royal Hospital in Chelsea, to rural Devon, the London court, the grandeur of the Dukeries and, later, France and Russia, one encounters the Hanoverian world in all its elegance and acidity, but also the tale of a woman bridling against history. In her publicity-hungry, wanderlustful, outrageously under- or overdressed self, Elizabeth Chudleigh was an anarchic woman, out of step with her own time.

Given her notoriety, it is not surprising that numerous writers were fascinated by her. The twists and turns of her progress, the whole cautionary tale, lived on after her death. Decades later, Thackeray drew on Elizabeth for inspiration in his fiction—for calculating yet irresistible Becky Sharp in Vanity Fair, chilly beauty Beatrix Esmond in Esmond, rackety much-married Baroness Bernstein in the sequel The Virginians, and the bigamous Blanche Clavering in Pendennis.

Dickens's Household Words[2] and Virginia Woolf's essays[3] both contain anecdotes from her life. Coleridge, bewailing his own faux naivety in a letter to Wordsworth, described himself as resembling "the Duchess of Kingston, who masqueraded in the character of 'Eve before the Fall' in flesh-coloured Silk."[4] She even inspired a hoax novel—I, Libertine—on American radio in the 1950s.*

Accounts of her life, her trial, even her will were published within days of her death. In a merging of fact and fiction, she was damned by the popular press as a grotesque, sexually heartless, with a lust for diamonds; objectified as that sexist cliché, the aging femme fatale. In death, as in life, the bile and condemnation continued.

The purpose of biography is to understand rather than justify, but it is impossible to ignore the fact that Elizabeth was put on trial all over again after her death by her startlingly unsympathetic early biographers. She was obviously flawed and complex—by turns brave, reckless, insecure, loving, greedy, resilient, depressive—a woman totally unwilling to accept the female status of underdog or to hand over all the power, the glory, and the adventures of life to men.

My intention is not to exonerate Elizabeth, but to retread the path of her life, and re-examine her trajectory in the context of her era,

---

* It became a real novel, I, Libertine, by the imaginary author Frederick R. Ewing (in reality, Theodore Sturgeon), after broadcaster Jean Shepherd's radio hoax on the bestseller lists. His listeners went into bookshops and ordered the nonexistent title, propelling it onto the bestseller lists. As a result, the actual book—a bodice-ripping yarn about an eighteenth-century roué, based on Elizabeth's life—was written.

and thereby take her out of caricature and back to womanhood. To reappraise a woman who became that contemporary phenomenon: the criticized celebrity, loathed and envied in an age when women were seen through the filter of a misogynistic culture, noted for virtue or lack of it. To restore her as a woman with the burden of tragedy and great loss; with the pressure of secrets; who fell in love, but made a mistake; who showed physical endurance and personal courage at the courts of Europe. A woman who could show herself to be trusting, generous, forgiving, although she was a restless soul, impulsive, hotheaded, and her overwhelming priority was her own survival at any cost.

From her birth in the fractious early years of the Hanoverian ascent, in the aftermath of the South Sea Bubble, to her trial as America rebelled and her death in exile in Paris among the sounds of fireworks, the first stirrings of the French Revolution, her life provides an insight into her seismic age. She became an early European; one of the first women to travel and settle in various corners of the world by necessity, but also by instinct and inclination.

During that period, many of our habits—news, novels, gossip, fashion, coffee, consumerism—took hold. War overturned the world order: Russia became a superpower, the Jacobite threat was extinguished, and although America was lost, the battle for the British Empire was increasingly won. In romantic matters there was one rule for men—including a succession of promiscuous kings and prime ministers—and another for women. As marriage changed from a matter of the head to a matter for the heart, the shift bred much confusion along the way.

Through a contemporary lens, many of the issues that surround Elizabeth would be well understood: a struggle with mental health, for female empowerment, for civilized divorce laws, the cost of fame-seeking. Annual sales of British newspapers had risen from 2.5 million in 1713 to 12.6 million in 1775,[5] the year before her trial, and as a fashionable woman connected to royalty, accused of a crime, she could not have been a better subject. But she toyed with publications herself like any controlling celebrity today, paying numerous publicists, lawyers, and editors to defend her. Her story was read in coffee shops and drawing rooms from St. Petersburg to Rome.

Elizabeth used her beauty, wit, and connections to further her own position. She tried to remove the obstacles in a woman's way: the lack of income, the lack of male relatives, the entrapment of an unwise marriage. For women of Elizabeth's ilk, born into gentry but not well-off, the only respectable salvation, bar a convent or becoming a governess—and Elizabeth was palpably unsuited to both—was marriage. Women were dollhouse figures, expected to lead small, decorative, confined lives traipsing in a carriage between town and country, drawing room and ballroom. Elizabeth Chudleigh shamelessly disregarded both the role and its constraints.

Piecing her story together is an imprecise enterprise. Even while she lived, fiction gnawed on truth. Thousands of words were written about her trial, yet it lacked clarity and fairness; cross-examination was somewhat random, palpable corruption and witness inconsistencies ignored. However, it does expose the female plight then, that even someone as privileged and well-connected as Elizabeth was condemned to remain in her first unhappy marriage by the law and by an unforgiving society.

In the eighteenth-century oligarchy, the lack of social mobility, the reliance on inheritance, and the status that came with it snared those hoping for legacies into endless legal quests. Those with no prospects were left hopelessly insecure. Most particularly, women, who could so easily (like some associates of Elizabeth's) become destitute. Downward social mobility was easy—the Duchess-Countess was no stranger to the pawnshop. Women of all classes looked to men for support.

If the Kingston case served to expose anything, it was the trap in which eighteenth-century women were placed. Elizabeth was the manifestation of women's humiliating, claustrophobic lack of autonomy and their lack of independence.

In this, she was just like America.

PROLOGUE

Before dawn on the morning of April 15, 1776, a handsome middle-aged woman nervously prepares herself with the help of her maid. She sits in the most private of spaces in her Knightsbridge house, her intricate dressing room with its fine needlework furniture and crimson silk upholstery. Corset, whalebones, and finally a bombazine dress of black silk, à la polonaise, swagged and draped over an underskirt. A hairdresser covers her hair with a black hood. Pale and imperious, like Mary, Queen of Scots going to her execution, she has scarcely recovered from a nervous illness of two months' standing, and is attended by a chaplain, a physician, and an apothecary—and by the Gentleman Usher of the Black Rod, Sir Francis Molyneux, who is responsible for preventing her from flight.

Somewhere en route, she discreetly swaps from a sedan chair to the Duke of Newcastle's carriage on the way to his house in Palace Yard, Westminster. The crowds have lined the streets, waving and calling out. For weeks now, the papers and the coffeehouses have been full of her story: the woman they have read about since girl-hood when she was the most lively, most beautiful maid of honour at the court of the Prince of Wales now stands trial for bigamy.

As she dismounts, she meets the men who have agreed to stand bail for her: the Duke of Newcastle, Bristol magnate James Laroche, and Lord Mount Stuart, son of the former prime minister, Lord Bute. Yet she is essentially alone, with no children, siblings, parents, or relations of any kind to support her since the death of her husband the Duke of Kingston three years earlier. There are few she can trust.

Will the Duchess of Kingston, Countess of Bristol, the Honourable Elizabeth Chudleigh, be found guilty of bigamy, that most scandalous of crimes?

Just before eleven o'clock, an impatient hush of expectation falls upon the ancient cavern of Westminster Hall, the flag-stoned, oak-roofed chamber that since the time of William Rufus has seen royal feasts, coronation banquets, and Charles I, Sir Thomas More, and Guy Fawkes condemned to their deaths. This spring morning is a modish affair—a trial with the feeling of a gala day. Diamonds catch sharp flashes of sunlight, pouring in shafts through the high windows, and compete with the lush silk finery of the ladies and the sumptuous velvet and ermine of the peers. There is a procession of sergeants, judges, bishops, peers; Black Rod, the Lord High Steward; teams of lawyers for each side; journalists covering the trial. High in the rafters sits Queen Charlotte with some of her brood, including two future kings, George IV and William IV, as well as Prince Frederick, Prince Edward,* and the Princess Royal. The queen is two weeks from giving birth to her eleventh child, but insists on being there nonetheless. She is joined elsewhere in the crowd by oligarchy and intelligentsia, from Boswell to the king's brother, the Duke of Cumberland, European royalty such as the Duke of Württemberg, and every peeress and coffeehouse aficionado in the city connected or cunning enough to get a ticket from one of the peers allotted them. An audience of thousands, complete with programs, are ready for the performance, some drinking coffee bought through the window from stalls outside, some solemn, some jovial; others pay a guinea just to look through the window.

"Oyez oyez oyez!" calls the Serjeant at Arms, as he raps his rod upon the floor and makes the proclamation for silence.

There are stage whispers, shuffling, coughing. Outside, the carriages stop rattling and the rustling and shouting die down. A vanishing scent of incense hangs in the air.

All pause for the incongruous, diminutive pale figure in thick black mourning fabric who takes leaden steps forward to meet her

---

* Prince Edward, then age eight, the future Duke of Kent and Strathearn, father of Queen Victoria.

fate. Like a sepulchral bride, she is followed by two ghostly attendants in white satin, who stand close to her, anxious and unhappy.

Here is Elizabeth Chudleigh whose story, the roots of her ambition and her attitude to men, began many years before, in her childhood on the banks of the river in Chelsea.

I

COUNTESS

CHAPTER ONE

A Town of Palaces

In the first quarter of the eighteenth century, the London metropolis sprawls from the tar-caked wharves of Wapping in the east to the walls of Hyde Park in the west: the greatest, richest, most rapidly expanding trading city in the world.

St. Paul's dominates the skyline in the City, as brick and stone rise from the ashes of the Great Fire. Mayfair is a neoclassical building site—the finest architectural period in England's history is underway. Terraces of houses, church spires with glinting weather vanes are interspersed with swathes of parkland and open fields along the city's artery, the salmon-rich silent highway, the Thames, which teems with sailing boats, pleasure boats, merchant ships, barges, small craft, and yachts.

A visitor in the summer of 1717 might witness the royal party, the new Hanoverian King George I and his attendants, on their stately barge, followed by an orchestra of fifty on another, playing Handel's *Water Music*. They board at Whitechapel, pass marshes and heathland, and disembark at Chelsea, two miles upstream. The banks shine with beauty on either side of the river; it compares only to the river "Tyber . . . nothing in the world can imitate it."[1]

Daniel Defoe calls London a "Great and Monstrous Thing,"[2] but Chelsea is a village outside the city, an airy "town of palaces"[3] where the river breeze shakes the boughs of the fertile gardens, none so spacious as those of the Royal Hospital.[4] Prosperous townspeople head for Chelsea on Sundays for fresh, clean air. Here there are market gardens supplying fruit and vegetables for the town, alongside the graceful houses of noble families.[5] At the hospital, the grounds are designed in French formal style, front and back; two L-shaped canals lined with swan houses flow from the river up the sweeping gardens. At the bank of the Thames, there is a terrace, pavilions, and steps down to the water. On the south side lies open country—trees, fields, homesteads, and windmills, like a scene painted by a Dutch old master. The river can only be crossed by ferry here and sheep are driven through the streets from local farms.

The austere redbrick splendor of Wren's home for old soldiers contains a gracious three-story, high-ceilinged apartment in a river-facing wing. In 1726, this forms the light-filled London home of the lieutenant governor, Colonel Thomas Chudleigh, his wife Harriet, and the two children who have survived infancy: dutiful, seven-year-old Thomas and the angelic-looking, adored five-year-old Elizabeth. The hospital estate is their playground: they run along stone-flagged corridors and through colonnades of Doric columns under the inscription "IN SUBSIDIUM ET LEVAMEN, EMERITORUM SENIO, BELLOQUE FRACTORUM"* towards the chapel and the dining hall, past the gilded statue of founder Charles II cast as a Roman emperor, near-blinding when the sun hits it, and the royal portraits, across lawns lined with limes and chestnut trees, orchards, and their family kitchen garden, all the way down to the river.

The Chudleigh children grow up accustomed to a degree of stately grandeur and plenty. They have several playmates, the children of hospital staff—the secretary, the clerk of works, the physician[6]—and they live alongside the elderly majority, 400 old or wounded soldiers. Chelsea, like its inspiration, Louis XIV's Hôtel des Invalides, is an architectural celebration of both military courage and a king's benevolence. It is said that in England, the hospitals resemble palaces, and the palaces resemble prisons.[7] Although the men sleep in small wooden berths and the stairs have shallow risers to aid their superannuated frames, prayers are said in the chapel beneath a glorious Resurrection by Sebastiano Ricci, and the Great Hall is fit for a medieval king. Governor Charles Churchill and Lt. Governor Chudleigh dine on a high table on a dais and the pensioners eat beneath

---

* "For the succour and relief of veterans, broken by age and war."

them at long tables. Flags of battlefield triumph and portraits of princes line the walls, most prominently, Antonio Verrio's mural of Charles II, crowned by the winged figure of Victory.

Within the institution live a chaplain, a porter, a baker, a brewer, an apothecary, a physician, a wardrobe keeper, linen-women, a sexton, cooks, butlers, gardeners, matrons, housekeepers, an organist, a barber, a treasurer, a canal keeper. The clerk of works oversees the building.[8] Most senior of all the residents are the paymaster—in 1720, it was Robert Walpole, who became prime minister[9] the following year—the governor, and the lieutenant governor.

As the children are aware as they weave their way through the faltering steps of the pensioners, with pats and smiles, the hospital is also a garrison, the men subject to military discipline: chapel twice a day, a roll call, and gate-closing time at 10 P.M. Some men—they are all men[10]—stand sentinel. A drumbeat calls them to the hall for lunch, between eleven and twelve. Food is served on pewter dishes; tablecloths reach to the floor, to double up as napkins; mugs of beer are poured from leather "jacks" or jugs, and the undercroft below the hall contains a brewery with six weeks' supply.[11] Pensioners wear variations of crimson cloth coats and tricorne hats, depending on rank and regiment. It is such a picturesque scene that tourists such as a young Benjamin Franklin* come to watch them from the gallery.

It is an idyllic place to grow up. The Chudleigh children's earliest years are spent among the gracious architecture of this strange palace of military heroes, a compressed version of the strict hierarchy of Georgian society itself, with their father, a man of high status, respected by all.

Constant entertainment is provided by the river, which represents the chaotic world on the edge of the estate, a globe on the fringe of their consciousness. By the hospital stairs† on the river, numbered, lightweight boats, painted red or green, wait on the water ready to take passengers: "oars" have two boatmen;

---

* In 1725, when the founding father was a trainee printer in London. He swam back down the Thames from Chelsea to Blackfriars.
† Stairs: a flight of steps down to the water, which led to a stop for watermen to pick up passengers at high tide. Often situated next to a pub.

"scullers" one. When a person approaches, the boatmen, dressed in velvet caps and red or green doublets, run to meet them, calling out "lustily 'oars, oars!' or 'Sculler, sculler!'" When the passenger chooses a boat, the others "unite in abusive language at the offending boatman."[12]

The hospital is bookended by plutocrats' villas, one the house of Lord Ranelagh, the late, corrupt hospital treasurer and army paymaster, to Swift, "the vainest old fool I ever saw."[13] Now lived in by his widow, its garden is known as the most resplendent in England, a "paradise"[14] to Defoe. One day Elizabeth will frequent the same spot when it becomes the Ranelagh pleasure gardens, a lamplit land of nocturnal delight.

On the other side is the house of the Walpole family, with its octagonal riverside summerhouse topped with a golden pineapple, its Vanbrugh orangery, and its grotto. The Princess of Wales (the future queen, Caroline) and the court are frequent visitors, along with the *ton*,[15] the fashionable set, such as the peripatetic writer Lady Mary Wortley Montagu,[16] of whom we will hear more. Proximity to power is part of the climate.

Politics is discussed constantly in Chelsea. Writer, Whig Richard Steele (Col. Chudleigh subscribed to his entire *Spectator* when it was published in 1721) and scientist philosopher Isaac Newton meet at Don Saltero's, the whimsical coffeehouse on nearby Cheyne Walk, where the cabinet of curiosities includes attractions such as a nun's whip, "the Pope's infallible candle," and a bat with four ears.*

The Botanick Gardens nearby with their cedar trees, the first in England, now belong to Saltero's regular physician and naturalist Hans Sloane, whose collection of rare artifacts will one day become the British Museum.[17]

A child in this environment learns the importance of the monarch, military might, and courage. Young Elizabeth Chudleigh, with her

---

* Also: "21 Petrified crab from China; 27 The Worm that eats into the Piles in Holland; 31 A piece of rotten wood not to be consumed by fire; 67 A pair of Nun's stockings; 76 A little Lobster; 102 A curious snuffbox, adorn'd with ivory figures; 119 the Hand of an Egyptian Mummy; 135 An Ostrich's Leg; 142 A Cat of Mountain; 302 A Whale's pizzle." From *A Catalogue of the Rarities to be seen at Don Saltero's Coffee-House in Chelsea* (1729).

expressive blue eyes, fair wavy hair, and the peachy plump cheeks inherited from her father, is armed with natural beauty and bravado. She has an intrepid, unconquerable spirit worthy of the military herself. She wears a simple bodice-and-skirt dress of pale calico, cap and apron, having graduated out of the padded infant "pudding" hat that protected her while she learned to walk. Her constant companion, her brother Thomas, now in breeches, wants to be a soldier like his father and the old war chroniclers who surround him with their stories. The Chelsea veterans of the Duke of Marlborough's decisive battles against the French in Flanders and Germany[18] dote on the children and their playmates, Horace Walpole, the prime minister's son,[19] diarist to be, a delicate child of eight, and Horace Mann, future diplomat in Florence, and his four younger siblings.

The hospital is a place of ritual, celebration, and pride. The children munch their way through the Ceremony of the Cheese at Christmas, where donated cheeses are cut and distributed; Restoration Day in May, when all wear oak leaves to commemorate Charles II hiding in the oak tree from Cromwell's troops; and the Festival dinner for the reigning monarch, George I, when pensioners fire their muskets. They visit the Old Church, whose lonely spire dominates the river view on the north bank, and feast on piping-hot sugary buns from the nearby Chelsea Bun House, "a Zephyr in taste! As fragrant as honey,"[20] which has royal custom and a cheerful queue.

As an indulged youngest child, Elizabeth is used to being the center of attention and is always at ease, fearless around men, especially, we can assume, military men.

Fifty years later, at her trial, Elizabeth proudly described the Chudleighs as "ancient, not ignoble"; the women "distinguished for their virtue," the men "for their valour."[21] Family was always important to Elizabeth, partly because she was a Chudleigh twice over: her parents were first cousins. The name itself was of profound significance to her. By the time she died, she had convinced two monarchs— Louis XVI and Catherine the Great—to let her rename two estates in countries hundreds of miles apart Chudleigh, and attempted to coerce heirs into changing their names to that of her waning tribe.

Some of the brave Chudleighs were as reckless as they were adventurous. Although one naval officer "distinguished himself" against the Spanish Armada, another, John "Chidley," a privateer who had sailed with his Devon kinsman Walter Raleigh in the search for El Dorado,[22] sold his estate for an expedition and died in the Strait of Magellan, losing his investors' money along with his own. Others were sheriffs, lawyers, and men who—a notable family characteristic—made advantageous marriages. In the English Civil War, a George Chudleigh raised the family to a baronetcy when he swapped allegiance from Parliament to king.[23]

Less was said of other ancestors, such as Elizabeth's maternal great-grandfather Sir Richard Strode, an MP from the Devon gentry, "a man of unquiet spirit and contentious nature"[24] who was incarcerated in Fleet Prison for debt and became mentally unstable. Or of Henry VIII's wily minister Thomas Cromwell, eventually executed for treason, of whom she was also a direct descendant. Ambition sometimes blighted reason.

Many centuries earlier, marriage had brought into the family her father's childhood home, a woodland manor house and estate near Higher Ashton, in a river valley ten miles from Exeter. Elizabeth's grandfather Sir George, 3rd Baronet, was a man of books and a landowner. Yet for all the male forbears, Elizabeth Chudleigh's most remarkable ancestor was a woman. Her grandmother Lady Mary Chudleigh was an early pioneer of independent female thought, in spite of the fact that she lived an isolated life among the remote rural backwaters of Devon, a week's carriage ride from the cultural center of the metropolis. She was a proto-feminist composer of lyrics, verses, essays, tragedies, satires, and operas. Sloe-eyed, dark-haired, witty, and opinionated, she was a friend of Dryden,[25] who asked her opinion on his works. Her best-known poem, "The Ladies' Defense," is a riposte in rhyming couplets to a sermon on marriage, "The Bride-Woman's Counsellor,"* in which women, who have "weaker capacities to learn than men" were advised that "the love of a husband very much does depend on the obedience of

---

* The sermon was made by the Rev. John Sprint at a wedding in Dorset, on May 11, 1699.

a wife." Mary wrote in retort: "Wife and servant are the same/ But only differ in the name."

Mary was one of only two published female poets in the first decade of the eighteenth century.[26] Her family were Puritan thinkers and she corresponded with a circle—the poet Elizabeth Thomas, "the first English feminist"[27] Mary Astell, the Rev. John Norris— who believed in women's intellectual autonomy.

She achieved her writerly success in spite of ill health and much bereavement: of her six children, only two, George and Elizabeth's father, Thomas, survived into adulthood. A devout Anglican and royalist, she dedicated one book to the Electress Sophia of Hanover, the cerebral woman who would have succeeded Queen Anne if she had lived three months longer, and another poem to Anne herself, after the death of her son, the Duke of Gloucester, at the age of eleven. Mary's "Ode to the young Duke of Gloucester" was written from one heartbroken mother to another:

> His Face was Charming, and his Make Divine
> As if in him assembl'd did combine
> The num'rous Graces of his Royal Line.

Lady Mary was much admired—one contemporary writer said she was the "Glory of her Sex and the Ornament of her Country."[28] Her sons must have been brought up with the peculiar idea that women's mental prowess, their dignity, was somehow equal to men's, their emotional life something to be expressed, not buried.

The elder George would lead a quietly opulent upper-class life in the country, while the younger Thomas, Elizabeth's father, fought his way to a position as an accomplished courtier and soldier. He was born in 1687, a year before the Glorious Revolution that secured the Protestant succession. As his brother was the heir, his father bought him an army commission when he was a child.[29] In May 1702, the expansion of the War of the Spanish Succession meant that the new queen, Anne, had to raise an army.[30] Charles II, the Hapsburg King of Spain, had died childless and as his closest heirs were either an Austrian Hapsburg or a French Bourbon, the succession threatened the delicate balance of power in Europe. The English

Parliament was united in wanting to thwart French supremacy. In December, when he had just turned fifteen, Thomas became second lieutenant in a new regiment of marines,[31] and was promoted to captain five years later.[32]

The War of the Spanish Succession saw over a decade of murderous belligerence waged across Europe with resolute John Churchill, 1st Duke of Marlborough, at the fore. Chudleigh was among that daunting "scarlet caterpillar, upon which all eyes were once fixed, [that] began to crawl steadfastly day by day across the map of Europe, dragging the whole war with it."[33] He served "with reputation"[34] in the march through Flanders, "from the ocean to the Danube," passing impregnable lines, laying siege to fortresses, and prompting surrenders under Marlborough.

The Chudleighs were related to the Churchills, another Devon family: John Churchill's uncle had married a Strode, Harriet's mother's line, and they therefore considered each other cousins. Marlborough's nephew, Charles Churchill, was governor of the Royal Hospital when Elizabeth was born. The duke was England's great Royal military hero, and even after her husband's death in 1722, the duchess was its alternative queen. With her boundless influence, one contemporary branded her "the evil genius of the whole state."[35]

The connection was a tangible advantage. Marlborough wrote to Robert Walpole, then secretary of war, in 1709 angling for him to ask the queen to promote Chudleigh,[36] who was rewarded for his "meritorious conduct" in November 1711 with a lieutenant colonelcy,[37] and in November 1712, days before his marriage, the queen gave him the colonelcy of his own regiment, Chudleigh's Regiment of Foot. This regiment was a colorful and dashing sight, the uniform a "tri-corned hat, a full-skirted scarlet coat, turned up with brightest yellow facings, a scarlet waistcoat, white trimmings and white gaiters."[38]

Army life meant periods of intense, heroic activity interspersed with expensive, alcohol-sodden inaction. After war ended in 1713, the regiment dispersed, to be reformed by Colonel Chudleigh in the summer of 1715, when George I arrived from Hanover and the Old

Pretender* reignited his mission to reclaim the crown for the Catholics.[39] In the autumn of 1719, Elizabeth's father fought in Spain in the Vigo Expedition, with his regiment seizing seven ships, settlements, and arms waiting for the Pretender. They returned victorious and the King of Spain pressed for peace.

On January 14, 1715, while his regiment was out of service, Chudleigh also became the lieutenant governor of the Royal Hospital at Chelsea, a role that included intermittently supervising the Plymouth garrison.† At twenty-seven, he was young for the position, but the appointment was in the gift of the queen, with whom he had ties through the Marlboroughs and his parents-in-law.[40] The lieutenant governor was responsible for the day-to-day running of the Royal Hospital. In this nepotistic era, it meant he had grace-and-favor accommodation and two salaries, and one when his regiment was not required. Chudleigh was companionable, hearty, and fond of brandy.[41] A 1715 portrait shows a charmingly chubby-cheeked, affable-looking fellow with bountiful curly hair, a double chin, an epicurean dressed in full armor topped off with a lace cravat. He exudes bonhomie, a quality his daughter would inherit.

He had not looked far for a bride: in 1712, he married his first cousin Henrietta Chudleigh, known as Harriet. She was a child of the court: her father, Hugh Chudleigh, younger brother of Thomas's father,[42] had been Marlborough's adjutant in the army, and later became Queen Anne's commissioner of the Master of the Horse,[43] and her mother Susannah was the courtier who alerted the Duchess of Marlborough—herself a former maid of honour[44]—to the plight of their mutual relation, Abigail Hill,[45] who then supplanted the duchess as royal favorite.[46] The Marlborough allegiance was of such importance to the family that in 1717, when Colonel Thomas and Harriet Chudleigh entertained the duke and duchess at dinner at Chelsea, they fanfared the occasion in the press.[47]

---

* The "Old Pretender," James Francis Edward Stuart, son of James II of England and VII of Scotland: the first of the fifty-seven Catholics who could claim the British throne by bloodline ahead of George I.
† In times of conflict, the Chelsea Corps of Invalids was drafted back into the army to defend a garrison, in order to free up the regiment for foreign service.

As Whig followers of Marlborough, the wider Chudleigh family was staunchly loyal to the Hanovers. Both of Harriet's brothers, George and John—the latter, a former page to Anne's husband, had once killed a man in a duel[48]—and her brother-in-law William Hanmer were in the same regiment, the aristocratic Coldstream Guards, under the Earl of Scarborough. All became colonels.

Yet as the family rose, Thomas and Harriet's financial affairs remained stubbornly precarious. In 1719, Colonel Chudleigh's father died and left him £1,000 and the minor Hall estate in Devon.[49] The bulk of the family fortune went to the elder son, George. Harriet had had a middling £1,500 dowry, and she and her husband were not well-off by the standards of their class.[50] And they—along with the whole country—were in for a brutal shock. In 1720, the South Sea Company, established to provide funds for the national debt built up by warfare, had become a bubble that was about to burst. Neither the hospital itself, which had invested in the stock,[51] nor Elizabeth's parents would escape the feverish gold rush unscathed. Colonel Chudleigh had sunk his entire cash inheritance into the South Sea Company.[52]

Like her mother-in-law, Harriet was weighed down by numerous pregnancies and the devastation of infant mortality. Four of her children died within months of their birth. Only two survived: Thomas, born June 9, 1718,* and Elizabeth, born March 8, 1721, baptized on March 27, at St. Martin-in-the-Fields. After the South Sea Bubble, the two Chudleigh children would have to make their own way.

Advancement in eighteenth-century England meant reliance on networks and tribal support. The Chudleighs were royalists, Whigs, military, a Chelsea family, and a Devonian one; an interdependent web of connected families, kin, and allegiances.

Such a matrix would prove crucial. Elizabeth's father sold his army commission in 1723—either through ill health, financial need, or a desire never to leave Chelsea and his children again. Three years later, in the cold, damp spring of 1726, he fell sick at Chelsea.

---

* Baptized June 23, 1718, at Chelsea.

In spite of having Chelsea's whole medical team at his disposal, he could not be saved.

He died, on April 14, at the age of thirty-eight.

Before Elizabeth's sixth birthday, the blithe surroundings of her riverside infancy were gone, all security and serenity lost. Nothing was to be quite straightforward for Elizabeth ever again.

CHAPTER TWO

SUCCESSION

Colonel Chudleigh was buried in the cemetery at the Royal Hospital, where his simple gravestone still stands. His widow and children were evicted from the quiet grace-and-favor apartment with its view of the vibrant river through the sash windows.

Within days, the hospital demanded an inventory to check what the next lieutenant governor might receive. Colonel Chudleigh's belongings—"rich Genoa damask, plate, his Berlin and Chariot"*— were auctioned off in a Covent Garden coffeehouse.[1] His wake made a gothic scene: the custom was to line the walls with black fabric as the body lay in state, by the light of tapers, while claret, ale, and cake were distributed to the mourners.

The newly widowed Mrs. Chudleigh and her two children moved to a noisy rented house in a Maddox Street stable yard, Mayfair, then a building site on the edge of the fashionable but unfinished Hanover Square, named after the new royal line and populated by Whigs and military men. There, they had to take in a female lodger to boost their income. The grieving mother leaned on her wider family: her brother George, his wife Isabella, daughter of Chelsea's apothecary, Isaac Garnier, and their four daughters lived around the corner in Great George Street. Their second daughter Isabella, known as Bell, two years younger than Elizabeth, would become her closest companion.

---

* A Berlin was a covered, suspended carriage used for longer distances; a chariot was a lighter vehicle with back seats only.

As their mother mourned, her two children had to adjust to being evicted from their airy, ample Chelsea home and into a new urban reality. Taken away from home, gardens, playmates, elderly friends, and, worst of all, their father, they would not have been too young to sense their slippage in having to live with a stranger, cooped up in the city. Such lessened circumstances might easily have wounded their mother's pride, and no doubt they would have felt her shame. But inevitably, they became streetwise before their time, negotiating traffic, traders, strangers: they were striding distance from Piccadilly, then an open road with a few houses on it, and St. James's Street, with its coffeehouses and "mug houses," and their swinging signs with names like "The Blue Boar."

Unlike the sleepy Royal Hospital, this was London proper: dusty, muddy, loud, and brightly lit, teeming with life, crime, and trade. Incessant building work and coaches caused circling dust. Lanterns and globes of light, "the little Suns of the Night,"[2] one at least outside every house, burned in the dark. Traveling by coach was a bone-shaking experience as the road was so rough, though the pavements were smooth. Mud was everywhere—passersby got dirty fast, if not knocked down by a speedy sedan chair. In every street, there was a watchman, carrying a stick and a lantern, who called out the state of the weather and the hour on the hour, checked if doors were fastened, and found the owner if they were not. Footpads,* often armed with pistols, and pickpockets jostled for business, as Harriet Chudleigh experienced firsthand. A story of her chutzpah in this circumstance survives her. One night in 1723 she had been returning to the hospital on the notoriously dangerous, unlit country lane that led from London to Chelsea, "late at night, with two of the old pensioners as patrol, walking behind the coach. She was asleep and was awakened by three footpads, one of whom held a pistol at her breast. She coolly put her head out of the other window and said 'Fire!' The patrol fired and shot the robber."[3] "What a heroine" was Horace Walpole's verdict. If caught, pickpockets were dunked in the nearest fountain or well until nearly drowned. Serial offenders were sent to America to be

---

* Highwaymen on foot rather than horseback.

slaves. Horse thieves, or those who broke into houses, were shown no mercy and hanged.

Alongside such rough justice there were signs of London's growing sophistication: a penny post; insurance for fire; and plentiful water in the houses or street pumps, only used for cleaning, not drinking, because everyone, high and low, drank beer (small beer, porter, or ale) or wine, mostly port, sometimes claret, or punch, made of brandy, rum, or arak, and was therefore semi-drunk most of the time. Otherwise there was coffee, tea, or chocolate, often with liquor, consumed in a coffeehouse, alongside the newspapers, all Englishmen being "great newsmongers."[4] In 1726 there were already a dozen different papers, divided down party lines. London was full of building noise and the cries of street traders selling their wares in the morning: fish from baskets, oysters, nuts, "sweet china oranges,"* crabs, cherries, gingerbread, shrimps, cheesecakes, apples. Those selling pies, muffins, and milk from tubs and pails offered good value. There were other more exotic sights too—snake charmers, jugglers, puppeteers with theaters on their backs. But in summer there was a pervasive stink—the stench of the drains, even in Mayfair. No wonder anyone who could escape London in the summer went to the country.

A Swiss traveler[5] observed that London houses—such as the one now inhabited by Elizabeth and her family—were built quickly, but with taste: a "moat" was built on the earth level in front of a basement, and edged onto the street with an iron railing, containing servants' quarters and a kitchen; the coal was kept in the cellar; walls were lined with wood to prevent damp, but hangings (such as tapestries) were rare because the coal smoke ruined them. Nearby in St. James's Park, there were wild geese, ducks, and tame deer that ate out of one's hand, and avenues of trees to promenade between at dusk.

Rent books show that in 1730 Mrs. Chudleigh was disputing the rise in the poor rate (the levy to help the local poor)—she was probably struggling financially—and by 1733 she had moved nearer to her two married sisters in the new Golden Square further east.

---

* A familiar street cry.

By this time, she was paying rates for the Hall estate in Devon, and spent time there, too, although she rented out parts of that estate to boost her income. For a while, she let Hall to her cousin, George Gibbon, the lieutenant governor of Plymouth town and citadel.

The money was found to send Thomas Chudleigh to Eton, which was socially elite, yet, in relative terms, much cheaper than it is now—the fees then were about a tenth of today's.[6] Pupils were the sons of the nobility, who had to be nominated to attend. Alongside lessons in Latin and Greek, maths, geography, and cricket, Thomas was being carefully raised to restore the family fortune.

Elizabeth had only one possible route to success: to win herself a husband. The aim was to train her to impress the people of fashion, the beau monde, and thereby find herself a secure marriage. All her learning was to that end. Elizabeth's education amounted to an informal hotchpotch of upper-class fare conducted at home: written and spoken French, Latin, geography, dancing, music, needlework, and how to run a household. And yet, however ad hoc the setup of female education, as Elizabeth's grandmother Mary showed, women could be highly educated, through reading, conversation, and parental encouragement.

Elizabeth was no scholarly autodidact in the mold of her grandmother, yet her education was taken more seriously than most. Although her ambitions were worldly, she was remarkably well-equipped by the standards of the day. Girls such as Elizabeth were encouraged to be pleasing conversationalists, and this was regarded as an accomplishment in itself, an important aspect of politeness. There were governesses or tutors for music or dancing—in Elizabeth's case, probably with her cousins in George Street, or in Devon. Elizabeth could converse with anyone on paper or in person. Even those she fell out with called her a "great wit."[7] She could speak and write in French. Of her education, and character, it was later assumed that "She did not get much instruction in her youth, or rather she did not take that which was offered her, for although masters of all kinds were employed for her education, the vivacity of her disposition prevented her from being an attentive pupil."[8]

According to her early biographers, Elizabeth spent much of her time growing up on the Hall estate in Devon. There, according to one unkind account, she contracted smallpox at the age of fifteen, yet survived unscarred; and had her first love affair shortly afterwards. The nameless swain, "gallant, devoted, handsome," died of the same illness in a matter of days; the "Adonis died and she went to bed early but by breakfast was fine."[9] By the time that was written, the idea that she was callous was carved in stone.

In the West Country, Elizabeth stayed not only at Hall, in the green, wooded Teign Valley, but also at the houses of her paternal uncle George, first at Place Barton, then at nearby, hilltop Haldon; and at Chalmington, the seat her maternal uncle had inherited from his mother, just over the border into Dorset. Hall was by far the most unassuming. Just outside Plymouth, it is still a setting that seems to exist outside of time: now a slate-roofed farmhouse, then a manor, it was a "pleasure house" among the wild country in South Hams, between the edge of Dartmoor and the sea, a remote spot where the skies are vast, the hedgerows are high, and birds of prey soar above the landscape. "This Fairy Land . . . will always be a friendly spot,"[10] wrote Elizabeth of Hall.

In the country, Elizabeth learned the pursuits for which she showed enthusiasm as an adult: gardening, fishing, seafaring. Many years later there was an imaginative version of her youth:[11] "Reared at the country seat of her father, her childhood passed happily and innocently, and to this period she ever looked back with pleasure . . . The peasantry on her father's estate said that she was *charmed*, that the beasts would follow her without being called, and that no person could know her without loving her."

But in Devon, there must have been a growing awareness for Elizabeth of her "poor-relation" status: her cousins were enjoying a reverse trajectory with a satisfying rise in the magnificence of their surroundings. Elizabeth's uncle Sir George Chudleigh abandoned the old family seat at Place Barton and let it fall to ruin. With the immense new wealth of his heiress wife,[12] and his own inheritance, he built the palatial Haldon House nearby, on the top of Haldon Hill. It was an intimidating edifice, a colossus to the model and scale of London's Buckingham House. Centuries later, when Haldon came tumbling down, its trappings, such as the giant wooden doors, were so grandiose that they were bought by William Randolph Hearst for

Hearst Castle. Hall was a pauper to Haldon's prince. Sir George's four daughters, Elizabeth's first cousins, had vast dowries. It has been said that the combination of poverty and expectations of gentility invariably produce ambition. Like a Jane Austen heroine a few decades later, Elizabeth was in that awkward spot for a woman of the time: a penniless, dowerless girl from the gentry. The likely reaction for such a child was to rebalance the scales in their own favor.

For all Haldon's magnificence, fate intervened with its own plans: Sir George Chudleigh died in 1738 before it was completed.* His death meant that Elizabeth's brother Thomas inherited the baronetcy and, by the terms of Sir George's will, much of the family estate. With this, his title, and his Eton education, he would rebuild the family and restore the Chudleigh name. It was time for a fresh generation of Chudleighs to prosper.

In 1737, at eighteen, Thomas put on the same dazzling scarlet uniform his father had worn, and took up the army commission he had been bought as a baby. He enrolled as a lieutenant in his father's old regiment of foot, the 34th,[13] now led by Lord James Cavendish. (One can imagine Harriet and Elizabeth's reaction on seeing him in it for the first time.) In 1740, when Thomas Chudleigh appeared in the army list, the British had allied with Austria in the War of the Austrian Succession, defending Maria Theresa's right to succeed her father as the Hapsburg monarch, against the French and the Spanish who wanted to thwart Hapsburg power.

The inheritance from his uncle was not forthcoming, however, and by 1740, in his bid to restore the family fortune as befitted his title, Thomas was involved in a legal battle with Sir George's widow Frances. He argued, as the male heir, that the executors had not correctly fulfilled Sir George's wishes; she argued that it was a Davie, not Chudleigh, estate, and hers to leave to her daughters.[14]

In the spring of 1741, before he was sent to Aix-la-Chapelle to fight, Thomas Chudleigh wrote a short will,[15] leaving everything to

---

* In the same year, Col. George Chudleigh, Elizabeth's maternal uncle, Mayfair neighbor, and father of her friend Bell, died too, "seized with a pain in the stomach having been playing cricket and bowls that day," leaving eight children without a father, and his wife expecting a ninth child. Harriet's brother John had already died in 1729 of consumption.

his "dear mother" and saying that if he should die abroad, he should be buried late in the evening, as privately as possible, in a very plain coffin, with no pall, and "no marks left for anybody to know the spot of ground where I am deposited." Perhaps he wanted to save his mother money if he died. Mother and sister Elizabeth must have waved him off in trepidation, hoping for him to emulate his father, and achieve promotion and glory.

It was not to be. Only a few weeks later, in June 1741, at the age of twenty-two, Sir Thomas Chudleigh, 5th Baronet, died on duty, and with him his dreams of rebuilding the Chudleighs. Harriet and Elizabeth felt the loss of income, the loss of hope, and the grief. He was indeed buried late in the evening privately, at Chelsea Old Church, on Sunday July 12. There is no mark of him anywhere.

It was devastating enough that, at twenty, Elizabeth had lost her only sibling, but in a practical sense, her chances of fortune and happiness were diminished, too. In the absence of a father, a brother would have helped broker his sister's marriage. Thomas Chudleigh, with his Eton education, his familiarity with the legal profession, and military courage, would undoubtedly have had an influence on her. We do not know the details of their relationship—perhaps she would not have listened to him anyway—but, certainly, now there was no close male relative to handle the financial negotiations that came with upper- and upper-middle-class marriage, or to steer Elizabeth away from disastrous choices.

By now, part of Elizabeth's romantic pattern was set: she would be drawn to military men like her father and brother. Yet in this she would have to find a way to flourish without her confidant.

In 1743, when Elizabeth was twenty-two, she had a stroke of luck. Her uncle's closest friend was the man who is sometimes said to have had the shortest term of any British prime minister,[*] William Pulteney, 1st Earl of Bath, charismatic, rich, effortlessly the finest orator in the Commons, and Walpole's bitterest rival in the Whig

---

[*] George II asked Pulteney to form a ministry when Henry Pelham resigned on February 10, 1746; Pulteney could not persuade anyone to serve him. Pelham therefore resumed office after "forty-eight hours, three quarters, eleven minutes and seven seconds." Pulteney was therefore appointed, but never served in office.

party. He had just lost his own daughter, Anna Maria, at the age of fourteen. As leader of the "Patriot Whigs,"* he was at the heart of the court of the Prince of Wales, probably its most influential figure bar the future king himself, and his own loss made him sympathize with Elizabeth's predicament.

He had a role in mind for the vivacious girl, and he was in just the position, and frame of mind, to make a recommendation—one that would elevate her from rural obscurity to the center of the British Empire.

---

* Dissidents within the Whig party.

CHAPTER THREE

THE HOUSE OF HANOVER

Befriending the politician William Pulteney was Elizabeth's first brush with power on her own account, and she quickly learned the advantages such connections could bestow. A later, fanciful version of events claimed that he had come across a teenage Elizabeth "breaking in a horse" on Dartmoor and declared, "Madam, it is a fortunate hunter who can come out of a wood and meet a divinity."[1] Actually, he was a family friend, who had served with Colonel Chudleigh on the board of the Royal Hospital.[2] His closest associate had been Elizabeth's uncle, John Merrill, husband of Harriet's sister Susannah,[3] MP for Tregony in Cornwall and, afterwards, St. Albans, a seat that lay under the patronage of Sarah, Duchess of Marlborough.[4]

Elizabeth's champion was a descendant of Leicestershire landowners and politicians. A handsome, rotund figure, he had "remarkably penetrating and brilliant"[5] dark brown eyes that shone with intelligence. In the summer of 1741, Walpole's ministry had collapsed after an unbeaten twenty-one years, largely due to Pulteney's machinations. The Earl of Wilmington, a "plodding, heavy fellow, with great application but no talents,"[6] had become prime minister, and Pulteney had accepted the Earldom of Bath (a decision he regretted—a supreme orator could no longer make havoc in the Commons).

Some gossips imagined an affair between Pulteney and Elizabeth, partly because his heiress wife was despised because of her "past": before marriage she had been mistress to the (married) statesman

Lord Bolingbroke—cartoons showed him using her naked backside as a desk to sign the Treaty of Utrecht.[7] (With a thirty-seven-year age gap between Elizabeth and Pulteney, and no record of infidelity on his part or attraction to much older men on hers, it seems unlikely.)[8] Lord Hervey, the most famous courtier in England, best friend to the queen, sworn enemy and perhaps lover of Prince Frederick, who became the definitive diarist of George II's court, denied the Countess of Bath "any one good, agreeable, or amiable quality but beauty";[9] a satirist called her a "vixen."[10]

The Pulteneys had had three children, a son who had died age two, a second boy, William,[11] and the "sensible and handsome" Anna Maria, who had died on March 9, 1742, just a few months after Thomas Chudleigh was killed at Aix-la-Chapelle. Elizabeth later said that Pulteney had adopted her "as his daughter"[12] and that he had left her an estate. One source claims he tried to embellish her education, lending her books and corresponding with her, but she was not an assiduous student. Her maxim was said to be that one should be "short, clear, and surprising."[13]

Pulteney often composed short, persuasive letters of recommendation in his clear hand, and however tumultuous his career, he did have one very advantageous friendship: that of Frederick, the Prince of Wales. Elizabeth was just eighteen months younger than Frederick's wife Augusta, and had the fluency, good looks, and background for court. According to one historian, Elizabeth had "provoking beauty, the combined brilliancy and delicacy of her complexion, her sparkling eyes and natural wit . . . exceedingly bright eyes and mobile features. She had little of the goddess and plenty of the woman, and her charm lay, not in her beauty, but in her piquant expression, her varied moods, and her fascinating manner. She had a temper, and one can conceive that when put out she did not take refuge in the chilly silence of the stately beauty."[14]

Pulteney recommended Elizabeth for a position at Frederick's court. At Christmas 1743, at the age of twenty-two, she was appointed maid of honour to Princess Augusta, who had been married for seven years and was already a mother of five. At this moment, Elizabeth's public life began, with the announcement of her appointment in the newspapers: "Miss Chudleigh, sister to Sir

——Chudleigh, Bart. and Miss Drax, Daughter of Henry Drax, Esq. Member of parliament for Wareham in Dorsetshire, are both appointed Maids of honour to her Royal Highness the Princess of Wales."[15] The opportunity to join the court of the Prince and Princess of Wales, as an attendant to the young future queen, was the most glamorous position available to a single girl of Elizabeth's background. However, before she arrived, the enmity between father King George II and son Frederick, Prince of Wales, had crystalized.

Two rival courts had emerged, just as they had in the previous generation.

In Augusta's train, Elizabeth stepped into the psychodrama of the Hanoverian succession that had its roots back in the second decade of the century, when the death of Queen Anne without an heir (in spite of seventeen pregnancies) had drawn the Elector of Hanover from the baroque summer palace of Herrenhausen to assume the British throne. The family Elizabeth's new mistress had married into was the height of dysfunction.

It had begun with George I, Augusta's husband's grandfather, Anne's second cousin. He was a jowly man with bulging blue eyes who spoke no English, "so cold he turns everything to ice."[16] He was not a model monarch. His wife, Sophia Dorothea of Celle, had been incarcerated in a castle as punishment for an affair, and her lover had been murdered. George entertained himself with two mistresses, nicknamed the "Elephant and Castle," both of whom accompanied him to London. The "Elephant" was his illegitimate half sister, Sophia Charlotte von Kielmansegg, Countess of Darlington; the "Castle," otherwise known as the maypole, bone-thin and tall, was Ehrengard Melusine von der Schulenburg, Duchess of Kendal. George decided that in a dynastic show of strength and continuity—there were plenty of people still agitating for a Catholic succession—his son and heir George Augustus; his wife Caroline; and their children, Princesses Anne, Amelia, and Caroline, should all leave Herrenhausen for England too.

Relations between the two Georges had never been good: the younger George annoyed his father purely by resembling his detested mother. Though musical, brave in battle, and intellectually in awe of his wife, the younger George was also foulmouthed and sexually rapacious.

George I chose to leave his seven-year-old grandson, Prince Frederick, behind in Hanover as the family representative. Frederick had already had a precarious start. Born in 1707, he had had rickets, jaundice, and been nicknamed *Wechselbalg* (changeling), as his father thought the yellowish infant could not be his. As his mother contracted smallpox soon after his birth, he was initially brought up by his great-grandmother, the Electress of Hanover.* He did not set eyes on his parents between the ages of seven and twenty-one, and they ignored his twenty-first birthday. After the death of his grandfather and the coronation of his father as George II in 1727, he was seized from a ball in the clothes he was wearing, and left the splendor of Herrenhausen, which had been the backdrop of his entire life, to be brought to London. He would never return.

George II had had four more children in England and by now barely knew his firstborn son, but he loathed him anyway, just as he had been loathed by his father. He said, "My dear first-born is the greatest ass and the greatest liar and the greatest canaille [one of the masses] and the greatest beast in the whole world, and I heartily wish he was out of it."[17] The king was a philistine and Queen Caroline a cultured, intelligent woman, but on the subject of their firstborn son they were as one. Although peculiarly tolerant of her husband's affairs, Caroline was vitriolic about Frederick.[18] She herself had had a desolate upbringing—her father had died when she was three, her mother, after an unhappy second marriage, when she was thirteen. Their cruelty was unwarranted, for Frederick was apparently a delightful child. But without parental check, he had run wild; he had an affair with a woman said to have been his father's and grandfather's mistress.[19] He was courteous and good-humored, but years of abandonment ensured that he never quite grew up, and he lent a childish, impulsive atmosphere to the establishment Elizabeth joined.

---

* Sophia, Electress of Hanover, was a granddaughter of James I. Her mother was James's second child, Elizabeth Stuart, Queen of Bohemia—she was called the Winter Queen as her reign was only a year long.

Nevertheless, Frederick was an enthusiastic arts patron, and an informal, intelligent friend to Alexander Pope and patron to James Thomson and Philippe Mercier.[20] The paintings he bought formed much of the Royal Academy. He commissioned silverware, architecture, and music; he started a fashion for the harpsichord, played the cello, wrote songs, and sang French madrigals, as well as playing cricket, learning languages, and supporting drama and the navy. But he was also a gambler and juvenile prankster, capable of holding puerile grudges.

Unlike his father, he was enthusiastically sociable. He established two drinking clubs: La Table Ronde (King Arthur's round table), and "Henry V,"* aligning himself with the paragons of patriotic British kingship, rather than with his remote, German father, who chased mistresses around Hanover while making no effort to be liked in England.[21]

Elizabeth's new mistress Augusta was the result of a long search for a bride. There had been a moment when it seemed that Frederick might marry Wilhelmina, sister of Frederick the Great, but negotiations between George II and her father went awry.[22] By the time Frederick arrived in London, his marriage was not a priority for his parents: his younger sister's marriage to the Prince of Orange was arranged, complete with generous settlement, first. In 1735, the Duchess of Marlborough's scheme to marry Frederick to her granddaughter, Lady Diana Spencer, was thwarted by Prime Minister Walpole, but her machinations prompted the king finally to fix on the then fifteen-year-old Augusta, a sweet-natured princess of Saxe-Gotha, in the forest lands of Weimar. "Tall . . . modest . . . good-natured . . . awkward,"[23] Augusta, daughter of the Duke of Saxe-Coburg-Altenburg and his first cousin, a princess of Anhalt-Zerbst, was born in the baroque Friedenstein Palace in a German hinterland. Her father had died when she was twelve. As the nineteenth of twenty children,[24] born when her mother was forty, she cannot have received any attention from anyone, nor could she expect any in the future.

In order to marry, Frederick needed his mistress, one of his

---

* Henry V, the Gang, or Harry the Fifth.

mother's maids of honour, Anne Vane, and their son, Cornwell Fitz-
Frederick Vane,* to disappear. She was reluctant, and Lord Hervey,
to whom she had also been mistress, was piqued at having been
displaced by Frederick in her affections. Whether or not Hervey and
Frederick had ever been lovers,[25] as was rumored, they had certainly
been close, and now detested each other. Vane published a letter,
secretly written by Hervey, claiming Frederick had treated her with
appalling cruelty, triggering a crisis for Frederick's reputation. He
was forever indebted to Pulteney, who brokered peace, removing
Vane and the boy to Bath with a pension.[26]

When Augusta arrived in London in May 1736, she was accompanied by a chaperone and a large doll with jointed limbs. She was
sixteen, and spoke no English. Her mother had assured her that as
the royal family was from Hanover, the British people now spoke
German.

Although a persistent irritant in his parents' eyes, Frederick was
affectionate and chatty, keen to love and be loved, and he fell for
Augusta immediately. On the journey to England to marry a man
she had never met, she had shown nothing but good humor. The
verdict was that she was affable, obliging to everyone she met, and
that she displayed "strong marks of contentment and good humor."[27]
Frederick met her in Greenwich, where she disembarked. He had
commissioned William Kent[28] to design him a magnificent barge,
still regarded by some as "the most beautiful boat in the world,"[29]
and on this he showed her the river and the wonders of London.

Not that his family did anything to make Augusta feel welcome.
There was a sibling fight at the wedding supper, which started
because Frederick had ordered stools for his siblings and chairs with
arms for himself and his bride. The siblings insisted on bringing their
own serving staff, and refused coffee in case it was poisoned. Queen
Caroline mocked her son's nightcap when the pair were put to bed,†
and her friend Lord Hervey encouraged her to believe that her son

---

* Fitz meaning "son of," as in son of Frederick. However, Lord Hervey and Lord
Harrington also believed the boy was theirs.
† Upper-class men wore embroidered caps when they removed their wigs as
part of their "undress."

was impotent. They laughed at how "refreshed"[30] Augusta seemed the next morning, the implication being obvious.

The "birthing row" the following year soured relations between mother and son irreversibly. In the summer of 1737, Frederick told his parents Augusta was pregnant; they were furious they had not been told earlier. Queen Caroline wanted to be present at the birth at Hampton Court, to verify the genes of the royal heir. Frederick, however, determined to thwart his interfering mother, moved his wife in the early stages of labor to St. James's Palace in the middle of the night. According to Lord Hervey (who, it must be remembered, hated Frederick), Augusta writhed with pain during the fifteen-mile carriage ride and the palace furniture was draped in dust covers; she gave birth on a tablecloth. Caroline dashed in fury to St. James's as soon as she heard. When she finally saw the baby, she called her a "poor, little, ugly she-mouse,"[31] and speculated she would soon die. She would have been far more suspicious, she said, had the child been a healthy boy.

Augusta never overreacted to the hostilities of her in-laws. She patiently learned English and astonishingly maintained their grudging approval, despite her mother-in-law believing her to have a "flat stupidity."[32] But as a result of the birth row the young royal couple were slung out of St. James's Palace, possessions in baskets,[33] and relations between parents and son were never restored. Queen Caroline died a few months later. So strong were the tribal loyalties that Frederick's friend Sarah, Duchess of Marlborough, wrote, "I freely own that I am glad she is dead,"[34] and Pope wrote savage verses about her as she lay dying.*

By the time Elizabeth joined the court, George II was a widower and Augusta had given birth to five children. Having put so much effort into Frederick's marriage, Pulteney was invested in the domestic happiness of his ally. It was typical of his maneuverings to fix one problem with another: finding Elizabeth a livelihood at the same time as supporting Augusta with a new maid of honour.

---

* "On Queen Caroline's death-bed" is an anonymous epigram, attributed to Pope: "Here lies wrapt up in forty thousand towels/ the only proof that C*** had bowels."

When Elizabeth arrived, the parallel courts of father and son were entrenched enemy camps. The battle had moved on to Frederick's allowance: George II had given Frederick much less than he himself had enjoyed as Prince of Wales.[35] Pulteney had helped Frederick achieve a rise to £100,000 a year, but the king had only paid a quarter of the agreed sum. In tilting for position, courtiers were effectively placing bets on the length of the king's life; was it better to stick with George or to align oneself with Frederick? The atmosphere was more strained than ever, the factions as viciously divided as any in British history.[36]

Thus in 1743, just before Christmas, Elizabeth became part of not just a household, but a coterie, an alliance of young aspirants and seasoned combatants around the Prince and Princess of Wales. Though young, she was well prepared for the role. She had grown up around the military, in another hierarchy; she had experienced tragedy twice over, so had nothing to fear; she came from a family of courtiers with a literary bent, and had a natural quick wit and intelligence, easy French, and an ability to dance. She had always mixed in a variety of society. She had escaped an uncertain future with her widowed mother and, although her new world was full of unknowns, it was undoubtedly the best thing to have happened to her.

Despite the setbacks she had encountered, it was hard to imagine a more perfect candidate for the role, or someone keener to embrace it. In the absence of her brother, she would be the one to restore the family to their rightful status.

CHAPTER FOUR

MAID OF HONOUR

The court of the Prince of Wales sprang up as a reaction to that of his father, and soon began to eclipse it. Courts were not necessarily agreeable places. Even before Caroline died in 1737, the king and queen's magnificent drawing room at Kensington Palace had become notoriously frothless, offering "little but the gloomy pomp of state and court etiquette."[1]

George could not bear male competition, so the wits and thinkers congregated round Frederick rather than risk outshining the king. Lord Hervey had described the monotony of George II's court thus: "No mill horse ever went in a more constant track." Night after minute-stretching night, the portly, pompous king played commerce* and backgammon, the queen quadrille, while Lord Grantham (the queen's Lord Chamberlain) had strolled around in silence trying to think of ways to create excitement where there was none to be had.

Years before, George's court as Prince of Wales—at Leicester House, where Frederick and Augusta now lived—had been intensely glamorous and lit up with "frizelation,"[2] their word for flirtation, by Caroline's young maids of honour. The buoyancy seemed to have stayed with the house and the Wales title, rather than moving with the original occupants.

Augusta, like Caroline, had three groups of attendants, in order

---

* Commerce is a poker-style card game.

of rank: the ladies of the bedchamber, all peeresses, headed by the groom of the stole; the bedchamber women, who dressed her and attended her in her bedchamber; and the tinsel of the drawing room, the maids of honour. In the bedchamber, the ladies remained in office for decades until death or illness removed them; maids of honour, on the other hand, had a high turnover rate because after a few years they were expected to marry and move on. These positions were highly sought-after. Since before Tudor times, court roles were the only occupations inside British institutions open to women.

Court ladies, according to Lady Mary Wortley Montagu, all looked the same—snowy-white skin, jet-black brows, scarlet lips. Elizabeth was a more delicate, elusive girl, with long, thick, light brown hair, "blue eyes like stars,"[3] pure white skin, and a slender, petite figure. Her face was described as "not only beautiful, but fascinating, from a glowing complexion and piercing eyes, which created desire in the beholder."[4] By all accounts, she was exceptionally beautiful; loveliness lit up by strength of character.

Women at court were the celebrities of the day, and it was the junior rank, the maids of honour, who attracted the most scrutiny. As Elizabeth, as everyone, would have known, there had been twin stars among Caroline's maids, Molly Lepel and Mary Bellenden, favorites of poets, papers, balladeers, and painters. Alongside them had been sensible Margaret Meadows and gregarious Sophie Howe. Usually wellborn, witty, and beautiful, a maid of honour's position at court meant, with luck, an introduction to an eligible husband. This was always a game of both chance and skill, like the faro* they liked to play until the early hours. Caroline's maids had had varying fortunes: Molly married the aforementioned Lord Hervey; Mary Bellenden became Duchess of Argyll; Sophie died young of a broken heart after a betrayal; and Margaret remained unmarried. Whose fate would Elizabeth follow?

Augusta's maids provided youth, energy, and enthusiasm in contrast to the gloomy, faded grandeur of the king's court, and once Caroline was dead, the highest-ranking female court was Augusta's.

---

* Faro (or pharo) is a gambling card game originally from France: easy to learn, with better odds than most. One deck of cards, any number of players.

As the princess's paid companions, they were expected to be vivacious, morale-raising, polite, and entertaining, though their duties were largely nonspecific. Being a maid of honour could be arduous. They could not cross their arms, sit down without permission, or speak to anyone more important than themselves unless spoken to first. Some found royal service insufferable, with no time to oneself, a form of marriage to the court without a groom.[5]

The most vivid account of their daily life comes from Pope, who, after speaking with Molly Lepel, Mary Bellenden, and Mrs. Howard,[6] wrote of the life of a maid of honour:

> We all agreed that the life of a maid of honour was of all things the most miserable, and wished that every woman who envied it, had a specimen of it. To eat Westphalian ham in a morning, ride over hedges and ditches on borrowed hacks, come home in the heat of the day with a fever[7] . . . as soon as they can wipe off the sweat of the day, they must simper an hour and catch cold in the Princess's apartment; from thence . . . to dinner with what appetite they may . . . and after that, till midnight walk, work, or think, which they please.[8]

As well as being born into the right family, accomplishments were necessary: a good speaking voice (reading aloud was frequently required), written and spoken French, possibly German, some Latin, the ability to dance, sing, play music, and ride. Elizabeth had to be punctual, willing, quick, cheerful, and discreet. Some aspects of her life were luxurious. There were servants to attend maids at table, and one maid[9] described how when traveling [to Holland]: "We have people found us that clean our rooms and wash for us, so there is no expense of that kind; sheets and towels are also found, silver candlesticks, and china, (tea-things, I mean,) and sugar . . . we have by much the best table; no allowance of wine, but may call for what quantity and what sort we please: we have two men to wait."

In some ways, court was like the Royal Hospital, but with younger men: a hierarchical institution with its own rules and codes. Only this time, Elizabeth's job was to look decorative in the drawing room, make amusing conversation, watch, and wait; her spirits and those of her fellow maids maintained by shenanigans, jokes, gossip, and flirting. The maids of honour inspired not only fascination, but also envy and contempt. Jokes and criticisms about them abounded; one wag claimed they had "never met one [i.e., a maid] who was not eager not to be"; a coachman, it was said, offered his son a vast sum if he promised not to marry one. Swift, after a visit to Pope, made "strange reports of the phraseologies of persons about the court,"[10] in particular the maids of honour. They made a habit of "selling bargains," which meant teasing someone loudly if they took a remark with a double meaning at face value. They were also known for being "free-thinking," that is, making disrespectful jibes about the clergy. They spent too much time simpering over "romance" novels, plotting stupid shenanigans, and ordering new dresses for birthday parties. And they were often thought to be promiscuous. The maids of honour of the late queen had been so unruly and coquettish during services that they had been moved behind a screen at the Chapel Royal.

So disparaging were the literary set of the maids of honour that Swift and Arbuthnot set up a hoax subscription to a publication called *A History of the Maids of Honour since Henry the Eighth, showing they make the best wives*.[11] Even Swift's Gulliver joined in, calling the Brobdingnagian maids of honour indecent, in a graphic passage that ends: "They would strip me naked from top to toe . . . the handsomest of these maids of honour, a pleasant frolicsome girl of sixteen, would sometimes set me astride on one of her nipples."[12]

In spite of the jibes, it was a social opportunity for Elizabeth second to none, a unique position between debutante and lady-in-waiting, the first step on a well-trodden ladder to an advantageous marriage. Those without a title, like Elizabeth, became the "Honourable," and she was to be paid a salary of £200 a year.

There were, of course, expenses. Getting the court wardrobe right was crucial, court dress being a society, and newspaper, obsession. New, splendid clothes were an expression of loyalty, like court attendance itself. They had to be pitched correctly: a maid of honour should be finely, but not too finely, dressed. Court dressing was both opulent and anachronistic. Elizabeth wore silk gowns consisting of oblong or fan-shaped hoops under a skirt; stays (a boned bodice); a mantua (a single length of cloth that hung from the shoulders), a low neckline

fringed with lace, and voluminous sleeves. Faces were painted, powdered, and patched, to cover up any smallpox scars. Hoops necessitated walking in tiny steps and made sitting down a challenge. As
successive Georges came to the throne, the hoops grew wider and
wider.* Elizabeth's hair was curled and powdered, though she might
wear a cap with laced lappets or ribbons tied under the chin. On top,
a satin cloak lined with fur, such as ermine or squirrel, was worn.

Fashions floated over from France: pink, for example, was made the
color in the 1740s by Louis XV's mistress, Madame de Pompadour.
Dressing was important at the thrice-weekly drawing rooms, those
regular royal gatherings at which courtiers battled for favor, but most
intense at royal birthday parties, which usually culminated in a ball.
Elizabeth's fellow maid of honour Elizabeth Granville, for example,
made a vivid impression in "rich pink satin trimmed with silver"[13] at
the Princess of Wales's birthday party in 1742.

Embroidered, colored, silk, and satin—the prestige was in the
fabric: how fine the silk, how exotic and exclusive the pattern, how
much silver and gold thread, the damask and brocades woven by the
Huguenots in Spitalfields. Such delights were expensive. As one courtier wrote around this time, "Yesterday I bespoke a hoop petticoat, of
the exact dimensions of my old one; the fashionable hoops are made
of the richest damask, trimmed with gold and silver, fourteen guineas a hoop."[14] There was no ceiling to possible expenditure: Anne,
Countess of Strafford, had spent £100 on one dress back in 1711.
There was a red-carpet, wear-only-once element to these extravagant
dresses. By the 1740s, the fashion at court was for "flowered silks,"
serpentine, botanic designs often shining with metallic threads; the
more imaginative the design, the better.[15] Here, Elizabeth spent much
of her salary, though her clothes must have been at the plainer end of
the scale. The men had to be polished for court, too, in white powder
and wigs, canes, swords, silk—clothes that, if they were seen in the
streets, would prompt derogatory shouts of "French dog!"[16]

When Elizabeth set her dainty slipper into Augusta's court at
twenty-two, the position was more sought-after than ever. Augusta

---

* Until they collapsed, like a deflated balloon, in the Regency.

was the first lady of the nation, and the sole royal consort. By now, the Princess of Wales was richly dressed and quietly confident, but her husband was the showman, ostentatiously dressed with long, flowing, curly hair, always accompanied by a boisterous entourage.

The country, and Parliament, were as divided as ever: Whigs against Tories; Whigs for, and against, Walpole; Jacobites and Hanoverians; town and country.[17] Walpole had long been pro-peace and low tax, where his rival Whig, Pulteney, styled himself as a "Patriot Whig," on the side of the patriot Prince of Wales (like half the Tories, too), the challengers to rampant patronage, venality, and appeasement in foreign policy.

Christmas 1743, when Elizabeth joined the court, was the height of faction fever: Walpole had finally been overthrown to Frederick's (and Pulteney's) delight, although the British victory over the French, at the Battle of Dettingen in Germany the previous June, had ensured the popularity of his father and rival George II, who had led the British troops into battle.[18] To make matters more irritating, the king's favored younger son, the Duke of Cumberland, was by his father's side as aide-de-camp, while foppish Frederick was fiddling on his harpsichord in London. Cumberland was even wounded in the leg in battle, all the better for his heroic reputation.

Elizabeth became part of an establishment that saw itself as cultured and family-minded. Frederick and Augusta had several summer retreats: the White House at Kew (opposite Kew Palace, remodeled for Frederick by William Kent), Cliveden House in Buckinghamshire (rented from the Countess of Orkney), Park Place near Henley (a shooting lodge bought from Lord Archibald Hamilton in 1738), and Durdans near Epsom (for hawking and hunting on the Downs). The court principally assembled in London between October and May.

Elizabeth was now part of the Leicester House set. Frederick's court had outgrown the London residencies of Norfolk House, St. James's, and Carlton House on the Mall.[19] They moved into Leicester House on Leicester Square, then called Leicester Fields, a "very handsome square railed about, and gravelled within." In the center of the square, Frederick was to put up an equestrian statue of his grandfather George I, modeled on one of Marcus Aurelius in Rome, to annoy his father.

It was an artistic, somewhat eccentric area. William Hogarth lived at 30 Leicester Fields; Philippe Mercier, painter and librarian to Frederick and Augusta, lived nearby for a time. Another house was a bagnio* inhabited by the notorious Mary Tofts, who fooled the medical establishment into believing that she had given birth to multiple rabbits.

Leicester House itself had been built by Sydney, 2nd Earl of Leicester, in 1631, for a private family "rather than a levée."† Nevertheless, it took up the whole of the north side of the square. Two decades earlier, in the 1720s, it had become "the pouting-place of Princes,"[20] as George II lived here as Prince of Wales while quarreling with his father, and then his son Frederick did exactly the same. The house faced onto the square, behind a high wall with a gatehouse and small shops in front of it. At the rear, there was a shady garden with a gravel walk bordered by statues, as well as cypress, pine, and fruit trees.

An invitation to an assembly here was much sought-after because the vigor was in Frederick and Augusta's house: it was full of children, music, plotting, and politics. Elizabeth found plenty of jokes, quips, and pretty young people like herself. It was a small but brilliant setup of aristocrats, men of letters, Patriot Whigs, and rebels that gathered around the flame of the reversionary interest: "All the freedom of private life, all the festivity of wit, all the elegance of literature" was there.[21]

Now in his heyday, Frederick had set himself up as the affable English patriot in contrast to his father's brooding, distant, German monarch. He would celebrate the navy, rather than the army. He had commissioned two busts for his lavish "fine bathing room" at Carlton House: Edward, the Black Prince, and King Alfred, both role models for a British patriot king.

---

* Bagnio: brothel or boardinghouse, or some mixture of both.
† Levée: an intimate reception with royalty, usually held around noon, originally on rising.

Those who wanted to cultivate the first pro-British Hanoverian clustered round the princely flame.

*

A drawing-room gathering in 1744, as we might imagine it: Elizabeth, an exhilarated new maid of honour, sees carriages drawing up at the door of Leicester House to drop the guests for a royal assembly. An elegant London house on the outside, it is palatial within.

Through the front door, footmen guide the guests up the staircase at the eastern end of the house with gilt leather hangings on the walls to the piano nobile, where they enter a suite of rooms of increasing grandeur. Frederick's carvers, painters, and paper hangers have embellished the interior. Above the wainscot hangs mohair, which gives way to damask, and glossy lustring* curtains shine under carved wood pelmets. The fireplaces are black and white marble, the ceilings fretwork. There are internal balconies and carved wooden cornices, the whole gently lit by warm candles in girandoles and chandeliers hanging from gilt roses, glittering against majestic looking glasses that dwarf the inhabitants.

Finally, as violins play, guests arrive in the state chamber in the west where among the Doric columns there are two state chairs and a crimson damask canopy above them. Here sit Frederick and Augusta, Prince and Princess of Wales. In the room are his favorites and her attendant maids of honour, including Elizabeth. Just as they eye up the company, so everyone looks at them, as they whisper to each other, joking, laughing, gossiping. They have been trained to stand still without "tottering."[22] There are gilded chairs, stools, tables, and a Turkish carpet; next door, in the green state bedroom with its bed from Paris, Princess Augusta sometimes receives visitors. It is the room in which she gives birth.

Balls, concerts, plays, dinners—all are held here. When Augusta has a new baby—which is often—it lies in the state cradle, decorated by Indian quilting, gold lace, and crimson silk. Frederick frequently moves pictures and furniture around between rooms, for parties and dinners and plays, and between Leicester House and Carlton

---

* Lustrous silk.

House, because he wants everything to be displayed in the finest possible position. Works by Rubens and tapestries of landscapes line the walls; the nurseries are decorated in yellow damask. The whole is glowing with red, green, yellow, silks, velvets, satins. There are many staff, but only six principal bedrooms. It is all so crowded that the maids of honour lodge elsewhere nearby, in the "Maids of honour" house in Duke Street, or at 18 Leicester Fields.[23]

Of all the women in the room, the most important is of course Augusta, and she is the focus of the maids' attention when required. She had "a peculiar affability of behavior, and a very great sweetness of countenance, mixed with innocence, cheerfulness and sense."[24] The princess had five white-blond, blue-eyed children under seven: Princess Augusta, Prince George,[25] Prince Edward, Princess Elizabeth, and Prince William, the last-named born at Leicester House just a month before Elizabeth's arrival.[26]

When Elizabeth becomes maid of honour, one woman—other than Augusta—is predominant in the drawing room. The maids of honour answer to the Mistress of the Robes, Lady Jane Hamilton. Third wife of the much older Lord Archibald, she is a mother of ten, paid £900 a year, and lives close to Frederick's other house, Carlton House. She is also mistress to the Prince of Wales, because as much as he loves Augusta, he is after all a Hanoverian prince. Powerful, jealous, and cunning, she keeps order in the household. Courtier Lord Shelburne says Hamilton is "always in charge." Hamilton's daughter is the same age as Elizabeth, a maid of honour who has just relinquished her role to become Lady Brooke, the future Countess of Warwick, a fine, envy-provoking match for the other maids.

Alongside Elizabeth are her fellow maids of honour, including the one with whom she is announced in the *Penny London Advertiser* in January 1744:* the "very pretty" dark-haired, dark-eyed girl, Elizabeth Drax, daughter of Henry Drax, MP for Wareham in Dorset.[27] In May, within six months of her arrival, Elizabeth Drax married the Earl of Berkeley and later returned, once married, as a lady of the bedchamber. The other maids are Charlotte Dives or Dyves (of

---

* The warrant, dated March 20, 1744, states that Elizabeth started at Christmas 1743.

an army family), in her early thirties, who became a lifelong friend to Elizabeth; Albinia Selwyn (daughter of Henry Selwyn, Receiver General of HM Customs); Lucy Boscawen (sister of the famous admiral, great-niece of the Duke of Marlborough); and Lady Elizabeth/Eliza Granville, a daughter of Lord Lansdowne, "a fair, red-headed girl, scarce pretty."[28] Elizabeth is the beauty but, compared to the others, she is not as assured in money or family connections.

There are all sorts of men congregating at Leicester House; rogues, has-beens, will-bes, wags, philosophers, fools. Soldiers, such as Lord Falmouth, brother of Lucy Boscawen, and the elderly Earl of Stair, who is particularly fond of Elizabeth; idlers and wits, like the outrageously rich George Bubb Dodington,[29] the "fat Mephistopheles," who subsidizes the prince and plays the tubby fool (he once allowed Frederick and friends to roll him down some steps wrapped in a blanket), and Lord Chesterfield, married to the daughter of George I's mistress. Politicians, such as Lord Bolingbroke; Lord Carteret, former ambassador to Sweden; future prime minister William Pitt; George Lyttelton, Frederick's principal secretary, poet, and MP for Okehampton who had married a Chudleigh relation, Lucy Fortescue. Writers such as James Thomson, author of "Rule, Britannia!," first performed at Cliveden for Frederick,[30] and his collaborator David Mallet, undersecretary to Frederick.

In theory, anyone in the right dress can attend a royal court, but each room becomes progressively more select until the inner sanctum is court proper only: friends, aristocrats, people of consequence, foreign ambassadors. However, Frederick does not draw social boundaries along class lines. One of his closest associates is the omnipresent family dance master George Desnoyers, who skips in and out of the picture with everyone confiding in him along the way.[31] A stage performer, too, he was the most fashionable dance master in London, and dancing was the town's most fashionable activity. Maids of honour were often given dancing lessons to make sure they were up to scratch. Presumably Desnoyers helped Elizabeth practice her steps; she became a keen, impressive dancer.

At Leicester House, there is always music playing. Sometimes Handel, finely balancing his relationship with both father George II and son Frederick, conducts morning concerts in front of the children. Tutors visit at all times of day. The young are not hidden at Leicester House; indeed, Frederick is an affectionate parent. Augusta is more aloof, exhausted by pregnancy and anxious about her offspring's health. They are both devoted parents and go to ever more extravagant ends for each birthday. For one, a Lilliputian band of children under twelve was assembled to serenade the infant Prince George, too young to notice.

If the house is a hub of art, music, political gossip, and plotting, it is also exceptionally well-supplied and run. Surviving accounts show the lavish style in which the residents, including Elizabeth, are fed: ingredients include "Jordan almonds, sago, nutmeg, pistachio kernels, fresh salmon, large lobsters, crayfish, shrimps, mullets, ox heads, sheep trotters, partridges, ortolan*."[32] There are running accounts with a bacon man, an oyster man, a salt purveyor, an oil purveyor (who also sells anchovies, capers, mango, parmesan cheese, and olives), a pastry cook who supplies ham and beef pies, apple pies, tarts, and cheesecakes. There are two roasters, and two "turnbroaches," employed to turn the spit. The servants have servants. Food is served on Dresden china, with plenty of ale and wines sourced by a Mr. Jephson. Courtier Lord Baltimore helps Frederick commission rococo silverware from Nicholas Sprimont, such as the ornate "Neptune" centerpiece in the Marine service, used to serve fish soup and seafood. The salt is in silver-gilt dishes in the shape of crayfish. Elizabeth will quickly become accustomed to the most exotic and expensive provisions that eighteenth-century London can furnish. To all this we can perhaps attribute her taste for luxury.

In this select, charged atmosphere, the new maid of honour, a fresh face from the West Country with a quick wit and social skills, made lifelong friends—notably, fellow maid Charlotte Dives—and attracted admirers. She was not, however, particularly a man's woman, nor did she alienate the other maids; she was charismatic, gregarious, a woman who attracted people to her. Whether she admitted it or not, circumstance dictated what she hoped to achieve:

---

* Ortolan: food of royalty and rich gourmands, tiny—thumb-sized—rare songbird eaten whole.

a good marriage, really, her only hope of survival. For magnetic Elizabeth, finding a suitable candidate would surely not be that onerous a task: the court was full of possibilities.

The most ardent of all her new acquaintances was young James Hamilton, the 6th Duke of Hamilton and 3rd Duke of Brandon, holder of Scotland's oldest dukedom, hereditary keeper of the royal Palace of Holyrood, with royal (Stuart) blood in his veins.[33] He was, on paper, a prize salmon for Elizabeth to catch. He had a labyrinth of family connections at court. A great-nephew of Lady Jane Hamilton by marriage, and nephew of another lady of the bedchamber, Hamilton was three years or so younger than Elizabeth and only nineteen or twenty when he met her, but he had already come into his title after the death of his father at forty. His mother had died a month after his birth.

After Winchester, Hamilton had studied law at Oxford, and was a member of Edinburgh's Select Society, which included David Hume, Adam Smith, and Allan Ramsay—but he was also an impulsive, reckless, addictive figure rather like his grandfather, who had died in a duel.[34] Portraits show a thin, pale, uneasy-looking young man. He was a chaotic figure who liked dogs, hunting, women, and drink. Later described by Horace Walpole as "hot, debauched, extravagant and wholly damaged in his fortune and his person,"[35] he became a well-known rake who worked his way through his inheritance with gusto and was rarely sober. He was a "gamester, turf lover" with his school friend Lord March, and a frequenter of bagnios. Another contemporary[36] observed that as louche as he was with "bad" women, he could be the politest and best-behaved gentleman with "ladies." In spite of his faults, he inspired loyalty in his friends—Baron Mure, his lawyer Andrew Stuart, and the old Duke of Douglas.

The orphan duke's lineage was impressive, in an age when such things equated to the financial security that came with land ownership. Such were the original riches of the Hamiltons that Defoe called them the "great possessors," pointing out that their seat, Hamilton Palace in Lanarkshire, was more fit for king than subject. At the time, it was probably the most magnificent country house in Britain. The family finances had been much diminished by his grandfather's investment in the spectacularly doomed Darien scheme,[37] while that grandfather had also missed his chance to declare himself the rightful successor to the Scottish throne.

According to one version, Elizabeth's "appearance caused a great sensation, and she was soon surrounded by lovers and admirers . . . the one she most esteemed was the duke of Hamilton, a young man of great wealth, who soon laid his coronet at her feet."[38] However, there were those who could not tolerate a penniless maid of honour attaching herself to Scotland's premier dukedom. When the "brilliant prospect" became known, it excited the envy of "many, who would willingly have taken her place, and no calumny was spared that was thought likely to prevent the marriage." Hamilton "refused to believe aught that could be said against her," but Elizabeth "lent a willing ear to the slanderous reports," and finally, "in a fit of displeasure, excited by the report of his infidelity, to her, she wrote to her lover forbidding him her presence, and saying that she would never again receive him."[39] We have no way of knowing how much truth this version of events contains, but certainly, they parted.

Leicester House was a champagne bubble of a place—fleeting flirtations, an atmosphere of intrigue, gossip, and scheming, all conducive to a hotheaded romance. Whatever young Hamilton's personal failings (and within a few years, it was clear there were many), he was a quasi-royal duke with a palace, a forbidding yet impressive pile of stone, so white it looked like marble, in a fertile valley forty miles from Edinburgh, and he had very obviously fallen in love with the non-heiress new maid of honour. They were secret lovers, perhaps even privately engaged. But he was about to head off on his Grand Tour, that obligatory jaunt round Europe for young nobles where classical antiquity, art buying, and bacchanalian excess went hand in hand. He went with his physician and tutor, Dr. William Pitcairn, who had already accompanied him to Oxford.* It was said that relatives encouraged him to go to

* It was not unusual for an aristocrat to take his own tutor to university as well as on the Grand Tour, and if they were a physician, too, so much the better. Scottish Pitcairn was also a botanist, and later FRS.

separate him from Elizabeth. He might have been parentless, but it is likely that some of the Hamiltons at court would have opined on the matter.

Hamilton left, and what remained, whoever's decision it was, was the anguish of vanishing hope. Something had been promised, and evaporated. It must have been upsetting, as well as publicly humiliating, for Elizabeth nearly to have become Duchess of Hamilton, Duchess of Brandon, mistress of a palace, and then suddenly to be thrust back into the lonely, financial, and romantic uncertainty of her position. Her distress must have been acute, whatever the reason for the breach. It was quite understandable for her to have hoped for an early engagement, like that of Lady Jane Hamilton's daughter.

As Hamilton embarked on his travels, Elizabeth remained at court, which disbanded every summer to avoid the stench and the heat of the city. By May 14, 1744, Frederick, Augusta, and children had gone to Cliveden with a much-reduced entourage. "Airing" was seen as the key to health and happiness. Once the prince and princess had left, the maids of honour found themselves alternative drawing rooms to adorn around the country.

Elizabeth made her way down to her cousin's house in Hampshire. If she was expecting an uneventful summer with her relations, she would turn out to be profoundly mistaken.

CHAPTER FIVE

"The English Casanova"

We can well imagine Elizabeth's state of mind as she arrived at her cousin John Merrill's seat, Lainston House in Hampshire. Humiliated, lonely; relieved, perhaps, to be out of town, and yet emotionally overwrought.

Lainston and its grounds were the most exquisite consolation for an aggrieved soul: a perfectly proportioned H-shaped, red-brick seventeenth-century house built on the former royal park-lands of Winchester, with sweet-smelling gardens and the tiny twelfth-century chapel of St. Peter a short stroll from the house. All around it was the abundance of nature. There was a dairy farm, a park, and fishing nearby on the River Itchen. Rumor had it that Charles II leased Lainston for his baby-faced mistress and spy for the French, Louise de Kérouaille, Duchess of Portsmouth, who had herself once been a maid of honour. It is an intensely romantic spot, just the sort of place a king might rent for his mistress, and where an aesthetically appreciative pleasure-seeker, desperate for distraction from a broken romance, like Elizabeth, might flourish.* Inside, there were wooden carvings by Grinling Gibbons; Delft tiles; outside, a hexagonal walled garden with a sundial and, in the height of sum-

---

* Lainston was the sort of trophy house that appealed to the socially ambitious. Elizabeth's uncle bought it from Sir Philip Meadows, MP, Knight Marshal, comptroller of the army, who owned it for less than a decade. In an ironic twist, his family reappears later in our story.

mer, plump greengages growing on the walls and falling onto the grass below.

Now the chapel lies in ruins, but one can still envisage a warm summer evening in 1744, with the scent of honeysuckle and roses in the air, doves cooing from the new dovecote, and the lime avenue on the far side of the house, stretching down through the valley to infinity.[1]

Elizabeth, who had spent so much time in rural Devon, was always at ease in the country, as her later letters illustrated.[2] She could fish for hours happily without result and had an in-depth knowledge of plants. Amusement of all kinds, many of which could be found in the country, appealed to her—drinking wines, eating fine food, reading books in the oak-paneled library.

Among the scenery alongside Elizabeth on this visit we would find her host, John Merrill, a widower in his thirties with a daughter, Mary, age six. The only child of the late John Merrill MP and his late wife Susannah née Chudleigh,[3] cousin Merrill was a graduate of Jesus College, Cambridge, and the Inner and Middle Temple,[4] mathematician, and future Fellow of the Royal Society. He had married an heiress in 1737; the following year she died, not long after giving birth.[5] Merrill was left a widower, single father, and rich man who seemed to do little other than take part in lawsuits to extract money from relations.

We would also see Elizabeth's chaperone and companion on this visit, her maternal aunt, Ann, who had left her house in Upper Grosvenor Street, Mayfair, for the summer to stay with her nephew. On her shoulders fell the responsibility for her niece's behavior. (Her mother, presumably, was in London or Devon. We cannot know why she did not join them.) Ann, the sister of Harriet, was the widow of Colonel William Hanmer, who had been in the aristocratic Coldstream Guards alongside two Chudleigh uncles. Hanmer had distinguished himself at Malplaquet.[6] As a result, he was one of four men selected by Walpole to lead a marine force onto land at Cartagena.* But the siege was

---

* A failed siege in 1741 of the port in present-day Colombia, in which the British were defeated by the Spanish. It lasted sixty-seven days.

a disaster and, to compound it, Hanmer caught yellow fever there, returned to England, and died at Lainston in September 1741.

In spite of the elegant setting and the entertaining season, most of the house's occupants were thus bereft. In the summer of 1744, one might have found wandering in the garden or sitting in the bright drawing room that ran the whole depth of the house, playing cards, sewing embroidery, or drinking tea: Merrill himself; his daughter Mary; a friend of Merrill's, Edward Mounteney, "goldsmith of London,"[7] then living at Lainston; the widow Ann Hanmer; and Elizabeth, recovering from the severing of ties with the Duke of Hamilton.

Waiting on them were a number of servants, including a butler, two housemaids, a laundry maid, and a kitchen maid. Also present was Mrs. Hanmer's ever-watchful lady's maid, Ann Walton, later Ann Craddock, from whom much will be heard down the line.

As lovely as Lainston was, being isolated in the country could starve a single maid of honour of romantic opportunities.

All was not lost, however: one of the attractions of the place was its proximity to the annual Winchester races, which took place in June at Worthy Down, four miles northwest of the ancient city of Winchester. There were public breakfasts in the morning, balls in the evening, a great deal of "frizelation," dancing, concerts, and carousing around the clock. For Elizabeth, the races were a welcome diversion and a chance to socialize. And they were held just four miles from Lainston.

The crowds were dressed up, "the Lords and the Ladies . . . satine'd and ermined,"* the tradespeople ready for their annual jackpot. This "fresh" country, a "dry chalky down where the air is worth six pence a pint,"[8] saw Elizabeth, maid of honour of six months' standing, in her finest, silkiest garb, embellished with ribbons, feathers, and flowers, attend the social occasion at which three popular pastimes— gambling, racing, and drinking—giddily coincided. In marquees, "tea, wines etc" were served for the gentry on race days and there

---

* From Jane Austen's last poem "Venta," July 15, 1817, dictated to her sister Cassandra three days before her death in Winchester.

was cockfighting, bullbaiting, bowling, and billiards, a theater, the St. John's Assembly Rooms, coffeehouses, and inns to visit.

England in the first half of the eighteenth century was racing mad. Pulteney described the attractions of the sport as "the splendor, language, obsession with pedigree, the great reputation of British breeds throughout Europe,"[9] and the "many hundreds of thousands of pounds" at stake; war, sex, and politics were all kindred spirits to the feverish, adrenaline-pumping intoxication of race days. It was the sport of kings and royalists, Whigs, and peers.[10] In 1739, Parliament passed an act to "restrain and prevent the excessive increase of horse races," and, by the 1750s, Winchester would have turnpikes on the road during race season for crowd control, and to make money out of the surge. Some race meetings only consisted of owners betting against each other, but Winchester was more prestigious, with royal connections since the visits of Charles II. Hence there was the King's Plate,[11] a four-mile flat race for six-year-old horses. In 1744, the year Elizabeth was there, the winner was Bucephalus, a chestnut horse, the best gelding of his time, bred by William Aislabie of Studley Park, the son of a Whig Chancellor of the Exchequer. If the society and the stakes were high, it was also sometimes indecorous—brothel keepers and illiterate touts mixed with fur-clad nobility. There was danger, too: there were no barriers to stop the horses running amok through the crowds.

As Hamilton went on tour, Elizabeth would have been acutely aware of her failure to find a husband. Before Lainston, she may have attended the wedding of the maid of honour with whom she had joined court, the ample-dowried Elizabeth Drax, to Augustus, 4th Earl of Berkeley, on May 7, on the Berkeley estate in Middlesex. Drax's husband was a lieutenant colonel and an earl with a baronial castle in Gloucestershire.[12] Such an occasion is only likely to have accentuated Elizabeth's eagerness for distraction.

No wonder Elizabeth was so drawn to the adolescent thrill-seeker she met at the races. The Hon. Augustus Hervey, son of the late queen's beloved courtier, Lord Hervey, had only just turned twenty when he arrived at Worthy Down, but he was at home strutting on the turf. Racing was in his blood: his grandfather, the 1st Earl of Bristol, was one of the leading racehorse owners in England, an owner so successful his rivals paid him not to race.*

Augustus also had the attraction of being in the Royal Navy. Four years after Frederick had first commissioned a performance of "Rule, Britannia!,"[13] Britannia ruled the waves in a spirit of imperial expansion. England was in a state of patriotic fervor, and Augustus was the epitome of the dashing young sailor. When he met Elizabeth, he was on the crew of the HMS *Cornwall*, an eighty-gun third-rate ship of the line,† preparing to sail from Spithead, Portsmouth, for the West Indies as part of Admiral Thomas Davers's squadron to protect trade in wartime.

Augustus was already beguilingly full of sea stories. After a brief spell at Westminster School, he had joined the navy under his uncle's command in 1735 at the age of eleven, first on the HMS *Pembroke* as cabin boy and captain's servant, and then on the *Superb*. Influence and connections mattered more than ability upon entrance into the navy, and the rewards could be substantial. The enterprise of the Royal Navy was driven by a manifest incentive: those on board when another ship was taken won a share of the spoils plus "head money" for each enemy captive. The more senior the sailor, the more generous his cut. The financial potential of a naval career then lay not in the salary, but in the value of captured vessels.

Aunt Hanmer, accompanying Elizabeth, seems to have taken to Augustus straightaway. It is likely she valued military courage above all. It must have helped that where her late husband had been defeated at Cartagena, Augustus had not only fought in the same battle,[14] but he had also been part of a slender British victory in that corner of the world, over her husband's enemies.[15] Under the command of his uncle, Captain (William) Hervey, on the HMS *Superb*, Hervey had captured a Spanish ship full of cocoa in the West Indies. At the same time, Captain Hervey had reported the most welcome news back to London: the death of Don Blas de Lezo, the crafty,

---

* Bristol was a politician ennobled in 1714, because he supported the Protestant succession and enjoyed the goodwill of the omnipotent Duchess of Marlborough. He owned a stud not far from his estate at Ickworth, Suffolk, and also rode his own horses in races.
† A ship of the line was a warship, as in fit for the frontline of battle.

peg-legged, one-eyed Spanish victor of Cartagena who had defeated Colonel Hanmer.[16] The following year, Augustus had to find another patron when uncle William, one of his four wicked uncles,* was court-martialed for brutality on board ship. After a stint on HMS *Sutherland* with Admiral Byng, Davers had taken Augustus on as a second lieutenant in June 1744, because grandfather Bristol, a Suffolk neighbor, implored him to do so.

Going to sea so young had made Augustus worldly for his age. Portraits show an attractive, even-featured mariner, who exuded confidence, rather cockiness, to the point of haughtiness.[17] He seems to have been irresistible. So wide was his appeal to the female sex he was later called "the English Casanova." Slim, athletic, and good-looking, he was a crafty, articulate young man, as well as a serial seducer. He rode, he danced, he fenced, he played the harpsichord. And he was a compulsive flirt. Although Elizabeth was three years older than him, he had had much more experience than her with the opposite sex: he already had women in two ports by the time they met. When his ship had docked in Lisbon (when he was sixteen) he had had an affair with Elena Paghetti, a married, Italian opera singer several years older than him. In Yarmouth, it was the turn of Mrs. Artis, the young wife of the aged postmaster there. He was a persuasive youth. Unsurprisingly, he was an adept press-ganger for his uncle's ships.

In gauging Augustus's frame of mind, two other factors must be considered. He was in a rush for romance, with a deadline in sight: he was soon to go to the West Indies, then a hellishly unhealthy place sailors tried to avoid because so many fell ill there, just as Uncle Hanmer had done. And, just like the Lainston party, he had suffered recent loss: his father, Lord Hervey, had died just a few months ear-

---

* Apart from the court-martialed Captain William, there was Henry, a gambler, who fought his own brothers over the family parliamentary seat of Bury (though he later reformed, and became a clergyman); Felton, who was expelled from Eton and dismissed as an equerry; and, worst of all, Thomas, who ran off with his own godfather's wife—the wife of Sir Thomas Hanmer, a relation of Col. William. He taunted him in a pamphlet, writing, "Our wife, for, in heaven, whose wife shall she be?" Three of Augustus's aunts died young.

lier, in August 1743, at the age of forty-six. Like Elizabeth, he was seeking consolation and adventure.

Having Lord Hervey for a father meant paternal neglect and all the consequences of that on Augustus's character—no male role model, and a lack of discipline—plus fame and familiarity in Elizabeth's eyes. The Herveys were one of the luminary families of the Whig oligarchy. Augustus might not have been a duke of royal blood with a palace, but the Herveys were an immensely wealthy, politically ambitious, intoxicating family. He was more than a sailor: he was a child of the court. Everybody—Elizabeth, Mrs. Hanmer, John Merrill—had heard of the Herveys. To the military gentry of the Chudleigh/Hanmer variety, a Hervey was of bluer, nobler blood.[18]

Augustus's parents were court celebrities, too. Lord Hervey had been Queen Caroline's closest advisor, and once the intimate, later the enemy of Prince Frederick.[19] He wrote about everyone, and everyone wrote about him, as "remorseless Hervey of the coffin face and painted cheeks,"[20] or "the third sex."[21]

As an enemy of Frederick, he was also a foe of Pulteney—they had fought a duel many years before, in a proxy war for king and prince.[22] He was ingenious, striking, fragile in health, and always pale (he lived on ass's milk and biscuits to control his epilepsy).[23] His effeminate looks inspired jealousy and mocking poetry, by Pope, for example (who was on Pulteney's side—everyone was on one or the other, Pulteney and the prince's, or Hervey, the king, and Walpole's), who wrote of him:

> Let Sporus tremble—A "What? that thing of silk,
> Sporus, that mere white curd of ass's milk?
> Satire or sense, alas! can Sporus feel?
> Who breaks a butterfly upon a wheel?"*

---

* "Sporus" was the castrated catamite Nero married. Pope also called Hervey "amphibious thing," Adonis, Narcissus, and "Lord Fanny." "Now high, now low, now Master up, now Miss,/ And he himself one vile Antithesis . . ./ Fop at the Toilet, Flatt'rer at the Board,/ Now trips a Lady, and now struts a Lord." Both quotes are from *Epistle to Dr. Arbuthnot* (written 1734). A—Arbuthnot's imagined answers to Pope.

His mother was Molly Lepel, once a maid of honour herself, that bright star of Caroline's court, toast of a previous Leicester House generation. She inspired poetry through admiration rather than scorn. Pope, Pulteney, and Voltaire wrote about her, the last-named: "Hervey, would you know the passion/ You have kindled in my breast?" Like Elizabeth, she was an army child: her father was a courtier/soldier, Brigadier General Nicholas Lepel, formerly colonel of a regiment of foot. A 1720s portrait shows her serene and Madonna-like with wide cherubic blue eyes, fair hair, and pale skin.[24] She had married John Hervey in 1720 in secret and they had had eight children together. People were fascinated by the pretty pair, the new golden couple. In 1720, Gay[25] wrote: "Now Hervey, fair of Face, I mark full well,/ With thee, Youth's youngest Daughter, sweet Lepell!"*

But Hervey became an absent father, preoccupied with court politics and love affairs. The recipient of his most passionate letters was the young Stephen Fox MP.[26] For the formative years of Augustus's childhood—from the age of two until twelve, by which time he had gone to sea—his father was obsessed with "Ste," traveling abroad with him on the pretext of his health, and living with him in London while Molly was abandoned at Ickworth, her "hermitage."[27] It was said the Herveys lived like "a French couple," i.e., in a detached fashion.

For all Augustus's charm and intelligence, guidance was scarce. John Hervey never entirely grew up himself, relying on his own father to be the paterfamilias. Molly was the wiser, fonder parent, and Augustus was her favorite. She, however, had seven others to fret about. When Augustus met Elizabeth at the races, Molly was at Ickworth, concerned about her daughter Lepel Phipps, who had just given birth to her first child on May 19, Augustus's twentieth birthday.[28] According to one source,[29] Molly was "a model of the highly polished, finely bred, genuine woman of fashion," although

---

* Another popular ballad, by Chesterfield and Pulteney:
  So Venus had never seen bedded
  so handsome a beau and a belle,
  As when Hervey the Handsome was wedded
  to the beautiful Molly Lepell.

her manners had a "foreign tinge" that some found affected.* Lady Mary Wortley Montagu called her (not entirely politely) "the top figure in town." She was a first-rate conversationalist. All of which must have helped breed that instant reaction when Augustus met Elizabeth: she reminded him of his mother.

The Earl of Bristol, Augustus's grandfather, had had twenty children[30] by two wives, both, conveniently, heiresses. He juggled his children and grandchildren's requests for money with advice and affection. Molly and her father-in-law shared concerns about Augustus's safety in the navy. In 1740, Bristol wrote that he was pleased about Augustus's "reformation,"[31] without specifying quite what he was reforming himself from.

Augustus was the rebellious second son to a studious older one. This made him both less eligible, and probably more attractive to Elizabeth. Herveys and Chudleighs were Hanoverian, Protestant, Whigs of the same military cast. Elizabeth must have felt an emotional, tribal connection—particularly as Augustus's elder brother George had fought alongside her own brother as a captain in the Chudleigh regiment. Unlike Elizabeth's brother Thomas, George Hervey survived, but resigned his commission in 1742 and became a diplomat. Three years older than Augustus, intellectual, possibly asexual, a future ambassador, delicate George was a sickly, effeminate-looking man like his father, who was "born to the gout from his mother's family but starved himself to keep it off."[32] He was a frequent object of ridicule: Lord Cobham once spat in his hat for a wager.† When his grandfather died, George would inherit the earldom, the seat in the Lords, the townhouse in St. James's Square, the silverware, and 30,000 acres of East Anglia and Lincolnshire—for all of which, his many proposals of marriage were rejected. George Hervey was tantalizingly, intermittently at "death's door,"[33] which meant that Augustus always seemed to be on the brink of becoming

---

* She was suspected of being a Jacobite at heart.
† George Hervey was said, by Horace Walpole, to have a "delicate constitution and an overbearing pride."

the heir to the earldom and estates himself if George died without having any children.

Augustus did not know which way the dice would fall, or when. This cannot have escaped either Aunt Hanmer or Elizabeth's notice, because George, now Lord Hervey, was a figure at court, and raking over uncertain expectations like these was the fuel that kept courts going.

Such was the background of Augustus Hervey when he met Elizabeth at the races, where the holiday atmosphere was charged with danger, gambling, and flirtation. Races began at four or five in the afternoon, and festivities continued long into the night. Here the naval officer and the maid of honour formed a connection. If Elizabeth's feelings were raw, here was her rebound. Hervey's man-servant William Craddock recalled the smitten pair dancing with each other at a ball there: he "well" remembered "attending him to the Assembly then held there . . . seeing [them] upon the Ball."[34] Craddock said that they had almost instantly "contracted an intimacy and friendship for each other." Presumably they confided in each other. Neither had a father; both resembled an adored parent; they seemed intensely attractive to the other. The relationship began at a gallop. Among the many things they had in common, alongside good looks and pleasure-seeking, was that they were both impulsive characters, often inclined to act first, and think later. This shared trait was to be their downfall.

Augustus was invited over to Lainston. He had an advantage over court beaux: in the country, he had no competition. Over the following few days, he asked the Lainston party to accompany him on a round trip of thirty miles to see the renowned HMS *Victory*, "man of war" and the finest ship of the day with its three decks and 110 bronze cannons, at the docks in Portsmouth.[35] This would no doubt have impressed Elizabeth, who had nurtured a love of all things maritime from childhood, when she watched the boats sail past the Royal Hospital and heard her father's tales of the sea. Augustus returned to Lainston for the nearby Magdalen Hill Fair. This ancient annual fair once featured "a real mermaid" from the Isle of Wight, and a unicorn from Tangier.[36] There were fortune-tellers, bear-baiting, and goods for sale, particularly hops, cheese, leather, and horses.

On those warm summer afternoons at Lainston, Elizabeth and Augustus might have taken part in salmon and trout fishing on the pristine River Itchen, archery (said to show off the female figure), croquet, or shuttlecock. Picnics by day, perhaps, and in the evening, moonlight and lanterns would have turned the grounds into a mini Vauxhall pleasure gardens. There might have been dinner, tea, syllabub, music, and dancing, served any time between 3 and 7 P.M., sometimes in the garden.

Augustus managed to ingratiate himself with Aunt Hanmer, who encouraged his suit. Of all the peculiar behavior in Elizabeth's story, that of Aunt Hanmer during that country summer is perhaps the most perplexing. Contemporary biographers tell us that the Duke of Hamilton had continued to write letters to Elizabeth from his Grand Tour. In Hamilton's mind, they were separated geographically, but not romantically. Aunt Hanmer was said to have intercepted the letters and got rid of them, either because she knew Hamilton was a reprobate, or because she was being paid off, or somehow persuaded, by his relatives to do so. This is not as unlikely as it sounds. The institution of marriage at that time was in transition from a familial, dynastic concern to a personal matter for the heart, and the grander the family, the more likely they were to regard marriage as a business decision. Or perhaps Mrs. Hanmer hid them because she was a romantic, who had decided she infinitely preferred young "Hervey the handsome,"[37] like most of womankind. But if Elizabeth was expecting letters and none came, one can only imagine the extent of her pique. Particularly if, as some said, there had been a private engagement.

On Hervey's part, the attractions of Elizabeth were undeniable. For a start, she was very beautiful. When she went to stay with a naval family called the Parkers at their country house, Saltram, she was painted by the then unknown but already discerning judge of female beauty, Joshua Reynolds, who recalled that Elizabeth was "eminently beautiful, and possessed the most delicate person he had ever seen."[38]

Like Augustus, Elizabeth was a wit. Like him, she was impetuous to the point of occasional recklessness, hot-blooded and a lover of attention. The two of them were a fatal mix: a passionate love affair was one thing, but, caught up in the moment, with the naivety of youth, Augustus proposed marriage and, presumably out of some combination of escapism, revenge on Hamilton or the world, love, loneliness, lust, and folly, Elizabeth accepted.

It was not until more than thirty years later that the events of the night of Tuesday, August 4, 1744, became clear and, even then, they emerged from the sketchy testimony of one corrupt, elderly servant woman in a courtroom. Yet, the story of Mrs. Hanmer's maid, Ann Craddock (then Walton), rings as true now as it unfortunately did then.

In a matter of weeks, although he was impecunious and about to go to sea for months, Augustus had successfully wooed Elizabeth. Given that her whole life plan, her only option, was to make a good marriage, she had become the mistress of her own misfortune. Always more excitable than considered, she must have been swept away. He was swashbuckling and attentive, and as she described him, a "gallant and gay lothario."[39]

A few weeks after the visit to the glorious, ill-fated HMS *Victory*[40] at Portsmouth—a backdrop that would have shown the young officer at his naval best as he explained his knowledge of seafaring—Mrs. Hanmer told Ann Craddock that Augustus was going abroad, but was to marry her niece Elizabeth before he went. She confided that although she would rather they waited until his return, they had decided to be married privately at Lainston straightaway.

If delay was Aunt Hanmer's preference, she does not seem to have made any proper attempt to enact it.

CHAPTER SIX

THE CLANDESTINE MARRIAGE

This was how Ann Craddock told the story:

On the night in question John Merrill and Ann Hanmer had gone out to dine elsewhere. No banns were read, although Merrill's friend Mounteney may have gone to get a marriage license; if he did, no trace of it was ever found. So as not to arouse the suspicion of the servants, Elizabeth and Hervey went out of the house as if going for a late stroll on that sultry August night. Mounteney took some air in the garden separately, and when Merrill and Mrs. Hanmer returned from dinner, as prearranged, they sloped straight from their carriage into the ancient chapel of St. Peter that lay a short distance across the luscious rose-scented garden away from the house. The chapel was unused, a small deserted family mausoleum, as Elizabeth later described it, more of "a summerhouse"[1] than a proper church. It had been built centuries before the house itself for the long-vanished hamlet of Lainston. Her Strode great-grandmother's remains lay under a gravestone in the nave—they lie there still, the floor open to the stars now the chapel is a crumbling hollow of stone walls—having been removed from a church in Covent Garden when the Merrills bought the house twenty years earlier.

The house party assembled in the cool pitch-darkness of the spartan stone interior. The Reverend Thomas Amis, the local vicar from Sparsholt, and a minor canon of Winchester Cathedral, had been hauled out at night to perform the ceremony. He was already waiting in there.

It was about eleven o'clock by the time the group came together. They huddled around the wooden reading desk, their shadowy faces thrown into silhouette by the light of a wax taper held by Mr. Mounteney and shaded by the brim of his hat, so that Amis could read softly from the *Book of Common Prayer*. Augustus stood on the right, Elizabeth on the left in front of him, as Amis began:

"DEARLY beloved, we are gathered together here in the sight of God, and in the face of this Congregation, to join together this man and this woman in holy Matrimony . . ."

Amis asked Augustus: "Wilt thou love her, comfort her, honour, and keep her, in sickness and in health; and, forsaking all other, keep thee only unto her, so long as ye both shall live?"

To which Augustus answered, "I will."

He asked Elizabeth: "Wilt thou obey him, and serve him, love, honour, and keep him, in sickness and in health; and, forsaking all other, keep thee only unto him, so long as ye both shall live?"

To which she answered, "I will."

Merrill played "father," as Craddock recounted, and gave Elizabeth away. Mrs. Hanmer sat on a bench in the aisle. Elizabeth and Augustus were pronounced lawful man and wife. They prayed for children. We can presume there was no music, organ, or singing, no parents or grandparents, silks or family jewels, attendants, or flowers other than those growing round the chapel in the garden. Craddock said that she saw it all from a "yard" away, but that none of the other servants knew anything about it.

Ann Craddock was dispatched to see if the garden was clear so that the party could return observed only by the fluttering moths around the flowerbeds. Apart from Amis, everyone went back to the house, some by the front door, some by the side door, and had a quotidian supper. This was certainly no celebratory banquet or wedding breakfast.[2]

Elizabeth and Augustus rushed upstairs and locked the door of the paneled corner bedroom on the first floor, which by day had a picturesque view of the lime avenue, but Mrs. Hanmer made them get up again, as she thought the servants would suspect something if they were alone. "Bundling"—a courting couple staying up for hours together, clothed, but not all night, and usually with someone else in the room—was customary for courting couples; it was a bit late for such niceties from Mrs. Hanmer.[3] After she fell asleep, the couple went upstairs to bed again.

Ann Craddock said that Elizabeth and Augustus "lay together in one and the same bed naked and alone . . . verily believes they consummated their marriage by having carnal knowledge of one another's bodies." She said that all this happened without either the servants or anyone else in the family knowing. They carried on thus for three nights.

Craddock saw them in bed on the morning Hervey left, as she was the one who had to raise him at 5 A.M. "They were very sorry to take leave," she said. As he went away from the house, he asked Craddock to go upstairs and give Elizabeth "all the comfort she could." She found Elizabeth "in a flood of tears," because Augustus was going to Jamaica with Admiral Davers, and her brief honeymoon was already over. Was she crying because he was leaving, because she realized she had yoked herself to a man who was going to sea for the foreseeable future, or because she knew she had made a mistake? Craddock would testify that she herself later married Augustus's manservant William Craddock, who went to Jamaica with him. Like a Shakespearean comedy, the servants were having their own parallel flirtation.

And that was it: a flicker of a moment in a candlelit mausoleum that would dictate the rest of Elizabeth's life. No procession, no gathering of friends or family—even her own mother was absent. No feast, wedding dress, or dancing. We cannot know what Elizabeth or Augustus wore—brides (and grooms) often wore white trimmed with silver, but also other colors such as blue and lilac.[4] (There would have been no time or money for a new dress—aside from the secrecy question.) No dowry, trousseau, linen, or plans for somewhere to live. The details of financial arrangements negotiated by father or brother, which often enriched the groom and protected the bride, did not happen here. John Merrill only acted as "father" in that brief moment of giving her away. There was not even a certificate or a register, because the chapel did not have one.

They did, however, have one thing: an agreement between everyone in the church to keep the marriage a secret.

*

There were many reasons, mostly financial, why Elizabeth and Augustus decided not to announce to the world that they were Mr. and Mrs. Augustus Hervey. Augustus was about to go to sea and, as a married woman, Elizabeth would have to forsake her position as maid of honour to Princess Augusta and the salary, accommodation, and other benefits that came with it. Some maids came back in other roles after marriage—Elizabeth Drax, for example, returned after a few months as a lady of the bedchamber. But Drax's husband was a court figure. A penniless sailor husband, however aristocratic, did not facilitate such a promotion. Augustus, meanwhile, feared his family's reaction. Not only was he still underage at twenty, but in the absence of a father, grandfather Bristol was the man to whom all applications must be made. It seemed unlikely that the sagacious politician who had vastly inflated his fortune twice over through marriage would look kindly on young Augustus, with his uncertain future, marrying someone who brought not so much as a hunk of bread to the table. The idea of a clandestine marriage was familiar to Augustus, however, because his own parents had had one, for much the same reason. His mother had not wanted to lose her position and salary as maid of honour.[5] His parents had created another problem: the enmity between the late Lord Hervey and Frederick, Prince of Wales, meant that of all the surnames that might appear at Leicester House, Hervey was the most unwelcome.

The question is why, if they had such pressing reasons to keep it secret, did they do it at all? It will always be an approximation, diagnosing people down the centuries, but from what we know of Elizabeth's behavior, psychiatrist Dr. James Arkell believes she may fit the profile for borderline personality disorder, a trauma-based form of emotional instability in which fear of abandonment and impulsivity play a part: she married Hervey on an impulse because she did not want him to abandon her, as Hamilton had done.[6] The trauma—the death of her father so early in her life, the move, and later her brother's death—might have triggered this. Those with borderline personality disorder, notes Arkell, are also often charismatic performer types, like Elizabeth: "mad, bad and dangerous to know," as Lady Caroline Lamb said of Lord Byron.

Contemporaneous biographers blame Mrs. Hanmer, reading too many novels to the point where she convinced herself that Hervey was a romantic hero instead of little more than a schoolboy, and believing him to be a catch through her social insecurity. Perhaps there was already some danger of pregnancy and Mrs. Hanmer (although Craddock said she wanted to delay it) or Mr. Merrill thought they were protecting Elizabeth, given that Augustus was about to set sail. "Bundling" often failed in its supposed limits: half of all children at the time were conceived out of wedlock. Women occupied a contradictory position: they had a fair amount of autonomy and could go around alone, particularly in that period between childhood and marriage, but should anything untoward happen, they were ruined.[7]

For many reasons—an increase in female literacy, the rise of the novel, the stirrings of the Enlightenment, and the "revelation" that women had an inner life (in which grandmother Lady Mary Chudleigh was so ahead of her time) and the right to happiness—personal feelings were beginning to take priority over dynastic family interest.

And yet among the upper classes, an economic pact was still expected. In a romantic attachment, the bride's family or friends would still make arrangements for her or advise against a match, as would the groom's.[8] Sailors, however, always aware they might get struck down by a cannonball or yellow fever, were frequently the most devil-may-care sorts who often got married in a hurry before they went on board.[9] The rashness was often alcohol-fueled—they never drank fresh water at sea and kept up their habits on land. On Elizabeth's side, Mrs. Hanmer and Mr. Merrill seem negligent in the extreme, particularly as Merrill, a lawyer who had himself carefully married an heiress, would have known exactly the predicament Elizabeth was getting into. Perhaps Mrs. Hanmer, as the elder sister—she was eighteen months older than Harriet—thought she knew best. Mothers often did weigh in in the absence of anyone else, but it does not seem that Harriet Chudleigh was ever consulted.

The Herveys, too, were unaware of the match. Augustus left Lainston at dawn that August morning and returned to HMS *Cornwall*. While waiting to finally embark for the West Indies in November, he did not reveal a word of what had happened to his fond mother, grandfather, or elder brother George, who were all preoccupied that summer with his siblings, gossip, and affairs of state. Lady Hervey was writing to her younger sons' tutor from under her father-in-law's roof at Ickworth about politics and books, her stay at the Duke of Buckingham's Buckingham House, and worrying about her new granddaughter,[10] with no mention of Augustus at all.

Augustus returned to ship with his family knowing nothing about his dead-of-night wedding.

And eventually, come autumn, Elizabeth returned once again to Leicester House and resumed her duties as maid of honour to the Princess of Wales. To all appearances, she was as available as ever.

CHAPTER SEVEN

PRETENDER

After the wedding, Lieutenant Hervey set sail for Jamaica on board HMS *Cornwall*, the flagship of the fleet of Admiral Davers, commander in chief of the Jamaica Station. Now that he was a secretly married man, Hervey was full of ambition for glory and spoils, and particularly irritated not to have risen beyond second lieutenant. He blamed Davers, whom he neither liked nor respected. The West Indies had been designated a strategic part of the British campaign against Spanish trading might in the War of Jenkins's Ear.* This maritime conflict had expanded into a global skirmish as France had sided with Spain, and the Holy Roman Empire and Piedmont with England.

Fortified by rum, salt beef and pork, dice, cards, and singing, life as a young officer was not all misery at that time, but conditions in the West Indies were an exception. It was both gruesome and dull. In a period of intense military activity, the action was elsewhere— almost everywhere else. Crews were lackluster in the heat, and they battled to stay alive rather than to triumph; only about half the men were ever well enough to do anything. The ship became a feverish floating hospital. Far from making a fortune with which to start married life, the highlight of Augustus's voyage, before he too fell ill,

---

* The War of Jenkins's Ear started when the British captain, Jenkins, had his ear cut off by Spanish sailors who had boarded his merchant ship. It merged into a trade war and the War of the Austrian Succession.

was capturing some canoes off the locals, a half-hearted, consciously dishonorable mission. His lot was an exasperating one.

Once Augustus had left Lainston, Elizabeth may have continued west along the south coast from Hampshire into Devon, to her family house at Hall and to Saltram, outside Plymouth, before she returned to court. Saltram House was the gracious home of the Parker family, connected to the Chudleighs by Devon kinship and friendship. It was here that Elizabeth sat for the Joshua Reynolds portrait. Reynolds's mother was a friend of the "proud and wilful" Lady Catherine Parker, who had set about aggrandizing Saltram.[1]

Born in nearby Plympton, Reynolds was then living with his two unmarried sisters in the Plymouth garrison, where Harriet Chudleigh's cousin George Gibbon was lieutenant governor and her father had been regularly stationed. In his picture of Elizabeth, of which only an etching in Horace Walpole's diaries remains,[*] the fresh-faced maid of honour wears an open, low-cut pale gown and dark cape, her hair hanging in a long, glossy rope over one shoulder, her face youthfully round and innocent looking, with huge sparkling eyes and full lips. What did she think about during those hours when she sat for the amusing, extroverted young man, who would still talk about her beauty decades later? Gazing into the middle distance with a faint, enigmatic smile, she seems lost in private thought—a woman with a secret. One of his sitters remarked that Reynolds would "walk away several feet, then take a long look at me and the picture as we stood side by side, then rush up to the portrait and dash at it in a kind of fury. I sometimes thought he would make a mistake and paint on me instead of the picture."[2]

For all these picturesque diversions in the West Country, come autumn, Elizabeth was nearer the axis of power than Augustus. The royal court reassembled before the return of Parliament. The Prince and Princess of Wales were going to and from Cliveden until mid-October, when they settled again at Leicester House. In January, the prince turned forty-one, and "their Royal Highnesses received the Compliment of the Nobility, foreign ministers &c at Leicester

---

[*] A Victorian engraving of Joshua Reynolds's picture by S. Bull survives in a book of Horace Walpole's.

House in the morning, where there was a great Court. The Day was usher'd in with the ringing of Bells, and the Evening concluded with Bonfires," it was reported.[3] Elizabeth, a lover of spectacle, would have reveled in it.

Leicester House continued as a milieu of parties and politics, and, with its lively young family, exemplary domestic bliss. The two oldest sons, the future King George III and his chatterbox brother Prince Edward, were under a distinguished tutor, Dr. Francis Ayscough,[4] who found both had a "good disposition." There were dramatic performances and birthday parties alongside lessons in arithmetic, Latin, geometry, writing, religion, French, German, Greek; and dancing under the ever-present Desnoyers. In 1745, there were five children in the house and a sixth on the way in November. By the age of eight, in 1746, Prince George, the first British monarch to study science, could read and write in both English and German and comment on politics.

As well he might—because it was almost all anyone talked about at Leicester House. Alongside the War of Jenkins's Ear and War of the Austrian Succession—which had claimed not only Elizabeth's brother, but, in August 1745, her first cousin, the last of the Chudleigh baronets, Sir John,* who died at eighteen—there was the looming, ground-shaking threat of another Jacobite rising. Robert Walpole, now displaced into the Lords as the 1st Earl of Orford, made one last, powerful, eloquent speech before he died in March, in which he warned of imminent invasion. Frederick was listening in the Lords.

The threat of invasion became reality. Encouraged by the French, who hoped to distract the British from operations abroad, the Young Pretender, Charles Edward Stuart, grandson of James II (and son of the Old Pretender), armed with his belief in his divine right to the kingship, landed in Scotland from France at the end of August. His aim: to reclaim the crown for the Catholics from the Protestant interlopers. Edinburgh surrendered immediately, through "supine-

---

* The only son of Harriet's brother George, Sir John Chudleigh, sixth and last Chudleigh baronet, died in the siege of Ostend, six months after being "given a pair of colors in the Second Regiment of Foot Guards."

ness," according to Horace Walpole. By early September, Walpole regarded Scotland as "gone!"[5] All was confusion and danger. Rumor had it that 10,000 men were ready to cross from Dunkirk by ship to support the Pretender. Dutch regiments were summoned for backup. General Sir Charles Cope, leader of the government troops, marched 2,000 men north; in September, they met the Pretender and his army of clansmen at Prestonpans. Cope was defeated; his men fled "without striking a blow," and he left for Berwick by boat. The Jacobites, a 6,000-strong force, began the march south. By mid-November they had crossed the border into England.

Back at Leicester House, the talk was of the Jacobite threat, night and day. Was Elizabeth missing her absent naval husband, or had doubts begun to creep in? Anxious about his safety, her own actions, or her own lies, she was busy playing the part of carefree maid of honour in the middle of a court of rising tension.

Frederick, Prince of Wales, talked politics to anyone who would listen. He had been banned from joining the army by his detested father, in spite of pleading to do so, leaving the favored younger brother, the Duke of Cumberland, a clear run at becoming England's military hero. William, "Billy the Bold," at just twenty-five, already celebrated alongside his father after the Battle of Dettingen,[6] was now commander in chief of the allied forces. Excluded from military planning, Frederick tried to interest Elizabeth and her fellow maids of honour in his political views, as the princess waited to have her sixth child, due any moment. Frederick sat "at the head of the table, drinks and harangues to all this medley til nine at night,"[7] his captive audience, including Elizabeth, listening and murmuring in agreement with him, as courtiers must.

Among all this fear and inaction, Elizabeth attracted attention, and not always of the most flattering sort. Either she already had a sense of humor about herself, or she had to find one. When Prime Minister Henry Pelham[8] tried to make William Pitt secretary of war (the Hanoverians hated Pitt, because he objected to subsidies paid to Hanover out of the British purse), Frederick, whose favorite pastime was complaining about the present ministry and composing imaginary future ones, was so outraged that he made Elizabeth write a letter to Lord Harrington, Secretary of State for the Northern Department,[9] stating that she was more fit for the employment than Pitt was. Frederick dictated as she dipped a quill pen in black ink and wrote, in her fluent girlish hand, in front of the whole room at Leicester House, that the warrant should be given to her, the Hon. Elizabeth Chudleigh, instead. Fourteen people at the table were to sign it, although two refused—Pitt's friend the Duke of Queensberry and Mrs. Layton, a bedchamber woman. As Horace Walpole related to Horace Mann, diplomat in Florence (both Horaces had been Elizabeth's Chelsea childhood playmates), with glee, "It was actually sent."[10]

We can deduce from this that of all the fops, beauties, and reprobates at court who might serve in the government, the idea of Elizabeth being in charge of the war effort was the most ridiculous. Although, less humiliatingly, it is also clear that Harrington would have known exactly who she was.

This prank was typical of Frederick. The Jacobite invasion threatened to displace not only the king, but the Prince of Wales and the entire court, too. Although Frederick had so much to lose, he was reduced, drone-like, to fretting in his many houses. His answer was to fiddle while Rome burned. He was a regular at the theater. In order to minimize his fear, he treated the threat with excruciatingly forced gaiety and levity.

In spite of the mounting suspense, life was civilized at Leicester House. The food was extraordinary by the standards of the time—Lady Jane Hamilton's brother Charles and a Scotsman, James Douglas, were responsible for the catering supplies; and the court, including Elizabeth, got to share the self-indulgent habits of their royal masters. Sometimes, suppers lasted until 5 A.M. Most aristocrats had French chefs, but Frederick had two Germans. Elizabeth's mistress Princess Augusta had breakfast in her room, which consisted of coffee or hot chocolate, bread and butter, and muffins. After dinner, Augusta drank tea in the drawing room, which she brewed herself in a silver kettle. She also liked Rhenish wine, bottled spa water from Bristol, and eating outside whenever she could. At the beginning of November, she gave birth to her fourth son, Prince Henry, at Leicester House. By then, strict Lady Jane Hamilton had been displaced as royal mistress and Mistress of the Robes, queen of the maids of honour, by Lady Middlesex, a "very short, very plain and very yellow" woman, according to Horace Walpole, but also educated, "with a headful of Greek and Latin," musical, artistic, and much more convivial than Hamilton.[11]

By now the Pretender and his men had reached Carlisle, where they captured the castle after a siege. The whole city surrendered through fear, illness, and confusion.

The Leicester House atmosphere was summed up in the fact that while his brother Cumberland had been recalled from Flanders to pursue the enemy in the north, Frederick's response was to have an edible citadel of Carlisle made out of sugar. This creation was presented as the pudding at the three-week-old Prince Henry's christening dinner on November 30.[12] Elizabeth, alongside her fellow maids of honour, pelted it with sugarplums in a siege of confectionery. The elderly courtier, war hero Lord Stair,* and the Prince of Wales joined in. Was Frederick trying to make light of the threat, demeaning his brother by making the thing a practical joke? Or was he showing contempt for the whole enterprise because he was not allowed to take a more active role?

Despite the frivolity at Leicester House, the Pretender and his men continued their march south—Lancaster, Preston, Manchester all fell to him without one shot being fired. On December 4 they reached Derby, only 130 miles from London. Terrible stories flew round the country: one was that children were being tied to the walls of Carlisle Castle, so that if government troops attacked, they would die. In the midst of such talk, the messenger sent to Leicester House to inform Frederick that the enemy was at Derby found a blindfolded figure pawing at the raucous creatures around him. The Prince of Wales and his pages were playing blindman's buff. But the foolery was a facade. Privately, he wrote to his father again begging to join the army. Again, he was refused.

Even the capital seemed threatened now. It was rumored that the Pretender and his forces would reach London any minute. Men signed up to the militia. Four regiments were ordered to camp at Finchley, ready to defend London when the moment of invasion

---

* The snuffbox Stair had given to her was the only thing, Augustus Hervey wrote to Lord Barrington thirty years later, that Elizabeth ever gave him.

came. On December 6, "Black Friday," there was a run on the Bank of England just as the tide turned: finding little support in England and fearing their route back north might be cut off, the Jacobites decided to retreat to Scotland. The promised French troops, whose army was already battered by war and uncertain of Jacobite strategy, never arrived. In January 1746, the Jacobites won a battle at Falkirk Muir in Scotland in wind and torrential rain, although the Pretender's men were much reduced.

Courtiers responded to the terror with intense patriotism and pleasure-seeking. Elizabeth sang the new anthem "God Save the King"* along with them. Her response to the internal stress of marrying a man she hardly knew, keeping it to herself, and not knowing if, or when, he would return, and the external stress of invasion, was to lark about, in true maid of honour style. Regular trips to Vauxhall Gardens, the pleasure grounds on the south bank of the river, alleviated anxiety, as did indulging in current crazes: collecting chinoiserie, bareback riding, visiting the opera, and playing with French paper puppets, called *pantins*. The more serious the threat, the more childish the court at Leicester House became.

Parliament was in pandemonium, too. In February, Pelham resigned because the king, who disagreed with his strategies—in particular, like his son, with making Pitt secretary of war—had gone behind his back and asked Elizabeth's surrogate father and pivotal supporter, Pulteney, now Earl of Bath, to form a ministry. Two days later, it was apparent that Bath did not have the support of the Commons; the forty-eight-hour attempt to form a government became known as the "Silly Little Ministry" and Elizabeth's mentor, Britain's most briefly appointed prime minister. After the failed coup, Pelham reassumed his position.

The rising finally came to a head in April 1746 at Culloden, four miles east of Inverness. The Duke of Cumberland and Field Marshal Wade led the royalist soldiers, including the Duke of Argyll and a

---

* After the defeat at Prestonpans, the Thomas Arne arrangement, 1745—"God save great George our King, God save our noble King, God save the King!"—was repeated nightly after each performance by Arne's daughter-in-law Mrs. Cibber and two actors on stage at the Theater Royal, Drury Lane, from where it spread across the nation.

cavalry troop raised by the Duke of Kingston, of whom we will hear much more. On the Pretender's side were Frasers, Camerons, Macdonalds, and others, aristocratic clan chiefs leading motley tenants, plus some Irish and French. The royalist troops were nearly double in number and better armed with cannons and bayonets, and they destroyed their opponents. The battle was over within an hour: around 1,500 Jacobites were dead and 700 wounded. The heavy-drinking Pretender, "Bonnie Prince Charlie," was taken to Skye by a young sympathizer, Flora Macdonald, and from there, to France. Finally, it was the death knell of the Jacobite threat.

It was not always clear where Frederick's sympathies lay. Although Culloden was a relief for the Hanoverian line, the battle had maddeningly made a hero out of his younger brother yet again. Handel composed *Judas Maccabaeus*, in particular the chorus "See the Conquering Hero Comes," to commemorate Cumberland's victory. But Cumberland had shown no mercy in leaving the battlefield, a barbarous departure in which men, women, and children were killed. After that, Frederick took every opportunity to refer to his brother as "the Butcher." He refused to fire Catherine Walkinshaw, the sister of the Pretender's mistress, who was in his household.[13] He even met the imprisoned Flora Macdonald and ensured her freedom.

London erupted in a state of jubilation. The excitement of peace was just the sort of mood in which maids of honour were feted. Elizabeth was by now becoming a court celebrity in the mold of Molly Lepel (her secret mother-in-law) and Mary Bellenden. In June, she was mentioned in *The Beauties: An Epistle to Mr. Eckardt the Painter*, a poem in which Horace Walpole defended well-known contemporary belles such as Elizabeth, her former fellow maid the Countess of Berkeley, and Augustus Hervey's sister Mrs. Phipps against classical perfection: "Whose Eyes shall try your Pencil's Art/ And in my Numbers claim a Part?/ Our Sister Muses must describe/ CHUDLEIGH, or name her with the tribe."

Among the euphoria, by August, wedding bells rang out for two more of Elizabeth's fellow maids. With the exception of Elizabeth, they were moving up and on. Albinia Selwyn married Sir William Irby MP, later Lord Boston; he was Frederick and Augusta's vice-chamberlain and known as a decent sort. "Lucky girl," wrote

Horace Walpole of the match. Lucy Boscawen, a distant cousin of Elizabeth, a Cornish mining heiress, married Charles Frederick MP. On marriage, she became a lady of the bedchamber.

Thirty of the Pretender's Scottish lords were brought down to London for trial amidst the rejoicing. Their plight so aroused the sympathies of the fashionable world that some ladies started speaking French in their honor (the French were in league with the cause), and others, like Lady Townshend,* developed a crush on them—in her case, on Lord Kilmarnock.

Lord Cromartie's wife appeared with her children before Princess Augusta and begged for clemency, mother to mother, and won her husband a pardon. The trials bred turmoil for Elizabeth when she should have been joining in the elation. As she would have heard, a nobleman turned up at St. James's and secured an audience with the king to plead for the life of Lord Kilmarnock. It was none other than the Duke of Hamilton, back from his Grand Tour at last.

The king was unmoved, seeing Hamilton as more foe than friend. Not only had the duke's ancestor, the 1st Lord Hamilton, married Mary Stewart, daughter of the deposed Catholic James II, but while he had been away the Pretender had, for a time, lodged in Hamilton Palace. There, he had shot pheasants, partridge, and a deer, and borrowed Hamilton's horses.[14] Hamilton's allegiances looked somewhat suspect.

As Elizabeth was in the country and Hamilton would shortly leave London, they did not encounter each other. But when in town, she had had plenty of other admirers, such as Peregrine Bertie, the 3rd Duke of Ancaster and Kesteven, Lord Great Chamberlain and a recent widower, who had raised a regiment of foot during the uprising. Elizabeth's position was bewildering. If she had to pretend to be single, how could she not encourage them a little? And yet, she had to keep her distance, which only made her admirers keener.

Despite protests, the first two of the Scots lords, Kilmarnock and Balmerino, were beheaded in August 1746 at the Tower of London. "Hamilton's intercession for Lord Kilmarnock hurried him to the block," was Horace Walpole's view.[15] Crowds clung to the masts of

---

* Wit and estranged wife of Viscount Townshend, politician.

ships moored on the river and crammed into windows to watch, and spyglasses were rented at halfpenny a time. The heads of those who had been found guilty of treason were stuck on Temple Bar.

Elizabeth had gone down to the West Country to escape the frenzy, and the day after the beheadings, a ship called the *Seahorse* landed in Dover from the West Indies. With no warning, and after nearly two years' absence, Augustus Hervey, Elizabeth's secret husband, had returned home.

CHAPTER EIGHT

MARRIAGE REDUX

Jamaica had been a luckless enterprise for Augustus Hervey. He had found Admiral Davers untrustworthy and divisive. After refusing to do his admiral's bidding, he was confined on board ship. He ended this unsatisfactory state of affairs in June 1746, by resigning his commission as a second lieutenant on the *Cornwall*, and returning to England as a passenger on board the frigate, the *Seahorse*.[1] According to his diary,[2] he was not rushing back, lovestruck, to see his spouse. He had made many friends on the island, such as the governor, Edward Trelawny, James Ord, a merchant, and his wife Anna Petronilla, to whom he became suspiciously close, though he claimed it was "in the most virtuous sense."[3] He wrote that it was "with regret I left the island, very great regret." A leaving dinner was thrown for him at one of the plantation houses, and a party, including the governor, came down to the harbor to see him off.

Sunbaked and seaworn, 22-year-old Hervey arrived at Dover two months later on August 19 alongside a fellow naval officer.[4] They slept at Canterbury, admired the harvest from their carriage, and dined at the Star and Garter Inn on Pall Mall. Hervey stayed at the sign of the Golden Ball, the premises of his tailor on Pall Mall. Submerged straight back into the beau monde as quickly as waves close over a shipwreck, he set about making visits. The boundless confidence with which he attempted to further his own cause at such a young age is striking. He delivered one letter from Governor Trelawny to the Duke of Newcastle, Secretary of State for the Southern

Department, at a wedding party at the Duke of Grafton's house,[5] and another to Prime Minister Pelham (Newcastle's brother) at the Queen's House in Greenwich.[6] He had extended talks with both of them, even though he knew that they had blocked his promotion because they were irritated by his elder brother's politics. The Royal Navy was just as riven by political factions as the court itself, often with even more drastic consequences. Family connections could as easily sink a career as float one.

Preoccupied as he was with his unsteady naval progress, it did not take long for Hervey to realize that his marital adventures were not quite as secret as planned. The evening he returned from Greenwich, his second night in London, he went at a late hour to see his brother Lord Hervey at the stately townhouse at 6 St. James's Square. His brother calmly confronted him with the astounding rumor he had heard: both he and grandfather Bristol had been told that Augustus was married to a maid of honour by the name of Elizabeth Chudleigh. Was it true? If so, Lord Hervey had persuaded Lord Bristol to receive her.

The marriage was not yet common knowledge—hence others were trying to woo Elizabeth—but someone, somewhere had revealed the secret. Augustus, always looser-lipped than Elizabeth, had told at least one friend; equally, it could have got out through the notoriously efficient servant network.

Augustus evaded the unwelcome question. Lord Hervey told him that Miss Chudleigh herself did not deny it. Augustus did not deny it, either, nor did he want to continue the conversation until he knew "how things were, or were likely to be," as he wrote in his diary.

An air of uncertainty hovered over Augustus's life. His feelings towards Elizabeth had been overshadowed by financial reality. He recorded resentfully that his family had never shown him any support, in "interest or fortune," and that marriage was a state he was "wholly incapable of supporting," being worth only £300 in the world, with "£50 a year left by my father until my grandfather's death . . . then £200 a year annuity." It seems that he believed by now—he had had two years on a tropical, faraway island with not much to do other than think about it—that he had made a significant mistake, putting himself in a position he could neither afford nor easily extract himself from.

The reports of Elizabeth that he had heard around town, both from those who knew nothing of the marriage rumors and those few who did, were not promising, either. He dined with his uncle Tom Hervey at White's, the aristocratic chocolate house turned gaming club, and went to see his friend Lady Townshend, in whom he had confided.[7] She dropped hints to him that Miss Chudleigh had not been as "altogether vestal-like as might have been wished."

He refused to be alarmed until he had found out the truth for himself. He knew "how ready people are to censure others or level them with themselves"—a reference to the state of the Townshends' own marriage and Lady T's shaky reputation. Elizabeth was pretending to be a single maid of honour, so was possibly entertaining advances because she had no excuse not to do so.

Plunged back into society, Augustus was offered the position of master and commander of a sloop, a smaller ship, to sail to Barbados (although he would have to pay to refurbish it himself); was presented to a "sour" king at court at Kensington Palace;[8] played cards with the Duchess of Richmond and admired the wife of the Venetian ambassador;[9] and met with his ally and mentor, Admiral Byng. He noted with annoyance that one friend[10] was already a captain in spite of joining the navy two years after him. Everything was "useless," he wrote, in ennui.

His family were ready to help, to a degree. He returned to Ickworth, then a country manor house in Suffolk parkland,* to see his mother and to celebrate his grandfather's birthday, at which lords, ladies, butlers, and kitchen maids all danced together. He only stayed for a few days, because his mother and grandfather thought that he should be "furthering his interest." He left Ickworth with letters written on his behalf to the top of the Admiralty.[11] His grandfather gave him eight guineas† "and his blessing!" The exclamation mark indicated despair over the paltry amount.

His uncles were more generous. His former captain, Uncle Wil-

---

* The neoclassical rotunda house, an Italianate palace, was built fifty years later by Augustus's younger brother Frederick.
† Eight guineas = nine pounds and forty pence (one guinea being one pound and one shilling, or £1.05).

liam, settled his debts and Uncle Henry, now a clergyman who had taken his heiress wife's name of Aston, offered advice. Eventually, he raised the money he needed for fitting out the sloop.[12]

While Augustus was trying to raise funds, Elizabeth was in the West Country enjoying her pastoral summer, staying at Hall, Lainston, Chalmington, Saltram, riding, fishing, picnicking, just as she had done before the wedding. It does not seem to have occurred to either Elizabeth or Augustus to make the effort to visit the other. "I was amazed in all this time not to have heard from Miss Chudleigh, and that she did not come to town," Augustus wrote in mid-September. Presumably, he had written to her and received no reply. He made no attempt to go to the country, either—perhaps he felt he could not as the relationship was a secret. Her silence "made me suspect there might be something in the reports I had heard of her conduct," he wrote. As neither traveled to see the other the romance, if not yet extinguished, was certainly not aflame.

We can only surmise that for Elizabeth, with her growing fame and band of admirers, regrets had seeped in, although it would have been impossible for her to arrange transport to London in the summer season with no good excuse. (It is unclear whether her mother knew about her marriage.) Devon to London was an arduous, expensive journey that took at least three days by stagecoach in the 1740s.[13]

Augustus was feeling humiliated. Fellow sailors had risen over him, his wife was ignoring him, and, if he believed the gossip, flirting with other men. His sloop, the *Porcupine*, could be stationed at home or abroad; he chose the latter, a decisive reading of the temperature of his marriage to Elizabeth.

Hervey urgently needed more money for this voyage, and after pleading, his grandfather would only give him £100, a third of what he needed. Bristol was pained in paying out: "I must own you ought to have lived upon much less." Augustus had taken the enormous sum of £1,500 in prizewinnings at sea in 1741, and spent the lot. His grandfather not unreasonably thought he should have saved £1,000 for exigencies such as this.

But behind his back, his prospects were rising. Inside the Admiralty, Lord Vere Beauclerk wrote to the Duke of Bedford, "If he has his faults . . . it is not [for] want of spirit or for knowledge of his profession."[14]

Dubiously, given both his lack of money and his claims of a "virtuous" relationship with Mrs. Ord in Jamaica, Augustus sent her "a very pretty onyx toothpick-case with an enamelled picture of me on the top." Neither cheap, nor platonic-sounding, a miniature in any form was often a love token.[15]

He did not hear from "Miss Chudleigh," as he referred to Elizabeth, "tho I did of her." Being still only twenty-two—in spite of one secret marriage, eleven years at sea, and six as a lieutenant—he wrote in his diary, in self-justification, that "being young and much about it was not surprising I got hold of some things." To a Georgian buck, "things" meant women beneath their own class, such as the starlets at Covent Garden Opera House, as Hervey put it, "famous in their way on the stage." Less than two months after his return, he was playing the lothario again, if he had ever stopped. Two performers "admitted [his] attentions": "the Galli"—Signora (Caterina) Galli, a mezzo-soprano, student of Handel, wife of a musician—and "the Campioni," Signora Campioni, an opera dancer, known as "one of the finest women of her time."[16] Campioni would not accept anything from Augustus but a diamond ring he bought her, which only seems to back up his grandfather's objections. He gathered women as quickly as he spent money.

On October 16, two months after Augustus had landed, the court reassembled from the country and Elizabeth was back in town. She sent for Hervey to meet her at Aunt Hanmer's house in Upper Grosvenor Street.* Here they set eyes on each other after a two-year absence in the discreet elegance of Mrs. Hanmer's first-floor drawing room. Heated "mutual reproaches" ensued; Elizabeth thought he should have gone to Devon, Augustus that she should have come up to London to see him.

Initially they were unsure of each other, but however many diver-

---

* Now number 48. The Hanmers were the first residents. It was later home to another scandalous duchess: Margaret, Duchess of Argyll, or "Marg of Arg." Her divorce case was a sensation in 1963.

sions they had enjoyed, physical attraction clearly remained: the reunion became a passionate one. He wrote: "However being both very young, this little quarrel passed off, nor did we let it break in on our pleasures." While Mrs. Hanmer was away, they spent nights, from midnight until 5 A.M., in her house. Hervey took on debts to settle Elizabeth's—her spending far outranked her salary[17]—and gave her an "onyx watch set with diamonds."

Things rapidly curdled. Lack of money and trust began to hang between them in the Mayfair air in the early hours. Augustus could ill afford watches and extra debt. He found Elizabeth preoccupied with her court connections, which "chill[ed]" his feelings, although he still wanted to please her. He was tired of London. What had begun as youthful exuberance had descended into intrigue, jealousy, and hesitation. Both determined, energetic, uncertain young people, they were too similar not to be irritated by each other. With Elizabeth trapped in a web of court gossip and Augustus engrossed with his naval career, they were ambitious in different directions. Elizabeth began to wish him away: sometimes she refused to see him, "though I knew her at home," he wrote in his diary.

It was an intolerable situation for a proud buccaneer. Aside from his relationships with singers, like any sailor of the day, he consoled himself with the bottle. On November 1, he reported that many "of the Admiralty" dined on board his sloop and staggered off inebriated at 2 A.M. One onlooker recorded that he saw Augustus at Vauxhall pleasure gardens around this time, on a drunken rampage with his school friend Sir Charles Sedley.[18] A party had just sat down to supper when they were "alarmed at a loaded plug [a sword that fits onto a rifle's muzzle] coming through the window and falling in the middle of a codling [apple] pie and cream which broke the dish and splashed us all over." They went to "chastise the ruffians who had been guilty of the outrage" and "who should [we] meet at the door but Sir Charles Sedley and Captain Hervey, drunk, and in a fury to find one of the waiters" who had refused to give them any more wine . . ." The riotous pair were so enraged that "they broke the lamps, beat not only the waiters" but also two others, "for remonstrating with them for the ravages they were committing."[19]

Augustus and friend ended up with a hefty fine. The writer added that, "I had not the honour of knowing . . . Hervey; but he had so many friends and admirers, that amidst all his madcappery he must have had inherent good qualities to balance his policoneries [pranks]."[20]

In early December, Augustus was out of town. He boarded his new ship, the *Porcupine*, and was ready to sail from Plymouth. Mrs. Hanmer wrote, full of regret, to tell him that Elizabeth was receiving none other than the Duke of Hamilton in his absence and they were "very often together." There was nothing she seemed to be able to do to prevent it. As recorded in his diary, Hervey wrote to his wife "in vain." Mrs. Hanmer seemed more interested in Augustus's feelings than Elizabeth's, as she had been around the wedding. Or perhaps she felt responsible for the state of the marriage.

But Mrs. Hanmer was right: a few days before she wrote her disquieting letter, on December 2, the Duke of Hamilton had arrived in London from his seat in Hampshire. His London house on Grosvenor Street, a wide, spacious residence on the south side, was uncomfortably close to Mrs. Hanmer's, and only a few minutes' walk away from Leicester House and Mrs. Chudleigh's house in Conduit Street. Ignorant of Elizabeth's marriage, he had renewed his suit with enthusiasm. Any attempts to keep them apart failed. Whatever was said, it must have become clear to her that, in his mind, he had not abandoned her at all.

In terms of Augustus's naval career, however, things were looking up: his friend Admiral Byng had asked him to be a captain under his squadron to be sent to the Mediterranean to gain dominance of those waters over the French and Spanish, a far superior position than that of the sloop headed for Barbados. He accepted, and in the interim, on December 18, he sailed off the south coast on a short voyage on the sloop. The timbers were too new, so all the men fell sick (through inhaling the dry rot that flourishes in unseasoned timber). But he was in luck: by the end of the month he had run one French ship aground and captured another, winning a concomitant three-eighths share of the prize money. He also received orders to take charge of the seventy-four-gun *Princessa*: a proper captaincy at last.

Before he could rejoice, however, Hervey heard desperate news even more overwhelming than the Hamilton rumors: Elizabeth was at death's door after taking an overdose of laudanum.

He set off on horseback from Plymouth to London, in the New Year freeze, "having no chaises in those days to travel with."

He arrived in London on January 9 at 6 A.M., having ridden all through the night.

Elizabeth's plight was so serious it found its way into the newspapers.

One report read: "A few days ago a melancholy accident happened to Miss Chudleigh, one of the Maids of honour to her Royal Highness the Princess of Wales . . . the young lady having caught a cold, which had occasioned her to be thick of hearing . . . was advised to drop a small quantity of laudanum into her ear . . . sending for a bottle, she did as prescribed. A medicine being sent some time after for her to take inwardly, she ordered her servant, a young country girl, to pour it out, and give it to her, but she mistaking the bottle, gave her the laudanum instead."[21] Mrs. Chudleigh came into the room, discovered what had happened, and sent for a doctor, who "advised them by all means to keep her awake, for if she went to sleep she would certainly die; which by shaking and other methods they have hitherto effected, and there are great hopes of her recovery." (This is a rare mention of Elizabeth's mother, Mrs. Chudleigh. She is peculiarly elusive in Elizabeth's story.)

There were rumors that it was not an accident.[22] Had the torment of the secret marriage to Hervey, and the agony of having to reject Hamilton, prompted a suicide attempt? By the mid-eighteenth century, laudanum, an opium tincture mixed with alcohol, was seen as a cure-all, and sometimes as a means of suicide, too, because it was toxic even in small quantities.[23] Raised in a Christian framework, although she was hardly saintly, she continuously referred to her faith through her life and would have seen suicide as "self-murder." But the possibility of borderline personality disorder (as first mentioned on p. 73) makes a suicide attempt much more likely, self-harming being part of that impulsive, "black and white thinking" profile.[24] It also might explain her reaction to Hervey's return: she hated him for having abandoned her. (The fact that he had to leave for naval duties would make no difference.)

It was not just Elizabeth who suffered. Hamilton had returned from his travels just as devoted as ever. How tantalizing for the maid of honour, with debts piling up (overspending itself being a trait of borderline personality disorder), who had realized the folly of her marriage to a boisterous, libidinous stripling who could not provide her with a carriage, let alone anywhere to live. The whole misunderstanding of 1744 may well have been made plain to her, even the missing letters, if true. Elizabeth's admirer with the palace in Scotland, the double dukedom, the country estate in Hampshire, the townhouse, the apartment in Holyroodhouse, the retinue, the royal blood and, more than all of that, the man who had inspired her love and commitment before he left, had returned to propose marriage, and to the amazement of nearly everyone she knew and much to her own—and his—consternation, she had had to turn him down. Whether she actually told him the truth, we will never know.

The result of this upset was deep malaise in both parties. Newspapers reported that after the rebuff, the Duke of Hamilton, now twenty-two, was lying seriously ill in Portsmouth, where he had fled with the intention of traveling abroad. By January, both Elizabeth and Hamilton were bedridden and dejected; she in London, he in Portsmouth. As she awaited the return of Hervey, Elizabeth had taken the laudanum, accidentally or otherwise, and Hamilton had turned to the bottle.

Augustus arrived in London after his night on horseback, half-expecting, half-hoping, perhaps, to find Elizabeth dead; instead, he "found her very much alive," having recovered at her mother's home in Conduit Street. Rather than relief and a touching reconciliation, any love between them was flickering out. While in town, he met Elizabeth every night and wrote, "There was some underhand game going on that I did not comprehend . . . great mysteries, great falseness, and every mark of what I wholly disapproved." He resolved to put his discomfort out of his mind, "to shut my eyes and ears as much as I could to it all, as I was shortly to go abroad."

On January 16, Augustus had the "great joy," the moment he had longed for, of being sworn in as the captain of Byng's flagship, the "glorious" *Princessa*.[25] At twenty-three, he was now one of the youngest captains in the navy, in the sea lane towards the Admiralty.

There was one more encounter between the two of them before he left. One version claims he had insisted she came to his lodgings on pain of exposing the marriage, as she was refusing to see him. Another, that they met at Conduit Street while her mother was out and that the door was locked to prevent her escape.

It may have been hypocritical, given his two mistresses and his "friend" in Jamaica, but Hervey had become jealous and possessive. At the time, male infidelity was a trifle, female infidelity significant, as reputation, legitimacy, and inheritance were jeopardized by it. Elizabeth and Augustus had similar temperaments, but Augustus could get away with what Elizabeth could not. As Augustus was never very discreet about his liaisons, it is likely that Elizabeth felt no particular loyalty to him, especially given her forced rejection of the Duke of Hamilton. Hervey's response to their increasingly unsatisfactory situation was to concentrate instead on his overriding concern, his naval career. There was no such distraction for Elizabeth.

Hamilton, meanwhile, still lay in bed at Portsmouth at the end of the month. It was reported that one Saturday: "Dr. Pringle, Physician to his Royal Highness the Duke [of Cumberland] set out for Portsmouth, to attend his Grace the Duke of Hamilton who is taken very dangerously ill there."[26] By Tuesday, January 27, his condition had declined further. "We have heard that the Duke of Hamilton is so ill at Portsmouth, that his Life is thought to be in Danger."[27]

In what amounted to an act of espionage, Augustus Hervey—who wrote that he was in a "miserable situation" out of town, waiting for his ship to sail, longing to be among the "Wise Great" again—found an excuse to see Hamilton on his sickbed in Portsmouth. He claimed in a letter[28] to his friend Lady Townshend that he was planning to help Hamilton with supplies for his trip abroad in exchange for money, but he must have been hoping to discover what had passed between him and his wife. He found him "so weak, he can't undertake the voyage . . . having been twice taken with very severe vomiting of blood. They say he can't (poor man) live many days longer; no wonder! For the instant he recovers a little, he drinks 'till four, five & six in the morning."[29]

In February, Hamilton began to recover, and in April he was on board ship, bound for the spas of Portugal to convalesce, leaving England and Elizabeth behind him.

Waiting at the coast to depart for the Mediterranean, it was Hervey's turn to sink into illness and emotional confusion. Baffled and upset—although now a proper captain—he contracted painful rheumatic pleurisy and consulted two doctors, Dr. Monsey* and Dr. Dawson. It took a full two months to recover and he then "made merry" with companions such as his school friend Lord Darnley, a lord of the bedchamber to Frederick, Prince of Wales. With such friends, it was impossible for Hervey not to hear news of Elizabeth from the heart of Leicester House before he set sail in June.

As fragile, penniless, and noncommittal as the clandestine marriage was, in spring, Elizabeth realized she was expecting a baby. There is no mention of this in Hervey's journal, which he transcribed from his original diaries. (Whether he ever wrote about it before he chose to draw a veil over it, we will of course never know.)[30]

She was not the first maid of honour to have been in this position.[31] The form was to disappear to somewhere like Bath, for one's "health," for a few months, with permission from the royal mistress. By the time Elizabeth's pregnancy started to show, the court had dispersed for the summer. In May she went to Chelsea, land of her childhood, still, perhaps, the place where she felt safest, and at home, to conceal herself. We cannot be sure exactly where she went—probably lodgings of some kind, readily available in Chelsea. The Rev. Hon. Henry Hervey Aston, Augustus's clergyman uncle and most supportive relative, and his wife, acted as go-betweens for Elizabeth and Augustus when he was at sea.

Perhaps Elizabeth felt a mixture of trepidation and excitement. Certainly, she took great care over the childbirth. She borrowed £100 from Mrs. Hanmer to buy baby clothes[32] and she must have confided in Princess Augusta because she was attended by one of Leicester House's physicians, Caesar Hawkins. He did not breathe

---

* Messenger Monsey was the doctor at the Royal Hospital, Chelsea. His method of pulling teeth was to wrap catgut round the tooth, the other end around a bullet in a gun, and fire.

a word about it for over twenty years, when he was made to speak at her trial.[33] Then, he could not remember the time or the exact place—other than the fact that it was in Chelsea, near the Royal Hospital. Hawkins said, "I was desired to attend, with a view and purpose that I might be witness to the birth of that child." Though the birth was largely secret, Elizabeth wanted a reliable witness, and the best medical advice.

Hawkins did not deliver the child: that would have been done by a midwife. Childbirth at the time was usually a social affair, with female helps—"gossips"—gathering round the draped bed, but, given the circumstances, it is likely Elizabeth's was quite the reverse.[34] With no husband to support her (even if they were not allowed in the bedchamber, they were usually nearby), Elizabeth's must have been a traumatic experience, her fear perhaps intensified by the knowledge of all those babies her own mother had lost. At the birth itself, cold air, smells, and sounds had to be kept out of the room; everything was kept clean; but Elizabeth's options for pain relief consisted only of prayer, herbs, compresses, opiates, being bled (to induce syncope, to erase memory), and various forms of alcohol. Once the baby was born, the placenta was examined and Elizabeth's pulse taken. Like all new mothers, she was given caudle—a sugar, fortified egg, and nutmeg drink—and the baby sweet almond oil for colic. Elizabeth lived on broth, caudle, and tea for two days and stayed in bed for several more: "lying-in" could last for weeks. It does not seem that her mother visited her. At her trial, Aunt Hanmer's servant Ann Craddock claimed that Elizabeth had the baby in Chelsea specifically because her mother could not go there, because her "late husband and son were buried there." (Presumably, Craddock meant that Mrs. Chudleigh would be too upset to visit Chelsea.) Either her mother did not know because Elizabeth did not want her to, or she did not want to know.

So it was that Elizabeth was delivered of a baby boy in September 1747, three months after Augustus had gone to sea. He was christened Augustus Henry Hervey on November 2 by his father's uncle, his own namesake, the Rev. Hon. Henry Hervey Aston, in Chelsea, in the church where his maternal uncle Sir Thomas Chudleigh was buried. Christenings usually happened within days, but there was no father around to organize it, or perhaps the baby or Elizabeth were ill. Augustus sent Elizabeth £200 via Uncle Hervey Aston a few weeks before the birth, from his winnings at sea. Again, his son's birth is not mentioned in his journal. He wrote, instead, about the numerous other women he was chasing.[35]

As the whole affair was to be kept under the covers, a wet nurse was found in Chelsea. Doctors were beginning to advise that infant mortality might be reduced if women nursed their own children, but to feed one's own child was not upper-class behavior and, it was believed, ruined the mother's health and figure as well as interfering with the social round. In Elizabeth's case, with no father and the weight of the secret, she would have felt she had no choice. Wet nurses often lived in reduced circumstances, some given "to drinking and other vices";[36] the health of the baby was jeopardized by their displaced environment as well as by the lack of maternal bond. Infant mortality ran as high as 75 percent in some areas of London. No wonder, with such unhygienic practices as feeding "pap," a kind of gruel, chewed and spat out by the wet nurse and given to the baby before it was put to the breast.

Three months after giving birth, Elizabeth was seen in Bath, presumably recovering her health. On December 28, 1747, a fellow spa visitor wrote,[37] "Here are many whom I know, but few whom I like; the rooms are very full of noise and whisk . . . We have here Miss Chudleigh, [and] a very pretty daughter of Lord Chief Justice; but they are ill provided with beaus, so that it is scarce worth their while to be so handsome."

We do not know if the baby went to Bath or whether he was with the wet nurse then, but she had not abandoned him. When he fell ill in London, Elizabeth asked Caesar Hawkins to attend him. Evidently there was little he could do, because baby Augustus died in the cold of January 1748, at less than four months old. He was buried at the Chelsea church where he had been christened, again by his great-uncle Hervey Aston. His father never laid eyes on him. His mother's situation, agonizingly, did not allow her to reveal how distraught she felt.

The only word about his tragically short life that survived from Elizabeth was years after, from Ann Craddock, who although she betrayed Elizabeth at every turn insisted at the trial that when Elizabeth told her that her baby, who looked just like "Mr. Hervey," was dead, the maid of honour was in "great grief." Later biographers would cast Elizabeth as heartless, but it seems that Craddock spoke with honesty here. Craddock added that when she and Elizabeth were once in a coach together going in the direction of Chelsea, Elizabeth was "much affected," as her boy was buried there.[38]

CHAPTER NINE

IPHIGENIA

An elegant woman, in vast hoops that emphasize the slender waist of her pale, extravagant gown, stands on the sunny Upper Walk of Tunbridge Wells, with its colonnade, post office, and coffee shop. Two dandyish gentlemen on either side of her are vying for her attention. They are potentates of society and politics. One is Beau Nash, man of fashion, master of ceremonies, architect of the social scene in here and in Bath; the other, the promising William Pitt, paymaster of the forces, a future prime minister—the man she once suggested she should replace. With her hair in a long knot topped by a lace cap, this graceful figure eclipses the other women by the showiness of her dress and the confidence of her bearing.

So, in a contemporary drawing, Elizabeth Chudleigh is represented center stage on the promenade of the spa town she visited in the summer of 1748. Between the shops and the spreading shade of the trees, there were also Dr. (Samuel) Johnson, the Duchess of Norfolk, the Bishop of Salisbury, actors Colley Cibber and David Garrick, and the former Speaker of the House of Commons, Arthur Onslow, as recorded by their fellow pilgrim to the waters, the novelist Samuel Richardson.*

---

* The drawing, by "Loggan the dwarf," a painter known for his "accuracy and spirit," was found in Richardson's possessions after he died. Loggan was a renowned fan painter who had his own shop under the sign of The Little Fanmaker.

Tunbridge Wells was the nearest spa town to London, and had been distinguished with royal patronage since the early seventeenth century when Queen Henrietta Maria[1] was sent there by doctors to recover after childbirth. Queen Anne, and more recently Frederick and Augusta, had been visitors. Built by aristocrats, for aristocrats, it conveniently combined the pursuit of health, happiness, and pleasure. The air was said to be "benign, pure and wholesome," the native "chalybeate"* water invigorating and attributed with miraculous restorative powers, for low spirits as well as infirm bodies. The founder, Lord North,[2] had a doctor who wrote:

> These waters youth in age renew
> Strength to the weak and sickly add
> Give the pale cheek a rosy hue
> And cheerful spirits to the sad.

It was now fashionable because Beau Nash ruled the walks as the "despot of the beau monde," just as he had ruled Bath. (Bath was his "kingdom"; Tunbridge Wells a "colony of that kingdom.") He decreed that every visitor should live in public. Each hour had its custom: devotees, including Elizabeth, rose between seven and eight to drink the waters and then took a walk before breakfast. They ate buttered rolls or toasted muffins, which in dry weather were served under the trees, accompanied by music; then chapel, an excursion by coach or on horseback, or a browse around the bookshop; followed by "dinner" at two, a hearty affair of, say, pheasant, duck, or "excellent fish" such as mackerel. Everyone changed into "full and splendid attire"—a quite dazzling transformation[3]—and the orchestra struck up, to accompany tea-drinking at six, and gaming. Supper was at nine. Twice a week, on Tuesdays and Fridays, balls took place in the assembly rooms. Silk dresses would swish across the marble floor as the music floated through the chatter. It was not a place to hide away from the world.

In July 1748, just a few months after the death of baby Augustus, Elizabeth could be found in the midst of the social scene at

---

* Chalybeate: mineral spring waters containing iron salts.

Tunbridge Wells. Such a public choice does not mean she was unfeeling—far from it. It was a contemporary belief that the best thing for low spirits was company; the worst, solitude.

Elizabeth was plagued by either hypochondria, ill health, or some curious mix of both; she became a frequenter of spa towns, for the cures as well as the decorative social life. If she already had borderline personality disorder, the trauma of losing a baby in secret would only have exacerbated it. She could cover up her past, but this meant she could confide in no one, certainly not tentative spa acquaintances. One contemporary biographer, who demonized her, wrote with no evidence that she was relieved when her child died. But not only did Ann Craddock, as a trial witness, contradict that, but Elizabeth's later letters show her to be a deeply affectionate sort who adored children and had a strong interest in education.[4]

Elizabeth had returned to court as maid of honour from her Bath visit in December, and her secrets, for the moment, seemed safe. In spring, after eight rumbling years, the War of the Austrian Succession, which had claimed the life of Elizabeth's brother, had at last come to a halt, with victory for the allies. The peace treaty was in the process of negotiation at Aix-la-Chapelle. Once the prince and princess had gone to the country in the summer of 1748, Elizabeth was free to go to Tunbridge Wells. The form might have been to rise early to drink the waters—hard because the spa induced such "sleepiness"[5]—but by the convivial nature of the place, cards and drinking commenced alongside the promenades, concerts, and shopping; and because of the peace, this season, the mood was one of celebration.

A sign of the state of nerves Elizabeth was attempting to conceal was described by a young politician in a letter to a friend in July:[6] "After drinking four bottles, which had made me mad, and the rest of the company drunk, I strapped and carried Baron Newman, alias Crook-fingered Jack,[7] in a chair, quite up to the end of Joy's long room, at nine o'clock, where all the company then in Tunbridge were assembled." The pair opened the door and fell straight over "to all appearances" as if they were dead. Elizabeth had a dramatic response: "Miss Chudleigh, who is very subject to fits, struck with the odd appearance, fainted, and was carried off. This, in less than a quarter of an hour, spread among the contagion; I am informed of eight at least, who fell into fits."

For a determined and intelligent woman, this would appear to be an overreaction. Nevertheless, Elizabeth had developed an uncontainable horror of death, and her response was to be repeated many times. At the time, such behavior was deemed to be attention-seeking hysteria: the men were cavorting about, the women fainted. But surely the strain of her unwise marriage, secret childbirth, and recent loss—particularly in the context of general jubilation at the end of the war—were taking their toll. There are several possible explanations: a fit of "hysteria" was much more common then than now, as "culture-bound" emotional reactions change, like everything else, through history. It could also have been a physical reaction prompted by a phobia of death,[8] or a psychosomatic or pseudo-seizure, which has been described as coming from "sadness . . . so overwhelming that they cannot bear to feel it . . . in its place they develop physical disabilities . . . against all logic their subconscious chooses to be crippled by convulsions . . . rather than experience the anguish that exists inside them."[9]

It was thought that women's "hysteria" came from their fragile nature and, more specifically, the womb. Pope's Belinda in *The Rape of the Lock* collapses into the "Cave of Spleen" at the loss of two ringlets: "She sighs for ever on her pensive bed/ Pain at her side. And Megrim at her head."[10] The writer Mary Wollstonecraft, a generation later, began to analyze "hysteria" as the outlet of women's silent sorrow, the "very echo of their grief." This was a society that had not yet found the language for emotional suffering, and for women, "hysteria" was the term for a limbic response.[11] Diarist Hester Thrale Piozzi at the same time wrote that grim childbirth, infant illness, and tragedy could "tear mind and body" to pieces, and it would be all the worse with a cruel, or absent, husband.[12] With Hervey estranged and abroad, and Elizabeth's unacknowledged experience of motherhood such a terrible and lonely one, it is no wonder self-control and consciousness sometimes deserted her.

Aside from this highly strung episode, the impression Elizabeth made was glorious. Richardson described how Elizabeth was the best example of the "Wells belle" phenomenon to a friend that summer:

New faces, my dear, are more sought after than fine faces . . . Miss
Chudleigh was the triumphant toast: a lively, sweet-tempered,
gay, self-admired, and, not altogether without reason, generally
admired lady—She moved not without crowds after her. She
smiled at every one. Every one smiled before they saw her, when
they heard she was on the Walk. She played, she won, she lost—all
with equal good-humor . . . But alas, she went off, before she was
wished to go.[13]

The belle who followed her, recorded Richardson, was found to
"want spirit and life. Miss Chudleigh was remembered by those who
wished for the brilliant mistress, and scorned the wife-like quality
of sedateness."

Now a young woman of twenty-seven, a sharper picture of a
more mature Elizabeth Chudleigh emerges. With one clandestine
marriage and one baby behind her, she was determined to present
herself as socially available. Her appeal was in her charisma just as
much as her beauty. There was never anything bland or subdued
about Elizabeth. At Chelsea, and at court, she engaged in playful
exchanges with multitudes of people. The admiral's wife Fanny
Boscawen wrote of the *élite de la jeunesse*, of which Elizabeth was
at the heart, who frequented the balls at Ranelagh (the pleasure
gardens that had opened next to the Royal Hospital), which in June
1748 included "Lady Tufton, Lady Falkener, Mrs. Pitt, Lady Charlotte Johnston, Miss Chudleigh, [her fellow maid of honour] Miss
Nevill, Miss Howe, Lord Eglinton, Lord Lauderdale, Lord Bute,
Mr. Pitt, Lord Barrington, Horace Townshend, etc."[14] Many of this
group, Bute, Barrington, and Sophia Howe, for example, became
her lifelong friends. She was an extrovert and might have been an
actress, had she been born into another era or class. She flirted as a
performance, even, according to Richardson, with the elderly actor-
manager and poet laureate Colley Cibber[15] at Tunbridge Wells, who
was fifty years her senior.

Mr. Cibber was over head and ears in love with Chudleigh. Her
admirers were not jealous of him: but pleased with that wit in
him which they had not, were always calling him to her. She

said pretty things—for she was Miss Chudleigh. He said pretty things—for he was Mr. Cibber; and all the company . . . had an interest in what was said, and were half as well pleased as if they had said the sprightly things themselves . . . But once I faced the laureate squatted upon one of the benches, with a face more wrinkled than ordinary with disappointment . . . said I, "Miss Chudleigh is gone into the tea-room." "Pshaw!" said he, "there is no coming at her, she is so surrounded by toupets"* . . . But he was called to her soon after; and in flew, and his face shone again, and he looked smooth.[16]

Some of her friends were posing pranksters: the Duke of Grafton's beautiful but "nymphomaniac" daughter Lady Petersham (née Caroline Fitzroy—Hervey had attended her wedding party on his first night back from the West Indies), and "little Miss Ashe," another Elizabeth. Known about London as the "Pollard Ashe," she was a diminutive girl with a lovely face and a ceaseless appetite for madcappery. One story, from a French biography written many years later, purports to relate the pack's sense of humor. While in Tunbridge Wells, the three were incensed "by the intrusion into their circle of a Mrs. Wildman, a rich widow of low origin, who wished to pose as a lady of fashion." Her vulgarity and airs of affectation excited the derision of the ladies of the *ton*, who formed a small committee, at the head of which was Elizabeth and her two friends, "to invent some method of heaping ridicule" upon her.

Elizabeth and her friends were said to have convinced this blunderer that it was the fashion to turn up to parties dressed asymmetrically, with unmatching gloves, slippers, earrings, face—one cheek "rouged excessively, the other had but a dab of white powder."[17] Wildman followed their lead at the next ridotto,[18] to her exquisite humiliation. This was exactly the sort of maid of honour escapade, outlandish and cruel, that gave them all ill repute. Perhaps Elizabeth had a mean streak with friends. But given it took so many years to emerge, it may not be true: Elizabeth became so famous that such stories began to involve her in their retelling. Society women

* Toupets were the young bucks in periwigs.

were subject to even more malicious gossip than other women then. According to another account, it was agreed, however, that Elizabeth, Miss Ashe, and Lady Petersham "vied in horsemanship" and were the handsomest women at court. Those women who were most praised were most open to criticism.

Augustus Hervey had also distinguished himself—for courage rather than capers. Having made a fortune capturing French ships, he became a hero at Leghorn.* A fire had broken out on a merchant ship, the *Calidonia*, which was moored among 300 others in the port. A "great quantity of powder" was on board. No one would go near it, so Hervey climbed aboard the burning ship and cut the cables that tied ship to harbor, burning his coat off in the process. He towed the *Calidonia* single-handedly out to sea, dived in, and swam back to shore. The ship blew up in a "violent blast," clear of harbor, ships, storehouses, and town, all of which would have caught fire without his action. He had saved the harbor. The episode gives insight into his brave, impulsive nature. Even grandfather Bristol, although he had to be prompted to do so by Augustus's brother George, wrote a letter of congratulation to his "gallant grandson." He wrote to George that Augustus's "late behavior on this last lucky occasion shall cancel all former prejudices"[19]—those being that he only heard from his grandson when he was after money. In between bouts of fighting with the French, Hervey threw balls and concerts on board his ship for the local nobility. One night he gave orders to "light up the whole town" with fireworks.

Guilt, lingering affection, and a sense of duty meant that Hervey had not quite given up on Elizabeth. He wrote offering to pay all her debts, "if she let me know what they were." Via an intermediary, he paid her £500 anyway. By July, peace had come, and Hervey the aesthete, appreciator of art and women, was in Florence admiring the Medici collection and the local nuns. Husband and wife shared an appetite for flirtation, although Hervey never stopped there. In peacetime, his naval life consisted of dining in palaces, and pursuing or being pursued by women. He returned to Leghorn to see two

* The Tuscan trading port of Livorno, then the chief port of the Mediterranean.

pretty wives, "the Bonfiglio" and "the Bonaini." The former presented him with a ring displaying her portrait set in diamonds, while
the latter gave him a "dinner, concert, ball and supper." He was
now in no rush to get back to England. He sailed across the Mediterranean, to Minorca, then Lisbon, where he renewed intimacy
with his first love, the singer Elena Paghetti, because not only was
she still "very handsome" but she also had "all the conversazioni"
(i.e., social gatherings) at her house, so it was convenient as well as
entertaining. At twenty-four, his Casanova life was well underway.
In Lisbon one morning, in the company of a French count and a
young Spanish duke, all three disguised in cloaks, he wrote in his
journal that he went to upwards of "thirty ladies' houses"—"Ladies
of pleasure, I mean."

Elizabeth, meanwhile, was at Leicester House as maid of honour
for the winter season. As a later biographer wrote, she was by now
"the favorite toast of the bon ton, the idol of the men, the envy of
the women . . . leading the fashion in all things, and her caprice or
whim, the most extravagant, was law to the courtiers," with "a train
of captives at her heels."[20] Apart from the Duke of Hamilton and the
Duke of Ancaster—she later wrote that Hervey knew well she had
had "two Dukedoms" at her "option," but did not think that either
of them would have suited her[21]—she had also had admirers in the
politician Lord Hillsborough* and in Lord Howe, the 3rd Viscount
Howe, army officer, elder brother of the two Howes who became
naval and army commanders in the American War of Independence.
It was said that Howe, a masterful, innovative military leader, was
the only person "she did not repel with indifference."[22]

    In truth, she could have been a duchess or countess several times
over.

Peacetime meant a return to England, and the Admiralty ordered
Hervey home. By December 2, 1748, he was on British soil once
more, and a reunion of some kind was inevitable. His uncle, Hervey
Aston—who seems to have cared for Hervey more than anyone else,

_____

* Later the Marquess of Downshire, Secretary of State for the Colonies, 1768–1772.

given that he was the only relation who regularly wrote to him, and knew about his wife and child—had recently died. Hervey stayed with his widow, Mrs. Aston, in Bond Street. Elizabeth and Augustus's relationship appears by now to have become primarily financial, unless he was not quite open with his diary. He gave her £500 for her debts. She gave him a list; he gave her another £200, then another £100. By now he was rich, having made a staggering £9,000 the previous year through capturing those enemy ships. But it was a cheerless time. He wrote, "I was very much displeased of many things I heard of Miss Chudleigh's conduct, especially from her own relations, too, which put me out of humor and made me mind several little circumstances that perhaps otherwise would have passed with me as nothing." "Her own relations" presumably refers to Aunt Hanmer, his usual source for Elizabeth's misbehavior. Out of either love or pride, he was deeply hurt by Elizabeth, and he chose to leave London to stay with Admiral Byng in the country. "On my return I carried it very cool with Miss Chudleigh wherever I met her. On 25th January I had come *eclairissements** as to Miss Chudleigh's conduct with her, which she did not approve, and Mrs. Aston was present the whole time. In short, I took a resolution from this afternoon of going abroad and never having any more to do in that affair."

The fact that a cloaked Hervey might visit thirty ladies of pleasure in one morning but fall out with Elizabeth over her "conduct" marks him out merely as a man of his era. By now, Mrs. Aston was their closest ally in their hidden marriage; it is notable that they didn't meet at Mrs. Chudleigh's house. (Details about Mrs. Chudleigh at this time are sketchy, apart from the fact she was at her daughter's side during the laudanum episode.)

By now, neither Elizabeth nor Augustus had any desire to stay properly married to the other, let alone acknowledge that the marriage had taken place. This left Elizabeth in the precarious and exasperating position of having to live on her inadequate salary and intermittent handouts from a husband who loathed her, and with a train of admirers she could not marry. By comparison, as she

---

* OED: "An enlightening explanation of something that has hitherto been obscure or inexplicable."

would have been uncomfortably aware, her first cousins, with their generous dowries, were marrying eligible West Country gentry.[23] The maid of honour she had originally joined with, Elizabeth Drax, Countess of Berkeley, had just had her second child.

Unlike her Chudleigh cousins (or many of her fellow maids of honour) Elizabeth was no heiress. But she had become a name by now. Such was her social capital that she could even sell face cream. John Gowland, Frederick's apothecary, made up a lotion that cleared up her blotchy skin, perhaps caused by too much makeup. It was made of bitter almonds, sugar, and tiny amounts of a corrosive, sulphuric substance—a mercuric chloride—and took off a layer of epidermis. In an early example, possibly the first, of celebrity endorsement turning a branded beauty product into a profitable business, word got out that the glamorous Elizabeth swore by it; he sold it as "Gowland's Lotion," and made a small fortune.* In Jane Austen's *Persuasion*, Sir Walter Elliot suggests his daughter Anne might try it† as it has worked so well on her friend Mrs. Clay. The business was still a going concern in the Regency over half a century later.

At the end of April 1749, London exploded into a month of fireworks, balls, and concerts. Peace was finally proclaimed at Aix-la-Chapelle on Tuesday 25th, after months of haggling over the treaty, and the whole town was illuminated that night. The first spectacular party of many was the next day, "a jubilee-masquerade in the Venetian manner at Ranelagh" by command of the king. Even the normally waspish Horace Walpole was overwhelmed by the atmosphere, writing, "It had nothing Venetian in it, but was by the far the prettiest spectacle I ever saw; nothing in a fairy tale ever surpassed it."[24]

It began at three o'clock in the afternoon and at five, the "peo-

---

* John Gowland, *Epitome of a Manuscript Essay on Cutaneous Diseases* (1794): "The fineness of [Miss Chudleigh's] skin actually became proverbial."
† "I should recommend Gowland, the constant use of Gowland, during the Spring months," says Sir Walter to Anne. Mrs. Clay had used it on his recommendation, and "you can see how it has carried away her freckles." Jane Austen, *Persuasion*, ch. 16.

ple of fashion began to go," including Elizabeth and her friends. Ranelagh Gardens,[25] Chelsea, was adjacent to the Royal Hospital of her infancy. There was dancing around a garlanded maypole, tents all over the lawn, masked huntsmen with French horns, a troop of harlequins and commedia dell'arte characters who formed a band. On the canal floated a gondola, fluttering with flags. The amphitheater had been transformed into a circular bower made up of 30-foot fir trees in pots, orange trees with small lamps in them, and festoons of flowers hanging from tree to tree. Tea and wine were served in booths; 2,000 people rejoiced, danced, and played at the gaming tables.

The following night there were fireworks from the specially built "Temple of Peace" in St. James's Park,* for which Handel composed the *Music for the Royal Fireworks*. Crowds gathered and people crammed onto balconies to watch. Even in times of national celebration, the king was divisive. He asked his children the Duke of Cumberland and Princess Amelia to watch them with him in the park itself; the uninvited Frederick and Augusta, with her maids of honour, had to watch from Lady Middlesex's house. As if in retribution, the display was a failure: some of the fireworks failed to go off and the pavilion (which measured 410 foot long by 110 foot high, and involved 100 synchronized cannons and 112 musicians) burst into flames.[26] On the Saturday, there was a performance of *Peace in Europe*, a serenata at the Opera House. "Wretched," was Horace Walpole's verdict on that one.[27]

Elizabeth attended all these events but her most elaborate preparations were for the following week's more exclusive subscription fete at Drury Lane in the presence of the king: "On Monday evening there was a Masquerade at the Haymarket, at which were present above a thousand Persons of the first Distinction, all dress'd very richly; and most of the Company unmask'd about an Hour after the Curtain was drawn up."[28]

At a costumed ball, masks were usually worn until after supper

---

* As the scaffolding took a week, and £90,000 and three lives spent, it was not a bargain ninety minutes.

at least. The sense of intrigue was pervasive; there was unrestrained eating, drinking, and gambling. An anti-masquerade movement denounced these carnivals as decadent, a place of moral danger: in Hogarth's *Marriage A-la-Mode* series the newly, unfortunately married viscountess's discarded mask lies alongside her playing cards on the floor; in *A Harlot's Progress*, a prostitute has a mask among her paraphernalia.

The movement had not yet gathered enough pace to prevent "respectable" women from attending. The bluestocking Elizabeth Montagu[29] went as a "Van Dyke Queen Mother" (that is, after Van Dyck's portrait of Henrietta Maria, mother of Charles II)—in a white satin dress with a pearl necklace and earrings, pearls and diamonds on her head. "Many ladies looked handsome, and many rich: there was as great a quantity of diamonds as the town could produce," she wrote. One woman was dressed as "Rubens' wife"; another as a "starry night." Horace Walpole admired the Duchess of Richmond as a "lady mayoress in the time of James the First," Mrs. Pitt as a canoness, looking "gloriously handsome" in a red veil, and Mr. Conway, the "finest figure I ever saw" as the Duke in *Don Quixote*. There were monks and nuns, sultans and Cossacks, and a plethora of dominos.* While the favorite son, the Duke of Cumberland, looked "immensely corpulent," the king was "much pleased" because he was so "well disguised in an old-fashioned English habit" that somebody "desired him to hold their cup, as they were drinking tea."[30]

But in spite of the monarch's successful disguise, the festive spirit, the range of court beauties in brilliant and inventive costumes at the end of a long, bitter, complex war, there was only one thing anyone talked about that night—and they talked about it for years after—and that was exactly what Elizabeth Chudleigh was wearing, or, more accurately, what she was not.

So drawn, so alluded to, so notorious did Elizabeth's outfit that night become that it is hard to ascertain what it actually looked

---

* Consisting of cloak, mask, and tricorne hat, the domino was the Venetian trademark masquerade costume that could be worn by men or women.

like. It has become an idea, an impression, more a symbol of mid-eighteenth-century exuberance than a costume. What is tangible is the effect that it had on everyone, which can be summed up in one word: sensation. It was the outfit that made her name, for better or for worse.

Elizabeth claimed to be dressed as "Iphigenia, ready for the sacrifice." Horace Walpole to Horace Mann: "Miss Chudleigh was Iphigenia, but so naked you would have taken her for Andromeda."* Elizabeth Montagu wrote that Elizabeth's "dress or undress was remarkable, she was Iphigenia for the sacrifice but so naked the high Priest might easily inspect the entrails of the victim. The Maids of honour (not of maids the strictest) were so offended they would not speak to her."[31] Masquerade costumes might be inspired by the commedia dell'arte, concepts such as abstract nouns, e.g., "pride," or figures from classical myth. Frederick's favored playwright James Thomson had staged his *Agamemnon* a few years before, and the print copy was a bestseller. The "celebrated Mrs. Cibber"—daughter-in-law of Tunbridge Wells's Colley,† a tragedian actress who had starred in Thomson's *Agamemnon*—had helped Elizabeth design her raffish costume. It was a crafted performance.

What Elizabeth seems to have been wearing was a dress or chemise (a thin undergarment) of either sheer or flesh-colored silk. Drawings show a gossamer Grecian-goddess-style drape with ivy strategically arranged around her waist, like Eve. In the candlelight, she appeared as good as naked. No wonder everyone wanted to have a look. It was a high-risk, scene-stealing, attention-seeking, maid-of-honour stunt. The Duke of Cumberland was agog. Even the king was impressed. The story evolved that he had asked if he

---

* In Greek myth, Iphigenia was the daughter sacrificed by Agamemnon to appease Artemis so his troops could reach Troy. Euripides, Ovid, Boccaccio, and John Dryden had all told Iphigenia's story. Andromeda, daughter of Cepheus, chained to a rock (and sometimes rescued by Perseus), was often portrayed half-dressed or undressed.
† Susannah Maria Cibber, estranged wife of Colley Cibber's son, was sister of the composer Thomas Arne and a singer beloved of Handel, who wrote parts for her. She was the highest-paid actress in England, at the center of a *ménage à trois* scandal herself.

could feel her breast through her scanty costume: she picked up his hand, said she would put it in a "far softer place,"[32] and placed it onto his own bald head. But it was a gamble: some other women, as Mrs. Montagu wrote, were outraged; not that anything came of that—her place at court ensured her social position. If Elizabeth knew how women felt, she did not seem to care. She was always remarkably unselfconscious. Perhaps those early days at Chelsea made her comfortable with male attention; or perhaps she was embracing her status as object of gossip.

The first print of Elizabeth in costume was advertised in July.[33] It was copied, adapted, and redrawn until pictures multiplied of Elizabeth alone, Elizabeth with Mr. Punch and another reveler, Elizabeth abducted by two dominos. The moment appeared in poetry too, for example in Charles Churchill's "Gotham":[34]

> SUMMER, in light transparent Gawze array'd,
> Like Maids of honour at a Masquerade,
> In bawdry Gawze, for which our daughters leave
> The Fig, more modest, first brought up by EVE,
> Panting for breath, enflam'd with lustful fires,
> Yet wanting strength to perfect her desires.

Another, in a newspaper:

> But you, O C-h-y! born mankind to please,
> To dress with freedom, and gallant with ease;
> O learn my fair, all censure to despise,
> And trust alone the lighting of your eyes;
> Nay sometimes deign your snowy breast to show,
> For Beauty does still captivate the Beau.

Her costume "was so perfectly transparent as to display, at the same time, the graces of her person and the disposition of her mind," according to one Georgian writer.[35] The dress showed off her figure—indeed, no one could look away—but also said something about her mental state. Undoubtedly—but what, exactly?

The most likely explanation for Elizabeth's behavior is that in the knowledge of her marriage disintegrating, her future uncertain, and her baby dead, she was asserting herself as an independent being the only way she knew how: through an overt display of her sexuality. The long-standing need for, and pressure of, secrecy might well have bred a contrary desire for self-exposure.[36] If she had to risk her reputation to make her mark, so be it. She knew she was alluring; she would use it to control her own destiny. It was an unambiguous display of power. She had an exhibitionist streak: it was telling that her actress friend Mrs. Cibber helped her with the costume. In another era, she would have been the starlet attracting the paparazzi, seeking publicity at any cost. Now in her late twenties, she was no longer the naive Devon girl who had arrived at Leicester House so fresh-faced and full of frivolity. She seems to have been expanding her social circle: Mrs. Cibber had a Sunday-night salon of wits, poets, and musicians, types who flourished among the Leicester House set.

The attention-seeking had immediate effect: Elizabeth caught the eye of the king. Two weeks later he ordered further revels in her honor. Walpole wrote to Mann: "I told you we were to have another jubilee masquerade: there was one by the King's command for Miss Chudleigh, the maid of honour, with whom our gracious Monarch has a mind to believe himself in love."[37] At this next masquerade, the notoriously mean king bought her a "fairing,"* a watch on a chain, for thirty-five guineas; a vast amount for him.[38] Everyone noticed his interest, and courtiers asked each other: was Elizabeth about to become the new royal mistress? Perhaps the desperate gamble had paid off more handsomely than even Elizabeth might have predicted.

---

* A fairing: a present bought at a fair.

CHAPTER TEN

THE RIVALS

Naked ambition and the resulting attention could not pay the bills immediately. However hard Elizabeth scanned the horizon, when she needed to supplement her income a month after the jubilee masquerade, she had no choice other than to track down Augustus Hervey.

Like so many others, Hervey had decided that his best chance was to demonstrate his support for Frederick, putting him a rumor's distance from Elizabeth. He was reassured by Frederick telling him at Carlton House that "he would certainly serve me when in his power." The prince added, wrote Hervey, that he "knew more of me than I imagined" (i.e., about the marriage—we can presume Elizabeth had told Augusta something). Peacetime meant few serving naval officers, and those not on ship were reduced to half pay. For Augustus, whose money fell through his hands like sea water, that meant four shillings a day and little to occupy him. He wrote pamphlets about the inadequacies of the Admiralty and met his former lover, Mrs. Artis; but, overcome with ennui, he decided to visit France and Italy. The Admiralty gave him leave, which meant the half pay sank to no pay at all. He was to depart London on June 3, 1749.

The day before he left, he had a surprise and unwelcome visitor at Mrs. Aston's house in Bond Street. As he wrote: "Tho in all this time I had not heard from Miss Chudleigh, yet she suddenly came in upon me at Mrs. Aston's, which I impute to their having sent to her and told her of my design [to go abroad]. But I was deaf to all the siren's voice." And that awkward meeting, nearly five years after that first fateful encounter in the rush of Winchester races, according to Augustus's diary, is the last time Mr. and Mrs. Hervey ever set eyes on each other. According to one later account,[1] Elizabeth had regretted the marriage almost immediately, deciding Hervey was an unworthy spouse.[2] Whatever the truth of that, by now, frustrated with being asked for money, consumed with wanderlust, Hervey was no more a husband than Elizabeth was a wife.

Grandfather Bristol was probably not alone in being shocked that after such conspicuous bravery at Leghorn his grandson had not been rewarded with a prestigious naval role, but now Augustus had aligned himself with Frederick, his connections, at this point, were not in the camp with the power. He decided to spend on himself, rather than Elizabeth: he headed to Versailles where he met the king and queen, the dauphin and Madame de Pompadour, "the handsomest woman I ever saw." He rode, fenced, danced, played the harpsichord, admired art and tapestries, attended masquerades, and in November fell in love with "the most beautiful woman in France," Madame Caze, the nineteen-year-old wife of a court official.

Back in London, the king was known to be keen on Elizabeth. This could have alienated Frederick and Augusta but such were Elizabeth's skills as a courtier that she engendered no ill will. In February 1750 it was said that George II had planned to approach her "a fortnight ago at the masquerade—but at the last she had the gout and could not come";[3] he went away cross. Elizabeth, however keen she was to build alliances, was a romantic. She might flirt with all sorts, but she fell in love with handsome, sporting men. She was not about to devote herself to a paunchy man twice her age, even if he was the king of England.

Whatever her illness was (gout being the all-purpose diagnosis or excuse for any kind of physical or mental discomfort among the Georgian nobility), masquerades and the like were about to cease in London because of a bout of apocalyptic weather that shook the city in every sense. An earthquake in February was followed by another one exactly a month later; a madman[4] then forecast that a third, on the same date in April, would swallow up London entirely. Clergymen, such as the Bishops of London and Oxford, blamed the climate of licentiousness, a world of immoral masquerades where maids of honour appeared so gauzily, erotically underdressed. In other words, the earthquakes were Elizabeth's fault. Such was the fear of further divine intervention that by April 5 people were sleeping in carriages and boats, and rattling out of town in a constant flow. Women ordered warm "earthquake gowns" in case they had to stay out all night.[5]

The date passed, and with it the moralizing. By the end of the year, Elizabeth's royal flirtation had borne fruit. She would not supplant the royal mistress, the German Amalie Sophie van Walmoden, Countess of Yarmouth, but she could secure a living for her mother. The German ministers, for whom Yarmouth was the advocate, were much alarmed by the king's admiration for Elizabeth,[6] when he publicly gave her mother a plum job: "Two days ago at the Drawing-Room [the king] strode up to Miss Chudleigh," wrote Walpole, and told her that "he was glad to have an opportunity of obeying her commands, and that he appointed her mother housekeeper at Windsor, and hoped she would not think a kiss too great a reward—against all precedent he kissed her in the circle." Elizabeth, we can presume, had somehow let it be known that her mother desired such a role, a sign of the strength of that relationship, missing as her mother generally is from her known history. Walpole continued slyly that the king "has had a hankering these two years. Her life, which is now of thirty years' standing, has been a little historic. Why should not experience and a charming face on her side, and near seventy years on his, produce a title?"[7] From this reference to her life being "historic" and her "experience," we can glean that Elizabeth's "secret" marriage was by now probably nothing of the sort for those, like Horace Walpole, who made it their business to know court gossip.

Elizabeth's mother Harriet Chudleigh, Mrs. Chudleigh as she was known, did indeed become housekeeper of Windsor Castle.[8] This sought-after "above stairs" post was (like the lieutenant governorship of Chelsea) a secure job for life that came with a grace-and-favor apartment within the castle walls, good food and board, and a salary (variously reported as £320 and £800, but welcome as either). It was perfectly suited to an impecunious aristocratic or military widow, who knew how to run an establishment with taste and efficiency. She was in charge of dozens of housemaids and prepared the place for royal visits. When Augustus Hervey heard the news of her appointment he wrote of his irritation in his diary; he was not alone in his suspicions, however unfounded, as to how exactly the mother's sudden promotion had come about.[9]

Elizabeth's masquerade performance had paid off, unintentionally, in gaining security for her mother. In that way, it had been something of a coup. As she later noted (in a letter to George III),[10] Elizabeth alone had managed the remarkable feat of being welcome, cherished even, at both rival courts. She was a luminary in the court of the next king, and the current monarch was smitten with her. But she had not found any security for herself—and, as ever, new faces had irresistible allure.

Competition had arrived from Ireland, in the form of the Gunning sisters. They were young—still teenagers, twelve and thirteen years younger than Elizabeth—and exceptionally good-looking. They also benefited from the timeless appeal of being a pair, wrote one observer: "I think their being so handsome and both [having] such perfect figures is their chief excellence, for singly I have seen much handsomer women than either."[11] The elder, Maria, who was described[12] as "more beautiful than an angel," had large gleaming brown eyes and, as diarist, conchologist, and creator of cutouts Mrs. Delany put it, "a thousand dimples and prettiness in her cheeks." The younger, Elizabeth, had an oval face and marble-pale skin.

The daughters of a barrister with a gambling habit from Roscommon, John Gunning, and his ambitious wife the Hon. Bridget Bourke, daughter of Viscount Mayo, the Gunning girls did not have Elizabeth's wit, but their visual impact was undeniable. Maria was the dimmer one, Elizabeth the wilier one. Asked by the king what event she would most like to see, the tactless Maria answered, "A royal funeral." Unable to afford dresses, they had been lent the costumes of Juliet and Lady Macbeth to wear to a ball at Dublin Castle, where they were introduced to Lord Harrington, Lord Lieutenant of Ireland. Such was their effect on Dublin society that Harrington gave their mother a pension, and they were sent to England to hunt for husbands. By the time they were presented at St. James's in 1750, they were so well known that courtiers climbed on tables to get a look at them. Never mind the masquerading, quasi-naked Elizabeth—the sensation was elsewhere now.

The sisters' intention to snare aristocratic husbands was so obvious that they became the victims of a hoax. Mr. Thrale, a brewer, and Arthur Murphy, a dramatist, hired a smuggler to impersonate a lord, to see how they would treat him if they thought he was eligible. Gratifyingly, they "played off their best airs" until the "lord" suddenly revealed himself by pulling silk stockings out of his pocket and trying to flog them to the sisters. Elizabeth harbored a grudge about it and Maria pretended not to remember it.[13] But they were more often victorious: they were the (absent) toasts, for example, of a dinner at White's club in 1751, thrown by seven young men who declared themselves in love with them. The bill—with its multiple courses—gives a flavor of extravagant St. James's life.[14] Only one glass was drunk from each bottle of champagne before moving on to another.

For Elizabeth, the presence of these new beauties was unsettling enough, but further disruption was in store. In the late 1740s, Leicester House became more of a hotbed of political debate than ever. Frederick seemed convinced he was about to become king. At sixty-six, his father was in good health (apart from hemorrhoids and rumored senility—and that may have been wishful thinking) but Frederick was already promising his associates future Cabinet posts. Bubb Dodington was to be Secretary of State for the Southern Department; Sir Francis Dashwood, the able but rakish founder of the Dilettanti society,* would be the treasurer of the navy; while Frederick's new friend, John Stuart, 3rd Earl of Bute, who he had met in the rain at Egham races when short of a whist partner, had become groom in the bedchamber and would surely figure somewhere. Augusta was also keen on the ambitious Scot, said to have "the best legs in London."† Frederick launched his manifesto with all the swagger of an opposition on the verge of a landslide. He announced that he would alter the civil list, cap his own benefits,

---

* Dilettanti: a group of aesthetes, whose purpose was to study and promote classicism; all had been on a Grand Tour. Horace Walpole said that although the stated qualification was having "been in Italy," the real one was "being drunk."
† As men wore knee-length breeches at the time, their legs were on show. Bute took every possible opportunity to display his, according to Walpole.

and extinguish corruption, although his obsession was making sure that the crown was not diverted towards his younger brother. Leicester House vibrated with an air of hectic expectation. Policies were circulated by Frederick in what became known as the Carlton House Paper, and he set up his own periodical, the *Remembrancer.*

Frederick presented himself as the patriot-king in waiting, and a family man. Acts of kindness and generosity were publicized. Elizabeth was therefore immersed in something she did not have for herself: a happy family atmosphere. When not buying plants for his beloved gardens—at Cliveden, Carlton House, and Kew—Frederick would be drinking in the pub near Cliveden, playing cricket, or watching his children's theatrical performances. Leicester House followed a cycle of birthday parties, assemblies, and plays put on by the children—*Lady Jane Grey*, Addison's *Cato*; Elizabeth quoted the Stoicism of *Cato* for the rest of her life. Presumably she helped the children rehearse in that winter of 1748/9 and the lines stuck.[15] Or the court would go to the theater, to see plays such as *Romeo and Juliet,* or *The Merry Wives of Windsor* at the Theater Royal, Covent Garden. Frederick was a tenderly loving father, interested in his children's education. He himself hired Lord North[16] as governor and Francis Ayscough as tutor for his sons, and wrote letters full of affection from him and their "Mama" when not with them, chastising them for not writing to him more often. He advised Prince George that he must please the people he governed, because he would find that "If you don't please them, they won't please you in return" (a piece of advice George may have forgotten when it came to America all those years later). "*Mens sana in corpore sano*"[17] and "Pray God you may grow in every respect above me,"[18] he wrote. Nothing would make him happier than the prospect that his children would "turn out an honour to me, and a blessing to my country." He stressed the importance of reading to form one's character; it was he who drew up their daily timetable.

An enchanting portrait commissioned by Frederick in 1746 shows his vision of childhood.* His six eldest children are playing out-

---

* *The Children of Frederick, Prince of Wales* by the Swiss portrait painter Barthélemy du Pan, a vast informal conversation piece for which he was paid £100, and £75 for two copies. The remaining one hangs in Windsor Castle.

doors in a gentle, rural English landscape on the edge of woodland. The boys are sporty and vigorous: the future George III has shot a "popinjay,"[19] a wooden bird on a pole, with an arrow. The girls are playful and maternal. The oldest, Princess Augusta, holds the baby Prince Henry, and Princess Elizabeth rides in a miniature carriage decorated with doves, drawn by dogs.

By now, Frederick's younger brother the Duke of Cumberland was seen by the public as "the Butcher"[20] and Frederick as the future "people's king." His court at Leicester House lived up to the idea. In May 1750, Augusta gave birth to her eighth child, a boy, "without a groan," and before Christmas that year she was expecting another. The atmosphere was alternately serious and lighthearted; Bubb recounted in his diary how Frederick arranged for the dancing master Desnoyers to impersonate a fortune-teller to fool the wife of a German minister.[21] Apart from the jokes, Elizabeth got used to being surrounded by exquisite art and craftsmanship. Frederick was patron, buyer, and collector. The silverware, tapestries, furniture, and paintings in his houses were the finest he could procure.

But from somewhere—perhaps from one of the fortune-tellers he liked to visit—he had a premonition. In his "Instructions for my son George," which he left with Augusta, he wrote that his son should reduce the national debt, not surround himself with people who agree with him, and become a credible Englishman in every way. He concluded, "I shall have no regret never to have worn the Crown, if you do but fill it worthily."[22]

Apart from his legacy, his other obsession—one he shared with Augusta—was the garden of his house in Kew. He had commissioned a Chinese summerhouse, the House of Confucius, and was creating an aqueduct lined with busts of his favorite philosophers, underscoring his personal enlightenment for all to see. Bubb wrote gloomily in his diary in February 1750 that everyone at Kew, "men, women and children," worked on the Prince's New Walk in the chill; they were only given a "cold dinner" afterwards.[23] In March 1751, the prince caught a cold working in the Kew garden and his blood was let at Leicester House. He seemed to recover a couple of days later; then a pain in his side returned. He suffered a violent fit of coughing and spitting on March 20. One of his doctors, Wilmot, thought it would pass, as his pulse was "perfect"; the other, Caesar Hawkins, who had been at Elizabeth's bedside when she had given birth, was more anxious. And rightly so, because although he had eaten bread and butter and drunk coffee that afternoon, had Desnoyers playing the fiddle, and touchingly confided in twelve-year-old George how lonely his own childhood in Hanover had been (and how much he had relied on his grandfather George I, and looked forward to his visits), at a quarter to ten in the evening he put his hand on his stomach, cried out "*Je sens la mort*," and died.

The doctors had not noticed the ominous "black thrush" down his throat, and did not yet know about the burst abscess in his side, found when he was opened up by command of the king. Was it an old cricket or tennis ball injury that killed him? Or pleurisy?

Frederick, who had died at forty-four, was now the king who never was. Pregnant Augusta, only thirty-one, was plunged at first into sleepless grief but forced herself, after four hours alone by her husband's body, to deal with the most sensitive papers. She locked herself away with her late husband's advisors, Dr. Lee and Lord Egmont. Egmont retrieved the papers from Carlton House hidden in cushion covers and, at her instruction, Lee burned them in the fireplace. Historians are divided as to her motives, but any evidence of collusion with the opposition would now have to be destroyed given that her future, and that of her son's succession, were in the hands of her father-in-law.[24]

Word of his death spread fast. Diplomats, bishops, and nobility began to arrive at Leicester House to pay their respects. A few days later, Frederick had a sparse funeral at Westminster Abbey. Augusta went sadly in a coach in the rain without her children. Her father-in-law, although he had wept with her, did not go, and neither did her sisters-in-law. The king had encouraged the lords and bishops to stay away. No music was commissioned. According to Bubb, it was far from the honorable funeral the Prince of Wales should have had.

And the Hon. Elizabeth Chudleigh, now thirty, went from being a maid of honour in the household of the next monarch, the popular people's king to be, to the attendant of a brokenhearted widow dowager princess, with eight young children, who would never be queen. Although she was reappointed as maid of honour by Augusta when the household was reformed after Frederick's death, a court without its own monarch-in-waiting (although there was of course the new future George III, a gentle boy) was neither as secure nor as exciting a prospect. The flame had been extinguished. Although they were responsible for the education of the future king, even he was not actually in the same household anymore. George, now Prince of Wales, who had "an appearance of apathy," and his brother, Edward, ungenerously described as a "very plain boy with strange, loose eyes,"[25] had moved with their household to Savile House, next door, two years earlier.

Elizabeth's situation was now perilous. She was, relatively speaking, an aging maid of honour, who had been usurped by two young Irish beauties. She had played her trump card as Iphigenia at the masquerade, and now, with the demise of the court in which she had played such a key part, she was left with an uncertain future and fortune.

Augusta, Dowager Princess of Wales, was still in shock when Caroline Matilda, her ninth child, was born. Leicester House was still in mourning. Deep mourning (the first of two phases) for ladies including Elizabeth consisted of "black bombazine . . . crêpe hoods, chamois shoes . . . gloves and crêpe fans"; the men wore "black cloth, without buttons on . . . sleeves or pockets, plain muslin or long lawn cravats . . . chamois shoes and gloves, crêpe hat-bands . . . black swords and buckles."[26] Even the house itself went into mourning for six months, and then half-mourning for another six months. The state rooms were hung with black cloth, with the chairs and stools to match, followed by gray. The gilding on the lanterns was painted black, and gold tables and looking-glass frames were replaced with white ones. The staircase and hall were hung with baize. The world went from color to black and white.

With her friends and female attendants such as Elizabeth at her side, however, Princess Augusta did not collapse in grief. Instead, the dowager princess commissioned a quite different portrait to that innocent pastoral romp of six children painted by du Pan five years earlier. This was an immense group portrait of nine children, now with their mother, painted by George Knapton.* Far from a

---

* It now hangs in the State Dining Room at Windsor Castle.

sentimental act of dejected widowhood, it is a majestic statement of intent. Augusta sits in stately fashion in white mourning dress, black mantilla over her hair, with baby Caroline Matilda on her lap, in front of the royal coat of arms and swags of scarlet silk and velvet. Her two oldest sons, Princes George and Edward, point at a map of the fortifications at Portsmouth, and the two younger boys play with a ship, emphasizing Britain's supremacy as a maritime nation. The oldest girl stands by her mother, elegant in blue silk, no longer the "poor, little, ugly she-mouse" mocked by her grandmother; the younger plays the mandolin; over all of them to one side hangs a portrait of Frederick, pointing towards his family. On the other stands a statue of Britannia. A relief beneath her represents the Church of England, the Magna Carta, the cap of liberty, and the Act of Settlement. The dowager princess looks protectively at her eldest son. There are symbols of science, music, and the arts beloved at Leicester House. It is a portrait that says: Frederick and Britannia look over us, I look over my son, and with me as regent, he will rule.

Princess Augusta had gained importance in one way: if the king died before Prince George reached the age of majority, she would become regent. But she was no longer a future queen, and with the responsibility of so many children in a foreign land, she became a protective and insular mother at Leicester House and Kew Palace. The education of the next king was preeminent in her mind: she had been left to carry out her husband's wish that his son must "convince the nation that you are not only an Englishman born and bred, but you are also this by inclination."[27] Frederick had introduced his children to plays, music, architecture,[28] gardening, and painting. He wanted his heir to be the most cultured of monarchs. The task now fell to Augusta.

Elizabeth was plunged into a world of constant improvement. The boys' regime consisted of six days of lessons, starting with Latin translation at 7 A.M., before breakfast, followed by geometry, writing, arithmetic, and French. "From twelve o'clock riding and other exercises . . . until dinner" at three.[29] "After dinner, they visited their mother, where they had lessons in German and history. Every Sunday the Bishop of Norwich read them "a practical explanation of the principles of the Christian religion" after breakfast. Elizabeth is more likely to have joined in with the dancing, drama, and music lessons.[30]

The dowager princess employed an ever-shifting army of tutors, whose proximity to the next monarch meant the incumbents were regarded with suspicion and envy. There were so many of them vying for influence that they fell out with each other. "The civil wars of the tutorhood," Walpole called it.[31] A fragile peace was reached, with Lord Waldegrave and the Bishop of Peterborough in place. Walde-grave, former bedchamber gentleman to the king, found the young Prince of Wales full of "princely prejudices"; he spoke too much to the "women," that is, his mother's attendants—of which the most visible was Elizabeth.

After Frederick's death, the house was no longer the scene of glittering drawing rooms, nor was it all childhood innocence; the glamour that had evaporated when Frederick died was replaced by a battle for the soul of the future king. Elizabeth was there to maintain morale—to provide singing, dancing, amusing stories.

In Augusta's widowhood she relied on her female attendants to support her, and as such a long-standing maid of honour,* Elizabeth was a family favorite. She may have provided warmth lacking else-where to the children, who were constantly judged and restricted. Reticent George was not a natural learner. While Waldegrave sought to instruct him by "conversation rather than books," Augusta interpreted his shyness as an absence of a desire to please. Like Frederick, Augusta favored his younger brother, Edward, an easy-to-like, effervescent sort of boy. Bubb saw that the seclusion after Frederick's death was suffocating and suggested George mix more widely, but Augusta refused. When he grew up, one of his brothers, Prince William, said, "No boys were ever brought up in a greater ignorance of evil than the King and myself . . . we retained all our native innocence."[32] Bute's daughter Lady Louisa Stuart, who knew George throughout his childhood, believed he had an "unspeakably kind heart" and "innate rectitude." He was curious about music and

---

* After Charlotte Dives married in 1762, Elizabeth became the longest-serving maid of honour.

architecture. But his mother was always critical. She wanted him to be more "forward and less childish" when he was a sheltered fifteen-year-old (and she was only thirty-three herself).

Augusta was devoted to her children's education, but possibly had a cruel streak: she encouraged the other children to laugh "at the fool," as she called William, her third son.[33] When he bowed his head in response she accused him of sulking. He replied to his mother, "No, he was only thinking . . . what I should feel if I had a son as unhappy as you make me."[34] Her grief had changed her from an ever-smiling benign princess to a woman fraught with agitation. Her ebullient, emotional husband had been able to assuage her disquiet.

If Elizabeth seemed condemned to the claustrophobic atmosphere of the dowager princess's court, it was only a momentary lull. Fate was about to take another curious turn.

2

DUCHESS

CHAPTER ELEVEN

"The Handsomest Man in England"

In 1750, a name began to feature in the social columns. He was at *Othello* in the Upper Gallery at the Theater Royal, Drury Lane, in March, alongside Augusta, Princess of Wales, and other members of the royal family. In June, he "whom Lady Caroline says she has been trying for these seven years" (i.e., trying to seduce) was with Horace Walpole and Elizabeth's friends Lady Caroline Petersham and Miss Ashe, taking a barge to Vauxhall Gardens for a frantic night out. Somewhere on this circuit of pleasure gardens, plays, and court drawing rooms, Elizabeth met "the handsomest man in England"[1]—Evelyn Pierrepont, Duke of Kingston, Marquess of Dorchester, Earl of Kingston, Viscount Newark, Baron Pierrepont of Holme Pierrepont, Lieutenant General of His Majesty's forces, and Knight of the Most Noble Order of the Garter.

The country's "best nobleman shot" was then thirty-eight years old, with estates that stretched from Yorkshire to Hampshire, via Lincolnshire, Derbyshire, Shropshire, Somerset, Buckinghamshire, and Wiltshire. The family seat was at Thoresby, Nottinghamshire, on the edge of Sherwood Forest, and the imposing London townhouse in Arlington Street, between Green Park and St. James's. A single duke in possession of a good fortune, who, in the eyes of England's mothers, daughters, and press, must have been in want of a wife. A portrait of 1741 shows an open-faced, attractive man with kind, generous eyes, full, dark eyebrows, and a lustrous frock coat trimmed with gold embroidery. He wears a lace cravat and his Garter star on his left breast. It is a trustworthy, boyish visage.

Just as the fizz started to flatten at Leicester House, Elizabeth fell for Kingston. She was not about to desert her forlorn mistress, but as much as contemporary cynical biographers and envious society let-ter scribblers might embrace the archetype of the scheming penniless woman entrapping a rich man, they did become genuinely devoted to each other. Kingston's appeal went far beyond his status. In spite of "no man being a hero to his valet," even his valet said he had "many shining virtues":[2] he was infallibly polite; no rabble-rouser (so unlike Hervey); he was a good-natured, kind, decent gentleman, seemingly without ego. He was blessed with looks, grandeur, money, and connections, but his early life had been acutely painful. Unlike Augustus Hervey, his loyalty to and love for Elizabeth—and hers to him—would be beyond doubt. Without the rashness of youth, their connection led quickly from attraction to absolute commitment. As Elizabeth recorded later, she viewed him with a respect and tender-ness she had never shown for another man; he was observed to have a steadfast love for her that allowed for no distraction. Perhaps they consoled each other—they had both experienced disrupted child-hoods, tragedy, and personal scandal.

His famous writerly, convention-busting aunt Lady Mary Wortley Montagu, née Pierrepont, wrote of her lineage, "there is no nobler descent."[3] A Pierrepont had been a colonel in William the Con-queror's invading army and through several lucrative marriage bets—one to a daughter of England's richest woman, Bess of Hardwick—the Norman bloodline was mingled with nobility. Through his grandfather's political career,[4] a dukedom was con-ferred. Kingston's father was the 1st Duke's only son, William, an eighteen-year-old Cambridge undergraduate when he became engaged to Rachel Bayntun, a fifteen-year-old illegitimate heiress held in contempt by her clever sister-in-law Lady Mary. On April 3, 1712, Rachel was "brought to bed of a son," Evelyn, and just over a year later, a daughter, Frances. Within weeks of Frances's birth, William, not yet twenty-one, died of smallpox, in "dreadful pain, disfigurement and stench" in July 1713 at the family priory in Acton, leaving a teenage widow with two infants. His appalling death was witnessed by his adoring sister Lady Mary, who contracted it herself, but survived with scars and without eyelashes. It later inspired her to bring the concept of smallpox inoculation to the West from Constantinople, where she had accompanied her diplomat husband.[5] (In the Turkish harems, she witnessed women successfully "engrafting" skin from a smallpox victim to a healthy child,[*6] a process refined by Edward Jenner, and which led to vaccination. As they were about to leave Turkey, she impulsively decided to try it out on her own three-year-old son, with no ill effects.) The young widow Rachel embarked on an affair with Lord Lumley.[7] Evelyn and Frances called him "papa." But when Lumley came into his inheritance, he refused to marry her and she died of a broken heart. At ten and eight, Evelyn and Frances were bereaved again.

Kingston's misfortune was to be brought up by a grandfather who was "a haughty, selfish, licentious man . . . equally a tyrant in his family and out of it," believed a Victorian editor of Horace Walpole, who continued cruelly, "Thus Kingston became bashful and dull and displayed few if any of the talents which had characterized his race, and were so evident in his aunts, Lady Mary Wortley Montagu and Lady Mar."[8] When his grandfather died in 1726, Evelyn Pierrepont became England's boy duke, probably the richest, handsomest, and certainly the grandest orphan in the country. He was left in the care of the Kingston estate executors, who decided that even though he was only fourteen, rather than remain at Eton, he should embark on a Grand Tour to continue his education.

---

* Lady Mary wrote from Constantinople to a friend, April 1, 1717: "I am going to tell you a thing, that will make you wish yourself here. The small-pox, so fatal, and so general amongst us, is here entirely harmless . . . There is a set of old women, who make it their business to perform the operation, every autumn, in the month of September, when the great heat is abated. People send to one another to know if any of their family has a mind to have the small-pox; they make parties for this purpose, and when they are met (commonly fifteen or sixteen together) the old woman comes with a nut-shell full of the matter of the best sort of small-pox, and asks what vein you please to have opened. She immediately rips open that you offer her, with a large needle (which gives you no more pain than a common scratch) and puts into the vein as much matter as can lie upon the head of her needle, and after that, binds up the little wound with a hollow bit of shell."

He sailed to France with his governor, Dr. Nathaniel Hickman, a portly, pipe-smoking polymath, a fellow of the Royal Society, his preceptor, Peter Platel, the son of a French Huguenot silversmith, a valet, two footmen, and a coachman.[9] They arrived in Rouen, where the young duke had a seizure. As it was not a one-off, he may have had epilepsy. Like Elizabeth's, his health seems to have been erratic.[10] They took a house in Orléans for a winter of study, before moving on, first, to Dijon,[11] then beyond.

With Kingston on tour for most of a decade, his estates flourished under the care of the trustees, Lord Cheyne, Sir John Monson, and Thomas Bennett, who transformed the inheritance of the "spend-thrift and happy go lucky" boy duke from shaky to thriving: in a few years, he was in charge of "one of the largest estate incomes in the country."[12] The duke's grandfather had left woods part-planted, his magnificent library semi-cataloged, pictures[13] unpaid for, and one room half-painted in imitation marble. The trustees set up an office in Berkeley Street to supervise rent collection, bought land to streamline boundaries, found reliable tenants, diverted rivers, maximized coal production, cut charitable donations, all to ensure the future prosperity of the Kingston estate.

The boy duke, meanwhile, traveled on the Continent with "an entourage of servants and possessions in several coaches and stayed in magnificent lodgings for weeks or months on end."[14] He was received in a manner befitting his status. In 1729, the party were living in Dijon with a friend, the future naturalist, the Comte de Buffon.[15] When Hickman was absent, Buffon said he was "missed by honest people; as for painters and prostitutes, they are in mourning."[16] So much for the man who was in charge of Kingston's development. In Angers, Cardinal Fleury, Louis XV's prime minister, allowed Kingston to hunt in royal forests; in 1731 they crossed over the Alps to enroll at the University of Padua. Buffon met up with them again in Paris in 1732, when the city was in the grip of Anglomania. They mixed in Paris's beau monde. The Abbé Prévost, novelist, wrote that he had dined with Kingston and found him "an extremely likeable man whose intelligence is astonishing, for no matter what subject is put before him, he reasons with it as if he were the most accomplished master of the art."[17] This sort of compliment to his intelligence was not often leveled at him, because he was reserved, and most people could not see past his title. But that he was likable was never contested. He was admitted to the Society of Dilettanti and to an order of Freemasons in Paris. Being a young duke on tour, he started an affair—with a dancer at the Paris Opera.

But his scandal came in the form of Mme Françoise-Thérèse Fontaine de la Touche in the seductive surroundings of her mother's house, the Château de Passy, on the banks of the Seine outside Paris. "A fine comely woman, of a brown complexion, and black hair," according to Kingston's valet, she was the youngest of the "three graces," daughters of Mme Fontaine, a former actress and mistress of the richest financier in France, their father, Samuel Bernard.[18] This youngest daughter had been married at seventeen to a courtier and tax official, Nicholas Vallet de la Touche, then thirty-one. They had three children, but she loathed him. Kingston was not her first lover, or even her first ducal one. He was preceded by two French dukes.[19] An anonymous author claimed, in a published "apologie,"[20] that her behavior was only to be expected because her actress grandmother had been a prince's mistress, and her sister was mistress of the Prince of Condé. Her husband, who was unkind as well as unattractive, had informed her that they were separated before he went to Italy on business. In his absence, the young English Duke of Kingston arrived, "amiably formed" and "indefatigable in his pursuit"; soon they were "united in an ardent and reciprocal passion."[21] He was her "tender and engaging lover."[22]

When the politician Lord Cholmondeley, Prime Minister Walpole's son-in-law, advised Kingston to come back to England to seek a court position, and Hickman, too, decided his charge should return, Mme de la Touche declared she would die if he left her. Hickman suggested she come too. He was worried about the amount of money Kingston was spending—he was commissioning such wonders as rococo candelabras and silver tureens, fantastical shell-like creations embellished with silver artichokes, carrots, oysters, and partridges from the designer Meissonnier.[23] Kingston set off and, nine days later, "Madame," as she became known, followed, leaving her children behind, in case, she claimed, they had an accident en route and took with them the last of the de la Touche bloodline.

A married mother abandoning her husband and three children for a young English duke caused a bustle of the highest order in Paris. As Lord Hervey[24] wrote in 1736, the year of the flight, "One should have imagined the Duke of Kingston, by the manner the French people speak of this affair, had seduced a vestal from her sacred fire, rather than only suffered a forsaken mistress of the Duc de la Trémouille's to follow him to England." The furor saw de la Touche's banker father have Kingston's servants arrested. A prosecution for abduction was only stopped by Louis XV's personal intervention, after a counterattack was launched on M. de la Touche, saying he was intolerable and had even tried to make her wear a chastity belt he had bought in Italy.[25] So hot was the episode that the naval captain, Jonceur, who had brought Madame to England on his ship, had to stay in Kingston's Arlington Street house for weeks before it was safe for him to return to France.

Lady Mary Wortley Montagu despaired of her nephew. Although he had "spirit," she believed he had become as "great a rake as any in England" because his education had been "deplorable" at the hands of the "wretch," Hickman.[26] For all her own behavior—she wrote, said, and wore whatever she liked, challenged the medical establishment, and had eloped herself[27]—she was dismayed by the conduct of the now nominal head of the Pierrepont family. Not everybody held the Madame episode against him, though: in 1741 he was made a gentleman of the bedchamber to the king, although he resigned two years later because of ill health, just weeks before Elizabeth joined the rival, junior court.

When Kingston returned to England he lived with Madame at palatial Thoresby, but in April 1745, as if by divine disapproval, most of the house was burned to the ground in a fire.[28] He saved papers and paintings, but was reduced to living in the kitchen wing not only with Madame but also his sister Frances, her husband Philip Meadows, and their six young children. Madame became a British subject, joined the Church of England, and devoted herself to the duke entirely.

Within months the duke, as his valet put it, "won over the favor of the reigning Hanovers" by showing absolute loyalty when England was under the threat of the Jacobite invasion. At his own expense, he assembled the Duke of Kingston's Regiment of Light Horse, reported in February 1745 to be "exceedingly well-mounted and in top order." These volunteer soldiers, armed with light equipment on nimble horses, could "traverse hilly ground with facility."[29] They were the first to "break into the rebel army" at Culloden, where they fought mercilessly. When they were disbanded the following year, they had fought with such bloodlust that all of them were asked to join the service of the Duke of Cumberland. For raising such a deft troop in such a short space of time, Kingston was made a general. Other than his romantic escapades, the raising of this battalion was his single, dramatic, noteworthy act; but given how impressive they were as amateurs, it was a proper military achievement.[30]

Encouraging the affair between the Duke of Kingston and Madame de la Touche was his sister Lady Frances, who had eloped at twenty-one with Philip Meadows, the second son of Sir Philip Meadows, Knight Marshal,* with no inheritance coming his way. They had had six children in quick succession and now lived off, and with, her brother in London and at Thoresby. Naturally, they hoped that Kingston's relationship with Madame de la Touche would survive, because as long as there was no legitimate heir, the Kingston estates would be left to their children. There was no backup plan to seizing the Kingston inheritance, so when de la Touche was forsaken for Elizabeth, they loathed her immediately. De la Touche had been an entirely subservient, insecure, non-English-speaking married woman. Elizabeth was ostensibly single, opinionated, and clearly adored by Kingston.

The Meadowses viewed her as a mortal threat the moment they heard her name.

By the time Kingston met Elizabeth, he was engrossed in a gentleman's sporting life at Thoresby. The act of creating the Light Horse from scratch demonstrated his prowess with all things equestrian. He was a hunter and racehorse breeder at Newmarket and held the position of "Master of the Stag Hounds," north of the Trent,

---

* He was descended from Suffolk squire Daniel Meadows of Chattisham Hall, an ancestor of Kate Middleton.

in charge of the royal hunting dogs.[31] He played cricket, fished, and shot with his friends, such as the Marquess of Granby and his brother Lord Robert Sutton (fellow soldiers at Culloden and sons of the Duke of Rutland).[32] "Not fond of new faces,"[33] he was most at home with the men who had been in his regiment, such as Colonel Litchfield and Captain George Brown, who had their own bedrooms at Thoresby. Among his many fine qualities, wrote his valet, he kept "good hours"; he was temperate and cautious, apart from in love and war; he was agreeably introverted, well-dressed, and sweet-smelling (violet and juniper "perfum'd water" appear in his accounts).[34] He was planning a new Thoresby, building and grounds. When in London, he sat in the House of Lords and attended court. When not with Madame, and before everyone knew about Elizabeth, he was sought-after by society women and their mothers.

According to the valet Thomas Whitehead (whose accounts of Elizabeth are likely to be biased—he hated her for disrupting his comfortable life with the duke), de la Touche "had the love of all the neighborhood for her bountiful disposition . . . her chief delight was in pleasing the Duke, and endeavouring to make him happy." She "welcomed his friends with respect." These included their equally scandalous friend, Lady Vane,[35] and her lover Seawallis Shirley. The Abbé le Blanc, art critic and later favorite of Madame de Pompadour, came for an extended stay, to the relief of de la Touche, whose English never much improved. Le Blanc wrote a series of letters about English manners, observing, for example, that unlike in France, the sexes barely socialized together unless they were in love. Englishmen treated women "as if they had been of another species as of another sex. For the most part they look on them as good for nothing but to dissipate their vapours, or ease the fatigue of business." The sexes were unable to communicate, he found: "The presence of one man here is sufficient to impose silence on a whole circle of women." The men drank too much and fought with each other; they lacked polish; they traveled too young to gain anything other than a taste for luxury. Unlike in France, where it was impossible to marry without parental permission, he noted the frequency of unwise clandestine marriages: "Youth is too blind, and too much abandoned to its passions, to discern its true interest." The work of "one moment's frailty" could mean misery for life, a sentiment with which Elizabeth would surely agree.[36]

In spite of Madame's accommodating nature, the affair with Kingston had faded out after fourteen years. The chronology of Elizabeth's arrival and Madame's downfall is lost in time, but when it did end, society felt sorry for her. The wildly attractive duke was in a swirl of rumor. "Poor Madame la Touche is, I think, to be pitied," wrote diarist Lady Mary Coke, "she must suffer extremely. The newspapers marry the Duke to Lady Juliana Collyer,[37] but I hear there is not the least foundation for the report, and the town says he is rather engaged in a flirtation than a matrimonial affair."[38] Lady Mary Coke was another uncharitable witness to Elizabeth's life. The daughter of the Duke of Argyll, she was estranged from her husband Viscount Coke, and is revealed by her writings to be unhappily full of envy, and fixated on royalty, as Horace Walpole believed. She loathed Elizabeth, ceaselessly offended by her social success.[39]

It was far more than a flirtation. When Kingston, "a very weak man, of the greatest beauty, and the finest person in England,"[40] met Elizabeth, they left all others behind.

CHAPTER TWELVE

A WOMAN OF PROPERTY

The female battleground over eligible men led to heartbreak, if not bloodshed. Madame de la Touche had never been on a secure footing in the Nottinghamshire soil. In 1739, just three years into her stay in England, a visitor to Thoresby had seen her walking forlorn and alone in the grounds with only a book for company. A crimson silk dress lay on her bed ready for her to change into, but with no one to admire it, as the duke was in London. Madame had the riches—the wardrobe, the servants—of a duchess, but none of the social life. Neighboring landowners' wives never regarded her as respectable company; village locals told the visitor that the duke was already tired of his French mistress. With Elizabeth in the ascendant, Madame was dispatched home to Paris with a maidservant, and a pension of £800 a year from Kingston. She had the comfort, at least, of a well-connected family.[1]

Sympathy for Madame was fleeting. These days, the gossip was all about those alluring upstarts, the Gunning sisters, trailing their silk mantuas in Elizabeth's wake. They attracted the same kind of attention—in fact, the same men—that Elizabeth had done, from the king downwards. Elizabeth's old suitor the Duke of Hamilton was one such example. Like Kingston, he had enjoyed an extended Grand Tour[2] and returned habitually drunk, "damaged in fortune and person."[3] He met the younger, more cunning Gunning, Elizabeth, at a masquerade in 1752. When he saw her again at Lord Chesterfield's unveiling of his London palace, Chesterfield House,* he was

---

* It had a French-inspired baroque interior. Chesterfield believed his library was "the finest room in London."

so distracted by her presence that he lost £1,000 at cards. Two nights later, finding himself alone with her, he persuaded her to marry him immediately. The wedding took place at half-past midnight, at the Mayfair Chapel, with a bed-curtain ring as a wedding ring, a ceremony almost as "scrappy" (Elizabeth's word for her own marriage) as the Chudleigh/Hervey one at Lainston. "The Scotch are enraged, and the women mad that so much beauty has had its effect,"[4] it was said of the match. Crowds gathered to see the new Duchess of Hamilton pass in her carriage, and "seven hundred people sat up all night [outside] . . . an inn in Yorkshire, to see her get her post-chaise the next morning." Three weeks later, it was the turn of her elder sister, Maria, who married the "grave young Lord" of Croome Court, Worcestershire, a politician and groom of the bedchamber to the king, the Earl of Coventry. The public were just as intrigued by the new countess. A shoemaker in Worcester charged a penny a time for a peek at a dainty shoe he was making for the Countess of Coventry.

The young Gunnings had arrived, found husbands, and moved on. The pressure was on Elizabeth to somehow secure her status: eligible men went quickly and younger models would replace the Gunnings. She was in an unwieldy position, with her secret marriage and scratched reputation: the furor over the Iphigenia costume had still not entirely blown over.[5]

Elizabeth—by now indifferent to the Duke of Hamilton—was attempting to consolidate her affair with Kingston, while knowing that marriage was not a possibility. As he was a rich, unmarried duke, ambitious mothers were steering daughters into his line of sight. Lady Juliana Collyer, a beady, dark-haired girl who eventually married the MP heir to a Jamaican plantation, was just one girl put forward by the newspapers. In 1751, it was the turn of Lady Elizabeth Bentinck, daughter of Thoresby neighbor the Duke of Portland, sixteen to Kingston's thirty-nine.[6]

It was to Elizabeth's advantage that her family did not, and could not, start a marriage negotiation. It was a courtship of camaraderie. She and Kingston shared trips to her mother at Windsor Castle, and country pursuits. He "chiefly amuses himself with cricket," wrote a Nottinghamshire grandee, disapprovingly, to Kingston's aunt, Lady Mary Wortley Montagu.[7]

By June 1752, the liaison was open knowledge in society. On Garter Day,[8] a fellow guest, Lady Jane Coke,[9] wrote to a friend of Elizabeth and Kingston as a pair that needed no explanation. After the installation of new knights, there was a ball at Windsor Castle, with dancing "in two rooms, several sideboards for lemonade and ice, tea, and coffee; all kinds of dessert-things and a supper at twelve o'clock . . . a great deal of finery." But Kingston "was so fatigued that he was forced to take drops during the ceremony"; he only stayed to dine and left before the ball; while "Miss Chudleigh was not here, she has been very ill, and was not enough recovered to venture."[10]

They had the inconvenience of fragile health in common, in which they tenderly sympathized with and nursed each other.

Kingston was extremely discreet. In his many years of service, his valet reported that he never saw him so much as kiss Elizabeth. We do not know exactly what Elizabeth told Kingston of her past; most likely that she had had an illicit, youthful marriage that she did not regard as legitimate. But her history was leaking out. For this, she had to thank the indiscreet Hervey, who had confided in his friend Lady Townshend, who in turn told William Pulteney's son. Young Pulteney made an enemy out of Lady Townshend by repeating her stories of "Miss Chudleigh" back to Miss Chudleigh. The Duke of Kingston went to "challenge" Lady Townshend about what she had said.[11] The rumor for which Lady Townshend was reprimanded, to her intense embarrassment, had started with Hervey's tortured confidences. Eventually, "everybody" knew. Sly verses appeared, alluding to Elizabeth's marriage and even to the baby. (If Elizabeth knew about this, she must have found it humiliating.) In 1755, Lady Jane Coke wrote to a friend that some "Bath wit" had composed the following verse about Elizabeth:

> A wife, who to her husband ne'er laid claim,
> A mother, who her children ne'er dare name,
> Is this a wonder, more yet be said,
> This wife, this mother still remains a Maid.[12]

In the summer of 1752, Elizabeth and Kingston were in Tunbridge Wells together; Elizabeth, in particular, in need of some elusive cure. Lady Jane Coke wrote in August, "Miss Chudleigh was there a fortnight, so altered, I was surprised to see her by daylight . . . The Duke of K was always with [her], that is a surprising affair, we are so used at Windsor to their coming together here to her mother, who is housekeeper, that now 'tis scarce mentioned."[13] Just a few months later, however, the newspapers reported that Elizabeth was "dangerous ill" again.[14]

Elizabeth could not orchestrate marriage, or good health, but her survival instinct did embolden her to embark on a new compulsion: property ownership. In this, her avowed single status worked in her favor: while a married woman's property belonged to her husband, a spinster or widow's property was her own. (Her ambitions also demonstrate that she did not accept the legality of her marriage to Hervey.) Born in a grace-and-favor apartment, partly raised in a rented townhouse, if she could not have the stability of marriage, she would have the feeling of prosperity and security that she, who had spent so much time at the gilded country seats of relatives and at court, had never known for herself. Her first mentor, William Pulteney, was known for his habit of acquisition. If he taught her anything, it was his belief in the importance of money, or rather, what it could buy.

Her first move on the Monopoly board of eighteenth-century London was on April 14, 1753, when she took a lease under her maiden name for eighty-seven years from Lord Berkeley of Stratton for a plot of empty land, 29 by 67 feet, in Hill Street, Mayfair. The Berkeley family* owned a section of the district, then a building site, and were selling off plots. He was a family friend: his younger brother was cousin John Merrill's brother-in-law.[15]

On the plot, Elizabeth had a house built with stables opening onto Farm Street. She moved in, and sold it five years later.[16] London society was not slow to observe that it was inconceivable she could have turned property developer on a maid-of-honour salary: she must have already prized open the stuffed Kingston coffers. (There are numerous unnamed withdrawals in the duke's account at his bank, Hoare & Co.; it is likely some were for Elizabeth. She opened

---

* After whom Berkeley Square was named.

her own account at Drummond's in 1755, with the staggering sum of £6,000.) It was later reported in *The Times* that rather than give her money directly, they played cards together and Kingston donated all his winnings to Elizabeth.

Soon it became apparent to everyone that they were devoted to each other. When Elizabeth fell ill again at Windsor in October 1753, Lady Jane Coke wrote, "Miss Chudleigh is still a nominal Maid of honour, she was here a fortnight, and the Duke of Kingston with her, and happened to be very ill, when he sat up all night with her, and the apothecary of this town."[17]

She recovered, but just a few months later, her nerves got the better of her in public, just as they had done in the assembly room at Tunbridge Wells. At the opera, a member of the cast fell flat on his face, motionless in "an apoplectic fit." Everyone thought he was dead. Elizabeth, who was in the box next to her mistress the Dowager Princess Augusta—who was "much affected" herself—and her children, fainted.[18] Walpole gave his own more colorful version: "The only event since you left London was the tragi-comedy . . . last Saturday at the opera. Miss Chudleigh, who *apparement* had never seen a man fall on his face before, went into the most theatric fit of kicking and shrieking that ever was seen. Several other women, who were preparing their fits, were so distanced that she had the whole house to herself, and indeed such a confusion for half an hour I never saw!"[19]

Since the death of the baby, she had perhaps developed a fear of mortality that caused her to pass out when she came across a sudden representation of it. In those vicious, misogynistic times there was little sympathy for her discomfort. Yet again, she was just seen as a melodramatic attention-seeker.

Whether these episodes were pseudo-seizures or a phobia of collapse, the pressure of a double life—the effervescent character with anguish at heart—was too much. Fainting, fading away in shock, was much more common then than now, but the regularity with which Elizabeth showed extreme distress, or succumbed to the "vapours,"[20] was startling even then.

At other times, Elizabeth still played the part of maid of honour with finesse. At the dowager princess's birthday in November 1754, a guest wrote that there was "more finery than usual. Miss Chudleigh danced minuets."[21] At Lord Holderness's ball, the king was noted as having danced with Lady Coventry, the elder Gunning. But Elizabeth "moved with all the grace and majesty of a goddess," wrote one contemporary biographer.[22] A minuet was a precise, mannered dance with bowing, curtsies, and hand movements that became popular at the court of Louis XIV, who prided himself on his mastery of it—not that anyone would have ever said otherwise. It was scrutinized by its audience, an opportunity to show off figure, dress, hair, and jewels.

Otherwise, Kingston and Elizabeth preferred being in the country. She rented a "villa at Finchley," and then Percy Lodge, Buckinghamshire, from her friend the Duchess of Northumberland, where she and Kingston met in private. Percy Lodge had *ferme ornée* grounds, Marie Antoinette–style.[23] There was a wood, a boating lake, "a cave overhung with periwinkles" with a spring gushing out of the back of it; "little arbours interwoven with lilacs," and an "astounding number of nightingales." It was "arcadia" on earth, wrote a previous owner.[24]

Elizabeth and Kingston seemed to have had the same idea of what was pleasurable—fishing trips, for example. There were trout to be caught a coach ride away from Percy Lodge by a farmhouse at Rickmansworth, where they would travel and often return having caught nothing. When Percy Lodge was given up, the farm at Rickmansworth was rented for fishing. The party met up at the White Horse Inn at Uxbridge, "Miss Chudleigh with a companion . . . man and maidservant";[25] Whitehead the valet brought cold provisions, beer, and rum for Elizabeth to stay warm. He stewed chickens in a silver pan over an iron heater, and made coffee and tea. They returned to the inn at night, and continued like this for three or four days. The whole enterprise cost Kingston a fortune, "five guineas a pound of fish," reckoned his valet.

In town, their less likely recreation was to observe criminal trials. They went to watch the proceedings at the new Bow Street Criminal Court, presided over by their friend (and Elizabeth's relative), the half-blind Sir John Fielding, of whom it was said he could recognize 3,000 known criminals by the sound of their voices alone. His novelist half brother Henry Fielding[26] had preceded him and started England's first police force, the Bow Street Runners, in 1749. London was in the middle of a gin-fueled crime wave: half the population was barely at survival level and many spent too much on gin, their only comfort.* When Fielding set up a charity to help poor girls and prostitutes, Elizabeth donated money.

They sought solace for their ailments at spas together. In September 1757 they were spotted in Bristol's Hotwells, with an army friend, "Col Prideaux and his lady."[27] The following August, they were in the Yorkshire seaside resort of Scarborough, where Elizabeth ordered a troop review.[28] A fellow tourist wrote: "The uniform is very pretty, and I never saw anywhere such good-looking men, and so exactly of a size . . . It was by Miss Chudleigh's desire, they exercised at this hour; all her party was there."[29]

Elizabeth's lust for property had not been sated by the Hill Street project. She decided to build a detached house in Knightsbridge, then "quite out of London,"[30] on the way to Kensington Palace. It was to be a country house near the market gardens just beyond the Hyde Park turnpike. Knightsbridge was a village with a maypole on its green. But west of Hyde Park Corner, the road was dangerous. On the edge of the park, just beyond Elizabeth's land, there was a "Half-way House," "a dissipated, rat-bitten tavern," an inn infested with footpads, highwaymen, and the spies who looked out for them.†

Not an obvious place to buy, but Elizabeth could be an astute opportunist. The appeal must partly have been the view: behind the plot there was a vista all the way down towards the Chelsea of her childhood. "The view over Hyde Park, and at the back over Chelsea, is considered with truth one of the finest that could be pictured," wrote one visitor.[31] The out-of-town element also suited her unconventional relationship. One of the other few houses to be built around the same time on that empty stretch was inhabited by

---

* The situation improved when the Gin Act was introduced in 1751, controlling its sale.
† When the tavern was demolished, a secret passage to the stables was discovered, for any patrons who needed to leave in a hurry.

another unmarried couple: Rutland House, built in 1753 by the 3rd Duke of Rutland who was living with a Mrs. Drake. The area had form—a few years later it was described as "concubine row."[32]

On February 3, 1757, Elizabeth bought three acres in Knightsbridge, as "copyholder and tenant," from the Dean and Chapter of Westminster Abbey, and commissioned a Palladian-style house. Two years later, Kingston bought a four-acre field to the west of the site, and Elizabeth bought six and a half acres to the east.

Chudleigh House, as Elizabeth named it (never mind that this style of appellation was usually reserved for grandee families such as the Spencers or the Devonshires), was designed by the architect Henry Flitcroft, Clerk of St. Paul's, who, as well as designing the Arlington Street townhouse for Kingston, had assisted Lord Burlington and worked for the Duke of Bedford at Woburn Abbey. (The Duke of Kingston paid Flitcroft regular sums from his Hoare & Co. account while Chudleigh House was being built.) This was the clientele with which Elizabeth aligned herself. For a cost of "many thousand pounds,"[33] he designed a three-story house with lower service wings linked by corridors to the stables and kitchens. The only visible decoration was Venetian-style windows in the center of the house under a pediment. Building such a house, embracing Palladian aesthetics, was seen as a noble endeavor. It was definitely not a house for a single woman, but for a grand couple who planned to entertain. There were formal gardens and a grotto behind the house. From the front, Chudleigh House looked out to the Serpentine, and the deer grazing in Hyde Park, into which a private gate was later granted by George III.

An impression of Chudleigh House was recorded by a German guest: "[Miss Chudleigh's] house can justly be called a gem; it contains a quantity of handsome and costly furniture and other curiosities and objects of value, chosen and arranged with the greatest taste, so that you cannot fail to admire it greatly. There is hardly a place in the whole house left bare or without decoration, like a doll's house. Everything is in perfect harmony."[34]

Not everyone liked it. Horace Walpole judged it "not fine nor in good taste."[35] The Gothic revivalist[36] was horrified by the sheer amount of clutter and dust-gathering *objets*. As he had gathered

4,000 curious *objets* of his own, this was somewhat hypocritical. Yet Walpole and Elizabeth were of different tribes, in aesthetics as well as in politics, Elizabeth being part of the Frederick/Pulteney camp who had opposed his father. He found Chudleigh House "loaded with finery . . . execrable varnished pictures, chests, cabinets, commodes, tables, stands, boxes, riding on one another's backs, and loaded with terrenes, filigree, figures and everything upon earth. Every favor she has bestowed is registered by a bit of Dresden china. There is a glass-case full of enamels, eggs, ambers, lapis lazuli, cameos, toothpick-cases, and all kinds of trinkets, things that she told me were her playthings." He was, however, impressed by the "conveniences in every bedchamber; great mahogany projections, with brass handles, cocks, &c." Elizabeth liked every modern convenience of heating or hygiene and gathering curiosities. "Overspending" and obsessive collecting were often criticized with a strain of misogyny, the townhouse being an emblem of feminine excess.[37]

The duke's valet, however, found it a "large and pleasant" house with "as good a garden and as well stocked with fruit and vegetables as anywhere within ten miles of the place." The maid of honour was now living in a house that bore her name, and her own produce—a gilded result for a woman who had started with nothing.

If helping to finance the house was not enough public proof of Kingston's love for Elizabeth, it came in January 1756, when Mrs. Chudleigh, still housekeeper at Windsor Castle, died. She was buried at Chelsea alongside her husband and son. Society could even be waspish about this. George Selwyn MP wrote the following verse on seeing Elizabeth crying in a royal drawing room:

> What filial piety! what mournful grace,
> For a lost parent, sits on Chudleigh's face!
> Fair virgin, weep no more, your anguish smother!
> You in this town can never want a mother.[38]

This was an allusion to her own experience of motherhood. (Mean-spirited—but then Selwyn was known for his sadistic tendencies: excited by suffering, he was rumored to watch executions dressed as a woman so he would not be recognized. The corrupt necrophiliac did not say a word in the Commons in his forty-four years of sitting in it. He had been sent down from Oxford for drinking toasts in blood to pagan gods. No wonder he lacked compassion for Elizabeth.)

Nevertheless, the death of Harriet Chudleigh confirmed one thing to all: Kingston was profoundly sympathetic and loyal to her grieving daughter. Newspapers, gossips, and mothers were forced to stop imagining he was about to marry anyone else. The Reverend Theophilus Lindsey wrote to the Earl of Huntingdon in May 1756: "The Duke of Kingston's marriage with the Duke of Marlborough's eldest daughter ceases now to be talked of [yet another mooted match] and his mistress is said once more to have resumed her ascendant. I fancy one may say—'Here end the Pierreponts.'"[39] A conclusion that of course means he, too, had heard of the Hervey marriage.

In spite of the Knightsbridge estate bearing her own name, the undoubted silk dresses and jewels, the various noble daughters who had been swiftly seen off with a graceful minuet and a flick of a fan, Elizabeth still felt insecure, like a premarriage Anne Boleyn with houses and titles but no wedding ring. She could not marry, and Kingston, now in his forties, was beset with mysterious and manifold ailments. In 1757 he was unable to meet the prime minister, the Duke of Newcastle, because a surgeon was treating him for "lameness in the foot."[40] There always seemed to be a malady of sorts. What if he died? Or abandoned her, as he had done Madame de la Touche?

In 1759, Elizabeth took an unexpected course of action, a gamble that would not come to light for nearly two decades.

Augustus Hervey's elder brother George, 2nd Earl of Bristol since the death of grandfather Bristol in 1751, had a delicate constitution, better suited to warmer climates. At the start of 1759, either he was having one of his momentary visits to the realm of the deathbed, or the mere fact of his going abroad again—he had just become ambassador in Madrid—refocused Elizabeth's mind on the Bristol succession. The urbane diplomat, "the effeminate son of an effeminate father," had failed to find himself a wife. Therefore, if he died, Augustus would become the 3rd Earl and inherit all the estate

and riches of the Bristol family, from the acres of oaks and deer at
Ickworth in Suffolk to the "great building" at 6 St. James's Square.
As his wife, Elizabeth would have security and status, in a way
that the Hon. Elizabeth Chudleigh of Chudleigh House could never
quite have, with her debts alongside her quasi-royal but unconventional lifestyle. As she and Hervey were estranged and the marriage
was still meant to be confidential, at the very least, with proof of
marriage, she would have leverage. Augustus Hervey would have
to subsidize her somehow, particularly if he wanted to remarry to
have a legitimate heir. In spite of her obvious and genuine feelings
for Kingston, Elizabeth was so desperate for security—or stifled by
her own lack of agency—that she made a bizarre decision.

    In mid-February, a 37-year-old Elizabeth, now older than her
father had been when he had died, arrived by carriage in the fading
dark of a freezing early morning at the medieval Blue Boar Inn, on a
hill overlooking Winchester. The Blue Boar was opposite the house
of the Reverend Thomas Amis, who had married her to Augustus
Hervey fifteen years before. At 6 A.M., she sent an anonymous message asking his wife, Judith Amis, to come to the inn. "Good God,
Madam, what can have brought you to such a house as this?" asked
Judith, surprised to find the maid of honour hiding in an ale-soaked,
sawdust-floored nook at such an odd hour. Elizabeth wanted to
know if Amis would provide her with a marriage register. As dawn
broke, the two women went over to the Amises' house in Kingsgate
Street. The aged clergyman was bedbound by illness, but agreed.
The women went into his bedchamber and cousin John Merrill
arrived from nearby Lainston. A local attorney, James Spearing,
was summoned; Elizabeth "said she did not care that Mr. Spearing
should know she was here and therefore she would conceal herself
in the closet . . . that opened on the staircase." While Elizabeth hid,
Spearing arrived and announced they must have a register book, and
that Elizabeth must be present. Judith Amis retrieved Elizabeth from
the closet; Spearing went to buy the register book. On his return,
frail Amis, propped up in bed, wrote out the entry and signed it.
According to Mrs. Amis,* Elizabeth thanked him and said, "It may

---

* At the trial, seventeen years later.

be a hundred thousand pounds in my way," and (according to her later testimony) told her that she had had a baby boy who had died, "by Mr. Hervey," and that she had borrowed £100 off Aunt Hanmer to "buy baby things."

Elizabeth sealed the book with strips of paper to prevent it from being opened and handed it to Mrs. Amis, asking her to take care of it until her husband's death, and then deliver it to John Merrill. Six weeks later, the reverend died, and his widow went to see Elizabeth at Chudleigh House to tell her that Merrill now had the register. When she found her in the garden, Elizabeth thanked her, and asked her to forget what had happened.

The register entitled "Marriages, Births, and Burials in the parish of Lainston" had only two entries. The first was: "4th August 1744 married the Honourable Augustus Hervey, Esq, to Miss Elizabeth Chudleigh, daughter of Colonel Thomas Chudleigh, late of Chelsea College, deceased, in the parish church of Lainston, by me Thomas Amis." To make it convincing, the other entry, added above it, referred to another Lainston event that had also had no record: "22nd of August, 1742, buried Mrs. Susannah Merrill, relict of John Merrill, Esq."

We only have this curious story from Mrs. Amis herself. Some parts are strange indeed. Why would Elizabeth mention the baby in conversation so long after the event? Conceivably, it was to show that it had been a real marriage that others had known about at the time, should she ever need to prove herself. Or perhaps Mrs. Amis elaborated her story at the trial to show how much she knew.

It seems that just at the time she might have wanted to demonstrate that she was able to wed Kingston, she had lost faith in ever being able to escape her first marriage. She had decided instead to risk all on a dramatic new strategy: to prove she was married to Hervey in case he came into his inheritance. She was defending her position in case Kingston died, or left; and yet, it is hard to avoid the conclusion that she was opening the door to blackmailing Hervey as a fallback option. Was there a streak of revenge in there, after the wretched birth, and the sad loss of the baby, during which she must have felt abandoned? In this gambling age, it was reckless, manipulative, and unwise, but the presence of cousin Merrill must have given it a veneer of reason.

Elizabeth Chudleigh left Winchester and the register went to Merrill for safekeeping after the reverend's death. Elizabeth had accomplished what she had set out to do, which was to establish evidence, should she ever need it, that her marriage to Hervey had taken place. But if she thought she had bought herself security for the future, she had drastically miscalculated.

CHAPTER THIRTEEN

FIREWORKS

By the mid-1750s, the country had tumbled back headlong into war, one that would involve every great power in Europe and span five continents. It became known as the Seven Years' War, but Winston Churchill later called it the "first world war."[1] As a rising sea captain, Augustus Hervey was in its midst. Part of Elizabeth's desire to provide herself with evidence of marriage was surely that in these years of bloody fighting with no end in sight, the odds of widowhood could hardly have been higher. Hervey was so often in the frontline of battle. Had George, 2nd Earl of Bristol, died first, or even if he had not, Augustus Hervey's widow would have found herself with an inheritance, including an Admiralty pension,[2] without the inconvenience of a husband, or the shame and complications of divorce. In 1756, Anglo-French tension, already being played out in combat in North America, erupted into conflict in Europe and intrepid Hervey was to become involved in one of the most traumatic episodes that the Royal Navy has ever seen.

After Elizabeth had met Kingston, estranged husband Hervey was entangling himself with women all over Europe, while angling for glory, adventure, and spoils. His ship, the twenty-four-gun HMS *Phoenix*, headed for Portugal where he flirted with nuns, lived with a Frenchwoman on board, and was abducted and blindfolded by a coachman at the request of a widow who had fallen for him on sight at a bullfight.* He lay under another woman's bed for two hours to

---

* This "much painted" rich widow was determined to make him her lover. They had anonymous liaisons at various country houses. He eventually worked out, by having her followed, that she was the Duchess of Cadaval, and the daughter of a prince.

avoid her husband. These women, according to his journal, always fell in love with him and sobbed when he left.

Hervey was forced to turn his exertions from women to war. The French had convinced Newcastle's government[3] that their target was England when it was, in fact, British-held Minorca. As a result, preparations for naval battle in the Mediterranean were woefully inadequate.[4] The French overran the island, bar the garrison, which was under siege. On May 20, Hervey fought at the Battle of Minorca under Admiral Byng: a mismatch of ships, men, weaponry, and, as the French got into port first, position.[5] In a four-hour skirmish, a chaos of sea spray, smoke, and cannon fire, half the British fleet was damaged. Despite failing to relieve the garrison, Byng felt they had no chance of resistance, so they headed for Gibraltar to repair their ships, leaving the French in possession of Minorca.

Byng was ordered back to England, arrested, and charged with "failing to do his utmost." The government, rather than be blamed for ordering a British naval defeat, made Byng the scapegoat. Hervey tried to exonerate his friend and, when he had been condemned to death at the court-martial, to get his sentence revoked. His efforts—pamphlets, visits, a performance in the witness box in which his testimony was described as "extempore . . . very candid . . . distinct and clear"[6]—are testament to Hervey's sense of honor, justice, and loyalty.[7] But his efforts failed—as did those of the next prime minister, William Pitt, who asked the king to spare Byng's life.*

On March 14, 1757, Admiral Byng walked out onto the quarter deck of HMS *Monarch* in Portsmouth, tied a white handkerchief across his eyes, knelt on a cushion, and dropped another white handkerchief to show he was ready. He was shot dead by firing squad[8]—a seismic event that reverberated throughout Europe. He was the first and last naval officer of his rank to be so treated. Voltaire satirized the moment in *Candide*; the eponymous hero witnesses such an event in Portsmouth and is told: "*Dans ce pays-ci, il est bon de tuer de temps en temps un amiral pour encourager les autres.*"†

---

* George II refused Pitt's request, saying of Byng, "This man will not fight!"
† "In this country, it is thought wise to kill an admiral from time to time to encourage the others."

It is to this hour that some trace the birth of Empire, the beginning of "a culture of aggressive determination which set British
officers apart from their foreign contemporaries, and which . . . gave
them a steadily mounting psychological ascendancy."[9]

Byng bequeathed Hervey a French clock "ornamented with Dresden flowers," bearing the inscription, "May time serve you better
than he has served me."

England, in uproar at the defeat, discussed little other than
the Byng affair, and the newspapers covered every word of the
battle, trial, and execution. Two cartoons survive from 1757 that
publicly made the connection between Elizabeth, Hervey, and the
Byng affair—a trial of a fashionably dressed lady for adultery, as
a satire of Byng's trial. The judges are ladies with reputations—
Elizabeth is captioned in one as "Miss Chide-a-lie, alias Hon
Mrs. Her-way."[10] Hervey's name and his exploits were everywhere—he was described as a "truly brave and active captain" in
one report, when a few months later he had "destroyed a French
frigate, taken six vessels and retaken two of our own."[11] Elizabeth
Chudleigh would have heard every detail, just as she would have
heard of the intermittent ill health and postings of his brother,
the Earl of Bristol; and that Augustus Hervey, by now MP for the
family constituency, Bury St. Edmunds, was commanded to assist
Admiral Hawke in another Seven Years' War encounter against
the French at Quiberon Bay.[12] That victory, in November 1759,
broke the morale of the French navy and ensured plans to invade
England were shelved forever. Hervey was acclaimed a hero. His
mother sent him these lines of verse from the *London Evening
Post*: "Britons exult! all Gallia trembling stands/ While Hervey
executes and Hawke commands."[13]

How did Elizabeth react to her husband defending a man seen
first as a coward, then as a victim of injustice, and two years later
playing his part in a heroic victory? As she was patriotic and emotional by nature, it is unlikely she was unmoved. It was after the
Byng affair that she secured the marriage register. Perhaps there was
a glimmer of admiration in her heart. However, she had responsibili-
ties closer to home, where a different kind of war was resolving itself.

*

The shining victor of Leicester House's lengthy tutor wars was John Stuart, 3rd Earl of Bute, now just as close to Augusta as he had ever been to her husband. He became "finishing tutor" in 1755, and he not only ran the children's education but also set the political line at Leicester House, as he was so implicitly trusted by both mother and son. His house on Kew Green had a private gate into the grounds of Kew Palace, where he helped Augusta nurture plants, as well as children. He was anti-war, in opposition to wartime leader William Pitt.[14] An honest, handsome, intelligent yet slightly pompous man, there were rumors of an affair between Bute and Augusta, alluded to by a stream of bawdy cartoons and poems, in spite of the fact that he was happily married to Lady Mary Wortley Montagu's daughter Mary, the Duke of Kingston's first cousin, with their eleventh child born in 1757. Prince George revered Bute, and his educational progress was transformed by his desire to please his new father figure. In 1756, the king suggested a new household at St. James's Palace for George, with an allowance of £40,000. George accepted the money but refused to move, and appointed Bute as his groom of the stole, his closest courtier. His frequent letters to Bute began, "My dearest friend . . ." Elizabeth became friends with Bute too, part of a protective, intimate circle. There was jollity, singing, and dancing among all the politics.[15]

Elizabeth was by Augusta's side for the highs and lows of her children's upbringing. Her frail second daughter, Princess Elizabeth, died in 1759, age eighteen, at Kew Palace, and was buried at Westminster Abbey. There to console Augusta in the abbey was Elizabeth, alongside her fellow maids of honour, her friend Charlotte Dives, Mary Bridget Mostyn, and a more recent appointment, Henrietta Egerton.[16]

With Augusta in mourning again, and Elizabeth now a woman of property, the shape of the new court had evolved: Elizabeth became a generous party hostess in Augusta's orbit. She put the dowager's court back into color. Birthday parties had always been the highlight of the Hanoverian court calendar, and the dowager princess must have been appreciative of her maid of honour's exertions; such events had been more Frederick's terrain than Augusta's. Elizabeth combined her mother's organizational skills with her father's bonhomie, dusted with her own exuberant glamour. She was an exemplary exerciser of soft power: in a time of frequent warfare, she enabled foreign ambassadors and statesmen to mix with each other, royalty, and British society. In March 1760, she held a breakfast and concert at Chudleigh House for the twenty-first birthday of the younger son, Prince Edward, who was by now a flirtatious naval captain. The music was followed by "a vast cold collation"* at 3 P.M. "All the town" attended.[17] In June, she hosted a ball for the twenty-second birthday of the Prince of Wales. The *Public Advertiser*: "Last night the Hon Miss Chudleigh gave a most splendid and elegant ball and entertainment to a numerous assembly of persons of the first rank, at her house at Brampton-park, in honour of the Day (the birthday of the Prince of Wales), at which was present many of the Foreign Ministers."[18]

Thrown on a balmy night in early summer, the ball was "magnificent,"[19] the forecourt illuminated by lamps on every wall. "The virgin-mistress"—as Walpole referred to Elizabeth—"began the ball with the Duke of York [Prince Edward], who was dressed in a pale blue watered tabby."†[20] Spain was an enemy, yet Elizabeth invited the Spanish ambassador and his wife. The latter, wrote Walpole, was "homely, but seems good-humored and civil," their son had a "high-born ugliness" and daughter-in-law "a good set of teeth as one can have, when one has but two and those black." The ambassadress "could see nothing; for Dodington stood before her the whole time,‡ sweating Spanish at her, of which it was evident by her civil nods without answers she did not understand a word." Elizabeth laid on card games upstairs.[21] "Everybody ran up: there is a low gallery with bookcases, and four chambers . . . each hung with the finest Indian pictures on [in] different colors, and with Chinese chairs of the same colors. Vases of flowers in each for nosegays." Of Kingston, Walpole wrote, "The lord of the festival was there, and seemed neither ashamed nor vain of the expense of his pleasures . . . On the sideboards, and even on the chairs, were pyramids and troughs of strawberries and cherries;

---

* A cold buffet.
† Watered tabby was fashionable silk taffeta with a wavy pattern.
‡ Bubb was a bulky fellow.

you would have thought she was kept by Vertumnus."* Kingston, we can assume, was quite content with the tableaux of society life Elizabeth was providing and he was paying for. She had embraced all the fashions: Tokay, Indian art, chinoiserie.

Kingston had provided a shift in status. With his backing, the whispers about Hervey, the Iphigenia cartoons, her unconventional relationship, were not so notorious that they weren't superseded by her royal connections. As Horace Walpole showed, even her detractors did not refuse her invitations.

Nor would they, because soon the Leicester House set was in the ascendant once more. After a thirty-three-year reign during which he had seen off the Jacobites, the French,[22] and his own son and heir, George II, half-blind and almost deaf, drank his hot chocolate in the early morning of October 25, 1760, and dropped down dead at the age of seventy-six "on the close stool." Under his 22-year-old successor, the new George III, there would be a reshuffle of the royal order. There was immense public joy at the transition: as Dr. Johnson said, the new king enjoyed the great advantage of not being his grandfather. He was the first king for generations to have been born and bred in England. He was civil, cultured, and educated. Elizabeth was safe in her position, being friendly with both mother, son, and "the Favorite,"[23] Lord Bute, who naturally became chief advisor and, eventually, prime minister.

In the 1760s, Elizabeth was frantically social. Closeness to court, her natural confidence, and Kingston's generosity meant she could attract the most glittering people to her parties, a fact that did not escape public notice. She was herself sought out by an opportunist: a Venetian opera singer–turned-impresario called Teresa Cornelys, former lover of Giacomo Casanova, with whom she had a daughter.[24] Cornelys had established herself at Carlisle House in Soho Square, filling it with Chippendale furniture and a crescent-shaped table that sat 400. Elizabeth was put in charge of the guest list at Cornelys's subscription balls, with a female committee including her friend, the "rowdy, Amazonian" Mary Bertie, Duchess of Ancaster,[25] all of whom were fans of fancy dress, gambling, and constant enter-

---

* Vertumnus: god of the seasons.

tainment. They persuaded Prince Edward, the Duchess of Argyll (as Elizabeth Gunning, widowed Duchess of Hamilton, had become on her second marriage), and the Duchess of Northumberland to join the setup, named the Society in Soho Square. The King of Denmark, the Prince of Monaco, and most of the royal family came to their events. Recruiting Elizabeth was a brilliant move: in 1763, the "fairy palace" took £24,000. Cornelys was full of gratitude: in the nineteenth century, a copper plate was found on the site of a garden pavilion commemorating Elizabeth laying its first stone.[26] But Cornelys spent more than she ever made back, hiring virtuoso musicians, such as Bach's youngest son Johann Christian; and serving an excess of jellies, syllabubs, crayfish, and exotica, and importing turf and Chinese bridges for "rural masquerades." Eventually the Society imploded and, after a stint selling ass's milk as a cure-all under an alias, Cornelys died in debt in the Fleet prison.

Cornelys's downfall is a reminder of just how high the stakes were for Elizabeth. In a period of conspicuous consumption, it had become more important to put on a show than to be able to pay for it. Yet glorious extravagance could easily end in financial ruin, debt, and prison. Elizabeth was at the pinnacle of her social success, and yet she was, as an unmarried woman, at the mercy of the men willing to support her. But in the early years of George III's reign, Cornelys's Carlisle House was the hub of the *bon ton* and Elizabeth, through connections, energy, and charm, had elevated herself to the position of London's preeminent independent social fixer.

Fluent French, diplomatic skills, and a discerning knowledge of music meant she could build alliances with ease. For example, George III had married a young German princess, Charlotte of Mecklenburg-Strelitz, and, a few months after the coronation (at which both Elizabeth and Kingston were in attendance, Kingston carrying St. Edward's staff),* Elizabeth held a concert in honor of Charlotte's brother, the twenty-year-old Prince Charles of Mecklenburg.

Hanoverian nobleman Count Frederick Kielmansegge recorded the event in March 1762:

---

* The golden scepter that symbolizes the monarch's temporal authority.

On the morning of the 15th we were invited by Miss Chudleigh to a concert; she does not live really in town, but opposite Hyde Park in a row of houses called Knightsbridge . . . At noon, a rather good concert began. Miss Brandt [Charlotte Brent, celebrated soprano]* . . . and an Italian called Tenducci† were the performers. The Prince of Mecklenburg and a large and select company were present. About half-past two, when the concert was over, we were invited to lunch in the dining-room downstairs, where music was going on with two good French horns; [a buffet] was served at a very long table, on which there was everything which could be brought together—cakes, sandwiches, cold and smoked meat, ham, jelly, fruit, etc. Small side-tables were arranged for coffee, tea, chocolate, etc., so that I must say it was the most perfect feast of its kind.[27]

The new young king and queen rejuvenated interest in royalty, and society clamored to go to the theater at Covent Garden, as the new queen had decided to go every week. Lady Mary Coke and Lord Strafford were irritated that the only box available on royal nights was above Elizabeth, who had a reputation for being noisy and drinking tea with her party.

At Christmas 1762, Elizabeth was entertaining on a more private scale with the Duke of Kingston at Pierrepont Lodge in Surrey, the house Kingston had bought and renamed in 1760. He had remodeled it with a picturesque pheasantry, dairy, water-powered corn mill, kitchen garden, ice house, and kennels. According to the valet, it now had a ballroom "capable of holding thirty couples with ease," an excellent kitchen, and even a new "coach-road over the heath to Farnham." That Christmas saw a party including two of Elizabeth's cousins—Miss Fielding, daughter of novelist Henry, and Bell Chudleigh—as well as Elizabeth's companion Miss Bate, her half brother Master Richard Shuckburgh, James Laroche‡ and his wife,

---

* Charlotte Brent was a pupil—and mistress of—Thomas Arne, the composer.
† Tenducci was an Italian castrato soprano who taught Mozart to sing.
‡ Laroche was an MP for Bodmin, a Bristol merchant, and a major slave trader after his uncle. He was the son of Isabella (Garnier) Chudleigh's sister Elizabeth. He became a baronet in 1776, and was declared bankrupt in 1778.

and others. Snowed in, they danced before supper every night for a month "apart from Sundays" to the tunes of a harpist and a violinist.

Energetic as she was as a hostess, Elizabeth was insecure about her status. If she could not marry, she wanted some kind of other official position to fall back on. Never shy about asking for favors, she wrote to Lord Bute, her old friend, royal tutor, and now prime minister, requesting the position of "Gardener of Kensington" in January 1763. Referring to herself as an "old maid" she wrote (in the third person) that "as ladies are not exempt from vanity she makes no doubt that she shall do herself credit in that employ; it has been held by a Duke of Ormond in former reigns, and therefore not unworthy of the acceptance of an old maid; and as much in character for a lady as ranger of a park is for Lady C Pelham." (The prime minister's widow enjoyed the Queen's House at Greenwich as a perk of being the ranger there.) She could not take the role, of course, if it meant giving up being maid of honour, as she had such "affectionate respect" for her mistress. She added, "If you will assist an old friend I may once more sing our old song, oh the merry merry hours of pleasure, the happy little hours of pleasure etc etc, and you will for ever oblige a person who has a grateful heart."[28]

Her timing was unfortunate: in April that year, demonized by the press over his relationship with the dowager princess, Bute resigned. Painfully for Elizabeth, her royal mistress was vilified, too. Against Bute were the following criticisms: he was a Scot; he had ousted the victorious Pitt; his peace with France was as unpopular as his cider tax; and, the final straw, he had helped to ennoble the loathed Henry Fox.[29] Worse still, he had fallen out with George III, too, as people recognized his former tutor's voice in his speeches, and the king felt Bute had made them overly authoritarian.

Misfortune in her faction did not deter Elizabeth. Just after Bute's resignation, his enemy John Wilkes* was imprisoned for criticizing the king's speech on peace with France in his periodical the *North Briton*, issue number 45,[30] and people gathered

---

* Wilkes was called the ugliest man in England. He said it took him "half an hour to talk away his face" with women.

in the streets, chanting "Wilkes, Liberty and Number 45." As Bute's friend, and no sympathizer with an angry mob, Elizabeth carried on doing what she did best in the face of a tempestuous London: she threw an explosive party. Part of her appeal to both the critical, nervous Dowager Princess Augusta and the reserved Duke of Kingston must have been her sheer willpower and social energy; she applied the sort of dogged determination to a birthday party that took others to victory on the frontline of battle. She put enormous effort and creativity into the planning, and then threw herself into the role of hostess with gusto. In May 1763, she held a great ball at Chudleigh House in honor of Queen Charlotte's nineteenth birthday. Horace Walpole's amused verdict: "to have spirits, a nation should be as . . . dashing as the Virgin Chudleigh. Oh, that you had been at her ball t'other night! History could never describe it."[31]

First there were fireworks, for which a scaffold was erected in Hyde Park. (No eighteenth-century celebration was complete without fireworks.) The assembled company watched the pyrotechnics from an unlit apartment: "If they gave rise to any more birthdays, who could help it?" asked a mischievous Walpole. Next, a "large scene" was lit up in the courtyard, representing the royal family; there were six obelisks, "painted with emblems, and illuminated," each with a Latin motto beneath, with its English translation:

1. For the Prince of Wales, a ship, *Multorum spes* [The hope of many];[32] 2. For the Princess Dowager, a bird of paradise, and two little ones, *Meos ad sidera tollo* ["I lift my young to the stars'].[33] People smiled; 3. Duke of York, a temple, *Virtuti et honori* [By virtue and honor]; 4. Princess Augusta, a bird of paradise, *Non habet parem*—unluckily this was translated, I have no peer. People laughed out, considering where this was exhibited [i.e., Elizabeth was not married to her peer]; 5. The three younger Princes, an orange-tree, *Promittit et dat* [He is promising]; 6. The two younger Princesses, the flower crown-imperial. I forget the Latin: the translation was silly enough: Bashful in youth, graceful in age.[34]

Most peculiar of all, there was a detonating memorial in rather dubious taste for the late Princess Elizabeth. "Behind the house was a cenotaph for the Princess Elizabeth, a kind of illuminated cradle; the motto, All the honours the dead can receive," wrote Walpole. "This burying-ground was a strange codicil to a festival; and, what was more strange, about one in the morning, this sarcophagus burst into crackers and guns."[35]

Elizabeth was self-deprecating: "The lady of the house made many apologies for the poorness of the performance, which she said was only oil-paper, painted by one of her servants; but it really was fine and pretty. The Duke of Kingston was in frock,* *comme chez lui*." But she also put herself center stage. As was her custom, she opened the dancing, this time with a German prince: "The Margrave of Anspach[36] began the ball with the Virgin," Walpole continued. "The supper was most sumptuous."

And yet, the past was inescapable. On December 10, 1764, Aunt Hanmer died at Lainston. John Merrill asked the local rector who had replaced Amis, the Reverend Stephen Kinchin, to record her death. In the absence of any other Lainston register, Merrill unsealed the book made on that icy dawn on the previous reverend's death-bed and gave it to Kinchin to add in a third entry, asking him not to mention the marriage above it. Kinchin then returned the book to Merrill.

Kinchin not only knew for certain about the wretched marriage between Elizabeth Chudleigh and Augustus Hervey, but had now seen proof. In the former, he was now one of an unknown number. After his night at Chudleigh House, Count Kielmansegge wrote:

Miss Chudleigh is Maid of honour to the Princess of Wales, but her fitness for the post may be gathered from the following facts. She has been married for many years to a captain in the Navy, called Hervey, a brother of my Lord Bristol; she had been sepa-rated from him for some time, and although everyone knows that she has a husband, she had kept on her appointment as Maid of

---

* Dressed as though at home.

Honour, and has never announced her marriage. That she has been kept all this time by the Duke of Kingston, from whom she receives all her riches, house, and garden, is just as well known.[37]

Despite the fact she continued to play the part of a supposedly unmarried maid of honour, Elizabeth was at the peak of her influence under the new king. Nevertheless, the threat to her status was growing, because it would appear that, by this time, everyone who was interested knew her secret.

CHAPTER FOURTEEN

A GRAND TOUR

Word spread among the beau monde in the winter of 1764 that Elizabeth Chudleigh was planning to travel abroad, and everyone wanted to know why. Horace Walpole, of course, thought he had answers. He had two theories: that she had had a colossal row with the duke and was an attention-seeking hypochondriac.[1] She had complained of pleurisy at the Dowager Princess Augusta's forty-fifth birthday party on November 30 and was seen "beating her sides in pain, so that people had to ask her what was wrong." She announced that she was going to try the baths of Carlsbad in Bohemia.

More dramatically, there was talk of the Duke of Kingston having fallen for another woman. According to Walpole, he had taken "a pretty milliner from Cranbourn Alley, and carried her to Thoresby." Cranbourn Alley was a passageway off Leicester Fields, lined with bonnet shops. Milliners, well dressed and good with customers, were of the "middling sort"; above domestic servants in status, but regarded as prey by rakes on the prowl. The duke's milliner seems, however, to have been just a rumor—wishful thinking on Walpole's part. She was never mentioned again. Lady Mary Coke joined in the waspish chorus about the trip, writing that the spa waters of Carlsbad "will be very famous if they can cleanse [Elizabeth] . . . of all her disorders."[2] Those expensive fireworks and flamboyant royal balls had aroused some envy and bile, the flip side of conspicuous social success. Elizabeth seemed vulnerable on three fronts: in the duke's affections, her health, and public opinion.

*

There was another reason for Elizabeth's choice of Carlsbad. Frederick and Augusta's first child, the opinionated Princess Augusta, had married Charles, Prince of Brunswick-Wolfenbüttel, in January 1764 at St. James's Palace, and had moved to Brunswick. There was talk of her unhappiness; the dowager princess presumably wanted the trusted Elizabeth to check on her. In addition, the Saxon envoy in London, Count Hans Moritz von Brühl, had sent such an enthusiastic report of his hostess at Chudleigh House that he had secured an invitation for Elizabeth from the Dowager Electress of Saxony to visit her at the court of Dresden. Of the nine prince electors entitled to choose the Holy Roman Emperor—of which, as Elector of Hanover, George III was one—the Saxons were the most cultured. Moreover, Charles of Brunswick-Wolfenbüttel's sister was due to marry the nephew and heir of Frederick the Great, King of Prussia. A British royal presence was required; this was to be Elizabeth's friend, King George III's younger brother, "the white prince,"* Prince Edward, the Duke of York and Albany.

As a culmination of these factors, the idea of a Continental trip, her very own Grand Tour, began to form in Elizabeth's mind in 1764. Although it was rare for a woman to travel alone—peace had inspired tourism, but nearly always with a male lead—Elizabeth had the connections, money, and motive. She also had the craving to escape her impossible position: her desire to marry a man when she was not free to do so, her ill-kept secret weighing on her.

And the thermal springs of Carlsbad were calling. Elizabeth's health had, since the death of her baby, propelled her towards spas. In July 1761, there was even an erroneous notice of the death of the Hon. Miss Chudleigh in a newspaper after a spell at Buxton Wells in Derbyshire.[3] The following year she wrote to request particular, airy apartments at Windsor Castle for the Garter investiture ceremony, because, she said, she was an invalid after a violent fit of rheumatism.

There did seem to be a physical component—pleurisy, or rheumatism—alongside her possible borderline personality disorder.

---

* Prince Edward was called the "white prince" because of his pallid coloring. He was Frederick and Augusta's second son, born March 25, 1739.

Physical and emotional distress were not helped by her awkward personal situation and her tendency to overindulge. She was a natural consumer—drink, food, jewels, parties, people, houses, and now countries—and her spirits seemed to swing from dejection to merriment in a minute. Indeed, she is recalled to have said, "I would hate myself if I remained more than an hour in one tone of mind." Her most likely form of instability[4] can cause great suffering to those afflicted, in impulsive spending, variable moods, and excessive consumption. Where the Duke of Kingston was "simple, gentle and retiring" and governed by a "deep and unconquerable passion" for Elizabeth, she was "exacting, vain and violent almost to fury."[5] Her own fluctuating emotions seemed to make her feel ill.

Carlsbad,* the "gem of Bohemia," "queen of all bathing places," set in the midst of a sublime ring of fir-clad blue mountains, had more varieties of bath than anywhere else, and miraculous claims were made for them. Peter the Great and various Hapsburgs had made its name. Elegant brick and stucco buildings were being constructed, and the waters' powers were marketed across Europe.

Now a creature of luxury, Elizabeth commissioned a carriage from the ingenious coachmaker, John Wright of Long Acre, Covent Garden, paid for by the Duke of Kingston.[6] Wright was the most technically advanced coachmaker of the day[7] in a competitive, lucrative market.[8] Fashionable society showed off new carriages at royal birthday parties, but Elizabeth went several steps further by ordering an elaborate carriage to her own unique specifications. It was to hold "four or five persons on occasion, to be made very strong." Instead of a box for the driver to sit on, a large trunk was created to hold her clothes, with a seat above it with a back and arms, "like an easy chair." Inside there was a "night-stool" open at the bottom "for the convenience of letting in fresh air"; another part of the interior seat concealed a drinks cabinet designed to hold bottles of her "favorite liquor Madeira" and "other cordials."†[9] Jewels and pistols traveled with her in special cases.

---

* Now Karlovy Vary in the Czech Republic. It had been the baths of Emperor Charles IV, Holy Roman Emperor and King of Bohemia, in the fourteenth century. The springs were the hottest in Europe.
† Where medicine met alcohol.

Traveling "alone" without a man in charge of the journey, she still had an entourage of impressive proportions, as Kingston's valet described. The company were no less eccentric than the means of transport. There was a "manservant of her own," and a hussar,* lent to her by the duke's friend the Marquess of Granby.† The Swiss hussar, named John Notzel, was a "very clever, active, handsome fellow" who rode alongside the carriage, his uniform, a "white dolman and blue pelisse, fur cap and red Hessian boots." (Joshua Reynolds had painted him holding Granby's charger in a portrait of that general.) There were two wellborn, impecunious female companions: the agreeable Miss Bate,‡ a talented singer and a long-standing favorite, and a teenage relative, a "fine beauty," Miss Penrose, daughter of a Cornish reverend. Kingston's valet claimed that Elizabeth called them her maids of honour, as if she was royalty herself. There was Thomas Evans, apothecary of Knightsbridge, subsequently famous for his worming powder, who administered Elizabeth's "vomits";[10] and Emanuel Siprutini, a cellist and composer who had been acclaimed a "virtuoso" by Mozart's father.[11] Elizabeth had a finely tuned ear, immersed as she had been in the arts patronage of Leicester House. She took plenty of money with her, borrowing £1,400 from Kingston's attorney in February, £1,000 from her banker Mr. Drummond, and £720 was paid into her own bank account, probably from the duke himself.[12]

The posse set off from Harwich in April 1765 to cross the Channel overnight to Hellevoetsluis. Elizabeth was welcomed by Frederick's nephew William V, Prince of Orange, at The Hague, and from there, she traveled over to Brunswick to see the younger Princess Augusta. The Brunswick-Wolfenbüttels had been aggrieved, as allies in the Seven Years' War, when a daughter of the humbler Mecklenburg-Strelitz duchy had been chosen for George III's bride. Augusta had been married to their hereditary prince, Charles, to placate them.

---

* A soldier from the light cavalry.
† Granby was a heroic general, and heir to the Duke of Rutland. He was so popular and generous that there were more pubs named after him than anyone else—he helped his veterans set up as publicans.
‡ Miss Bate was half sister to Sir George Shuckburgh, who appears later as Elizabeth's executor. She sang with Miss Brent at Elizabeth's concerts.

Outspoken, with an "earthy sense of humor," Augusta's character sat awkwardly with her status. A month after her marriage, she wrote to her brother the king about how uncouth her new countrymen were. One of her husband's family, she wrote, "holds his glass between his legs, and a lady today put her fan while she dines in the same place."[13] Not surprisingly, her new compatriots thought she was condescending.

In Brunswick, Elizabeth was spotted by the libidinous Venetian diarist Giacomo Casanova, whom she had last encountered in 1764, when he came off his horse and sprained his ankle outside Chudleigh House, and was carried into her drawing room to recover. Casanova saw Elizabeth "on a great plain some distance from the city," where Augusta's husband was reviewing 6,000 infantrymen. Casanova wrote of Elizabeth that, among the assorted nobles and in torrential rain: "that celebrated lady was wearing a muslin dress with nothing under it but a shift, and the heavy rain had so soaked it that she looked worse than naked. She seemed to enjoy it. The other ladies sheltered for the downpour under tents."[14] Undoubtedly, Casanova would have heard about Elizabeth's Iphigenia costume. Did he see what he wanted to see? Elizabeth was traveling on a diplomatic mission, but Casanova, full of innuendo, saw the sexualized exhibitionist of fifteen years earlier.

Elizabeth on tour was a spectacle, however, one that continued at the wedding of the Prince Royal of Prussia* to Princess Elizabeth of Brunswick, sister-in-law of Princess Augusta, which took place in July just outside Berlin at the rococo castle of Charlottenburg.[15] There was a church service, two balls, a fireworks display, and several suppers, the one after the wedding consisting of 200 guests at four tables: there was one for royalty, one for ambassadors, one for important foreign visitors, including Elizabeth, and one for everyone else. At the first ball, the dancing was opened by the Prussian prince and his new wife. The King and Queen of Prussia and the Duke of York danced next.

A few days later, Frederick the Great, the hero, philosopher king,[16] was writing to his friend, Maria Antonia, Dowager Electress of

---

* Frederick the Great's handsome nephew, and eventual heir.

Saxony, of the wedding's most memorable feature: an English lady called Madam Chudleigh, "who after draining a couple of bottles, staggered in dancing, and was about to fall on the floor. This adventure has much amused the public, unaccustomed to seeing ladies travelling alone, and even less prefer fumes of wine to the graces and the good disposition that suits them so well, and which is their finest adornment."[17] Free from home constraints, overfond of consumption, there was no check on her impulsive behavior. The party-loving aging maid of honour retained dignity at home, but indulged herself to the point of recklessness abroad.

The adventuress in Elizabeth was inclined to live life like a man—traveling, drinking, dancing as she desired, and being unashamed, perhaps even unaware, when she made an exhibition of herself. The papers reported that the day after the wedding "the Hon Miss Chudleigh" was presented at the court in Berlin and "received with remarkable politeness."[18] Her dress was "uncommonly magnificent; and we hear the very buckles in her shoes were £8000."[19]

The dowager electress replied to Frederick in early August. She had heard of the Englishwoman from the "Carlsbad water drinkers": "I would not be less happy to see a drunk woman dancing, although the honour of my sex would deprive me of the desire to laugh with English travelers, and it was said she would pass here; but she may have been afraid of finding no more wine from Hungary."[20] It seems even those she had never met knew Elizabeth was fond of Tokay. Elizabeth must have been on her way to the electress as the ink dried on the page, because days later she arrived in Dresden. The exchange about her dance-floor antics was an unpromising start to what turned out to be one of the most significant friendships of her life.

In passing from the Prussian to the Saxon dominions, from Berlin to Dresden, via an episode of boar shooting near Leipzig, the party experienced what one visitor[21] described as a change in the landscape, the "sandy plains of Brandenburg" are "exchanged for a rich, finely undulated, and populous country, covered with marks of opulence, industry and freedom." In place of the "melancholy and deserted magnificence of Berlin," a small capital was to be found, "cheerful, elegant and in a situation the most picturesque."

Less than a decade after Prussian occupation, Dresden still bore the scars of the Third Silesian War. Saxony was sandwiched between two rival powers: they had supported Austria over Prussia, and then swapped sides. In spite of the damage, Dresden was charmingly civilized, with its court art collection, its Grosser Garten, and the River Elbe dividing the old town from the new. The widow of the elector,[22] and her six children including Frederick Augustus, the fourteen-year-old son for whom she was co-regent,[23] were at their summer residence of Pillnitz Castle, a baroque palace full of chinoiserie to which the court traveled down the river by gondola.

The dowager electress, three years younger than Elizabeth, a Princess of Bavaria in her own right, was an erudite, multitalented woman who had received a wide-ranging education and musical training from the composers of Munich and Dresden. She was herself the composer of, among other pieces, two operas, *The Triumph of Fidelity* and *Talestri, Queen of the Amazons*.* At the first performance of *Talestri*, she sang the main role herself.[24] She was a poet, a patron of artists, and an accomplished painter. When her husband became elector in 1763, he put the entire state finances under her control. But within three months he was dead, and she was a widow at thirty-nine. She became an active diplomat on behalf of the Bavarians, with her own entrepreneurial drive: she set up two textile mills and a brewery in an attempt to revive the local economy after the war. Her contemporaries considered her "a model of extraordinary scholarship," a "magnanimous Minerva."[25]

Elizabeth and Maria Antonia shared more than a refusal to accept the prescribed limitations of female existence. Elizabeth could not write operas, but she appreciated such gifts in others. She was only the second woman to have applied for her own ticket to the British Museum library.[26] (The staff speculated she might publish a book.) To be friends with a woman like Maria Antonia, she had to be able to hold her own, just as she could with the ambassadors back at Chudleigh House. As with Maria Antonia's other correspondents, such as Frederick the Great, Elizabeth could pass as sharp enough to be an intellectual equal. Elizabeth's public persona—the hazy Iphigenia outfit, the chaotic love

---

* *The Triumph of Fidelity*, 1754, and *Talestri, Queen of the Amazons*, 1760. They are still performed today.

life, the dancing and prancing—was one side of her. Her curiosity and appetite for conversation was quite another.

By the time Elizabeth's carriage had left Dresden and rattled into Carlsbad in the middle of August, the two women had established what would be a lifelong friendship and correspondence. The electress had given Elizabeth a copy of one of her operas and commissioned her to satiate her voracious reading appetite by supplying her with English books when she got back to London. Elizabeth wrote to her in French "at the moment of her arrival" in Carlsbad, expressing her admiration for her talents and apologizing (quite unnecessarily) for her lack of linguistic proficiency.[27]

Behind her back, things were not so civil. Her seamless entry into the highest circles, and especially the warmth with which she was received by the electress, annoyed some people intensely. In August, the statesman and wit Lord Chesterfield replied to a letter from his son Philip Stanhope,* the British envoy in Dresden, who had told him how polite he had been to the most discussed English visitor in the city, the Hon. Miss Chudleigh. Chesterfield asked about society's main preoccupation: what on earth was Elizabeth Chudleigh playing at? He could not resist a jibe, presumably about both her weight and her sexual reputation: "As for the lady, if you should be very sharp set for some English flesh, she has it amply in her power to supply you, if she pleases," and he speculated on her motives for travel: "Your guest, Miss Chudleigh, is another problem which I cannot solve. She no more wanted the waters of Carlsbad, than you did. Is it to show the Duke of Kingston that he cannot live without her? A dangerous experiment! which may possibly convince him that he can. There is a trick, no doubt, in it; but what, I neither know or care; you did very well to show her civilities, *cela ne gate jamais rien*"[28] [that never goes amiss].

Elizabeth always attracted a mixed response, and not one divided down gender lines (although it is impossible, now, to miss Chesterfield's casual misogyny and innuendo). Courtiers at one remove found her irksome; those on whom the beam was turned found her irresistible.

---

* Philip was his adored, illegitimate son by a French governess, b. 1732.

Elizabeth considered Carlsbad miraculous (mineral water probably being what she needed after all that drunken dancing) and recommended it to everyone. After choosing to stay a month in that spa rather than return to England with the Prince and Princess of Brunswick in September,[29] she arrived back at Harwich after a "tedious and dangerous passage from Helveotfluys in perfect health" on Tuesday, October 15. What with the wedding, the new friendship, the dancing, boar shooting, and the waters, she had tasted freedom and ignited her wanderlust. On the Sunday, she waited on the king and queen and the Princess Dowager of Wales at court, to fill them in on all she had heard and seen. She was, reported the papers, "most graciously received,"[30] almost as if she were a British envoy herself.

While Elizabeth was away on her triumphant first trip abroad, the Duke of Kingston visited the city of which he had inherited a large part from his mother, Rachel Bayntun.* Bath was at the height of its expansion, the Kingston estate there in constant development. When workmen pulled down his Abbey House to make way for new streets in 1755, they had discovered the astounding remains of the Roman Baths. Using the original springs, Kingston had commissioned a bathhouse that opened in 1766, at the price of five shillings a visit. The Duke of Kingston's Baths contained five private baths and "sweating rooms," dressing rooms, and a waiting room for servants. Soon after the opening, Elizabeth's relation the Reverend John Penrose, father of Elizabeth's "maid of honour" Mary, wrote, "Some use them for privacy's sake, and for the sake of bathing naked."[31]

Come summer, the duke could be found at Weymouth, where he always stayed at Mrs. Templeman's lodgings near the seafront. His valet wrote that the duke "much regretted the absence of Miss Chudleigh, being a very shy man, and not fond of new faces." From abroad, Elizabeth had eyes on him: cousin Bell Chudleigh, whose mother lived twenty miles away at Chalmington, had been dis-

---

* Illegitimate daughter of landowner John Hall. Kingston's Bath inheritance in 1726 included the old Priory precinct and all the land that originally formed an orchard next to the abbey.

patched to check up on the duke at Weymouth, reasoned his valet, who was "certain they need not have doubted his constancy, as I could, I think, safely swear, that he never knew any other woman after his first connection with Miss Chudleigh; an instance of fidelity, which but few in his Grace's situation would have shown for her." (Half-barb, half-compliment.) Perhaps after the meekness of Madame de la Touche, Elizabeth's independence only galvanized Kingston's affections. Bell was the only woman he visited in Weymouth. The custom was to bathe in the sea before breakfast. The duke "rode in the morning, after bathing, until dinner-time, and in the afternoon paid Miss Bell a visit to tea. The Duke was ever fond of keeping good hours." While his beloved was stumbling over dance floors, Kingston was tucked up under his quilt.[32]

When Elizabeth was reunited with Kingston in the autumn, Lord Chesterfield had to eat his words about her risky venture. If her strategy was to make the duke miss her, it had worked perfectly. He wrote to his son at Dresden: "Miss Chudleigh is safely arrived here, and her Duke is fonder of her than ever. It was a dangerous experiment that she tried, in leaving him so long; but it seems she knew her man."[33]

At Christmas, they were together at Pierrepont Lodge. But by January, Elizabeth's health had declined again, and she was reported to be in Knightsbridge, "dangerously ill . . . of the gout in her head and eyes, attended with a severe cold."[34] When she recovered, she wrote to the Duke of Portland, the Lord Chamberlain, seeking a position at court for her apothecary, Evans: "I owe my life to his care and skill," she wrote loyally, but ill health demanded a return trip to Carlsbad. The normal progression from courtship to marriage to motherhood, from maid of honour to bedchamber lady, was denied her. The secret marriage meant that a subsequent conventional life could not be hers, however much she desired one. Yet she made a virtue of it: she had acquired a taste for escape, for unknown terrains and foreign encounters.

In early May 1766, Elizabeth returned to her European haunts, traveling across country to Harwich with Miss Bate, as the *Evening Post* reported: "She proposes to pass the summer at the Courts of

Dresden and Berlin, and at the famous baths in Bohemia."[35] The month before—presumably in order to pay for this trip—she had taken out a mortgage of £4,000 with Mr. Drummond against the Knightsbridge property.[36] Kingston stayed at Thoresby with those two friends from his Culloden regiment, Colonel Litchfield and Captain George Brown. According to the valet, they tried to get him to exchange Elizabeth for a younger woman so he could have an heir, but "Miss Chudleigh so hung on his heart that it was out of the power of any to persuade him to shake her off." (Kingston, in the meantime, returned to Weymouth, where Bell Chudleigh and Miss Fielding kept an eye on him quite unnecessarily.)

When Elizabeth returned to London in September, the news emerged that she had received the most extraordinary present from the electress: that lady's picture "magnificently set with brilliants" and "a magnificent set of jewels, valued at 12,000 crowns"* including "a pair of bracelets, earrings, eight buttons, two rings, a necklace and a pair of shoe buckles," as well as strings of pearls, sapphires, amethysts, and numerous other gems.[37] It is impossible to know for sure, but it seems that although she claimed the jewels were a gift, they were in part payment for a loan from the Knightsbridge mortgage to the electress, who was always in debt. (Elizabeth wrote later, desperate for some of her money back.) It is likely someone briefed the papers on Elizabeth's behalf; she seems to have become more conscious of her public profile around this time, if we can judge by the number of times her name appeared in print. She was a rarity then in being a society woman trying to control her image; the women who engaged with media tended to be either royalty or actresses, or women of business such as Mrs. Cornelys.[38] She valued status by association (in this case, to the electress), particularly as it was eluding her in marriage.

Lady Mary Coke wrote sarcastically that Elizabeth was boasting she had been given jewels of "considerable value. One must say her Royal highness bestows her favors with judgment."[39] And so an exchange of expensive gifts continued between Saxony and Chudleigh House. In 1768, Elizabeth arranged a selection of rare,

---

* A crown was five shillings: therefore four crowns were a pound: £3,000.

cream-colored horses to be sent to the new elector as his coming-of-age present.

Newspaper readers were also informed that "this lady received the most distinguished marks of respect from the several courts she visited on her way to and from the baths in Bohemia, where she had a dangerous illness, but ever since her recovery from it, has enjoyed a perfect state of health."[40] Furthermore, since returning, another newspaper related, she had received letters from both Frederick the Great and the electress, "containing the warmest professions of regard for that Lady." (Presumably, this leaked out as another public relations exercise.) The journalist speculated that Elizabeth's triumph over the Continental courts might start a trend: "The Lady has given such an account of her favorable and polite reception at the several courts abroad, that it has determined several other ladies of rank and distinction, next year, to visit the same; so that, in a short time, we may hear of the females of fortune making the grand tour, as well as noblemen and gentlemen."[41] Indeed, they did. Lady Mary Coke, for example, sought to emulate her, taking her first European trip in 1770.[42]

While Elizabeth was away this time, Chesterfield was forced to concede to his son at Dresden that she had extraordinary social powers (which he rated above anything): "Is the fair, or at least the fat, Miss Chudleigh with you still? It must be confessed that she knows the art of courts; to be so received at Dresden, and so connived at in Leicester Fields"[43]—i.e., that Elizabeth's past was so overlooked at Leicester Fields.

Elizabeth had made a new, powerful ally. That the electress held her in such regard was shown by the fact that when she contracted smallpox, she summoned Elizabeth to her all the way back from England. Within weeks of her return, Elizabeth was at Thoresby when she received a letter from the electress saying that Her Highness "could not die in peace, without once more beholding her dear Miss Chudleigh, and begging she would immediately set out for her palace."[44] The moment she read it, a great bustle commenced. Elizabeth set off at midnight "on a very dark night" to cross the twenty-three miles over the forest from Thoresby to Nottingham, and from there on to London. A few years later,[45] Elizabeth wrote to the electress reminding her of the journey she had made from London to Dresden without seeing a bed on the way. The electress recovered, and Elizabeth came home in mid-December. On her return, the maid-turned-envoy went to court to see Their Majesties the king and queen and the Dowager Princess Augusta, to let them know how things stood abroad.

Traveling across Europe, a confidante to highnesses at two of the most sought-after courts—Saxony and St. James's—Elizabeth was now at a zenith of sorts in her standing. She had established a connection with the electress that would have lifelong importance to her.

Back in London, Elizabeth resumed the role of society hostess with renewed vigor. In February 1768, the newspapers reported that she had given a "grand entertainment at her house" with "most of the foreign ministers, their graces the Duke and Duchess of Northumberland,"[46] and, according to Lady Mary Coke, "Lord and Lady Hertford, the Spanish ambassadress, the Duchess of Portland" too. In April, it was an "elegant breakfast and concert to a great many persons of the very first distinction . . . HRH the Dukes of Gloucester and Cumberland [George's younger brothers],[47] and His Serene Highness the Prince of Monaco . . . who made a very splendid appearance . . . some gentlemen of fashion performed on different instruments, and some ladies of quality sung in the concert."[48] In July, it was "a grand entertainment . . . Duke of Cumberland, two Princes of Saxe Gotha . . ."

With her frantic entertaining and flamboyant dress style, the more vicious commentators sniped that as Elizabeth approached fifty, she was trying to hang on to lost youth. Walpole wrote from Bath, "There is no keeping off age by sticking roses and sweet peas in one's hair, as Miss Chudleigh does still!"[49] (Hair—like hoops—was expanding and becoming more ornamental, and flowers were in fashion.) But with her frequent and well-attended parties, and new friendship in Dresden, Elizabeth was in a position strong enough to provoke envy: she was ostentatiously high-profile, her position in society fastened by her friendships and parties, an independent woman successfully, it appeared, consciously, proudly writing her own rules. Yet it was no more secure than one of her elaborate hairstyles, because she lacked a means to formalize her very public relationship with Kingston.

There were riots on the London streets that spring, accompanying the return from exile of John Wilkes, that rabble-rousing nemesis of Lord Bute.[50] Elizabeth played hostess regardless. In the Bute camp, she would not be restrained by the mob. (Lady Mary Coke dismissed Elizabeth's social success with: "Who may not have company that will give a grand dinner?")[51]

Elizabeth's own vulnerability meant she was sympathetic to it in others. She showed her kindness and self-image when she wrote to the now much-hated ex–prime minister, Lord Bute, who was in ill health. The Wilkes mob had smashed his windows in London; when he was about to sail for France to convalesce, he was forced to leave England in a small boat to avoid being attacked. He had to travel incognito, even abroad.

Just before he set off, Elizabeth wrote to him. As he was now the most unpopular man in England, she had nothing to gain. She asked him to accept "the sincere offering of my good wishes for the return of health to your mind and body," continuing, "My singularity need not surprise you, you have known me upwards of twenty years, always disinterested, loving merit, but disdaining to court it while sycophants followed its smiling fortune." Given how eagerly she grasped the opportunity to befriend those in power, she is generous to herself, but it is broadly accurate. She sought to console Bute: "The fickle turns of fortune which we all experience shows itself in depriving you of health, and the society of your friends . . . prudence commands your absence . . . yet your enemies . . . will lament it eternally. Where will they now blunt their arrows? On whom load their faults? . . . in your absence, envy may sleep . . . Justice by that time will assert her power, and do honour to your fame . . . drink a large draught of Lethe to man's ingratitude."* She concluded, "You have a sincere friend and well-wisher in your obedient humble servant, Elizabeth Chudleigh."[52]

It is written equal to equal. Elizabeth saw herself as not worth less than a man who had been prime minister and, in that way,

---

* Lethe: the river of forgetfulness in Hades.

she certainly was no sycophant. A combination of maternal example, paternal loss, and sheer necessity seems to have provoked self-confidence from an early age. At twenty, she could talk to a prince or a prime minister. No one intimidated her. She had spent her early childhood talking to the elderly; her youth without a father prompting self-reliance; and she had known Bute intimately for years, as her friend, fellow courtier, and princes' tutor before he ever became an exalted statesman. This self-belief and apparent fearlessness provoked her enemies. Her attitude did not suit a patriarchal, conventional society. How could this bumptious, penniless Devon courtier have so much more social capital, and sheer audacity, than a duke's daughter such as Lady Mary Coke?

When she wrote that reassuring letter to her old friend Bute, little did she know that they had a common enemy. Augustus Hervey was a prolific pseudonymous letter writer and columnist in the press, frequently attacking Bute on behalf of his friend, the short-lived Prime Minister George Grenville, who blamed Bute for his dismissal.[53]

In mid-August, London was abuzz with a shocking development. In spite of the events of that summer at Lainston having lain dormant for nearly a quarter of a century, Hervey had asked for a divorce from the woman who had never presented herself as married to him. His grounds were "the criminality of her conduct"—in other words, he was publicly accusing her of adultery.

It was sudden news to Elizabeth, but Hervey had been stewing on his plight and gathering evidence for years, partly because he wanted a legitimate heir and partly, one can assume, because she was so brazenly seeing somebody else. The more flamboyant she became, presenting herself as ambassador and hostess with a public profile, the more he wanted to cut her down to size. He could tolerate the "marriage" no longer.

CHAPTER FIFTEEN

MARRIAGE À LA MODE

Augustus Hervey first consulted his attorney, William Barkley, in May 1768, but thoughts of divorce had been simmering in the back of his mind for years. In 1761, a Gray's Inn lawyer heard from the West Indies that Captain Hervey out there "had full proof against another person,"[1] i.e., that he could prove Elizabeth's infidelity.

Naval activities meant that Hervey had held fire on the divorce front. He had played a vital role at the siege of Havana in 1762, giving the signal to attack and bearing the news of victory back to England (and seizing a large French frigate on the way). This was his finest hour in the navy. Or at least he certainly thought so: a full-size portrait by Thomas Gainsborough that hangs in the drawing room at Ickworth today shows him at his most swaggerish, holding a telescope, right foot crushing the Spanish ensign. In the background, his warship HMS *Dragon* lies at anchor and the Moro Fort he had captured is seen on the horizon. Painted in Gainsborough's Bath studio, five or six years and much claret after the siege, Horace Walpole considered it "one of the best modern portraits I have seen."[2] Imposing and aristocratic, Hervey was the archetypal Gainsborough subject. The artist was known for getting a true likeness: here Hervey looks as much Pall Mall gentleman as sailor, even though he is in uniform, a rarity in a Gainsborough.

Hervey had gone to Bath in 1767 to soothe his gout.[3] There he fell for the "virtuous, beautiful" Mary Moysey, twenty-four to his forty-four, daughter of the spa's most sought-after physician, Abel

Moysey,[4] and the gossip was that Hervey was seeking divorce to marry her. He denied that he had thoughts of marriage, although he admitted to friends that he was embarking on "an arduous task." He made it plain, as Elizabeth occasionally did, that the unresolved nature of the covert marriage haunted him. In August 1768, he wrote to George Grenville with emotional frankness and strained discretion, about his quest for divorce: "I am unfortunately plunging myself in a very troublesome, disagreeable, yet I think (for me and my family) necessary business, which has long employed more of my thoughts and time than my health could bestow . . . Excuse me saying no more . . . my lips have never been opened about it but where it was necessary."[5]

On the intended "marriage" to Miss Moysey, he wrote,[6] "I find this town has made me a much more intrepid person than I really am, for they have already given me another person for a wife, and such a one as I am sure I should never have thought of." According to Horace Walpole, the marriage came to nothing because "Miss Rhubarb"[*7] had been paid "5000l" (£5,000) by her father not to marry Hervey. Brave and patrician though he was, his reputation had unfortunately preceded him.

In this he had some help, although he was unaware of it. Hervey's younger brother, Frederick, Bishop of Derry, who stood in line for the earldom as long as Augustus had no legitimate heir, found himself in Bath that same year treating his own gout and, more importantly, ensuring that Dr. Moysey got to know all about his brother's checkered marital history. These two Hervey brothers had never got on. When they were young, Augustus had found a rude comment that Frederick had written about him in a French satirical book of personality types, "which fixed me in regard to him." In scuppering the marriage, Frederick was victorious.[8]

Even if he was not to marry Miss Rhubarb, Hervey still sought divorce. He yearned for freedom. Without one, his detested younger brother, the bishop, would inherit. It had become clear that his intellectually able but physically fragile elder brother, Lord Bristol, would

---

* Rhubarb was a frequently prescribed laxative, hence Walpole's nickname for the doctor's daughter.

never marry. By now, Augustus had had an illegitimate son with another maid of honour (to Queen Charlotte) Kitty Hunter,[9] daughter of an Admiralty lord and "a handsome girl with a fine person, but silly."[10] "Little Augustus," Augustus Henry Hervey (poignantly, he was given exactly the same name as Elizabeth's child),[11] born 1764, was now four. His illegitimacy must have focused his father's mind on his inconvenient marital state. His romance with Hunter did not last, although there was never any doubt of his love for his son, who was acknowledged by the Hervey family. Gainsborough later painted a touching, octagonal portrait of the boy, fashioned on a piece of tin, rather than canvas, so it could be taken to sea.

So began a game of legal chess. A man (not a woman) could sue for divorce, but only through an Act of Parliament at vast expense and with good reason, such as his wife's infidelity. Male infidelity was not grounds for divorce. Hervey had compiled ample evidence—presumably, servants' testimonies, which were often amenable to the highest bidder. Divorces, rare as they were, would come down to the word of a coachman seeing who alighted where, at what hour; a housemaid observing a dent in a pillow, a footmark on a sofa, or a cipher on a letter. Woe betide anyone who fell out with their servants.

Seven years later, at Elizabeth's trial, details of Hervey's actions emerged. He had run into Caesar Hawkins, the doctor who had witnessed the birth of the son he never saw, on a London street and asked the doctor to visit him at home to talk about an "old friend." Hawkins found Hervey sitting with a thick pile of papers on the table beside him "at his right hand" and he told Hawkins that, somehow, he wanted to separate from Elizabeth. The papers were "abundant proofs" of Elizabeth's "adulteries," collected over a long period. He did not want to "mix malice and ill temper" in the case as he still had "regard" and "respect" for his wife.[12] He only asked her not to put up any obstacle. Hawkins was asked to relay the message, which he did.

Hervey was not particularly discreet about his intentions, according to Horace Walpole, who wrote: "Augustus Hervey, thinking it the bel air [i.e., the height of fashion] is going to sue for a divorce from the Chudleigh. He asked Lord Bolingbroke t'other day who was his proctor [lawyer], as he would have asked for his tailor."[13]

Elizabeth's father, Thomas Chudleigh, above left, when he was colonel of his own regiment and lieutenant governor of the Royal Hospital, Chelsea. Elizabeth, above, as a young maid of honour in an engraving from a painting by Joshua Reynolds, who described her as "eminently beautiful."

The Royal Hospital, Chelsea. Elizabeth's family lived at the river end of the left wing. Here—with its old soldiers, swans, and stairs down to the frantic river—Elizabeth learned to walk and talk. Col. Chudleigh is buried in the graveyard.

The king and queen who never were: Frederick, Prince of Wales, above, presided over the rebellious, frivolous Leicester House set and was detested by his parents, George II and Queen Caroline. His wife Augusta, right, the affable German princess to whom Elizabeth was maid of honour—for twenty-five years.

Elizabeth's first orphan duke: the 6th Duke of Hamilton, left, "hot, debauched, extravagant" and the object of Elizabeth's affections before he went on his Grand Tour. By the time he returned, she was (secretly) married. Above, a miniature of Elizabeth as maid of honour, on the front of a snuffbox.

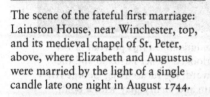

The scene of the fateful first marriage: Lainston House, near Winchester, top, and its medieval chapel of St. Peter, above, where Elizabeth and Augustus were married by the light of a single candle late one night in August 1744.

One woman, two husbands: First husband, the "gay and gallant lothario" Augustus Hervey, future 3rd Earl of Bristol, above, in 1750, wearing the blue and gold braid of the undress uniform of a naval captain, his ship in the background; and second husband Evelyn Pierrepont, 2nd Duke of Kingston, left, painted when he became a Garter Knight in 1741. He was a "man of great beauty and the finest person," according to Horace Walpole. He was also shy, sporty, and intensely loyal to Elizabeth.

After Frederick died in 1751, Augusta commissioned this portrait of her in mourning with her nine children, overlooked by her husband and the figure of Britannia. From left: Prince Edward, the future King George III; Princess Augusta, in blue; Princes William and Henry play with a boat; Caroline Matilda, future Queen of Denmark, on her mother's lap; Princess Elizabeth plays a lute; Princess Louisa in pink; and the child in the red dress with the dog is a boy—toddler Prince Frederick—still in "coats."

Myth-making: the most notorious outfit of the age. Images of Elizabeth dressed as Iphigenia at a masquerade, held in 1749 to celebrate the peace of Aix-la-Chapelle, were printed and reprinted.

Elizabeth's trial in April 1776 was described as "A festival for the whole nation." An engraving of Elizabeth at the bar, above, all in black like Mary, Queen of Scots; "she really looked handsome," wrote one observer. Right, Elizabeth appears in the center foreground of Westminster Hall before the royal family and every peer in the land—alongside anyone in the *ton* who could procure themselves a ticket.

Elizabeth, left, in bejewelled middle age and, below, her signature, as "Duchesse de Kingston." The tickets for her trial were color-coded for each day. Day five, right, was blue: this one was for the queen and Prince of Wales's box. The wording—"calling herself Duchess"—was ominous.

Enemies: Gainsborough's portrait of Augustus Hervey, left, foot triumphantly resting on the Spanish ensign after the capture of Moro Castle, Havana, painted in 1768 when he was determined to divorce Elizabeth. Lady Frances Meadows, above, sister of the Duke of Kingston. Her husband Philip and eldest son Evelyn brought the bigamy trial against Elizabeth in the hope of invalidating the marriage and inheriting the Kingston fortune—without Elizabeth running through it first.

Strategic sibling: Augustus's showy, acquisitive younger brother, Frederick Hervey, Bishop of Derry, above left, was determined to inherit the Bristol title. He traveled in such splendour that Hotel Bristols sprung up in his honour. The chorus: above right, Horace Walpole—who may have been Augustus Hervey's half brother—named Elizabeth the Duchess-Countess; right, the acerbic Lady Mary Coke. Both followed Elizabeth's wayward progress by pen.

Friends: Catherine the Great, left, welcomed Elizabeth at her summer palace and sat her at her right hand—after her conviction. The empress believed Elizabeth to be spirited; Elizabeth called Catherine her "great friend." Catherine's husband and co-ruler Prince Grigory Potemkin, above, shared Elizabeth's eye for luxury and lent her his adjutant to escort her across Europe. Many of Elizabeth's belongings—pictures, chandeliers, silver—are now in the Hermitage, St. Petersburg.

Patrons and protectors: Pope Clement XIV, above, the humorous Anglophile who treated Elizabeth "like a sovereign" in Rome. A self-portrait by the Dowager Electress of Saxony, right, Elizabeth's ally and her conduit to the courts of Europe.

A property empire: Kingston House, left, previously Chudleigh House, facing Hyde Park, was built for Elizabeth. There she threw parties—with fireworks and Hungarian wine—for princes and ambassadors, and always opened the dancing herself. Opinion was divided; Horace Walpole thought the house was full of "execrable" knick-knacks; another guest called it a "gem." The two Nottinghamshire houses of the Duke of Kingston: Thoresby Park, left, designed by John Carr of York and built on Elizabeth's watch, was the second of three Thoresbys and Holme Pierrepont Hall, below left, was used for shooting parties.

Reclaiming her family name: Elizabeth's remote manor house, above right, overlooking the Baltic in the wilds of Estonia, had its own vodka distillery and was renamed Chudleigh with the permission of Catherine the Great. The Château de Sainte-Assise on the banks of the Seine outside Paris, right, which she bought—at vast expense and in ill health—from the heirs of the Duc d'Orléans. With the permission of Louis XVI, she renamed it Chudleigh. When she died on the eve of the French Revolution, she had not finished paying for it.

In February 1768, the second Lord Bolingbroke had divorced Lady Diana Spencer in a sensational case: he alleged "criminal conversation," i.e., adultery, with her subsequent husband.[14] Hervey confided in a friend[15] that a few weeks later he had had no reply from Elizabeth. She felt blindsided, and she was not one to acquiesce and play by another's rules.

The rumor went round via the usual suspects—Horace Walpole and Lady Mary Coke, although they both later retracted it (one must have heard it from the other)—that Elizabeth had replied that she was £16,000 in debt, and if he was her husband he would be liable for it. Coke assumed Elizabeth would be glad to divorce so she could marry Kingston: "I make no doubt of Miss C being Duchess of Kingston. Infamy seems to prosper, while virtue appears under a cloud, neglected and oppressed,"[16] she wrote, seeing herself perched under that cloud.

But it was not that simple. Elizabeth did not want a divorce, for several reasons. First, her adultery would have to be proved, which required an action for "crim. con." as it was known in order to be successful; then a private Act of Parliament would have to be obtained. For Parliament to dissolve the marriage, there would therefore have to be a shameful parade through the marital history. Allegations of adultery and deceit would be publicly humiliating, and on a practical note, if she accepted she was married, her property belonged to Hervey, not her. As if that was not enough, it was unclear whether the Duke of Kingston would be willing to marry a divorcee with her reputation in shreds. Even Elizabeth was not that much of a risk-taker.

Elizabeth told Hawkins, it was said, that she was damned if she would "prove herself a whore." She had convinced herself that she had not properly married Augustus. She consulted a lawyer in the ecclesiastical courts, Dr. Arthur Collier, said to be "ingenious, but unsteady and eccentric."[17] Alongside her other lawyers, Dr. Peter Calvert and Dr. William Wynne, he came up with a bizarre, arcane legal solution.[18]

The ecclesiastical (or consistory) court was the legal system run by the church with its own lawyers, known as doctors or proctors. Part of the fabric of English society since the Norman Conquest, it had authority over church discipline, land, probate, and many cases to do with morality. Here, an injured party could bring "a clause of jactitation of marriage,"* which meant they could sue if someone boasted that they were married to them when they were not. If the accused could not prove the marriage had taken place, it was declared null and void. If that happened—Augustus claimed they were married, Elizabeth denied it, and he was unable to prove it—Elizabeth would be free to marry the Duke of Kingston without the embarrassment of divorce.† It was a cunning piece of legal sophistry.

On August 18, Elizabeth filed a caveat in the ecclesiastical court that meant that Hervey could not proceed without warning her proctor. She sent Hervey a message via Hawkins, "wishing him to understand she did not acknowledge him for her legal husband," that she would be fighting him in the ecclesiastical court, and that she trusted that he, "as a man of honour . . . [would] confine himself to proofs of marriage."[19]

She knew her man: even though he had "ample proof" of adultery, if there was one thing the naval hero and scion of the house of Bristol could not bear, it was the idea that anyone would consider him dishonorable. When confronted with the reality of bringing Elizabeth's sexual activity to the world's attention, it looked less ingenious. In spite of being one of the most—if not *the* most—notorious womanizers of his generation, he would not risk a reputation as a telltale. "Gallantry," as it was called,‡ was one thing; humiliating a woman—particularly his own wife—with lurid details of her behavior quite another. Once it had been pointed out, he could not do it. He agreed, saying he was indeed "too much of a gentleman" to serve up his "proof" for public consumption. That left jactitation rather than divorce: now the onus was on Augustus Hervey to prove that the marriage had taken place, and all his "abundant proofs" of Elizabeth's adultery were worthless.

---

* Jactitation: from *jactere*, to throw around, i.e., boast.
† Legal separation—in which both parties agreed to live apart, with a financial settlement—was easier and cheaper to achieve, but it suited neither party in this case as it meant they could not remarry. And they were not together anyway.
‡ "Gallantry" was a double-edged term: originally it had meant the chivalry of courtly love, but it had come to be a euphemism for womanizing and discreet adultery. Wollstonecraft saw it as a form of pretend servility, an abusive manipulation of women.

(Now Hervey had asked for divorce, it was too late for them to some-how agree that the marriage had never happened.)

Elizabeth and her lawyers had come up with a strong solution given their very weak hand. Augustus, after all, had plenty of evidence of adultery; their only option was to ensure he felt obliged to conceal it. Their knowledge of contemporary mores, that such a gentleman could never deliberately hold up a woman to public contempt, and Elizabeth's assessment of Augustus's idealized self-image, as military hero, aristocratic gentleman, and perfect English knight, were all played on by her lawyers with some psychological panache.

Hervey told Hawkins that he was ambivalent about his decision to accept the request, saying something like: "I doubt if I will find myself so free by this method as my own." Hervey's suspicions were well founded. Little did he know what that "honorable" decision would eventually cost them both.

When Elizabeth insisted that she did not regard herself as married, she was not being as disingenuous as it might sound. (In spite of the new register, she could argue it either way.) In 1744, the year of the Lainston ceremony, marriage as a legal entity was as clear as the turtle soup served in White's club, with the result that many people were simply not sure if they were married or not. Before 1753, there were three types of marriage: the church sort, per-formed within canonical hours by a priest, with witnesses and a register, which was not open to doubt; the clandestine marriage, involving a clergyman, but otherwise less formal; and, flimsiest of all, the "contract" marriage, made in the eyes of God only, which was somehow religiously binding but rarely legally so, consisting of a mutual promise in the present tense.

In the early thirteenth century, Pope Innocent III had decreed that the "free consent of both spouses" (rather than any form of religious ceremony) was the "sole essence" of marriage,[20] and since then, "contract marriages," where each pledged themselves to the other, had existed, although they were defenseless if one side denied the fact. The clandestine kind, though a ceremony performed by a priest (or someone who claimed to be one) following the ritual in the Book of Common Prayer, was somewhat furtive. Any of the following five conditions made a marriage clandestine: 1) no banns read, or special license granted; 2) outside the parish of both bride and groom, not necessarily in a church—it might be a house, coffee shop, or brothel; 3) outside the canonical hours of 8 A.M. and 12 P.M.; 4) not recorded in a parish register or priest's notebook; and 5) one or both parties a minor,* without parental consent.

Elizabeth's marriage was certainly of the clandestine kind. At twenty, Hervey had been underage and his mother had not given her consent. Indeed, she did not even know at the time (although perhaps she did later). The ceremony was not within canonical hours. It took place in the parish of neither the bride nor the groom, and no banns had been read. And, most significantly of all, it was held in secret. Although in 1744 that was not illegal, it was not watertight, either. After 1753, when the law changed to state that marriage must be public, with consent if underage, it would not have been legal at all.

Elizabeth's mentor William Pulteney suggested reform of these shambolic marriage laws in 1752, possibly to help his protégée Elizabeth. His idea was that all clandestine marriages should be nullified. Parliament believed that this was too extreme. The then secretary of war, Henry Fox, who had himself married the Duke of Richmond's daughter Lady Caroline Lennox in a clandestine ceremony, was particularly against it.[21] There was a year of debate in the House, so hotly contested was the subject between those who felt marriage should be out in the open, and those who felt love should take precedence over the wishes of financially or dynastically motivated, interfering parents. The debate reflected the mid-eighteenth-century shift between strategic marriage, particularly in the upper classes who were loath, like royalty, to give up control, and romantic marriage and the autonomy of the individual. Richardson's novels, for example, which described women's inner lives,[22] and the domestic happiness of Frederick, Prince of Wales, with Augusta (and, later, George III and Queen Charlotte), only served the idea that a love match was desirable.†

---

* Under twenty-one, then the age of majority.

† Although these romantic royal matches were in fact arranged, dynastic, *and* happy.

After the most impassioned and extended debate of eighteenth-century politics, the keenness to avoid uncertainty triumphed. Eventually, Lord Hardwicke's Marriage Act of 1753 was passed, which still sets most of the framework for today's weddings: two witnesses, minimum; a register; certain hours only; the reading of the banns; the wedding to take place in the parish of bride or groom;[23] church doors to be left open. This new law left Elizabeth in a marital shadowland in which she could convince herself that, as her marriage would not have been legal in 1768, perhaps it was barely legal twenty-four years earlier. The episode of the register drawn up on the Reverend Thomas Amis's deathbed only served to emphasize the ambiguity of the whole affair, as originally there had not been one. (There was now. Would Elizabeth destroy it?)

Now Hervey had made his move, Elizabeth had no choice but to respond, and respond she did. She gathered evidence against his claim of marriage, as Collier advised. In the meantime, to the intense annoyance of Lady Mary Coke, who could not believe Elizabeth's temerity, she continued her well-publicized social life and her summer at Thoresby, cool as an iced crayfish on a Meissonnier silver platter.

Negotiations via her "guardian angel," as she called Collier, were sensitive. He told her to tell no one. In gratitude she sent him a basket of fish, and venison to the other lawyers. She felt the "dawn of hope" for her liberty, but passed on the message that "he must be singularly clever to exact obedience and obtain it from those who have always received it."[24] This reference to Augustus and the need for secrecy might indicate some form of collusion on Hervey's part; that is, that he agreed to secretly go along with the jactitation suit rather than put up a decent fight.

Morale revived to the extent that in October she was at a masquerade given by the King of Denmark[25] in the Haymarket, at which "Miss Chudleigh seemed to outvie the ladies."[26] Elizabeth still managed to be the talking point, at nearly fifty. She was spotted dancing at the queen's ball, and playing "whist at the Princess's ball" with three secretaries of state: Lords Weymouth, Rochford, and Hillsborough. To Lady Mary Coke's annoyance, Elizabeth was one of "Lady Ailesbury's party" for a game of loo[27] at Syon House, the London home of the Duke and Duchess of Northumberland, the paint barely dry on its Robert Adam interior. Even a firework that fell through the window of her coach, burned its lining, and set fire to a "very fine lace ruffle" could not dent her bravado. Elizabeth told this story against herself, Coke recounted, and had everyone in laughter.

So eager was she to ingratiate herself with Dr. Collier that he was invited to Pierrepont Lodge around Christmas. He wrote "epitaphs," which summed up what he thought of each of the party. He showed the prejudices of the age. While the duke could do no wrong:

> 'Tis hardly fair to take his Grace,
> Without your leaving in his place
> a Man as Generous, Just, and kind,
> Of equal Merit, equal Mind.
> But yet 'tis best: we'll dry our Tears
> He goes to Heav'n to meet his Peers

And Bell Chudleigh was "My gentle Bella good and kind/ Of placid mien, of placid mind!" Elizabeth, in bed with a cold, for all her efforts and gratitude towards her "guardian angel," was dismissed with: "What have we here! a Maid upon her Back!/ Why that is as she should be, is it not? Good luck."[28] Like other men of the age—Chesterfield, Walpole—Collier divided women into two sorts: virtuous or not. As Elizabeth was put in the latter category, there was no need to be kind about her, or refer to her with anything other than sexual terminology.

Elizabeth's inner turmoil showed itself in letters to the electress, in which she chased the return of her money,[29] bemoaned that her health and "family affairs" would not permit her to see her friend for a few years,[30] and mysteriously wrote about men: "I am convinced that the only way to bend men is to smother them with indifference . . . they love difficulty . . . it is better to be respected than to respect them."[31] (Perhaps this demonstrates Elizabeth's tactics with the duke—that, as Chesterfield suspected, she had traveled to make him jealous.) In November, Elizabeth wrote, "I have too much heartache now." Although she expressed joy that the electress had received her present from Elizabeth, a "fat and pretty" little dog called Fifi.[32]

While gossip flew—in September, society insider Mrs. Delany*
wrote that Hervey and Elizabeth would "certainly be divorced"—
depositions were being gathered for examination at the London
Consistory Court.[33] This court was vying for supremacy with the
criminal and civil courts, as we shall discover later on.

Augustus Hervey was now (apparently) searching for proof of
marriage. Apart from the bride and groom, five people had been
present at that candlelit ceremony in the Lainston chapel so many
years before. To Elizabeth's advantage, four of them had died: the
Reverend Thomas Amis back in 1759, just after providing the register; Mrs. Hanmer in December 1764; and Mr. Mounteney and John
Merrill had both died at Lainston, the loss of the latter, her last male
relative, in February 1767, a most upsetting event for Elizabeth.

That left just one remaining witness: Mrs. Hanmer's servant,
Ann Craddock. There were also two living witnesses to the register
debacle: the Reverend Thomas Amis's widow Judith, and James
Spearing, the Winchester attorney (and one—the Reverend Stephen
Kinchin—who had later seen the result). But Hervey did not know
about the register.

Both of the women had married servants of Elizbeth's men.
Ann had married Hervey's steward William Craddock in 1752,
and stayed in contact with both Aunt Hanmer and Elizabeth; and
Mrs. Amis was "often invited to Knightsbridge by Miss Chudleigh
who made very much of her."[34] Kingston's valet claimed that Elizabeth had successfully "contrived" to get Judith Amis to marry the
duke's butler Thomas Phillips, and then provided him with a place
as steward of Holme Pierrepont, the implication being that she had
bought her silence.

Family, footmen, peers, and bankers were all asked by Elizabeth's
lawyers to write whether, in their opinion, Elizabeth was married
or single. Unless Hervey could prove for certain—which could only
be by producing a witness to the ceremony, or the certificate—that

---

* Daughter of a minor Jacobite aristocrat, Mary Granville, then Mrs. Pendarves,
finally Mrs. Delany, was a frequent letter writer who became known later in life
for floral découpage—botanical paper cutouts that she called "mosaicks"—still
on show in the British Museum.

the marriage had taken place, he would lose. (The question is, did Hervey sincerely pursue his cause, or was he colluding—i.e., pretending to seek proof, while secretly agreeing not to find it, and to end the marriage via the jactitation suit as the only—awkward—solution? He had already said he would not use his "abundant" evidence—which was irrelevant, anyway, without proof of marriage.) Bell testified that she and the late John Merrill knew their cousin as Miss Chudleigh, and that Aunt Hanmer had left Elizabeth "£100, a silver sugar urn and spoon" in her maiden name. Butler John Williams said she had never lived with Hervey, whom John Sprackling, footman, insisted he had never met. Under her maiden name, she had been paid her salary by William Watts, Augusta's treasurer; and vast sums of money—£1,000 here, the £4,000 mortgage on Knightsbridge there—by banker John Drummond, and William Feild of the Inner Temple (who had lent her £1,900, plus other, smaller, amounts). Even the Bishop of Exeter was invoked, as it was Miss Chudleigh who had presented the living of Harford to a Reverend Julian. Her Bank of England account, now down to £6 from £10,000, was under Chudleigh; Lord Berkeley of Stratton confirmed she had bought the Hill Street plot as Miss Chudleigh; Henry Flitcroft, the architect, said she paid him "many thousand pounds"[35] to build "Chudleigh" House—and so it went on. Leases and contracts were shown, although the Knightsbridge property deed that read "Elizabeth Hervey known as Chudleigh" was not produced.

On Hervey's side, the story was more ambiguous, but inconclusive. Hervey's former manservant William Craddock remembered well "attending Hervey to the assembly" held at Winchester races in 1744, seeing him "upon the ball" with Elizabeth, with whom his master had "contracted an intimacy," and accompanying him to Lainston for three or four visits. He had heard a "general public report of marriage" when he got back from the West Indies. Mary Edwards and Ann Hillam, Lainston servants, said there was a report "among servants of the family" that the pair had been married. Lieutenant John Robinson of HMS *Dragon*, Hervey's ship at Havana, had heard the same; as had James Hossack, surgeon on board HMS *Phoenix*, and one of Augustus's mother's servants, Richard

Edwards. But these things were hearsay, not proof, and, crucially, the one surviving witness, Ann Craddock—now married to Hervey's former manservant—refused to give evidence. In person to William Barkley and Augustus Hervey, she said that she was very old, infirm, it was a great many years ago and she could not remember a thing about it. Hervey later believed (or knew) that Elizabeth had "bought" her memory, and there is a payment of £28.12 to William Craddock from Elizabeth's bank on June 14, 1768—for what, we can only guess. For the Craddocks, this was an enormous amount of money (more than Ann Craddock's annual wage: £20 p.a. was a high salary for a lady's maid c.1760).[36]

William Barkley, Augustus Hervey's lawyer, failed to track down Judith Phillips, previously Mrs. Amis. He probably did not even know of her existence. As far as he and Hervey were concerned, she had not been present at the ceremony and, as they did not know about the new register, she would not have been able to add anything anyway. With the most damning evidence unsought, the scales of justice were tipping in Elizabeth's favor.

With such a lack of proof, there was little choice for the ecclesiastical court. It had been a masterful tactical display from Elizabeth's lawyers. In February 1769, the newspapers reported: "Yesterday was determined, in the Consistory Court of London, the case between the Hon. Mrs. Chudleigh and the Right Hon. Augustus John Hervey, Esq; when judgment was pronounced in favor of the lady, she was declared free from any matrimonial contract with the said gentleman."[37]

Better still, after nearly two decades together, the Duke of Kingston had already promised to marry Elizabeth if she could prove herself unwed in the eyes of the law. It is unknown when they first discussed it or what exactly she had told him, but the promise must have been there, ready and waiting for the verdict.

Elizabeth was ecstatic: she had been ruled a single woman at last. She wrote in happiness to the electress to say that she had won her case, with her honor intact; that Hervey could never claim marriage with her again on pain of excommunication (an unlikely scenario given how desperate he was to get out of it); that she was free to marry and in control of her own finances; that she did not bear the slightest ill will towards Hervey—although he had made her unhappy for twenty-five years, she "forgives him with all her heart and hopes that he will live to repent all the bad things he has done." She was "overwhelmed with all the congratulations." Deeply affectionate towards the electress, she wrote, "I am embracing you heart and soul, I am until I fall, your faithful friend."[38]

Hervey was left stranded like a beached sloop. All the costs were awarded against him. His lawyers had been outfoxed by Elizabeth's and, by bringing the suit, losing it, and not using any of his evidence, they had left him wide open to accusations of collusion. Indeed, many people believed he had been paid off to go along with what she wanted. (It is more likely that he was not paid, but went along with it because he could see no honorable way out for himself.) Worse still, he did not share Elizabeth's confidence about being free to marry again: too many people knew the truth.

Within days of the decision, the rumor was circling that his younger brother, Frederick Hervey, Bishop of Derry, disinherited by his own mother (Molly Hervey had died with Augustus at her side,[39] her last words—"Poor Augustus"—presumably a reference to his marital state), had arrived in London to ensure that whatever the court decided, he, and then his son, would inherit the title.* A cruel man of unlimited ambition and with extravagant taste,[40] he wanted as much inheritance as he could possibly get his hands on. If Elizabeth married, it might encourage Augustus to follow suit. According to the duke's valet, the bishop "hurried over [to London] to prevent" Elizabeth's wedding to the Duke of Kingston, "if not too late, well knowing, should it take place, it would give his brother an opportunity of marrying Miss Moysey, of Bath,"[41] which might prevent the bishop's children from enjoying the paternal estate. Elizabeth was spurred into action when she heard that the devious bishop was on the move. Her second wedding was destined to become almost as chaotic and impromptu as her first, even if it was more urban comedy of manners this time than clandestine country romp.

Whitehead the valet claimed that the duke had promised Eliza-

---

* The bishop had had seven children, five of whom were living.

beth "£10,000 a year" if she could prove herself to be single and he did not marry her. Lady Mary Coke found it odd that the duke was not concerned about Elizabeth's previous "marriage," but the signs were that he was extremely anxious about it. The valet reported not only that he spent a lot of time drinking with his friend Lord Masham,* when he was usually rather abstemious, but also that every morning he and James Laroche went to talk to Dr. Collier, even after the decision had been made by the consistory court. He wanted to be absolutely sure. Collier told him he was free to marry.

"Miss Chudleigh has taken an oath that she is not Mr. Hervey's wife; and though everybody knows she is, as the witnesses to the marriage are all dead, she intends marrying the Duke of Kingston," wrote a provoked Lady Mary Coke. Worse, it was said she was to be presented at court, in a "bespoke white gown trimmed with point lace and pearl." Coke took some comfort in the disapproval of other grandees; the Duchess of Norfolk, at least, "seemed surprised that the Duke of Kingston could think of marrying Mrs. Chudleigh when he knew her to be Mr. Hervey's wife," but not much, because, "'Tis indeed wonderful, but such encouragement does vice meet with that I'm persuaded she will be visited by half the people of fashion as soon as ever he calls her Duchess of Kingston."

The duke applied to the Archbishop of Canterbury in person for a special marriage license. Coke clutched at her final straw: "Lord Frederick Campbell† told us he heard the Archbishop had refused granting the license. It seemed to me worthy of the Archbishop's character, and I hope he will be steady in that refusal."[42] She hoped in vain: the archbishop[43] granted the license. On March 8, 1769, Kingston went to Dr. Collier's to collect it with James Laroche. But Collier was out, so they went to dine first in the first-floor club room of the Thatched House Tavern in St. James's.

Apparently spurred on by the envious glare of the Bishop of Derry, Elizabeth called at the Arlington Street house at one o'clock

---

* Masham was a lord of the bedchamber to the king, married to Elizabeth's friend, fellow former maid of honour Charlotte Dives. Masham's mother was the Chudleigh relation who supplanted the Duchess of Marlborough as Queen Anne's "favorite," Abigail Hill.
† Lord Frederick Campbell: Scottish MP and a cousin of Lady Mary Coke.

to ask if the duke was at home. When the porter told her he was out with Laroche, she departed in search of him and reappeared at half past three, "his Grace's usual time of coming home to dress . . . much agitated." Whitehead the valet was called; he said he did not know where His Grace was. She ordered her carriage back to Knightsbridge; the duke and Laroche returned very late at five, and an hour later Elizabeth returned "and was ushered into the Duke's apartment, he being just come home."

Within ten minutes, "all the footmen and chairmen" were dispatched hither and thither for lawyers and clergy, and within two hours all was assembled. Collier, it turned out, had delivered the license to the house himself while everyone was elsewhere searching for each other.

Whitehead told the "upper servants"* they could go into the duke's dressing room to watch the wedding if they wished. He wrote that no one accepted the invitation apart from himself, and that it was "the worst ceremony I ever saw in my life." He did not explain himself, but he was the embittered ex-employee par excellence.

On March 8, 1769—Elizabeth's forty-eighth birthday, although unconventionally, some would say unluckily, it also was Lent†—Evelyn Pierrepont and Elizabeth Chudleigh were married before about "40 persons"[44] by the duke's chaplain, the Rev. Samuel Harper.[45] Lord Masham had begged permission from the king to skip accompanying him to a performance of Handel's oratorio, and gave Elizabeth away. Whitehead wrote, "The ceremony was performed in the Duke's dressing-room, at his Grace's house in Arlington Street, in the parish of St. Margaret's, Westminster, at about eight o'clock in the evening."

The marriage was recorded thus:

The most noble Evelyn Pierrepont, Duke of Kingston, a bachelor, and the Honourable Elizabeth Chudleigh of Knightsbridge, in

---

* The upper servants, such as the steward, butler, valet, housekeeper, and lady's maid, supervised the lower servants, such as the footmen and kitchen maids.
† Marrying in Lent was once banned, and was still uncommon. There was a proverb: "Marry in Lent, you'll surely repent."

St. Margaret's, Westminster, a spinster, were married by special
license of the Archbishop of Canterbury this 8th of March, 1769,
by me, Samuel Harper, of the British Museum. This marriage was
solemnised between us.

Kingston
Elizabeth Chudleigh

In the presence of

Masham	J. Ross Mackye
William Yeo	E R A Laroche
AKF Gilbert	Arthur Collier
James Laroche, Jun	C Masham
Alice Yeo	

The wedding was the talk of London, but whispers of external intervention persisted. Countess Temple wrote ominously to her husband,
"They say the Bishop of Derry is coming to annul the match, and
that he has a living witness to produce." She added, "Politics subside,
and nobody talks of anything but the Chudleigh farce."[46] There was
no word around this time of the duke's sister, Lady Frances Meadows, who was certainly not at the wedding, but we can assume the
dismay in that branch of the family when they heard. They did not
want anyone coming between them and the inheritance they had so
long taken for granted.

But for Elizabeth, it was a moment of supreme happiness and
victory. After nearly twenty years with the Duke of Kingston, and
twenty-five of the bitterest remorse over events on that sweltering
night at Lainston, she finally had what she wanted.

Two days later she wrote to the electress describing her "hasty"
marriage: "At the end I find myself under the protection of the most
perfect man."[47]

From her earliest days she had sought security, a resumption of
status, and respect. Her ambitions had been fulfilled at last. She told
the electress that she was preparing to be presented at court, and,
with a big sweeping flourish of her pen, she wrote her new signature
in French—Elizabeth, Duchesse de Kingston.

CHAPTER SIXTEEN

A Duchess Meets a King

With a few days to spare before the presentation at court, the newspapers reported that "their Graces the Duke and Duchess of Kingston"[1] had set out from the renamed Kingston House in Knightsbridge for Pierrepont Lodge. They left for Surrey with a retinue, including Bell Chudleigh, Miss Bate, and various servants, and at every inn along the route the landlord or landlady "complimented them with, 'God bless ye both, my lady Duchess and my lord Duke! May you long be happy!'"[2]

After nearly two decades with the duke, how sweet those words must have sounded to Elizabeth. Whitehead the valet wrote that "the only person that seemed pleased with this journey was the Duchess . . . she smiled with an inward satisfaction . . . but the Duke . . . I never saw him cheerful as before, but always sighing and thoughtful." The valet's leisurely way of life as a gentleman's gentleman was disrupted by the marriage and he later fell out with the duchess completely; there were no other witnesses to such a change in Kingston.

Their Graces gave a "grand entertainment" at Pierrepont Lodge for the local "nobility and gentry" and, for several days after the wedding, they kept "open house" for the duke's tenants. "Great quantities of meat, bread, and strong beer" were "given daily to the neighboring poor."[3]

On their return to London, Lord Masham presented the Duke of Kingston to Their Majesties, King George III and Queen Charlotte, as a married man. Compared to the one that followed two days later, this was a subdued event. The elaborate preparations for Elizabeth's court presentation were a matter for much speculation in the press. It was a rare honor to be personally congratulated by the king and queen on one's marriage, and required costume of the highest order. It was said that the new duchess had turned away jewelers sent by the duke to make her "eight thousand pounds' worth of jewels." She did not need more, she had explained, because what with her own collection and the 40,000 pounds' worth of jewels given to her by the electress, she already had "the most of any Lady in England."[4] The Irish press reported that the dress she would wear to be presented as duchess at court, "white satin trimmed with the finest Brussels lace, and edged with oriental pearls," cost £8,000 (though undoubtedly expensive, this excessive figure was probably plucked out of the air).[5] At last, Elizabeth returned to court as duchess rather than maid of honour. After twenty-five years of loyal service, she passed the maid baton on to the Hon. Susan Keck, a relative of the Duke of Hamilton. On that Sunday, the courtyard outside St. James's Palace and the street beyond was thronging with spectators come to peek at the new Duchess of Kingston in her finery, that gauzy Iphigenia, court beauty, now all-conquering grande dame who carried a gratifying scent of scandal and glamour behind her like a train.

As she alighted from her chariot, the women who sold posies around St. James's threw flowers down before her, so that the middle-aged Cinderella walked across a carpet of petals. Inside, she swept up the staircase, through the anterooms, past the Yeoman of the Guard, and into the final room, the Presence Chamber, with its thrones under a crimson and gold canopy. The court was brimming over. She was worth waiting for: a sparkling vision in a rich white and silver dress and priceless jewels. On her throat, she wore the diamond necklace that Augusta had given her as a wedding present, and on her left shoulder, a miniature painting of the Electress of Saxony set with diamonds. In this she started a trend, according to a newspaper: "From her Grace's Example, it is become a fashion with several ladies of distinction at this court, who wear her majesty's picture in the same manner, in the form of an order."[6]

Whitehead the valet described her as "so loaded with jewels, pearls, etc, that she could scarcely move: indeed, it was thought that no bride ever appeared at St. James's so richly dressed." Another spectator wrote that not only did Her Grace "lead the fashions of the day," but she was also honored by Their Majesties wearing "her favors,"* as did "all the great officers of state."[7]

She was presented to the king she had known since he was a boy of six, and the queen. It was said she had sometimes advised on her wardrobe.[8]

Along with the wedding, this was Elizabeth's moment of triumph. Of course, there was a chorus of disapproval from her enemies behind her back. Countess Temple wrote to a friend, "She had a white and silver [dress] and pearl lappets [long lace trim] which were the most curious piece of workmanship that ever were seen," as her pearl gown was "not finished in time." Temple added that the king "hardly" spoke to the bride, the queen little more, and that "nobody talks about anything but the Chudleigh farce, which may end in tragedy."[9] Horace Walpole wrote with his usual raised eyebrow that those pearl lappets were "proof of her purity and poverty."[10] Another report noted that Augustus Hervey's brother Lord (George) Bristol, now Lord Privy Seal, had been in the Presence Chamber to see his sister-in-law presented. Lady Mary Coke reassured herself in her journal: "It would have vexed me if they had been more gracious." With relish, she related that Augustus Hervey's sister Lady Mary Fitzgerald said that night that, as family, "she ought to have had a [wedding] favor" too.[11]

Lord Buckingham, however, said that King George was in a fine mood, and others said both king and queen talked to the duchess and received her very politely, as might be expected.

Elizabeth herself was purring with delight, keen to inform the electress that the court had worn her wedding favors, "silver lace knots in the shape of large roses, close to their hearts" in honor of her marriage.[12] Decorated with jewels from two Royal Highnesses and presented as a duchess to the king and queen, for all the scandal and setbacks that attended her rise, Elizabeth had prevailed.

---

* A wedding favor was a small gift to bring good luck, here the traditional "love knot" of lace and ribbon.

Whitehead the valet later advanced his theory that, at this point, something changed for Elizabeth: that in her ascendancy lay the seeds of society's censure, as "not a single lady of society or fashion paid her a visit"; that those who might come to the parties of a maid of honour could not tolerate Elizabeth as a duchess. Was there any truth in it? The Duchess of Queensberry[13] and Lady Masham, her former fellow maid of honour, were her companions, although the occasional grandee, like the devoutly Catholic Duchess of Norfolk, refused to speak to her.

Anyway, what did it all matter? Now she had Kingston, most of Elizabeth's time would be spent at Thoresby, on which, it was reported in July, "above one hundred workmen" were "continually employed." When finished, Thoresby would be "one of the most elegant seats in England."[14] Kingston was paying, but it was to be Elizabeth's creation.

CHAPTER SEVENTEEN

THORESBY

Elizabeth was now the wife of one of England's great landowners, his principal estate a fifteen-mile circle, an arcadia at the heart of the "Dukeries," that part of Nottinghamshire around Sherwood Forest where four ducal estates met. Apart from Kingston at Thoresby, there was his friend, the Duke of Newcastle* at Clumber House; the Duke of Portland at Welbeck Abbey; and the Duke of Norfolk at Worksop Manor. The new duchess approached Thoresby by crossing through mile after mile of Pierrepont parkland and primeval forest, its floor covered with ferns, and green with oaks, Scotch firs, and beeches. The sweet scent of clouds of white hawthorn hung in the air, leading to an avenue of Spanish chestnuts towards a new Palladian villa in a sylvan setting.

"One of the most beautiful inland spots in all England," Whitehead called it. "One of the prettiest bits of park scenery in the world," wrote Dickens Jr. a century later.[1] A mile-wide lake had been built by damming a river, where pike and perch swam and coots nested in the rushes. In the center of the lake, "Kingston Island" had been constructed. Thoresby had its own water mill, bakehouse, dairy, brewhouse, kennels, greenhouses, a home farm, a church, and an estate village with an inn at Perlethorpe.

John Carr of York, the favorite architect of the northern Whig/

---

* When the former prime minister the Duke of Newcastle had died in 1768, his nephew Henry, Earl of Lincoln, had become the 2nd Duke.

Dilettanti set, who had worked on nearby Welbeck Abbey for the Duke of Portland,[2] had designed a house to replace the first Thoresby, the more magnificent structure that had been destroyed by fire in 1745, leaving only its capacious service wing standing. The replacement under construction was a classically symmetrical house of simplicity on the outside, with a "rustic stone basement and two stories of brick." A visitor in 1773 remarked on the "very neat and compact villa" that had been built, with its "noble piece of water" hidden by "offices that escaped the fire when the house was burnt."[3]

If it was relatively plain on the exterior—brick with stone columns, although the window frames were gilded—it was, with Elizabeth's help and taste, splendid within. There was chintz, Indian wallpaper, green damask in the bedrooms, Wilton and Axminster carpets, Dresden china, furniture by Thomas Chippendale, portraits, busts, brightly colored silk curtains, sets of tapestries. The place was a rich, bright, luxurious jewel box of a house. A central double-height circular saloon on the first floor, known as the "dome," was lit from above by a cupola, with a double staircase and a balustraded gallery, factitious verd marble pillars, and scagliola marble walls* below. That room alone cost £1,000 and took an Italian artist, Carlo Clerici, two years to complete. The marble chimney pieces cost £850. There was an octagonal drawing room decorated with crimson damask (then believed to be the best color for showing off pictures). The house was furnished with an appearance of "refined luxury, with an air of complete comfort."[4]

Like its chatelaine, it was not free from controversy: it was more to Continental taste than English country-house style. Diarist John Byng[5] thought that with all its French furniture it looked like a house in St. James's Square (given that men thought honest, sporting country houses superior to feminine townhouses, this was an insult): "foolish expense and vanity" visible in every room, with too much mock marble, gilding, shells. Foreign tourists, however, such as French politician Alexandre de La Rochefoucauld, pronounced it "simple but beautiful," "elegant, without magnificence."[6]

---

* Factitious verd—a man-made decorative rock; scagliola—a mixture of plaster, pigments, and glue, polished to look like marble.

Under Elizabeth's orders, the gardens were laid out "German style," inspired by those at Dresden, with arbors, cascades, and trellised foliage. A Russian visitor, the young Prince Alexander Kurakin, found "the paths shaded by dense foliage, waterfalls whose gentle babble tempts one to daydream, meadows carpeted with the best turf, red deer, fallow deer."[7] Those deer were said to provide the finest-flavored venison in England.

Every Sunday was a "public day," when Thoresby's eighteen or so racehorses would be ridden out by jockeys in the Kingston racing colors—crimson trimmed with white. On the lake, streamers and flags fluttered on the Thoresby flotilla as it undertook maneuvers for the spectators. In the fleet was a large, flat-bottomed yacht, with a cabin spacious enough for twelve to dine; a half-decked sailing boat; a fast, Dutch-style boat with "lee boards,"[8] and, most splendidly, a scale model of a fifty-gun frigate, 15 feet long, a present from James Laroche, who had to have a special carriage built to transfer her from Bristol to Thoresby.[9] Each boat had its own captain. There were several smaller vessels, Scarborough cobles (open fishing boats) and canoes, all moored together near the house so that from a distance they gave the impression of a navy. The Kingstons' friend, the blind magistrate Sir John Fielding, liked to go out on the boats and afterwards sit on the bank to fish for perch. Through the archway in the kennels, there was a picturesque view of the house, boats, and lake, which constantly refilled itself with water through an ingenious engineering system of cascades and canals.

Elizabeth's life sounds like a harmonious conversation piece, that kind of decorative domestic group picture beloved of the period. On a rainy morning, she might simultaneously organize an impromptu concert, dictate letters in English and French, and talk to the estate clerk of works, Mr. Simpson, about progress on the house and grounds. A mix of staff, such as her footman John Lilly, and houseguests, such as her cousin Colonel Glover, sang and played harpsichords, violins, cellos, and horns in her impromptu orchestra; to this end she tried to hire servants with musical ability. In setting up her house with musicians and artists, she was constructing her own cultured court, like the one she had known for so long at Leicester House. All was done, admitted Whitehead, "with the greatest ease and perspicuity imaginable"; "I never heard her equal; she being endowed with an uncommon share of good sense." He did not let it lie there, however, adding, "though too often it was applied to very bad purposes."

Music was played to guests as they went upstairs to tea and cards in the drawing room, with three "maids of honour" ushering ladies around the house. Her relationship with these young women seems to have been protective, somewhat maternal. She told them to beware of predatory men, supposedly saying: "Take care of the men; they will first squeeze your hand, next kiss you: growing bolder, they will attempt your bosom; which gained, they will soon try for something else."[10] There was Mrs. Sarah Coates, the housekeeper, and four housemaids on £6 a year, Mary and Elizabeth Always, Ann Pidding, and Mary Tudbury, alongside dozens of other staff including confectioners, bakers, brewers, and groundsmen. To Whitehead's annoyance, Elizabeth had the curtain removed "on the second-best staircase" so she could see who was staying up late to drink in the servants' hall and pack them off to bed.

A Hogarthian picture of Elizabeth was painted by the prejudiced Whitehead. He claimed she would eat too much, be sick in the neighboring room "to the hearing of all," say she had had a "fit of the gout in the stomach" and round off her performance with a glass of Madeira "as a bracer." All of which she then slept off on a sofa, snoring away until teatime, when she awoke with "a violent headache" and emerged with a white handkerchief tied around her head until it was time to play cards. She always had headaches and stomachaches; but no wonder, he wrote, "she never allowed nature sufficient time to digest her victuals." She was always eating: "Between breakfast and dinner [the midday meal] I have known her order the carriage home five or six times, and take tea, chocolate, sweet cakes, and Madeira, or some other damper, every time she returned."[11] (Binge eating and drinking fit with her possible borderline personality disorder.)

Even before Elizabeth's arrival, the food at Thoresby was lavish: in 1736, the duke spent £1,477 in twelve weeks on household expenses, of which £307 was on meat alone.[12] The scurrilous Whitehead was not alone in observing Elizabeth's constant consumption. In August 1769 she and Kingston were spotted with the Laroches at the Hotwells at Bristol, by a young fellow visitor, Thomas de Grey, who wrote: "The Duchess of Kingston and Mrs. Laroche with their husbands were at the play last night—the Duchess covered with diamonds." Elizabeth could not resist eating, even in the theater. She "had her tea, and food as is now often done at the opera in London, but I believe never at the play." De Grey added that "she was quite fashionable—for when a man had a fit in the second act, she went over all red til she was carried out."[13] This is a telling moment: in spite of her newfound happiness, she had not shaken off her instinctive pseudo-seizure or phobic reaction.

Happily married at last, Elizabeth's life at Thoresby should have been serenity itself. London gossip had moved on from her for now. But Elizabeth's life was never that straightforward. She thrived on, or attracted, conflict. Luckily, there was the occasional romantic drama at Thoresby to gratify her. The cellist, Emanuel Siprutini, his "very pretty" wife, and the painter, German-born Johann Zoffany,[14] a favorite of royalty, all stayed at Thoresby for weeks. Zoffany, claimed Whitehead, spent the night in a room with Siprutini's wife, and all the footmen listened to the cellist's drunken banging on the door. The story went round the neighborhood and the Siprutinis and Zoffany all returned to London early. And although relations with their neighbor the Duke of Newcastle were deeply affectionate, Elizabeth could not resist wading into a row. Miss Lion, houseguest at Thoresby, was engaged to Captain Roddam, a guest of Newcastle's at Clumber Park. While they were both staying on these neighboring estates, Miss Lion broke off the engagement, and Roddam wrote a "very rude" letter to Elizabeth accusing her of meddling. Enclosing the offending letter, Elizabeth wrote to Newcastle, "You will shudder at the contents . . . full of unmanly, rough, and I may add ungrateful reproaches." Elizabeth defended herself vigorously: "I endeavoured to make peace between them . . . [told her that] she ought to weigh the matter well before she gave her final refusal . . . that I wished them both happy." She had offered Miss Lion a wedding at Thoresby with her young ladies as bridesmaids, and the ladies and herself "all in new" clothes, "to quiet her [Miss Lion's] little discomposure at the appearance of being married in a mean manner, and going in a hackney post chaise from Retford."[15]

Elizabeth had become grand, but she was generous with her riches.

When two Russian aristocrats, Prince Alexander Kurakin and Count Nikolai Sheremetev, visited Thoresby unannounced at the end of 1771, they found the duchess's "fine manner" charming. The house was "furnished with an elegant simplicity." They were moved by the warmth of their welcome: "You have to have traveled yourself to understand how flattering such a kind welcome is when it comes from someone who has nothing to gain by it." The duke and duchess were out when they arrived, but when they came back, "not content with making us a thousand apologies for keeping us waiting such a long time, [they] lent us their carriage, so that they could organise the house during our drive. After we had toured the living quarters, we were shown into a room, where a magnificent table well stocked with all kinds of refreshments met our gaze. It was a very agreeable surprise, especially to travelers who were known to no one."[16]

Broken engagements aside, Elizabeth maintained a fond correspondence with the Duke of Newcastle. She implored him to "laugh with the Duchess and play at whist in Nottinghamshire rather than cough in Lincolnshire" when he was thinking about going to his damp estate there, and asked his whole house party for one New Year's Eve. She strained to console him when his son lost a fortune to fraudsters at a gaming table,[17] quoting her favorite mantra (from Francis Bacon), "Fortitude will conquer fortune," and saying that, as his son had owned up to his losses, "I am quite certain . . . that you would have given twice the sum in question to have been sure that the darling author of the alarming letter possess'd so much reflection, filial affection, good sense, and spirit to confess a fault with frankness."

She ended the letter poignantly, saying the Duke of Kingston came back from Clumber with a heart "full of sighs . . . longing for such a naughty boy to make us glad for we know not what."[18]

That is the sole mention in her writing of Elizabeth and Kingston's sadness at not having any children. This was the only dent in the happiness of their marriage: with Elizabeth now fifty (and the duke nearly sixty) it was too late. The Kingstons filled the house with friends instead. In another letter to Newcastle, Elizabeth wrote, "One House might hold two or three good friends." Newcastle's son and his tutor could study in the library (and, in neighborly fashion, could he let her have a supply of coffee).

Elizabeth's letters flew back and forth from Thoresby. She sent Frederick the Great *"une charrue anglaise"*—an English plow (presumably, an exemplary one)—all the way to Berlin. In December 1772, he wrote her a poem to thank her, invoking Circe, Europa, Nebuchadnezzar, and ending, *"Je la prendrai. Je vous le jure/ Si vous promettez de m'aimer"*—"I take it, I swear, if you promise to love me."[19]

When not at Thoresby, the duke and duchess continued with their sea and spa circuit of Weymouth and Bath, where Whitehead expressed outrage that Elizabeth engaged a pair of chairmen at twelve shillings a week and tried to renegotiate the price when they left Bath early, a claim that stands in contrast to his usual criticism of her, which was thoughtless extravagance.

Mostly they were calm and happy. There was a blissful three-week trip to Mount Gould, outside Plymouth, staying with a relation of Elizabeth's, Alice Yeo, widow of Captain John Yeo, at her "small, but neat palace, clean and compact, with a most delightful view of the sea in front . . . on the east Mr. Parker's country seat . . . no situation can be more delightful," with the hostess diffusing a "spirit of love and harmony." Even disgruntled Whitehead had to admit this trip was a delight, including a visit to Eddystone lighthouse with Admiral Spry[20] that had to be abandoned because of the weather, and fishing for mackerel on the way home: "I never ate them in such perfection before, or since." Whitehead was sometimes left behind to look after "Lion," Elizabeth's tiny lapdog, "the size of a rat." Once he thought he had drowned him while washing him (indeed, Lion could have easily been drowned in a teacup, he speculated), but a maid at Thoresby got there first. She ran along the gallery with the dog in her lap: "He gave a spring and fell upon his head, and died on the spot."[21] There were always animals: pointers, spaniels, greyhounds, horses.

Very occasionally, the Kingstons went to London. They made an appearance at Teresa Cornelys's masked ball in May 1770, at which costumes included "a nurse and a child intolerably troublesome and noisy" and "a chimneysweeper" who "displayed some humor."[22] Mrs. Charlotte Hayes "was the finest woman in the room, with respect to jewels." It seems that Mrs. Cornelys's heyday was over by now: Hayes was a famous brothel keeper. More provincial but more respectable were the balls and concerts they attended at the assembly rooms in Nottingham, where performers from as far as "Lincoln and Lichfield" played Handel's *Messiah*, *Judas Maccabeus*, and *Solomon*. They sat alongside fellow Nottinghamshire landowners Lord and Lady Ferrers,[23] Lord George Sutton, Sir Gervase, and Lady Clifton.[24] Complex, ruthless, loving Elizabeth could be the epitome of sedate county dignity when she wanted to be.

As the bills racked up at Thoresby, they decided to sell Arlington Street and Pierrepont Lodge. John Carr of York's new Thoresby, Elizabeth's "enchanted castle," cost £17,000—£6,000 more than its estimate. The stables, greenhouse, engine house (to work the lake), and other offices cost another £13,000. The furniture, some by Chippendale, cost £4,000; the saloon/dome, £1,000.[25] Auctioneers Mr. Langford & Son put Arlington Street under the hammer in May 1770: "The magnificent freehold mansion house of His Grace the Duke of Kingston ... commanding a beautiful view of Green Park and also a most extensive prospect of the Surrey Hills."[26] It sold for £16,850, "not thought dear." Langford's sold Pierrepont Lodge a month later. In a contrast of scale, Elizabeth attempted to sell her small Devon estate, Hall, to her neighbor, the shrewd lawyer and sometime MP Sir John Rogers, while on a trip to Plymouth. Her methods are revealing. In the time-honored manner of estate agents, she claimed to have had other offers but to be too discreet to name an exact price. She cajoled Rogers, wanting to "have the opportunity of laughing when at Blachford[27] at the great bustle people make about nothing." Conscious that her tactics might be perceived as unfeminine, Elizabeth wrote, "Pray observe that I do not deny my sex when I desire a great deal for a small matter, these small things have ruin'd many a man and made many a woman."[28]

Despite her animated efforts, Rogers responded, curtly, that he could not think why anyone else would want her estate as he owned the sporting rights anyway. There was no sale. A few decades later a map showed "Hall pleasure house in ruins," but that was a long time after. It would be tenanted in between.

The Duke of Kingston was a hunting, shooting, fishing man. He dressed for his pastimes with the utmost care, sometimes changing four times before breakfast when shooting to get it right. The valet wrote, "I shall give you a list of articles taken to Holme Pierrepont for one week's shooting . . . six frocks or jackets, twelve waistcoats . . . thirty pairs of breeches . . . twenty pair of different sorts of stockings, sixteen shirts. Six pair of boots, six pair of half boots, six pair of spatterdashes, six pair of shoes, six pair of gloves, three hats." The carriage was so loaded up with guns and equipment it looked "like a stage coach."

In 1770, the duke and duchess took a shooting party to stay at Holme Pierrepont, the dark redbrick Tudor manor house just outside Nottingham that was home to the family before Thoresby was built. Generations of Pierreponts were—are—buried in the vault of the neighboring church of St. Edmund's. Elizabeth hated the place so much that she only spent one night there. The church was so near the house, "it put her in mind of her mortality, to think her remains must lie there, made her very unhappy."[29] The party stayed on without her.

In a way, her omens were correct. Holme Pierrepont did play its part in her downfall. Elizabeth attempted to keep her enemies, or those who knew too much, close to her. Judith Amis, widow of the Reverend Thomas Amis of the Winchester register, had been introduced to the duke's butler Thomas Phillips with the aim, as Whitehead claimed, that they should marry. Once wed to Mrs. Amis, Phillips was promoted to stewardship of Holme Pierrepont, with a house of his own fifty yards away from the manor. Unfortunately, this attempt to buy Judith Amis/Phillips's silence turned into a disaster. Whitehead recounted, "Phillips now assumed the great man; screwing the tenants so intolerably that they made heavy complaints of him." He took hay, straw, and poultry off the tenants, and sold a poor woman's "sow with a litter of young pigs"[30] without her knowledge and kept the money. When the duke heard the stories of his behavior, he fired him. Judith Phillips wrote to Elizabeth in November 1771, imploring her to save her husband's job, "in return the remainder of our lives shall be passed in gratitude and duty,"[31] she promised, a dark hint towards the possible consequences for Elizabeth. It was to no avail—the duke was adamant he should go.

*

On February 8, 1772, Princess Augusta, Elizabeth's mistress for so many years, died at Carlton House at fifty-two, not long after learning that her youngest child Caroline Matilda, the baby born after Frederick's death, now Queen of Denmark, had been imprisoned in a palace coup. The news undoubtedly hastened her mother's death. Augusta had never recovered popularity after the Bute fiasco (the suspicion that he directed Leicester House when she was prospective regent and that, as prime minister, she directed him). When she was buried at night in the chapel of Henry VII at Westminster Abbey a week after her death, the black cloth that had been hung in the abbey was stripped by the mob, and insults were shouted at her coffin as it passed. No longer in attendance, Elizabeth was not asked to be in the procession, but she mourned her friend, mistress, and royal confidante. Bathos came in the form of Mrs. Cornelys's tribute, a "kind of funeral elegy" for Augusta. In an ill-lit room decked with black drapes, she displayed a white tomb with "Augusta" written on it under a black canopy. A man and woman on either side "sang forth the praises of the Princess." "A most ridiculous whim of the woman's," wrote one society matron.[32]

Newspaper reports rarely involved the Duke and Duchess of Kingston these days, apart from references to their health. Just a few months after the loss of Augusta, it was reported that Elizabeth was in the Bristol Hotwells in a "very bad state of health," while the duke was with his racehorses in Newmarket.[33] She recovered, only for the duke to decline. In July 1773 Kingston, now sixty, always fragile, had a frightening turn and lay "in a most dangerous and affecting situation, suddenly seized with palsy" which had "entirely taken away use of one side of the body."[34] (Most probably a stroke.) Elizabeth took him to Bath, concerned, but optimistic she could help him recover.

CHAPTER EIGHTEEN

THE LAST DUKE

Sandy-toned Bath in the mid-eighteenth century was like an unfolding opera, all illicit love affairs and illness, among a stage set in constant construction. The golden Assembly Rooms and the first bank had just opened, and the building of the Royal Crescent was underway. On this trip, flirtations, coffee, and concerts, the rigmarole of Bath life, all took place without the Kingstons' presence. The abbey bells rang out ominously over the ailing duke, who was fussed over by expensive doctors. The foremost was Dr. Raines, who had come with them from Nottinghamshire.

The situation seemed worrying, but not hopeless. In mid-August 1773, the *General Evening Post*, which had reported that the duke was "dangerously ill," updated their readers that he was "greatly recovered."[1] Elizabeth had already moved the whole Kingston party twice in displacement activity for her fear. Mrs. Hodgkinson's select boardinghouse by the abbey in Orange Grove, renowned for comfort and good food, "mahogany furniture, down beds and clothe presses" (ten shillings a room per week, five for the servants in the garret),[2] was exchanged for the Abbey Bath House, and then for Bath's most luxurious accommodation, the central house of John Wood's gracious South Parade, which overlooked the horses and cattle grazing on open fields by the River Avon.

At number 5 South Parade, Elizabeth sat by the duke's bed, prayer book in hand, as doctors monitored his every breath. She was already in severe distress, as she wrote to the Duke of Newcastle, because her cousin, Bell Chudleigh's sister Susannah Haines, had died, and she could not bear to tell her husband. He was taking "food and medicines from my hand, only, night and day," although she believed he was getting better. But Sir Charles Sedley,[3] writing to the Duke of Newcastle of their mutual "dear friend," saw differently, fearing that Elizabeth was consulting the wrong doctors: "The last stroke that the Duke had was so severe that I think it is impossible he can so far get the better of it."[4]

In September, the Kingstons' steward Samuel Sherring wrote to Newcastle, who had been to Bath to see his "unhappy friend." Where Elizabeth's letters were outpourings of incoherent grief, Sherring's were a detailed journal of this sorrowful time. The duke was subjected to the Bath regime: "The bathing and pumping he underwent on Wednesday exhausted his spirits and made him very low all the evening." Bath treatment for "palsy" included bathing up to the neck in warm water, affected limbs being pumped with water, and drinking 1½ to 2 pints of mineral water a day. The following day, the duke had had breakfast, and then turned "drowsy and could scarce be kept awake." Elizabeth took him out for "an airing" before and after dinner, but he was "dull," "heavy," and took no notice of anything. In the evening, he had "the most violent spasm of his lame arm, the tendons and muscles were drawn up into knots as big as hazelnuts for some hours."[5] He suffered from hiccups and lethargy; recovery and strength eluded him.

Everybody despaired; apart, unfortunately, from Elizabeth. Sherring wrote, "She does not see with the same eyes as other people . . . Your own tender feelings will suggest the eminent danger we apprehend his Grace to be in . . . and in some measure will prepare you for the doleful event that is expected to follow."[6] The desperate doctors had ordered "blisters," he added in a forlorn postscript (blisters were believed to convey fluid out of the body, aiding healing).

Far away in Dresden, Elizabeth's old enemy Lady Mary Coke was being questioned about the duke's health by the electress, who feared that her friend would fall ill with the stress of looking after her husband. (Coke was trying, to no avail, to befriend the electress herself.) Horace Walpole was speculating on the duke's will, writing to a friend that Elizabeth had already "made offers of the sale of Thoresby. Pious matrons have various ways of expressing decency."[7]

Of course, that was untrue. Anyone who saw her tending her husband with such tragic optimism and spaniel devotion could not have adopted such cynicism.

Elizabeth dictated a letter to Newcastle, via Miss Bate: "I bless God for his great mercy in giving me strength still to attend my dear friend with an unwearied spirit . . . last night my dear friend was given over by his three physicians. His senses remain perfect, and I had consent to call in Dr. Delacour, a physician who practis'ed in London, with great reputation."[8] Hope was now pinned on this new doctor, society favorite Dr. Philip Delacour,[9] who usually deemed his patients "bilious," and proposed emetics and evacuation by "warm nervous glisters."[10] Miss Bate added a postscript: "The Duchess is inconsolable, not only with grief, but with surprise, for the doctors have kept her in ignorance of the Duke's danger always telling her his Grace's pulse was good; and as he ate and slept well, she flattered herself that there was not that immediate danger." On Friday, thinking the duke stable, Elizabeth even offered Dr. Raines her "chaise" to go to the Bath races. But Kingston diminished in strength every day, until even Elizabeth began to adjust her expectations. Bate's postscript was written in distress, "I hope your Grace will pardon all faults as I hardly know what I write."

By the end, the duke's convulsions were so strong that "three men could scarcely hold him," and he bit his tongue "almost through."[11] He was tortured by doctors until the curtain fell. At 2 A.M. on Thursday, September 23, 1773, during a tempestuous gale howling across the city, the Duke of Kingston, at the age of sixty-one, took his last breath.

His body was taken to the vault of St. James's Church in Bath to await burial, with four chairmen watching over it.[12] Preparations began for a fittingly ducal funeral back in Nottinghamshire. In the meantime, Elizabeth returned to London for the reading of the will.

The newly widowed duchess was so upset it took her five days to reach London from Bath, about double the expected time, as "she moved to town with the pace of an interment" in a voluminous cloud of black crêpe. Even the usually unsympathetic Horace Walpole wrote that, "One may always venture to bet that the world's ill-nature will outgo anybody's deeds, and I am persuaded that Nero and Caesar Borgia will, as well as Richard III, come out much better characters at the Day of Judgment."[13] This was perhaps his grudging admission that even he could see that Elizabeth loved her husband. Mrs. Delany, however, wrote, "Her widowed Grace fell into fits at every turn on the road from Bath:—true affection and gratitude surely cannot inhabit such a breast?"[14] Lady Ossory was more sympathetic, and more accurate, writing that much "will be said that she does deserve, and more that she does not."[15]

In bereavement, Elizabeth had once again become the object of public fascination, most of which was salivating rather than sympathetic, because, as Delany wrote, "Everybody [was] gaping for the Duke of Kingston's will."[16] A colossal fortune was at stake: who would inherit the land, the houses, the pictures, the silver, the stud, the income?

The Meadowses, the family of the duke's sister, Lady Frances, had great expectations. So keen were they to enrich themselves that when the duke's body was barely cold, they took legal action before they knew the will's contents: "On 1 October, several caveats were entered at Doctors-Commons against the Heir at Law of the late Duke of Kingston taking out Letters of Administration."[17]

In panic, they were attempting to block the will. They had spent a sizable chunk of their expected inheritance already.

To understand the resentment that surrounded the duke's will, one has to wind the giltwood clock back nearly forty years to the elopement of Kingston's younger sister Lady Frances Pierrepont with Philip Meadows, against the wishes of her family.

Although she had been born into every aristocratic privilege, Lady Frances's life was a piteous one. She had been orphaned at six, and when her brother Evelyn set off on his lengthy Grand Tour, Frances had been placed first with her great-aunt Cheyne* and then, when she died in 1732, with her brilliant, judgmental, somewhat self-centered aunt, Lady Mary Wortley Montagu. Lady Mary never

---

* Gertrude Cheyne, sister to the 1st Duke of Kingston; her husband was William Cheyne, 2nd Viscount Newhaven.

took to her niece. Frances was a romantic, determined girl, friends with Lady Mary's own daughter, who went on to marry Lord Bute.

Wortley Montagu was even more critical of Lady Frances than she was of Kingston. Lady Mary had adored her younger brother and called her niece and nephew "my ever-dear brother's children," but when the responsibility for the girl's well-being fell to her,[18] she found it painful to be "undertaking the management of another's child." Her hostility had many reasons to flourish:[19] she had never liked the girl's mother and her father's death just a few weeks after her birth meant that Frances was forever associated with his loss in her aunt's mind. She looked at her niece and mourned her brother. But, most frustratingly, her niece would not take her advice. The disagreement, of course, was about whom to marry.

Kingston and Sarah, Dowager Duchess of Marlborough, had suggested her grandson the Hon. John Spencer, MP for New Woodstock, who would inherit Althorp and other estates. But he was a hard-faced, boorish rake in whom Frances had no interest.* She had met Philip Meadows, second son of the courtier Sir Philip Meadows, the Knight Marshal, MP, and envoy, who pursued her relentlessly. Lady Mary regarded Philip as a fortune hunter—he had previously been rumored to be marrying a wealthy widow. She tried to distract her niece with a visit to the Lichfield races; Frances fainted and had to be taken home.[20] Two weeks after she had turned twenty-one,[21] she eloped with Philip, probably already pregnant with their first child, Evelyn, who was born seven months later.

In the viciousness of the era, both men and women were unkind about Frances. Mrs. Delany believed she was right to seize her chance, "if she could not live without a husband, for nobody else would have cared for her notwithstanding her twenty thousand pounds,"[22] and Lord Hervey wrote that Meadows was "welcome to her for me; she has a sly, and at the same time determin'd look, that would have made me dislike her more for a wife than any woman I know."[23] Her aunt thought her stubborn and stupid in marrying a

---

* "Jack" Spencer once had a dinner party and asked only stutterers. They nearly came to blows as each thought the others were mocking them. Spencer was a fortune hunter, too: he married Lord Carteret's daughter, who came with £30,000.

man who, in her view, was only after her money. Given what happened later, she had a point.

Lady Mary had divined a seam of remorseless acquisitiveness in Meadows. It was an unattractive trait he passed on to his firstborn son, for whom an obsession with his uncle's estate would erode all industry, dignity, and happiness.

After Evelyn, the Meadowses had seven more children in quick succession. In their early marriage, they seemed to live off her brother Kingston,[24] hence their encouragement of his romance with the married de la Touche, who would have left their inheritance alone.

Life was unkind to Frances. Two of her eight children died in infancy. Her first child Evelyn grew up to lead the dissipated life of a rake. His younger brother Charles became a naval captain; then there was a daughter, Frances, followed by William and Edward, both in the military, and Thomas, who was disabled.

In September 1768, the only daughter, Frances, a maid of honour to Queen Charlotte, had married a dashing but impecunious soldier, Alexander Campbell,* "without asking either Her Majesty's leave or her father's consent; even her own maid knew nothing of it."[25] The news came out through the servant network. The new Mrs. Campbell wrote to ask forgiveness from the queen; all was forgiven, the bride presented at court. But just a few months later, soon after giving birth, Frances died, leaving Captain Campbell with their baby boy, Henry.[26] Her father Philip was, it was said, "much shocked," particularly as he had never been properly reconciled with his daughter since her marriage.

Even before the death of her only daughter, Lady Frances Meadows was incapacitated by fragile mental health. As Horace Walpole put it, she had "long been mad" by now.[27] There seems to have been a familial predisposition to instability. Her namesake, the Duke of Kingston's other aunt, Frances, Countess Mar, had suffered from depression and "unsound mind" and had spent years at the mercy of others, unable to look after herself.[28] The details of her niece Lady Frances's con-

_____

* Of the Campbell of Cawdor clan, his father John was a Treasury and Admiralty lord.

dition have not survived, but in the subsequent family story she was either silent or absent, her views and condition erased from history. Family lore in the nineteenth century was that sad Frances had been "confined twelve years in prison" by Philip Meadows.[29]

Elizabeth and Kingston had blamed Philip and his son Evelyn for Lady Frances's nameless condition, and for the fate of daughter Frances, too. They believed that Philip had tortured his wife, and that Evelyn Meadows had been "cruel to his sister and mother." Evelyn had also abandoned the army, and broken the heart of a "beautiful and virtuous" girl. Elizabeth later explained in a letter: "The eldest nephew for many reasons was disinherited. The principal cause was, that when he had the advantage of being an Aide de Camp to [the allied commander] Duke Ferdinand[30] in the late war . . . he quitted that post of honour . . . and afterwards without any property quitted the army entirely, living extravagantly, on the hopes of succession."[31]

To Kingston, a general who had raised his own regiment, such presumptious dereliction of duty was intolerable in the nephew who was meant to be his heir, compounded by the fact that "poor Lady Frances Meadows in her intervals of sense told the Duke that her unhappiness" proceeded from ill treatment by Evelyn Meadows, as well as her "barbarous husband." Elizabeth also believed that Evelyn Meadows's cruelty had helped kill his sister and her husband[32] and that father and son hated her because she had reconciled the duke to the Campbells before they died, and she herself had provided for their orphan child "as soon as I had the power."[33] Which is to say that not only did Elizabeth believe Evelyn Meadows to be an indolent, treacherous coward, but that he and his father had mistreated Frances and her husband; and that she herself had vouched for the family financially when they failed to support each other by providing for the late duke's great-nephew, the Campbell orphan.

Evelyn Meadows had publicly abandoned that "beautiful and virtuous" girl for a "dainty," "laughter-loving" actress/courtesan, Clarissa "Clara" Hayward, daughter of an oyster seller, who could drink three bottles of wine with composure, according to another lover.[34] Her most prominent role was as the unfaithful wife Calista in *The Fair Penitent*[35] at Samuel Foote's theater in the Haymarket (sample review: "very bad" although she had a "pretty figure").

Meadows had "rescued" her from Charlotte Hayes's brothel, paying for her by extending himself credit as the rightful heir to the Duke of Kingston.

His younger brother Charles, on the other hand, studied at Oxford, served with distinction as a naval captain, and retired in 1769. William by now was a lieutenant colonel, Edward a captain in the army.[36]

In the last few years of his life, the duke could not bear to set eyes on Evelyn Meadows. His porter had orders "never to let in the Captain on any account whatever." In spite of this obvious enmity, Evelyn Meadows had borrowed heavily against his "inheritance": £6,000 from his own brother Charles alone. His father Philip, himself a third son, also wanted the money.

Such was the tribe waiting to hear the Duke of Kingston's will.

In early October, all concerned were gathered around the table at Kingston House in Knightsbridge. The Duke of Newcastle, who had custody of his late friend's will, Philip Meadows, Elizabeth, and various lawyers were inside the house; the Meadows children and their cousin Spencer Boscawen* were pacing impatiently around outside.

The Meadows family were full of wishful thinking or misplaced confidence. One paper reported, "We are assured that the Right Hon. Lady Frances Meadows, only sister of the late Duke of Kingston, will become Countess of Kingston and Baroness of Pierrepont in her own Right."[37]

This was untrue. In fact, the will, written out by the duke, unconventionally, in his own hand in July 1769 so no one could dispute his intentions ("impregnable as the Rock of Gibraltar," one lawyer later called it) prioritized his adored wife. This was not unusual: the Meadowses' assumptions were based on debt and desire, rather than reality. The duke left Elizabeth all his wealth and the income from his estates for her lifetime—at least £4,000 a year—as long as she did not remarry. On her death, or remarriage, if there were no offspring—poignantly, the will mentioned possible children of the Kingstons' marriage—all would pass to the second son, Charles

---

* Then a lieutenant in the Coldstream Guards.

Meadows, and then to his heirs; if he did not have any, the estate passed in succession down the line of the younger brothers and their heirs, and if that failed, to the sons of the Duke of Newcastle. The Meadows boys would not receive their cash legacies, of £3,000 and £2,000, until Elizabeth was dead. Apart from £500 in a codicil, Evelyn Meadows had been cut out. There were gestures for staff, servants, family, and friends, including £500 a year for Samuel Sherring; £1,000 a year for Bell Chudleigh; and a mourning ring, to the value of £200, for the Duke of Newcastle.

Philip Meadows left the room in silence, tears streaming down his face. He was incandescent with shock and rage. The Meadowses saw Elizabeth as the alpine obstruction between them and the immense riches of the family into which Frances had been born. They were quite wrong, according to Elizabeth: such was the duke's love for her that he had wanted to leave his entire fortune to her alone, forever—to dispose of as she pleased after her death—but she had persuaded him to include his nephews through her own "generosity."

The Meadows family, and society at large, chose not to see it that way. They vilified the grieving widow. Whitehead the valet implied that the witnesses to the will were suspiciously lower class—Elizabeth must have forced it through. Gossips speculated on what she might have been called in the will—Duchess? Countess? Chudleigh? Horace Walpole joked that Augustus Hervey had been seen coming out of her house and perhaps would take her back "after the loan of her" to Kingston.[38] The level of bile directed at Elizabeth was astonishing, just as it had been towards the Dowager Princess Augusta; it was reserved for women who seemed to have "stolen" power. Eighteenth-century patriarchal society could not tolerate a rich widow,* particularly one who had long ago been condemned as without virtue. Evelyn Meadows, in particular, was determined to get his revenge.

Submerged in grief, Elizabeth had no idea how much visceral hatred she had provoked in the Meadows clan. Her heartbreak was so

---

* Most widows were not rich; they would have their dowry plus a jointure from their husband's heir, as agreed before marriage. They could inherit their husband's estate, but it was rare.

intense that quiet dignity would not do. For the first time in her life, she had the means to demonstrate her inner anguish, and demonstrate it she did. Kingston House was hung in black; black clothes were worn by staff; kitchen maids rubbed pots with black rags; horses were rubbed down with black cloths; the soles of shoes were blackened. Once visitors had gone past the "professional mourners"* holding black poles with plumage on them at the door, like a Swiss guard from the underworld, they were received by Elizabeth sitting up in a bed draped with black curtains, the room lit by a single candle. The funeral would reflect the scale of her sorrow. Kingston had been companion, lover, friend, husband; she was desperately unhappy at her loss. Like Queen Victoria in another generation, the mourning and the sorrow were overwhelming.

On October 13, church bells rang in Bath as His Grace's body was dispatched in a mourning coach on the six-day journey north. Mayors and dignitaries of towns along the route came out to pay their respects. At the Nottinghamshire border, the cortège was met by gentlemen in black cloaks with rosemary† in their buttonholes. Fifty carriages of mourners followed. At Nottingham, the final procession began: it was over a mile long. The final resting place was to be the family mausoleum in the church by the Tudor hall where Elizabeth had spent that gloomy night musing on her mortality, Holme Pierrepont.

Considerably more elaborate than many a royal funeral, with the College of Arms involved in the organization,[39] it was a theatrical event, and an outward expression of Elizabeth's character: her taste for drama, her love of grandeur and status, and, however much others doubted it, her love for the duke. It seems ironic that the most magnificent event she ever organized was a funeral—her two rushed, surreptitious weddings had had none of this opulence.

---

* Professional mourners were expensive, yet a frequent sight. To some, they were inherently comic; Dickens's *Martin Chuzzlewit* (1844): "two mutes were at the house and door, looking as mournful as could be expected of men with such a thriving job . . . feathers waved, horses snorted, silk and velvets fluttered; in a word, as Mr. Mould emphatically said, 'everything that money could do was done.'"

† Rosemary was a symbol of remembrance.

The procession included clergy, tenants on horseback holding "white staves," mounted tradesmen, men with torches, "mutes on horseback in black cloaks," and, for each coach, six horses wearing plumes of black feathers. "His Grace's gentleman" carried the ducal coronet on a cushion "on a led horse [the duke's favorite, Crony] in mourning supported by two pages." The body was in a hearse drawn by six long-tailed black horses covered with velvet drapes, ornamented with escutcheons [coats of arms] and streamers. "Lining the road all the way men, women and children an incredible number," recalled the valet, "I never saw so many on such an occasion, either before or since."

At noon, the cavalcade reached Holme Pierrepont, and the nobility and gentry went into the house. At four, the short funeral procession to the church of St. Edmund's on the drive began on foot. In the order of the funeral there were: "fourteen servants out of livery, in mourning; livery servants in mourning; twenty constables; the pall . . . supported by, amongst others . . . the Duke of Newcastle and two of his sons, the Duke of Portland, Lord Lincoln, Sir William Boothby, Lord George Sutton . . . the chief mourners including Samuel Sherring and army friends, Col Litchfield and Captain Brown . . . numerous gentlemen following 'in scarves and hatbands' and then the tenants . . ."

The boom of a cannon accompanied the duke's final journey: "During the cavalcade from the house to the sepulchre, minute guns were fired in Thoresby Park (25 miles distant) to the number of 61, his Grace's age, which were heard distinctly, by many people, near the Trent side, and as far as Newark, the wind being then favorable for conveying the report of the cannon."[40]

In a sea of black, the coffin was draped in crimson velvet. The church was hung with mourning and the family coat of arms. The mutes attended the coffin on each side, His Grace's gentleman at the head, with the ducal coronet on its cushion, while the duke's chaplain, the Reverend Nathan Haines, the widower of Elizabeth's cousin Susannah,* performed the "divine service." Elizabeth was surrounded by female attendants, all in black.

---

* Susannah Chudleigh, sister of Bell and daughter of Harriet's brother, Col. George Chudleigh.

The service over, the *Derby Mercury* reported that the church was open so that "the numerous spectators, tenants, &c. might take their final farewell, of one of the first and most illustrious peers of the realm; whose most amiable character and benevolent disposition, added to his many other virtues, procured him the universal esteem and real love of this country, and of all mankind." At Thoresby, the "colors of the vessels on the lake were struck half mast, and the bells were muffled and tolled."[41]

On his coffin was written:

The most high, mighty, and most noble Prince
EVELYN PIERREPONT,
Duke of Kingston upon Hull,
Marquess of Dorchester,
Earl of Kingston upon Hull,
Viscount Newark,
Baron Pierrepont of Holme Pierrepont,
Knight of the most noble Order of the Garter,
And
General in his Majesty's Army,
Died the 23rd Day of September,
MDCCLXXIII.
Aged 61 Years.

The family vault was opened for the first time in thirty-four years, and His Grace's coffin joined twenty-two of his ancestors deposited there. Such was the savagery and cynicism of eighteenth-century society that the Dowager Countess Gower wrote: "The Duchess of Kingston! (alias Mrs. Hervey) must have been struck with a whim for the Duke to appear a Grand Seignior [an Ottoman sultan] before he died. She and her six women attending with all humility gives me an idea of a seraglio [harem]."[42]

In the long list of mourners, the name Meadows does not appear.

After the show, the expense, and the tears, Elizabeth was left lost, heartbroken, and, on paper, rich.

She executed various parts of the will, instructing London jeweler

James Cox to make Newcastle's mourning ring. On a trip to Bath, she sat for a portrait in mourning dress by the artist William Hoare.* One visitor to his studio wrote: "I saw nothing very capital at the two painters, excepting a portrait of the Duchess of Kingston in her weeds, looking at a picture of the Duke, her robes carelessly behind her on a chair, & an hourglass & skull on the table, all her own device—she would have had some bones at her feet, but Hoare would not comply with that."[43]

The Meadows family were left plotting splenetically. It was not a good omen that less than two months after the funeral, a Meadows relative, Fanny Boscawen, was writing to a friend: "Mrs. Montagu wants to see the Duchess of Kingston, *alias* Hervey, burnt in the hand. Nobody would have any objection."[44] Being burned on the hand was the traditional punishment for bigamy, combining the penalty of physical pain with indelible public humiliation. Being branded was a literal mark of infamy.

No wonder that, after the duke's death, Elizabeth felt power and security ebbing away from her. Just when she most wanted to mourn her loss, she was facing jealous spite from several quarters, and a looming battle to hold on to an inheritance so extensive, it was inevitable that others would lay claim to it.

Under threat again, she formed a plan. When the duke's friend Sir Charles Sedley visited Elizabeth at Thoresby, he found the "apartments were stripped of everything of value."[45] She complained she had spent "sixteen hundred pounds in law" since the duke's death, mostly on legal advice from Lord Mansfield,[46] and that "she had been so ill-treated since her worthy lord's decease, that she was determined to quit this vile country and reside in France, where she should have proper respect shown to her."[47] For that reason, Elizabeth explained, she had sent away all the best furniture, with the pictures and plate. The duke's plate "was one of the finest in the kingdom." (Indeed it was, given that it included the Meissonnier collection he had commissioned in Paris.) Elizabeth was fighting back: she had

---

* Hoare shared a studio with Gainsborough. The whereabouts of this morbid picture are unknown.

mobilized her lawyers and started moving Thoresby's treasures out of temptation's way.

She decided to abandon cold, unfinished Thoresby for the solace of Rome rather than France. By mid-January she had departed. An introduction from the Electress of Saxony to the Anglophile pope, Clement XIV, drew her to the Holy City.

CHAPTER NINETEEN

CONVERSAZIONI

Rome was most familiar to the British from the recently published etchings by Giovanni Piranesi, which showed a bucolic wilderness among tumbling classical ruins: oxen lowing at the Colosseum, a cattle market at the forum, goats and hens scratching among temples, baths, and vineyards.

Visitors arrived across a panorama of open country, the dome of St. Peter's floating on the horizon like a vision. They entered the city through marble columns into the Piazza del Popolo, which had an Egyptian obelisk, a fountain, and two churches facing each other, "an august entrance which cannot fail to impress a stranger with a sublime idea of this venerable city."[1] Rome had shrunk within its walls, occupying a fraction of its original sprawl.[2] Country had come into the city, which was a mix of the "lordly and sordid": only pigs—and rainfall—cleared up; there were few pavements on the narrow cobblestone streets. Romans, like the animals they lived alongside, had no fear of relieving themselves in the street. And yet, it was the "smiling city," a tranquil, engaging place, where the gross—the surrounding swamps turned putrid in summer—met the beautiful—fairy-tale fountains, baroque churches and palaces, fat marble cherubs who knew their good fortune, and barley twist columns. Piazza Navona was one of the most spectacular squares in all Europe, its public fountains pouring forth "prodigious quantities of cool delicious water."[3] The Trevi Fountain and the sweeping steps by the Spanish embassy were recent papal commissions.

There was no sign of the industry that had enveloped London. From lunchtime until five or six in the afternoon, Rome slept in the heat. In the morning, the smell of coffee and fried fish wafted through the streets along with that of animal dung. Slices of watermelon, ices, and *sorbette** were sold, with fasts on Friday. Music floated through the air, from outdoor concerts, bands of singers, and church bells. The theater was a babble of talk and laughter, with picnics in the auditorium.† Apart from when the cardinals were in conclave, when candles were lit everywhere, the streets were plunged into darkness at night.

Only the richest and most determined English tourists made it to Rome. They were embraced because they carried with them the promise of money. Just as popes and princes had removed parts of the Colosseum to build their palaces, the English grand tourists plundered works of art, buying antiquities as well as commissioning portraits. Elizabeth was a rarity in being a new British widow alone in Rome (women came with their husbands and fathers, although more came alone in the years after). The Dowager Duchess of Beaufort was one other, but she was accompanied by a daughter she wanted to marry off.

Apart from money, the Romans loved a title more than anything. Their own nobility competed with their carriages, as only aristocratic families were allowed velvet linings and doors painted and gilded with their family crests. Their palazzos, built right next to other dwellings, were surprisingly somber with "mean stairs, dusty brick floors . . . crimson hangings laced with gold,"[4] religious pictures, busts, and urns. Fruit and flowers were unfashionable, but there was fine veal, white wine from Orvieto, and pyramids of ice cream.

Peasantry, clergy, aristocracy, and royalty all mingled on the Vatican steps, where Pope Clement XIV reigned supreme. Elected in 1769, he was the most talked-about man in Europe. In the summer of 1773, he had suppressed the Jesuits, whose order had a resented stranglehold on royal courts across the Continent. For this, and

---

* Iced froth with the juice of orange, apricot, or peach.
† Unlike in England, only men and castrati were allowed on stage.

because he was an urbane and humorous Anglophile, Rome had become more popular with the British than ever. His Holiness played billiards and bowls, snared birds, rode out in lay dress, and "liked to be liked."[5]

The city was evolving from Jacobite magnet to tourist destination for Hanoverians. Although Elizabeth was Anglican in that gentle way of the Church of England, the place with its grandeur, its music, hot, gloomy, holy, magnificent,[6] its sacred solace so theatrically presented, could not have been more suitable for a flamboyant duchess in the throes of grief.

When Elizabeth arrived in Rome in February 1774, Clement XIV* was at his apogee. And luckily for Elizabeth, he knew the dowager electress, who had enjoyed her own visit to Italy in 1772 and had suggested the idea to her overwrought friend.

Elizabeth's stay was recorded by the Jesuit father, agent, and art dealer John Thorpe in letters to his patron, Lord Arundell of Wardour. On February 26, he wrote that the Duchess of Kingston "shows great regard for the poor Irish Franciscans of St. Isidore's, keeps in deep mourning and does not see much company." The monks of St. Isidore's, in the north of the city, seemed to be the only beings the frail, sensitive Elizabeth could face. Within weeks of her arrival, however, she had recovered enough to meet the pope: "The Duchess of Kingston was presented to the pope at the Church of La Vittoria;[7] she told his Holiness she could not come to Jerusalem[8] without adoring; he raised her up and received her very graciously." She mostly attached herself to a Friar O'Kelly, however; after "a late fit of convulsions [she] would have the Father Guardian always near her." O'Kelly was soon "perpetually one of her company at table, and when she goes out to see any curiosities she will have him always within sight or within call."[9]

The city was full of splendid British visitors, at whose request the pope had "given license" for "a grand musical entertainment twice a week during Lent: many are much scandalized at it; but all frequent

---

* Clement XIV was born Giovanni Vincenzo Antonio Ganganelli, the son of a physician, in 1705.

it out of regard for the English, which is now the favorite nation of his Holiness."[10] But Elizabeth avoided the other British grandees, including the Duchess of Beaufort and the two younger brothers of George III who had made marriages that had alienated the king: the "dim-witted" Prince Henry, Duke of Cumberland, known as the "Royal idiot," and Prince William, Duke of Gloucester.[11] Thorpe believed Elizabeth did not want to alienate the king and queen by befriending the princes, although she had known them both since birth.

Perhaps she was just enamored with Rome and wanted to leave English court politics behind. A few days after her introduction to the pope, Thorpe wrote that Elizabeth was leaving but was "so pleased with it that she declared that if she could have the house she desires, she would take a lease of it and come hither every year . . . Some people imagine that she has a notion of religion,"[12] meaning, such was her enthusiasm for the place that people were speculating that she might become a Catholic.

She wrote to the electress sounding lighter than she had in England, complimenting her with "His Holiness was enchanted to hear that you were delighted by your stay in Rome, everyone I speak to says how gracious and full of spirit you are."[13] News of her impending Catholicism had flown back to Italy from England: Arundell's Wiltshire neighbor, Lord Pembroke, wrote to Sir William Hamilton, British ambassador in Naples: "The Duchess of Kingston should, in my opinion, turn Catholic, and end her days at Rome. Indeed, it would be a nobly proper measure, and answer all her purposes of pride, and éclat wonderfully well."[14] Her friendship with the pope had intensified: he sent her a "handsome" snuffbox bearing his portrait; she sent him a "rich present [via] Fra Buontempi," his favorite friar.[15]

While the pope's health wavered,[16] Thorpe recounted waspishly that Elizabeth was buying "a great number of wretched paintings, most of them not worth the carriage and duty . . . all pious subjects, except a Venus and two or three such like pieces." She was certainly making her way through money: £1,400 in three months via banker/agent Thomas Jenkins alone,[17] although back in England enough income (estate rents) was still coming into her Hoare's account to cover it. She was thinking of commissioning a monument to the duke, but with the extravagant taste that made her so easy to mock, Thorpe claimed she thought that only Michelangelo could "do justice to the noble figure of her dear Duke." She envisaged him sculpted in marble, placed "amidst the highest angels."

As her generosity and connection to the pope became known, Innocenzo Buontempi, the pope's secretary and only confidant, unsurprisingly paid "assiduous attendance" to her. The Franciscan friar was said to be more powerful than any Secretary of State.

Spring in Rome made Elizabeth gradually more sociable. She roamed around the Forum and the Colosseum, with its chapel and wild flowers; ate iced melon in the garden of the Villa Albani with its owner, Cardinal Albani;[18] and began holding court, with O'Kelly, Buontempi, and Abbé Turner, a master of languages: "her conversazione is very brilliant, much frequented by the gay Prelates, young noblemen," wrote Thorpe. "She sometimes has . . . literary academies, wherein each one of the company makes a short discourse upon some interesting subject. The sprightliness of her character and the singularity of her sentiments make many curious to see and converse with her."[19] At a conversazione,* there would be a hum of noise, with servants circulating with wafers, biscuits, and ices. The most exalted guests sat on upright chairs upholstered in silk or velvet, while others stood and mingled. Priests usually led the conversation.

The widowed Elizabeth, now fifty-three, who initially would see no one but the neighboring monks, was now hosting a salon. She had become an object of fascination for young Englishmen on their Grand Tour, and a sought-after client of artists. Such was her belief in the restorative powers of travel—and her eagerness to continue her self-imposed exile—that the poet Vasily Petrov started teaching her Russian.

Elizabeth furthered her acquaintance at another audience with the pope, who held her hand for a flatteringly long time. A story emerged that he kept his gloves on, turned to one of his prelates, and "bid him remember the Italian proverb, 'Love does not pass the

---

* A formal gathering, based around conversation.

glove.' "[20] Whether this unlikely pontiff cattiness was true or not, she was restored to such a level that she wrote to the Duke of Portland, "My sorrow knows no end, but at Rome I have found rest, sleep has restored me to a better state of health than when I left England, but happiness is not for me this side of the grave."[21]

Indeed, Elizabeth was "so charmed with Rome"[22] it was said that she had offered "£20,000" for the Villa Negroni, seat of a pope and then a cardinal, on the Esquiline Hill.* Most significantly for Elizabeth, it had an expansive garden with fountains, statuary, and walkways, the air full of murmurs of water trickling down basins of porphyry. As one visitor wrote, "There I found what my soul desired, thickets of jasmine, and wild spots overgrown with bay; long alleys of cypress totally neglected, and almost impassable through the luxuriance of the vegetation; on every side antique fragments, vases, sarcophagi . . . in deep, shady recesses."[23]

Unfortunately, it was now owned by two brothers who could not agree on the price, which was to include all the antiquities inside it, to sit alongside her furnishings from England. Other villas were suggested and rejected.[24] As she proposed to spend the winter months in Italy, it was said that Cardinal Albani might lend her his. Such was Elizabeth's fame that her plans were discussed at the highest levels of government. Sir Horace Mann, envoy in Florence, wrote to the Earl of Rochford, Secretary of State for the Southern Department, on May 10: "The Duchess of Kingston has broken off the treaty for the purchase of the Villa Negroni . . . for which she had offered sixty-two thousand crowns.[25] The proprietor of it who is at Genoa raised some difficulty and proposed to her to send a person thither to . . . conclude the negotiation with him, which gave her offense and furnished her with a pretext to break off the treaty, though it is supposed, that in the mean time she had repented of having gone so far in it."[26] (The purchase did eventually fall through.) Mann was expecting her in Florence on her way back to London.

From there she wrote a reverential, or unctuous letter (in French)

---

* Next to the Diocletian baths.

to the pope, which showed her ideology. She saw him as an ideal monarch rather than a spiritual guide:

Elizabeth to Pope Clement XIV, Florence, 15th of May 1774 (11th hour).
... I willingly surrender to my duty, which is to signify to Your Holiness the attachment I have for a sovereign so worthy of the state where the good God has placed you ... the glory which surrounds you takes its power over hearts more by the greatness of your spirit, and the rare qualities of your soul, than by sovereignty itself. If all kings ... governed like you, their people would be led, as yours are, without any chains other than those which lie within their hearts ...
  I have the honour to hold Your Holiness in the utmost respect
  Most sincere and very humble servant
  Elizabeth Duchess of Kingston
  Left Rome Wednesday
  arrived in Florence on Friday morning very early
  in a quarter of an hour I leave Florence
  Rome has no rival
  11 o'clock[27]

The rumors that she might become Catholic were unfounded—scurrilous, given that Jacobite century and her Hanoverian connections[28]—although she was enamored with Clement XIV. She was tribally Protestant, emotionally and aesthetically Catholic.

Mann, once her Chelsea neighbor (his younger sisters were her age, and would have been playmates) was a genial host in Florence where he kept open house. After dinner he took Elizabeth to the park, the Cascine,* which (he wrote to Walpole) "delighted her much, till their resemblance to some of her own parks where she had passed such delicious hours with the Duke produced a flood of tears."[29] She left

---

* The Parco delle Cascine: the vast green park on the north bank of the Arno in Florence.

Genoa in three feluccas, bound for Lerici and then Antibes, from where she continued the journey by land.*

At the end of June, she was in Paris, arranging to sell what she could not remove from Thoresby, such as the duke's stud; she wrote to the Duke of Portland to tell him how much she wanted him to have the duke's favorite horse, Crony. As soon as she arrived in Calais, her ship's commander, Captain Harden, took her back to her home shore in the comfort of her own ship, the *Minerva*.

While Elizabeth was recuperating in Rome, the Meadows family had been reacting to the shock of the will in their own fashion. The newly designated heir, second son Charles Meadows, now felt free to marry at thirty-six, in knowledge of the fortune that would be coming his way. In March 1774, he wed Miss Anne (Orton) Mills, daughter of William Mills Esq. of Richmond Hill.

The reaction of the elder brother Evelyn Meadows was more demonic than romantic. The moment the will had been read, he had set about trying to find proof of Elizabeth's first marriage in the hope of invalidating his uncle's wishes.

Unfortunately for Elizabeth, he happened upon a web of intermarried, disgruntled Chudleigh/Hervey/Kingston servants, some of whom, having watched their privileged masters and mistresses enjoying lives of capricious decadence for years while they endured lives of drudgery, were more than happy to bring them down for money or out of malice. Eighteenth-century hierarchy and power play could be a great deal more complicated than it looked on its showy surface; it was hard to know who was more dependent on whom.

First of all, Evelyn Meadows went to Bath to find Thomas Whitehead, the one-time valet of the Duke of Kingston who had always resented Elizabeth's arrival. Whitehead was now scraping a living as a music master, willing to conduct any tune for the highest bidder. "The year after his Grace's decease," Whitehead later recounted,

* A felucca was an open boat, rowed by "ten or twelve stout mariners." They waited to go between Lerici and Genoa, or Genoa and Nice, and elsewhere, as conveniently as the water taxis in London.

"Captain Evelyn Meadows came to Bath, and asked me some questions concerning the Duchess's behavior to the Duke, in order if possible to set the will aside." Whitehead told him of "her ill-treatment of my good lord; that he had no will to act as he pleased; that he could not even go an airing without her leave." Meadows asked him to make "a memorandum" of his memories for his attorney, and to "accompany him to Bristol, to find out Mr. Phillips' wife" (Rev. Thomas Amis's widow) and promised to reward him for his trouble. Whitehead added slyly, "You see how I have been rewarded on all sides for my faithful services."

Whitehead not only provided Meadows with the testimony he required—that the will was not what the duke had really wanted—but also introduced him to the Reverend Thomas Amis's widow Judith, now Mrs. Phillips. The woman whose first husband had created the register on his deathbed, and whose second husband, Thomas Phillips, had left Holme Pierrepont in such ignominy, was now in Bristol, simmering with resentment.

By a stroke of luck or by design, Evelyn Meadows kept his horses at livery at Hyde Park Corner in the well-known stables of John Fozard,[30] who had worked as a groom for the Duke of Kingston and married one of Elizabeth's maids. He told Meadows that he knew people who could prove the first marriage—Fozard's wife had heard Mrs. Craddock claim she saw Elizabeth and Hervey "married and bedded." Mrs. Craddock was in London, having fallen out with Elizabeth.

According to Whitehead, Craddock had indeed been bribed to stay silent: "Her Grace had promised her thirty pounds per annum for her life, with the proviso that she would live . . . in the North Riding of Yorkshire." Craddock did not want to be so far from London and from everyone she knew, but she told Elizabeth she was penniless. While Craddock was absent, Elizabeth (as she often did, according to Whitehead) opened a letter that showed Craddock in fact had £300 in stocks. When her lie was discovered, Craddock said Elizabeth should give her £20 instead and let her live in London. A furious Elizabeth refused.

To summarize Ann Craddock's history, she had been a single woman when she was first maid to Elizabeth's aunt, Ann Hanmer.

She had met her future husband at Lainston when he came to visit as Hervey's manservant, and was now the sole living witness to the candlelit vows. Craddock was willing to talk because Elizabeth, safe in the judgment of the ecclesiastical court, had refused to buy her off any further, once she had discovered that her pleas of poverty were false. Craddock, however, was quite aware of the value of her testimony.

Armed with this evidence, on May 17, Philip and Lady Frances Meadows filed a bill of complaint against her, including an accusation of collusion against Augustus Hervey.[31] Filed in the Court of Chancery,[32] this was a civil rather than a criminal action. It had to be received in London in person. In it, Elizabeth was accused of using "threats and menaces" to coerce Kingston into writing the will she desired. Her lawyers wrote to urge her not to come back.

Elizabeth never received their warning. In early July, her carriage drew through the gates of Kingston House. Inside, a letter was waiting for her. The familiar chorus of society scribblers recounted what happened next.

Horace Walpole wrote to Horace Mann: "Christina[33] Duchess of Kingston is arrived, in a great fright, I believe, for the Duke's nephews are going to prove her first marriage, and hope to set the will aside. It is a pity her friendship with the Pope had not begun earlier; he might have given her a dispensation. If she loses her cause, the best thing he can do, will be to give her the veil."[34]

On August 3, with breathless glee, he followed up with:

I told you in my last that her Grace of Kingston was arrived. Had I written it four and twenty hours later, I might have told you she was gone again, with much precipitation, and with none of the pomp of her usual progresses. In short, she had missed her lawyer's letters, which warned her against returning. A prosecution for bigamy was ready to meet her. She decamped in the middle of the night; and six hours after, the officers of justice were at her door to seize her . . . What will be the issue of the suit and law suit I cannot tell. As so vast an estate is the prize, the lawyers will probably protract it beyond this century.

He was right there. He added, "Her friend the Electress of Saxony said to the Duke of Gloucester, 'Poor thing! what could she do, she was so young when she was first married?'"[35]

Elizabeth had come to London to consult William Feild, her lawyer, who convinced her that the ecclesiastical judgment was watertight. A few years before, he had turned Ann Craddock away when she sought him out, so confident was he in this assertion—a decision that had sent Craddock catastrophically into the cabal of Evelyn Meadows.

On finding the letter stating intention of prosecution waiting for her at Kingston House, a panicking Elizabeth returned to Dover as quickly as she could. With no packet boats available, she was rowed out in an open boat to an Ostend merchant ship that was sailing for Calais. She arrived, as she would write bitterly to her persecutor later, with "only a young lady and not even a change of clothes or linen."[36]

From Calais, she explained her plight to her friend and neighbor the Duke of Portland: "I depended upon being in England, alas! I have been there! and the first melancholy object that presented itself to my view, was the attachment.* Mr. Meadows and his eldest son will soon end my wretched life; which though I am well apprised that is their aim . . . But as Mr. Addison says, 'while I yet live let me not live in vain.'"[37]

In the midst of her legal shock, she received a visit from Lord Mansfield, the Lord Chief Justice.[38] Their conversation remained private, but whatever he said reassured Elizabeth enough that she turned her mind to more positive matters: asking Portland to send her pineapples to Calais for her to give to the pope. "She would take it as a particular favor if his Grace should have any fit to cut, if he will spare her some of his. The pineapples should be just turning yellow, and cut with a long stem. Her Grace's hothouse has failed this year, or she would not have taken this liberty."[39]

---

* An attachment was a legal process that had to be served while the "debtor" was in the city, hence the lawyers trying to stop Elizabeth's return; it was also a way of freezing assets under investigation.

London was abuzz with Elizabeth's midnight flit. For example, George Selwyn MP, at Almack's,* wrote:

> The lawyers are going on furiously and sanguinely against the Duchess of Kingston, who is, they say, at Calais...Nobody doubts of her felony; the only debate in conversation is, whether she can have the benefit of her clergy [i.e., reduced punishment]. Some think she will turn Papist. All expect some untimely death.[40]

Courtier Lord Bruce had heard that "the Meadows are supposed to have secured in their favor a woman who was present at her Grace's marriage with Mr. Hervey."[41] Lady Mary Coke described a conversation she claimed to have had with the queen about Elizabeth: Queen Charlotte "said that things always came out at last, and did not seem sorry...that all that infamy was brought to light." On hearing that Elizabeth was complaining about the Meadows family, Coke wrote with her usual archness, "If, with all her crimes, her peace of mind is only disturbed by the Meadows family, 'tis extraordinary indeed."[42]

Horace Mann in Florence, as unsympathetic as the rest, blamed her greed, as he wrote to Walpole:

> How much happier she would have been, if she had been contented with a few thousands a year, and had let her fond Duke leave his estates to those who are now contending for the whole, the bare management of which for a woman of her age and asthmatic disposition is too great to consist with happiness. But would a little singe in her hand prevent her counting her vast riches!...We had been told her second marriage had been acknowledged in all the courts of justice. Oh! but you tell me that there is another [i.e., civil] court which does not act upon those principles...At all events this last attempt will make her Grace an exile for all her life, and will sound odd in the ears of all the foreign princesses with whom she proposed to associate, whatever indulgence the Electress of Saxony may have for her.[43]

---

* A club in Pall Mall.

An illustration of the venom Elizabeth was up against: in this one letter, Mann attacked her sex, age, health, ambitions, connections, and right to inheritance. Why should an "asthmatic" woman of her age inherit anything? Would all those princesses tolerate her when they discovered that she was in exile?

The *English Gazette*, briefed by the Meadows family, carried equally negative updates. Elizabeth wrote fretfully to the electress asking her not to believe them. Back in London, the affair had become a running joke. As Walpole wrote to another friend: "Why what should I have found, but the thing in the world that was most worth finding? a hidden treasure? . . . no, sir, nor the certificate of the Duchess of Kingston's first marriage . . . nor the philosopher's stone."[44]

In September, Elizabeth was on her way back to Rome,[45] expected at Civitavecchia, a port north of the city, when terrible news reached her in transit. Pope Clement XIV had taken to his bed on September 10 and two weeks later, possibly poisoned by his Jesuit enemies, had died. This changed everything for Elizabeth in Rome. He had been, she wrote, a "fortress against my enemies,"[46] according her various dispensations—no taxes or duties on her goods, permission to sail right up the Tiber to the last bridge, into the city—but more than that, their friendship meant no one in Rome would dare to take advantage of her.

When she heard, she wrote frantically to the electress that her "unhappy fate" pursued her. Since the death of her "dear husband," everything in England increased her sorrows. The persecution by his nephew and all the backbiting, "which by the grace of God I do not deserve," had filled her with disgust for everything there. As a result, she had left Rome thinking that "the Pope's kindness" would have made a six-month stay every winter "the most pleasant idea."[47] Now she knew she had to change her plans.

Full of anxiety, Elizabeth wondered if she should try France instead. Travel did not indicate a lack of grief for the duke—far from it—but it was a measure of her desire both to escape the Meadowses' legal maneuvers and to find a court, the patronage of a protector-figure, the only status she had known as a single woman. "Now my thoughts are turning to France, and I am convinced that you can obtain for me the protection and graces of that Court," she implored the electress. "You will recall, my dear friend, that I had the good fortune to make the Emperor's acquaintance with you, my dear friend, at Dresden.* And I do not doubt, that I enjoy the honour of his protection . . . in a few days I will be at Rome, since my baggage and my servants are leaving by sea to meet me."[48]

Might the electress write a letter of introduction to the queen, Marie Antoinette, for Elizabeth to take with her? "I will have the honour to write to you from Rome, perhaps to ask you for a letter for the Queen of France, which I would like to present myself on my return from Rome, but I would not want you to mention this before my arrival at Versailles. Your declared enemy, the Prince Xavier, who never liked me [as] I am your friend, would play some evil trick on me, and put me in a bad position in court."†

Elizabeth returned to Rome via Genoa and Florence, where she visited Leopold, Grand Duke of Tuscany, and his wife, Infanta Maria Luisa of Spain, the electress's niece.[49] She arrived in Rome in November. The *Notizia del Monde* (World News) announced that the "English Duchess would arrive on Thursday," November 10. Her servants and luggage arrived separately on her ship, the *Minerva*, in what Walpole described as a "shipload of plunder."

Meanwhile, back in England, there was a development within the Hervey family. Augustus's brother Lord Bristol was critically ill. If he died, Augustus would become earl, and as the most forensic in society such as Horace Walpole could envisage, the younger brother Frederick, Bishop of Derry, might well help the Meadows family in their quest for proof of the marriage. If a legitimate heir was out of the question for Augustus Hervey, the Bishop of Derry—and then his children—remained next in line to the Bristol title and fortune. As Walpole wrote to Mann on November 11, 1774:

---

* The Holy Roman Emperor, Joseph II, was Marie Antoinette's brother; Louis XVI the electress's nephew.
† Prince Francis Xavier of Saxony, who now lived in France, was the electress's brother-in-law (and uncle of Louis XVI). The electress had fallen out with him.

The bigamist Duchess is likely to become a real peeress at last. Lord Bristol has been struck with a palsy that has taken away the use of all his limbs. If he dies, and Augustus should take a fancy to marry again, as two or three years ago he had a mind to do, his next brother the Bishop may happen to assist the Duke of Kingston's relations with additional proofs of the first marriage. They now think they shall be able to intercept the receipt of the Duke's estate—but law is a horrid liar, and I never believe a word it says before the decision.

The cardinals were in conclave choosing the next pope when Elizabeth arrived in Rome. Thorpe wrote, "The Duchess of Kingston, Countess of Carlisle* and some other such characters are arrived to be in readiness for the opening of the Porta Santa, as soon as a Pope is chosen."[50] (The Porta Santa, the "Holy Door," was opened at St. Peter's Basilica once every twenty-five years.) Three weeks later, Thorpe wrote, "the Duchess of Kingston continues to make her figure here"; he had heard that she had accepted the offer of Albani's villa for the summer season.

In December, Elizabeth was so integrated into Roman society that she held two parties on successive nights with her friend, the Roman aristocrat la Marchesa de los Balbases, sister to the Constable Colonna.[51] Forty soldiers, wax torches burning in their hands, bandoleers slung over their shoulders, stood guard on the avenue leading up to the palace to escort visitors upstairs. It had all the flair of a Chudleigh House party in the old days.

Elizabeth had been lent the graceful Palazzo Ruffo in the Piazza dei Santi Apostoli by a Neapolitan cardinal. Thorpe noted that she was furnishing it with "the valuables and movables that she brought in her ship from England: which are all permitted to enter without paying any duty." Elizabeth, he had heard, had "one of the most elegantly furbished houses in England"[52] and she was emptying its

---

* The Countess of Carlisle was another scandalous woman abroad. When the Earl of Carlisle died, his widow Isabella née Byron had remarried, to Sir William Musgrave, a historian fourteen years her junior. They were estranged and she went off traveling and accumulating vast debts.

treasures into her boat, painting by painting, plate by plate, to bring it all safely away from the avaricious Meadows clan.

Rome was full of drifting aristocrats and English artists on the make, but as far as the locals were concerned, the voluptuous, peculiar, emotional Elizabeth was their most entertaining English visitor. They regarded her as a one-woman carnival, according to Thorpe: "The Romans are very anxious of being further acquainted with this extraordinary character." They were not disappointed. She rode around in an elaborate black and white mourning coach, "a white bear skin for her coach box . . . her servants' mourning is now trimmed with silver, which makes them look like so many Pantalones."* Jibes included the idea that her extended mourning was for the pope rather than for "him whom she calls her dear Duke, whose death is now at too great a distance and was too profitable, to be mourned." The gossipy priest continued: "The Duchess of Kingston continues to divert the Romans with her droll equipages and other whims: they say that the late Pope made her a Catholic and dispensed her from every practice of religion . . . She is hitherto resolved to have her English ship come up the Tiber to Rome, and outdo everything that Queen Christina of Sweden did, if she can: the Romans smile, and think that she will at least afford them sport."[53]

In London, excitement was mounting over something much more serious than melodramatic livery: a newspaper had run a "blind item" that the grand jury for the county of Middlesex at Hicks Hall had considered a Bill for Indictment against "a lady, for felony, in marrying a late nobleman, at the time she was actually the wife of another person," and had decided to proceed.

Below the item ran the following clue: "A celebrated lady has disposed of all her moveable effects in this kingdom, with a design of ending her days on the continent; on which account it is expected that an outlawry will take place without opposition."[54] This was a menacing hint from the Meadows family, who were hoping Elizabeth would stay away with what she had already taken and volun-

---

* Pantalone: a stock character of the commedia dell'arte—an old man obsessed with money.

tarily become an outlaw, rather than face a public criminal trial of certain expense and uncertain outcome.

One of the duke's trustees, Nottinghamshire lawyer Richard Heron, wrote to Elizabeth's steward Samuel Sherring to inform him of the Meadowses' latest move. Sherring replied in horror on December 12, 1774:

> I was dumbfounded last night when I opened your letter. What a scene doth this event open to my mind? I can remember what you once hinted might be done, I could never get it out of my mind, though I tried to forget it. Alas the time is come! Good God! How will the Duchess bear the shock when she is first made acquainted with this criminal process? It will require more firmness and fortitude than she is mistress of, I fear, to support herself under the tumultuous passions this injurious treatment will raise within her throbbing breast. She can lay no blame but on herself . . . This looks to me like the beginning of sorrows.[55]

There were now two legal actions targeting Elizabeth: one civil—the challenge to the will in Chancery; and one criminal—the charge of bigamy. This was a grave crime that ran contrary to the Christian framework of society. Once punishable by hanging, now by branding, transportation, or imprisonment, this was far more momentous than the Chancery case.

The Meadowses were convinced that Elizabeth was selling off their inheritance and spending the proceeds in Rome, so they tried to injunct the money she was being paid for the duke's horses and dogs by Tattersall's, and to block her selling or exporting "gold and silver plate, jewels, magnificent furniture, and valuable pictures . . . carriages" and further livestock. The Lord Chancellor, Lord Apsley (later Bathurst),[56] pointed out that the bill named Elizabeth Chudleigh rather than the Duchess of Kingston, and as the person called Elizabeth Chudleigh no longer existed, he threw out the action and ordered the money to be paid to the estate trustees. The Meadowses refiled their bill without the Chudleigh name in January. A delay in the civil case was small comfort for being accused of bigamy.

*

News of the bigamy accusation reached Elizabeth in Rome in mid-January 1775. She promised to send the judgment of the ecclesiastical court and the Archbishop of Canterbury's permission to the electress, because, if the word of Britain's most senior clergyman and its church court did not hold water, "there is no religion in our country."[57] Heron, the trustee, wrote to Elizabeth at the request of Sherring and her lawyer, William Feild, to offer his advice. He thought there was little point in trying to involve the king, as she had wildly suggested, as His Majesty would not feel it prudent to "interpose." Elizabeth's choices were to risk standing trial, or come to some kind of financial arrangement with her persecutors. Heron's preferred option was the latter: "I venture to advise it; the greatest Princes in Europe are obliged to pay for peace."[58] He added that Elizabeth should return to England as soon as possible to meet her advisors, and so her opponents did not think she was running away. And she must keep her counsel in Rome.

Elizabeth replied that she had resolved to stand trial. Other than that, she was suffering. She sent a list of complaints: asthma, even in a "fine clime," rheumatic attacks on the right, "threaten'd palsy" on the left, all compounded by her banker, Mr. Hoare, who would not give her any of her money, so that she was reduced to selling "trinkets" in a city where she had previously been "treated like a sovereign."[59] The Court of Chancery had ordered that she could not receive any more money from the duke's personal estate until she had responded to the complaint bill; as a result, Mr. Hoare had cut off her supply (she was spending vast sums—£4,900 in one month; far less than was coming into her Hoare's account. She retaliated by returning to Mr. Drummond, her premarriage banker). A story was circulating that her other Roman banker and art dealer, Thomas Jenkins,* was avoiding her, and that after repeated attempts to reclaim the jewels and money in his keeping she had hidden on his

---

* Devon-born Thomas Jenkins was a guide, painter, and dealer, who knew everyone and acted as a barrier/agent between the British, their art/antiquities, and their money in Rome. He was also an unofficial spy for the British government, with an eye out for Jacobites. In Elizabeth, he had met his match.

doorstep brandishing two loaded pistols, until she got what she wanted.

By the end of January, the news of the Meadowses' machinations had spread all over Rome. Italian author Alessandro Verri wrote to his brother: "The Duchess has been summoned to appear, her real estate has been seized, meanwhile she has transported all her rich furnishings and furniture to Rome, in addition to an extraordinary amount of bijoux."[60]

Her yacht, the *Minerva*, had brought her possessions right up the Tiber to the quay by the new customhouse. Curious Romans gathered on the riverbanks to see the vessel arrive to the sound of cannon fire. A newspaper reported in early February that,

> Last week, a ship arrived in the port . . . Very well equipped with all requirements, it was built from scratch in England for her own use by an English lady, the Duchess of Kingston, who has lived in this city for a while now, housed in a palazzo on Via Condotti, from where in a few days she will move to another palazzo in the piazza of SS XII Apostoli. People have been rushing to see this vessel for several days, and it has been praised by many, especially for the noble decoration of the cabins and the built-in comforts that serve for the aforementioned Duchess.[61]

The praise was not universal. Thorpe wrote that he found it a bit on the small side: "the Roman populace crowd to stare at the English Ton; as for the ship, they call it only a model, and say it would be a pretty thing to put upon the Lake at Albano and be a pleasure boat for the late Pope who so sweetly squeezed the hand of the owner."[62]

Elizabeth might have been immune to what others thought about the size of her yacht, but she was palpitating about the bigamy case. She wrote to the electress, recalling her husband, "so tender, so faithful, so worthy of being loved," and explaining the circumstances of the will, by which the nephew who had so "dishonoured the family name" was disinherited. The Meadowses had tried to get her property in Chancery, and failed; now the new "barbarous" process meant that if she did not get back to London by June, she would be outlawed, her property taken from her; "their malice is without equal." The journey would be so dangerous that she might die: rough, muddy, rocky summer roads were even more perilous than hard, frozen winter ones. In her desperation, she wondered again about asking George III to intervene. She felt very alone "without a father, mother, brother, sister, children! Without my dearest husband."[63]

By the time she sent her next letter, she had come up with a more cunning plan: rather than ask the king herself, in which case it might look like she had something to fear, might the electress, her son the Elector of Saxony, the Elector of Bavaria, and, indeed, the Holy Roman Emperor all ask King George III for help on her behalf— but not let on that it had been Elizabeth's idea? Would the electress arrange that for her? Elizabeth reminded her friend that she had once come to see her when she was ill, at risk, she claimed, of losing her future husband and without the permission of the Princess of Wales. Besides, George, surely, would love to be able to do the electress a favor?

Although she was throwing around fanciful ideas, she still retained (on her lawyer's counsel) confidence in the ecclesiastical court's judgment, and carried on building her life in Rome. On February 9 she was admitted to the literary Accademia dell' Arcadia.* Their mission was to "wage war on bad taste" by "purifying" Italian poetry; to encourage a "renaissance of the Renaissance." Members each adopted the name of an Arcadian shepherd, read and improvised poetry to each other, and met on the hills around Rome to discuss art and ethics. After a discourse from the General Custodian,[64] Elizabeth was acclaimed a member and took the name of Artemisia Ciparissia. The electress was one too: it was a clear sign of social acceptance.

But for now the muses of the academy would have to wait, because Elizabeth learned that she had to be in Paris by March 26 to answer the Court of Chancery on oath. She had to leave Rome immediately. As predicted, it was an appalling journey: the road was

---

* The Arcadian Academy aimed to conduct mental competitions, just as the Olympic Games had physical ones. Founded by Queen Christina of Sweden, a Catholic convert to whom Walpole once compared Elizabeth.

so rough between Rome and Florence that she burst an abscess in her side and had to be carried in a sedan chair all the way from Florence to Bologna. In spite of this, she still arrived in Paris before her lawyers. The electress advised her not to go to England until she was sure it was safe to do so.[65] She was "fatigue a mourier [*sic*]" (tired to death), she wrote, and shaken in bones and soul. "Poor woman, she is so melancholy she cannot bear the sight of anybody," wrote one of her compatriots in Paris.[66]

Elizabeth had not yet heard the one piece of news in her favor: George, Earl of Bristol, had died in Bath on March 20, 1775, "of a palsy from a repelled gout."[67] Horace Walpole noted that now Augustus Hervey had become the earl, Elizabeth was, at the very least, a countess. She did not yet realize the advantages this brought her: the right to trial by her peers, to bail, and to a reduced punishment if found guilty.

The electress, unfortunately, disagreed about the wisdom of involving George III. And Elizabeth had been told that she had become entangled in a systemic rivalry, as she explained to the electress: "I am made to believe that the gentleman of Ecclesiastical law and the gentlemen of the other law are in a scramble for supremacy, and the latter would like to have the final say in all disputes between them . . . if they come out stronger I could be the sacrifice."[68] In this fear, she was quite correct. The only current consolation was the kindness of the newly elected Pope Pius VI, Count Giovanni Angelo Braschi, and Frederick the Great, who had written a sympathetic letter.

Initially unaware that as a peeress she was entitled to bail, Elizabeth responded to the Chancery charge via her lawyers, but hesitated at Calais, worrying that she would be imprisoned if she landed on British soil. On May 19, the choice was taken away from her. She learned she had to be in London almost immediately for the hearing. As she was preparing to cross the Channel, the case was escalated from the lesser Hicks Hall to the Court of King's Bench, the highest common law court in England and Wales.* It took five days before she reached the British shore, because "a terrible tempest" delayed

---

* An ominous sign: it was being taken more seriously.

her departure, after which it took 120 men to drag her ship out of the harbor at Calais.

Now Elizabeth had to find four people to stand bail for her. The Duke of Rutland, Knightsbridge neighbor and friend of the late duke, woundingly refused. The Duke of Portland was slow to respond, but before he agreed, four others had loyally accepted: the kindly Duke of Newcastle; Lord Bute's son and heir, Lord Mount Stuart;* James Laroche MP; and Sir Thomas Clarges, Bart. For her first court appearance, Elizabeth arrived at the Duke of Newcastle's house by Westminster Hall, and from there entered with her four guarantors. The court treated her with exceptional civility and respect, and she was allowed, unusually, to sit down on the bench between a judge and Newcastle. She was in front of Lord Mansfield for ten minutes and the crowded courtroom observed that she was "somewhat thinner than when she left England."[69] Her bail was set at £8,000; half to be guaranteed by herself, and £1,000 by each guarantor.

As bail was granted, Elizabeth felt such a sense of relief that, "armed with innocence," she even started communicating on other matters—commissioning a new private yacht, in fact. She instructed her secretary, Captain Moreau, to ask for a "draft of a barge" that might be superior to her current one in the Mediterranean. Escape must have been on her mind. But she was in "good health [and] spirits," having safely received some pineapples, and now ordered supplies of venison from Thoresby.[70]

The following month, a judge in Chancery found in her favor concerning the Meadowses' first bill of complaint, deciding that her property was rightfully her own, as she wrote to the electress:

> It is with the greatest pleasure that I share the news with you that I have obtained a complete victory over my enemies. On Tuesday, the 27th, at about ten o'clock in the morning, my cause was brought in front of the Supreme Court of the Chancery. The next

---

* A relative by marriage: his mother Mary, Lady Mary Wortley Montagu's daughter, was first cousin of both Lady Frances Meadows and the Duke of Kingston. Sometimes spelled Mountstuart.

day, they used every imaginable rule against me that sophistry could invent. However, the court strongly and evidently convinced of my innocence, decided in my favor. This decree ... is so complete and decisive that I find myself clear of the danger of my enemies in future ...[71]

However, the taste of victory was fleeting, and Elizabeth's interpretation of events overly optimistic. A new enemy had appeared, in the most unlikely quarter.

Samuel Foote, one-legged transvestite satirist, playwright, actor, theater manager, and controversialist, was a theaterland celebrity and permanently hard up. Like Elizabeth, he was from obscure West Country gentry—in his case, Cornwall—and though his parents had intended for him to be a lawyer after Oxford, he had chosen to tread the boards. Sent down from university and finding himself in a debtors' jail, Foote received a letter from his mother asking for money because she was in one too. He refused. The family fortune had been entrapped in Chancery, in a lawsuit that outlasted a generation and inspired *Bleak House*'s Jarndyce v Jarndyce.

However, Foote always made an opportunity out of a crisis. When one of his uncles murdered another, he made money selling the story from their nephew's point of view. Through his friend Frank Delaval, reprobate, actor (most famously as Othello, seen by Elizabeth),[72] and heir to Seaton Delaval Hall in Northumberland, and via his friendship with Prince Edward, Duke of York, he had entered Elizabeth's orbit. He had observed her exuberant ways at close range, having attended Prince Edward's birthday party at Chudleigh House in 1760. The same age as Elizabeth, mixing in overlapping social circles, he was critical and competitive; he was a showman and social climber with an eye for an opening. And like "everyone" else in the *ton*, he knew her entire story.

For these reasons, he had written a play called *A Trip to Calais*, in which Elizabeth, thinly disguised as Lady Kitty Crocodile (originally "Lady Betty Bigamy"), was evidently the subject of his poisoned pen. "Crocodile"—a reference to crocodile tears—was an overweight widow who dressed in black because it made her look slimmer. The play is set in Calais, where everyone knew Elizabeth sometimes stayed. Crocodile is on the run from the law in France; she snaps at her maids, accusing them of flirting while being charming to them in front of others; she encourages bigamy and boasts about her friendship with the pope. Iphigenia is mentioned, along with a Lenten wedding (recalling Elizabeth's to Kingston). Foote was planning to play Crocodile himself, in drag.

It was said that Foote had met Elizabeth's ex-companion Miss Penrose, who had revealed all of her former mistress's foibles. But suspicion must also fall on Evelyn Meadows, who, one might surmise, had decided to attack Elizabeth on the public relations front. His mistress Clara Hayward was a friend of Foote's and had appeared in his productions. The connections were numerous and uncomfortable: Foote's friend Arthur Murphy had been a rival for the affections of an actress, Ann Elliot, with Augustus Hervey. One of his patrons was Lord Gower, first cousin of the Duke of Kingston. Another patron had been Lord Townshend, whose first wife was Hervey's confidante.

Word got out about Foote's nefarious play. Elizabeth's friends intervened and Lord Hertford, the Lord Chamberlain, refused him a license to put the play on that summer. A public relations battle ignited in the press. Foote's public reply to Hertford in early August was splashed across all newspapers; he told how Lord Mount Stuart had come to see him, and taken Elizabeth a copy of the play; how Foote himself had visited her, because, he claimed disingenuously, he could not see any characteristic of Lady Kitty Crocodile that resembled Elizabeth. He even tried to seize the moral high ground; he was not, he claimed, the "echo or instrument" of any man, however "exalted his station." (Not true, given that he was so clearly doing the Meadowses' bidding.) He suggested Elizabeth mark those passages she felt referred to her to identify the offense. She was not that foolish.[73]

In fact, Foote had also asked for money—£2,000—to suppress the play. Walpole wrote in excitement to a friend in Paris, "You have left England at an unhappy time, now the paper war is broke out between Duchess Kingston and Foote."[74] Everybody covered it in their letters, including the philosopher Jeremy Bentham and the actor David Garrick, who thought Foote was attempting to "bully 'em into a license."

If only Elizabeth had been wise enough to leave it there. But her friends, such as the pseudonymous "Verus," took revenge on her behalf, accusing Foote of malice and writing that although "there is nothing in the character like the Duchess," the situations given were "similar enough to force the audience"[75] to apply the character to Her Grace. Foote was accused of trying to prejudice the Meadowses' case, which presumably was what Evelyn Meadows was banking on.

In the midst of the conflict, Elizabeth was introduced to the Reverend William Jackson by one of her lawyers. Belligerent, attractive, and witty, the Irish journalist, editor of the *Public Ledger*, was hired to be her secretary, factotum or, in modern terms, publicist.

With Jackson's fresh ink—and a sense of injustice Elizabeth could not suppress—the madness escalated. Foote wrote to Elizabeth to say that the Duke of Newcastle had advised him that the timing of his play (as he well knew) was inconvenient and so, out of pity, he would refrain. She, unwisely, replied. He replied to that, and gave their entire correspondence to the press. She had written that she was insulted by his attempts at extortion—he was a "subservient vassal" who had insulted her dignity with his "pity"—but that as she was "clothed in my innocence as in a coat of mail, I am proof against a host of foes."[76] She could not resist being drawn into a public slanging match, just as the Meadows family were hoping. The heat of her anger made her look guilty.

Foote implied she must have been drunk when she had written to him; a public exchange with her was "too great an honour" for him to decline. It would have been prudent to have answered his letter before dinner, "or at least postponed it to the cool hour of the morning," when she would have found that he had already "granted that request which you had endeavoured by so many different ways, to obtain." As Lord Mount Stuart must recollect, when he met him at Kingston House at her request, he had rejected her "splendid offers to suppress *A Trip to Calais* with the contempt they deserved." He was "above . . . reach" of her bounty.

The dramatist continued, his quill pen like a turning knife:

But why, Madam, put on your coat of mail against me? I have no hostile intentions. Folly, not vice, is the game I pursue. In those scenes which you so unaccountably apply to yourself you must observe that there is not the slightest hint of the little incidents of your life which have excited the curiosity of the Grand Inquest for the county of Middlesex [i.e., the bigamy case]. I am happy, Madam, however, to hear that your role of innocence is in such perfect repair. I was afraid it might have been a little worse for wearing; may it hold out to keep you warm the next winter.[77]

Garrick wrote that Elizabeth had "made herself very ridiculous, and hurt herself much in the struggle."[78] By now numerous people aside from the Reverend William Jackson were involved on Elizabeth's behalf: the physician, Dr. Isaac Schomberg; William Feild, her lawyer; her chaplain, the Reverend John Forster, who signed in an affidavit that Foote had tried to extract money from Elizabeth, which Foote, of course, denied. It was too late to salvage her dignity. "The Pope will not be able to wash out the spots with all the holy water in the Tiber," wrote Walpole.[79] Cartoons appeared, Elizabeth fighting Foote clad in chain mail of "innocence."

In addition to making her a laughingstock, Elizabeth's spirited, undoubtedly sincere defense of herself had made it easier for those who might judge to find against her; and ensured universal fascination with whatever might come next.

CHAPTER TWENTY

THE CROWN AGAINST ELIZABETH

Elizabeth had won the Chancery case, and in one way at least—by stopping his wretched play—trounced Foote.[1] But she was unable to stop the criminal proceedings.

In November 1775, she asked for the hearing to be moved from the Court of King's Bench to the House of Lords, where punishments were more lenient. She sent a "circular note" to individual lords, confident they would support her; the prime minister's brother Brownlow North, Bishop of Worcester, was staggered by her self-assurance. He wrote to his father that it was a "dark business and everybody has a different story."[2] With Lord Mansfield's help, she was successful. Mansfield, the Lord Chief Justice, was friend by faction: a prominent Whig, he had counted Sarah, Duchess of Marlborough, among his clients, since both (along with Elizabeth) were related to the Fieldings by marriage. Mansfield was an enlightened figure, the man who began the abolition of slavery in British law with the celebrated Somerset case.[3] He was a modernizer who could see what others could not. He tried his best to stop Elizabeth's case coming before the peers at all, pointing out, not unreasonably, that it was not "the suit of the Crown; it was the prosecution of private individuals,"[4] connected with property matters, and in contravention of an existing ruling in the ecclesiastical court. The Meadowses were determined to press ahead, as their counsel had told the House. Mansfield reasoned that even if they won, the duke's will would not be overturned. And as Elizabeth was a peeress, guilty or not, there would, most likely, be no punishment, and therefore no subsequent deterrent for anyone else: "She makes your Lordships a curtsey, and you return the compliment with a bow,"[5] he said, asking: what was the point?

What he did not mention was the extraordinary timing for such an expensive, singular case. Perhaps when they first set the date for December 18, the Lords had not factored in that the trial would be as costly as a coronation, and necessitate the shutting down of all other parliamentary business while it proceeded. But not a man among them can have been unaware—in fact, most of the dramatis personae were only too acutely aware—that the pursuit of Elizabeth was coming in the middle of a crisis on which British citizens might reasonably have expected their lawmakers to be spending their time, in the form of the American War of Independence. In November, while the Americans established their own navy, the House of Lords argued about Elizabeth's trial. Even the military wrote about it: Lord Amherst, future commander in chief of the forces, wrote to his brother that there was no news from America but some were saying that "Her Grace will become a Countess."[6]

Elizabeth's household wrote to the Duke of Portland to tell him that her health was suffering under the strain. She was "very ill in a fever and inflammation in her bowels wore almost to death with sorrow and fatigue."[7] She was "seized with a fainting" and had to be carried home from a service at the Chapel Royal in St. James's in early December, an event Walpole described as a "scream that roused all the palace" and then "ripened to madness."[8] What he saw as attention-seeking was undoubtedly a resurgence of her anxiety disorder, those faints that overcame her at moments of intense fear. Her hopes for a *nolle prosequi* (dismissal of the case) looked vanishingly thin. The date was set and discussions about logistics were beginning. How much seating would be needed? And as Elizabeth heard—the Meadowses were only too keen to repeat it—as a suspect could not be tried from a state of freedom, should she be put in the Tower of London?

As she was "confined to her bed by a very severe illness," her three physicians, doctors Richard Warren,[9] Isaac Schomberg, and Nicholas Faulk, advised she could not possibly appear in court on the set date, and requested the trial be delayed by two months. By now, she was so desperate she took the step everyone had advised her against: she wrote to the king asking him to intercede, making an impassioned, personal plea for his sympathy, reminding him of the vitriol that had pursued his own mother:

> I am, my Lord, by this malicious prosecution detained in England at the hazard of my life . . . Our Lord Chief Justice [Mansfield] has publicly declared that the law stands in my favor; and he is the greatest judge and the ablest lawyer that this country ever boasted of. His Majesty is justified to all nations in not suffering an unhappy woman to die under persecutions when the prosecutors can only be benefited in gratifying an inveterate malice . . . Your feeling heart, I flatter myself, will enforce my plea, considering how every woman in every station who has the misfortune to survive a good husband stands exposed, and my fate may be that of every individual's wife or daughter. My dear and late Royal mistress died, as I shall, of a broke heart. His Majesty, I hope, will recollect I was a child of the Crown 21 years, being maid-of-honour, and was esteemed and honoured by His Royal father, and when faction and party unhappily divided the Royal family, I was the only person in the kingdom that was accepted and allowed at both Courts. I had His Majesty's consent, my Royal mistress's, the sentence in the Ecclesiastical Court, and the Archbishop's license, with every form of Church and State, to justify my marriage. And His Majesty and all the Royal family, and all the officers of State, wore my favors for a week. He will not surely now suffer a peeress to be disgraced with a trial, and break the heart of a most faithful and loyal subject, when every mouth will speak his praise for having rescued me from the hands of my enemies without doing an injury to any mortal.[10]

Perhaps the king, alone among all others, was focusing on the war in America: his reply, if there was one, has not survived, but nothing changed for Elizabeth. A few days later, on December 23, the king issued a royal proclamation closing the American colonies to all commerce and trade, to take effect in March 1776. This was a turning point in the war: until then, the American Congress had been unwilling to accept that King George III—as opposed to the current ministry—could be "seen as the author of our miseries." Meanwhile, Congress heard that France might support them against Britain.

Elizabeth's physicians did, however, convince the House in person that the trial must be delayed due to her health, because her memory was disordered in consequence of a fit "of a paralytic kind," and a "debility of the nervous system"[11] was impairing her faculties.

A new date was set: January 24. Next it had to be decided where, and how, she would be tried. Lord Mansfield's efforts to contain the trial within the privacy of the Lords chamber faltered in the face of those who wanted a public show in Westminster Hall, and the reality of the numbers who had to attend. The Lords were in no mood not to go to trial. The prevailing view was captured by Lord Lyttelton (a rake who had left his wife to go abroad with a barmaid), who found "the offense of so atrocious a nature as to affect civil society more than many other crimes which carried at first a blacker complexion . . . the line of peerage might be affected if such enormous crimes were suffered to go unexplored."[12] The Lord Chancellor, Lord Bathurst, felt it was "a crime of the blackest dye"[13] and suggested that only collusion had won the ecclesiastical case.

Elizabeth wrote to Portland of her horror at the prospect of Westminster Hall: "Surely you would not have your friend and the widow of your relation a public spectacle?"[14] But the Lords, and the press, were feverish about the trial. A clamoring was underway: they wanted the sport. "The tide was turned," wrote Walpole.[15] MP George Selwyn commented, "There is hardly a crime on earth for which she may not be tried . . . there is forgery, and perjuries without end; and a more complete rogue, fool and bitch I take for granted cannot be found in history than are represented by the three dramatis personae"[16]—i.e., Hervey, Kingston, and Elizabeth. The case was moved to Westminster Hall where there was room not only for all the peers, but a large audience, too. The date stalled again: the larger the scale, the more time was needed for the preparations.

The trial was deferred to February 28. The builder responsible for the seating announced it was out of the question; there was no way he could finish the job in less than five weeks. So it was moved again, to April 15. Elizabeth's one-time admirer Lord Hillsborough, who had been a disastrous Secretary of State for the Colonies,* tried to speak up on her behalf, but he was no more successful with Elizabeth's case than he was with America. He said there was no purpose other than to create a "public spectacle"; that the Jury[17] (i.e., the men who had signed the original bill) "were men of as unpleasant a cast as the refuse to human nature could produce" and, given that everyone had known about Elizabeth's marriage to the Duke of Kingston, "Why was it now arraigned, unless to answer some latent purpose?"[18] His points were all valid, but he was ignored. A public spectacle seems to be exactly what the House of Lords wanted after years of ill-tempered indecision about the American problem.

Selywn wrote with relish, "The D[uchess] of K[ingston] will afford conversation for two months, a great show for two days, and a trial for the astonishment of many years." To his friend Lord Carlisle at Castle Howard, he wrote, "You will be here for the Trial . . . It will be altogether the most extraordinary one that ever happened in this or I believe in any other country. It is a cursed, foul pool, which they are going to stir up, and how many rats, cats, and dogs, with other nuisances, will be seen floating at the top, nobody can tell. It will be as much a trial of the E[arl] of B[ristol] as of her, and in point of infamy, the issue of it will be the same, and the poor defunct Duke stand upon record as the completest Coglione†of his time."[19] He added that the Attorney General and Solicitor General had appointed that Friday for the final attempt by her lawyers to get the case thrown out.

As Selwyn predicted, this last bid for a *nolle prosequi* was turned down by Thurlow, the Attorney General. And once that had failed, there seemed to be no more options for Elizabeth, other than to stand trial.

Walpole wrote to Mann: "What this heroic lady will attempt next is very unknown. If she decamps, outlawry and forfeitures follow. Laudanum she had recourse to formerly on an emergency. If she

---

* Lord Hillsborough had authorized regular troops to suppress opposition in Boston, an act that led to the Boston massacre.
† *Coglione*: Italian swear word—fool or worse.

adheres to frenzy, she must retire to a madhouse. If she braves her fate—I shall not wonder if she escapes."[20] Flight? Suicide? Madness?

But in February, even Walpole, who had never written a kind word about Elizabeth, was mystified by the vitriol of Lord Bathurst, the Lord High Chancellor, in pursuing her. "The Earl's zeal against her was as marvellous to me as to you; I know reasons why he should have done the reverse [i.e., he could have argued the opposite and not gone ahead, as Mansfield advocated] and cannot reconcile contradictions."[21]

It was now too late to quibble. The Lord Chancellor had written to all the peers, demanding their presence; lawyers on both sides were burning candles late into the night looking up obscure precedents in dusty tomes; dressmakers were sewing tailored black silk for Elizabeth, and outfits for the many guests; carpenters were creating yard upon yard of crimson-covered seating for the hall; and the quest for tickets had already reached boiling point.

Meanwhile, the subject herself lay at home in Knightsbridge, surrounded by expensive doctors with no cure in sight for the intractable misery of her bizarre, public situation.

CHAPTER TWENTY-ONE

PRELUDE TO A TRIAL

Weeks before the trial was due to begin, peers were besieged for tickets by friends, acquaintances, tenants, and staff, for themselves and for others. The Lord Great Chamberlain, the Duke of Ancaster, another former admirer, had issued seven tickets per peer, per day, printed in different colors: day one was black, two red, three green, four yellow, five blue, each stamped to prevent forgery. The most important 350 had one "pass and repass" ticket for the entire trial. Committees had decided the seating, the security measures (a mounted guard outside), a ban on nearby carriages, and the running order of the trial. Most sought-after was a seat either in the queen and the Prince of Wales's box, or in the Duke of Newcastle's gallery, as it led through to his house, where there would be food and drink on offer. Even the most legally engaged knew that this variety of day out would be more enjoyable on a full stomach and with alcoholic fortification, in case the judges indulged their verbosity. A newspaper reported that a "kind of doorway has been made from the Duke of Newcastle's house, through a window in Westminster Hall, to his Grace's gallery on the left-hand side."[1] There was speculation that the queen, expecting her eleventh child any moment,[2] but still determined to attend, such was the draw, might come and go from here.

Unsettled, with days to go, were two matters: where should Elizabeth be held in custody? And what, exactly, should she be called? On the latter question: Chudleigh, Hervey, Kingston, Bristol? The Hon., Miss, Mrs. Duchess, Countess? References that emerged to

Elizabeth as "aka Countess of Bristol" showed that she was not regarded as innocent until proven guilty. The trial's outcome could be predicted from the tickets: "Tryal of Elizabeth Calling Herself Duchess Dowager of Kingston."

On the first question, Lord Sandwich's[3] committee had proposed that Elizabeth be held in the Tower of London if the trial lasted, as it inevitably would, more than one day. On April 2, the Duke of Portland received the following nervous missive from Kingston House: "The Duchess of Kingston's compliments to the Duke of Portland and is highly alarmed at a report in the Gazetteer of her being to be sent to the Tower. The Duchess is sorry it is there & is much surprised at the suggestion of such a thing. Recommends herself to his Grace's care this day, is for ever his most obedient servant."[4]

Nor were her nerves soothed by the Lord Chancellor's comment, that in criminal cases those convicted could have their entire estates confiscated on behalf of the Crown.

Whether it was thanks to Portland or not, two days before the trial it was decided that rather than incarcerate her in the Tower, as the Meadowses, with their unbounded malice, undoubtedly hoped, Elizabeth would stay at Kingston House in the custody of Black Rod. He, too, was an old friend, a Nottinghamshire neighbor, Sir Francis Molyneux. Many swains from her maid of honour days reappeared at the trial, gray-haired and benignly nostalgic towards the young beauty of the 1740s. Molyneux would be in charge of Elizabeth, taking her to and from Kingston House, sleeping there himself to ensure she did not abscond.

Westminster Hall had been filled with even more rows of seating than had been built for the last peer's trial, that of Lord Byron in 1765 (the poet's great-uncle).* Before the trial opened, Ancaster's servants were unbolting the doors to show where the queen might sit for a shilling a peek. Observers gazed on row upon row of crimson baize; it looked like an enormous bloodred amphitheater. The doorman collected £500.

---

* This Lord Byron, the Kingstons' Notts. neighbor at Newstead Abbey, had killed his cousin in a duel at the Star and Garter Tavern, Pall Mall, during a wine-fueled row about who had the most game on their estate.

After the publicity surrounding the Foote fight,* the trial became
the apotheosis of the *ton*, the fashionable set's chance to show off
and proselytize their superior morality at the same time. It would
be a spectacle, a circus, a feast for conversation—that Georgian
favorite, a sponge pudding of entertainment soaked with morality
sauce. Those who fed on the excesses of the *ton* saw a commercial
opportunity. As carriages full of aristocratic visitors poured in from
far-flung shires, Garrick put on a farewell run of his most surefire
hit, *Hamlet*, to tempt them in the evenings. Mrs. Cornelys, untrou-
bled by old loyalties, planned a masquerade for April 22 of "asiatic
magnificence with arcadian splendor," though she had to delay it
when the Duchess of Northumberland chose to hold an assembly
on the same night. A 60-foot decorated obelisk was put up to entice
guests into the rotunda at the Pantheon, the new assembly rooms
off Oxford Street. An enterprising publisher reissued an account
of the 1706 bigamy trial of Robert Fielding,† with prints of the
interior view, and a key of where famous people had sat. An anonymous pamphlet was sold, like a theater program, for Elizabeth's
trial; this "Ceremonial for the Trial of a Peer" showed the order
in which the peers and their attendants would arrive, illustrated
with explanatory diagrams. Elizabeth took her own precautions,
paying the Reverend William Jackson to feed her version of events
to the papers: £30 passed from her bank account into his hands on
March 25.

In spite of their eagerness to see the duchess humiliated, the
Meadows family suffered a momentary loss of confidence and let it
be known that £10,000 would settle the matter out of court. Elizabeth was advised to refuse by her lawyers, in whose financial interest
it was that the trial went ahead. One lawyer, a Serjeant Davy, on a
retainer of £20 per visit to Kingston House, changed his advice from
settling to going to trial, because he had been paid off by the other

---

* London alone had fourteen newspapers by 1790.
† Rake "Beau" Fielding married Charles II's onetime mistress Barbara Villiers,
Duchess of Cleveland, bigamously; he had already married a poor woman who
had posed as an heiress. He also had a relationship with Villiers's granddaughter.
He was found guilty of bigamy. Oddly enough, he was distantly related to
Elizabeth.

lawyers with "venison and madeira." Perhaps they really thought they could win.

The summoned witnesses were in a flurry, too. James Spearing, the attorney who had bought the marriage register on that February dawn in 1759, was now Mayor of Winchester. He found himself urgently detained abroad. Elizabeth's confidant Lord Barrington sought legal advice about whether he had to attend. Elizabeth's lawyer during the ecclesiastical court case, Dr. Arthur Collier, was conveniently, psychosomatically or not, bedridden.

Two days beforehand, tickets could be collected from the Prince's Chamber—an anteroom at Westminster Hall—or from the Lord Great Chamberlain's, the Duke of Ancaster's, house in Berkeley Square.

As the newspapers—some jovially in favor of the duchess ("why would she want two husbands? One is punishment enough!"), some against—fed the flames of anticipation, a black market in tickets sprang up. The going price was twenty guineas a ticket; one woman was said to have offered fifty. Royalty and aristocracy, such as Countess Castiglione from Milan and the Duke of Württemberg from Stuttgart, were crossing Europe to watch. Attendance had become a status symbol. The papers felt that blanket coverage was their solemn duty. The *Lady's Magazine* resolved that "the importance, the novelty of a case of this kind having excited the curiosity of every female in the kingdom . . . we thought it our duty to give them all the information they could have reaped from a ticket signed by the Lord Chancellor."[5]

The House of Commons, the House of Lords, and the rest of the British legal system was to be suspended while the trial went on, implausibly, given that, at that moment, the fate of New York City was on the brink. George Washington was setting up his headquarters in America's most prosperous city that was itself divided in its allegiances, and vulnerable to the British on the seaboard. Citizens were fleeing, replaced by soldiers.

But in London, people only talked about Elizabeth. "The whole world is occupied with the Duchess of Kingston's trial," wrote one;[6] a Prussian visitor, d'Archenholz, described it as a "festival for the whole nation," with the kind of pomp reserved for religious ceremonies in Catholic countries. He noted in amazement that it was "striking to other countries that in the midst of an unfortunate war" the country should make the "private affairs of a woman" the object of universal attention.[7]

Perhaps the strain of the American question—decisions about which were fraught with tension, with half the House of Commons advocating leniency, even liberty for the colony, and the other half wanting all-out, teach-them-a-lesson war—prompted a diverting, salacious, but less demanding kind of debate for the British psyche. Who would not rather pruriently peer over a promiscuous society upstart's past than deal with the awkward geopolitics of the day? Horace Mann asked questions about America from Florence, and Horace Walpole put him straight on London's insular priorities: you "do not know how superior fashion is in a great nation to national interests. Few people knew much of America before . . . now we forget it as if Columbus had not routed it out of the ocean."[8]

In a market competitive for detail, the London Chronicle printed the seating plan. Under that wooden hammer-beam ceiling, begun while Chaucer was alive,[9] raised seating stretched ten rows deep all the way up to the high windows. The Lords would sit in the middle, in order of precedence, their sons and wives at the side. There were private boxes for foreign ambassadors and royalty, including the king's brother, Prince Henry, the Duke of Cumberland. There were viewing galleries, just as there had been for the trial of Charles I. Westminster Hall was normally drafty, dirty, noisy, and lined with bookstalls and tradesmen, but the stud paneling had been taken down for the scaffolding that held the seating aloft, and the air was full of stench-quashing incense.[10]

With hours to go, the Duke of Ancaster banned viewings of the hall so that the workmen could finish their task. All the "constables and peace officers" within Middlesex, the City, and Westminster received commands to be outside the hall at 7 A.M. on Monday, April 15 in order to keep the peace. One colonel's guard would be mounted in Old Palace Yard and one in New Palace Yard, to ease the entrance of peers and peeresses going into the trial.

As if the trial really was a theatrical production, the Morning Post *and Daily Advertiser* complained about the flimsiness of tickets, which they found:

> ... meaner than those generally delivered for a puppet-show. On the top is the Duke of Ancaster's crest; in the body is

> TRIAL of ELIZABETH, calling herself
> Duchess Dowager of Kingston:
> ANCASTER
> Great Chamberlain

> Beneath are the Duke's arms: the whole is wretchedly engraved, and printed upon a narrow slip of paper; in short it has more the appearance of a wrapper of Hebb's best Virginia, than an admission ticket to the supreme tribunal of this great empire.[11]

On Sunday, April 14, Elizabeth received the sacrament at a service at the Chapel Royal, St. James's. She must have prayed for deliverance or divine intervention.

The Georgian era's greatest ever courtroom spectacle was about to begin.

CHAPTER TWENTY-TWO

IN WESTMINSTER HALL

DAY ONE: THE CASE FOR THE DEFENSE[1]

So it was that before dawn on the morning of April 15, 1776, the handsome middle-aged woman could be found nervously preparing herself with the help of her maid, in her intricate dressing room in Knightsbridge.

Dark clouds threatening showers hovered in the sky. We can only presume how sleepless a night frail Elizabeth had spent at Kingston House, under the intrusive eye of the "well-dressed, well-powdered"[2] Sir Francis Molyneux and the "tall beastly fellows" that were his guardsmen.[3] Strained by many weeks of illness, she collected herself and her papers, and, immaculate in her bombazine dress of black silk and black hood, climbed into an anonymous sedan chair, and set off from Kingston House at eight o'clock. She was met by the Duke of Newcastle's coach "on the road." At half past eight, he smuggled her into his house in New Palace Yard. There, she was greeted by two of the men who had stood bail for her, Lord Mount Stuart and Mr. Laroche. At ten o'clock she was taken by Newcastle and Laroche through a private door into a room prepared for her at the edge of the hall, where she waited to be called to the stand. Alongside her were a chaplain, an apothecary, a physician, and several female attendants. Dr. Warren blooded her to keep her calm. No wealth of entourage could disguise the fact that her fate was hers alone.

*

For the audience, the London air was alive with anticipation, like the day of a royal wedding or coronation. Women rose early to have their hair dressed before they secured their seats, as Mrs. Delany wrote: "The solicitude for tickets, the distress of rising early to be in time enough for a place, the anxiety about hairdressers (poor souls hurried out of their lives), mortifications that feathers and flying lappets should be laid aside for the day, as they would obstruct the view from those who sit behind—all these important matters were discussed in my little circle."[4] (Not everyone was so considerate.) Her friends met at seven and came together in a coach. Some had tickets from the Duke of Beaufort.

Eighteen-year-old Anna Porter had been with her hairdresser at five and was now waiting in a room in a coffeehouse next to Westminster Hall that Lady Bathurst, wife of the Lord High Chancellor, had taken for the whole trial. Anna was one of thirty-six people who would be sitting in Lord Bathurst's box. As breakfast was prepared, she watched the peers and peeresses alight from their carriages, their horses "full harnessed and ornamented."

Lord Bathurst, the Lord Chancellor[5] who temporarily became Lord High Steward to preside over that rare event, the trial of a peer—a peeress's trial was rarer still—entertained judges and nobility that morning at his house in Great Russell Street, "where an elegant breakfast was provided . . . his Lordships' Attendants breakfasting on cold tongue with a choice of rich wines."[6] He then set off, dressed in a gold gown, his state coach drawn by six black horses decorated with blue ribbons, with four footmen in new livery walking along on each side; the coach preceded by four painted green carriages, and a white one painted with the arms of the Bathurst family and their motto: "*Tien ta Foy*" (Steadfast Faith).

Crowds lined the roads around Westminster. Windows were let at one guinea each, so that people could watch the trail of nobility pass. So unruly was the heaving, curious mass that one onlooker was killed as he was thrust under a cart, his skull crushed.

Bluestocking Hannah More went along with Mrs. Garrick. She wrote of the "sight which, for beauty and magnificence, exceeded anything which those who were never present at a coronation, or a trial by peers, can have the least notion of. Mrs. Garrick and I were in full dress by seven. At eight we went to the Duke of Newcastle's, whose house adjoins Westminster Hall, in which he has a large gallery, communicating with the apartments in his house. You will imagine the bustle of five thousand people getting into one hall!"[7] Eight A.M. was quite restrained: some ticket-holders had arrived at three.

By nine o clock, it was reported that "peeresses, foreign ambassadors . . . had all taken their seats, and at half after ten her Majesty entered from the Duke of Newcastle's House in New Palace Yard, the center box of his Grace's gallery, which he had prepared for her and their Royal Highnesses the Prince of Wales, the Bishop of Osnaburgh [sic],* the Princess Royal, and two other young princes who accompanied her."[8]

By ten o'clock, "there was scarcely a seat that was not occupied."[9] Coffee was served through open windows on the lowest tier. Thousands of people were now crammed into the hall—one attendee estimated that there were 4,000 people there, of whom 2,500 were ladies, many wearing priceless diamonds. The sun broke through the clouds and bounced on jewels "like firelight." James Boswell "had not known there were so many fine women in the universe," their "mode of dressing, with a deal of hair and feathers and flowers more beautiful than what I had seen before."[10]

The shimmering ladies became restless. Two of them, waiting for the Lords' procession, rushed to the end of a gallery when they heard a noise and fell through a gap between the floorboards. One wrecked the elaborate hair of the woman who sat beneath, "dissipating the mock grass, flowers, fruits; uncasing the wool; and, by separation of the several component parts, showing to every beholder the simple and absurd materials which had helped to support the fabric." Her heel grazed the woman's cheek and "her bare bum squatted on a

---

* The queen came with the future George IV, then age thirteen; Prince Frederick, the Duke of York and Albany, otherwise known as the Prince-Bishop of Osnabruck, a Holy Roman Empire title with an income that went between a Protestant and a Catholic holder, twelve; Princess Charlotte, nine; Prince William, ten (future William IV); and Prince Edward (future Duke of York and Strathearn), eight.

gentleman's head." The other lady hung suspended from the gallery in midair.[11]

Guards' bayonets disheveled the hair of two other ladies as they entered; two more entangled caps in a gallery, and as their curls became entwined they started to blame the other, and had to be separated.

At 11:15, when "great impatience" had taken hold of the crowd, the procession started—in order: the Lord High Steward's domestics, the peers' eldest sons, "the Masters in Chancery; King's Serjeants, and Judges; Barons, Bishops, Viscounts, Earls, Marquesses, and Dukes; the Serjeant at Arms, the Lord High Steward, with Black Rod on his right, and Garter on his left; the Lord President and Lord Privy Seal. The Barons went to their seats . . . till the benches in the front of the Court were filled: Archbishops and Bishops to the side benches on the right, and the Dukes to the side benches from the Throne, down as far as the table."[12]

For Anna Porter, the highlight was the Lord High Steward's attendants: "twenty gentlemen walking two by two," a number of whom who were "pretty, genteel, well-dressed," and, after them, the "handsome set" of peers' eldest sons and peers' minors unrobed: these—a parade of the most eligible young men in the kingdom—were mostly "lads, some among them charming boys."

The last duke to enter the hall was the Duke of Cumberland, the king's brother, Prince Henry, now a thirty-year-old vice admiral of the white.[13]

Lord Bathurst sat on the woolsack and the Serjeant at Arms made that ill-observed proclamation for silence on pain of imprisonment, which began, "Oyez oyez oyez."[14]

The chatter dropped to a whispery hush and thousands of pairs of eyes turned as Elizabeth walked into the hall, accompanied by Black Rod, James Laroche, two elegant attendants, Mrs. Egerton and Mrs. Barrington,* the chaplain, physician, and apothecary.

---

* Mrs. Egerton was a "relation of the Duke of Bridgewater by marriage" and Mrs. Barrington was the widow of General Barrington, and Lord Barrington's sister-in-law.

A phalanx of lawyers was already waiting for her. She made a deep curtsy to the Lord High Steward, who called out "Madam, you may rise," to stop her. The peers made a slight bow in her direction.[15]

More described her appearance: "The prisoner [was] dressed in deep mourning; a black hood on her head; her hair modestly dressed and powdered; a black silk sacque, with crêpe trimmings; black gauze, deep ruffles, and black gloves, but small remains of the beauty of which kings and princes were once so enamoured ... nothing white but her face, and if it had not been for that, she looked exactly like a bale of bombazeen."*

Others were kinder. One newspaper reported that not only was Elizabeth "magnificently dressed," but that "she sat with the calmness and dignity of innocence, and all admitted that she looked more like a Queen surrounded by obedient subjects than a woman over whom was impending a disgraceful judgment." George III's chaplain Beilby Porteus, future Bishop of London, thought Elizabeth "very becoming," although "she looked very pale and a good deal agitated as well she might, with the first view of so tremendous a court; but she soon recovered herself."[16] Anna Porter admired her "long black hood most becomingly put on ... it came down in a point before to her forehead ... exactly the headdress of Mary Queen of Scots sold in the old pictures ... her aspect was unconcerned, seemingly unaffectedly so—she really looked handsome."†

The Lord High Steward instructed the Clerk of the Crown to read the indictment found by the grand jury for the county of Middlesex,[17] "which sets forth, that Elizabeth, Duchess of Kingston, indicted by the name of Elizabeth Hervey, wife of Augustus John Hervey, did, on the eighth of March, in the ninth of his present Majesty, marry the late Evelyn Pierrepont, Duke of Kingston, deceased, at the church of St. George's, Hanover Square, she being then the wife of the said Hervey, who is now living, and they likewise found

---

* Bombazeen, or bombazine, was a matte fabric, used for mourning.
† Mary Stuart was a romantic figure at the time and there was a lively market in portraits of her, in which she always wore her black cap.

that she was married to her said first husband Augustus John Hervey, on the 4th of August, in the 17th of the late King, at the parish of Medstone in the county of Southampton."

The Lord High Steward explained the offense, with a homily about how destructive the crime of bigamy was "to the peace and well-being of society, how hateful in the sight of God, and how much it behoved [Elizabeth] to manifest her own innocence against so heavy and criminal a charge." The Clerk of the Crown asked if she was guilty or not guilty to the felony whereof she was indicted, to which Elizabeth declared, "Not guilty, my Lords," with much bravura.

It did not bode well that she was indicted under the name of Elizabeth Hervey—it seemed to be a show trial, in every sense. But her lawyers, Mr. Wallace, Mr. Mansfield,[18] Dr. Calvert, and Dr. Wynne, had a strategy: to stop the trial before it began. Mr. Wallace claimed that overturning an ecclesiastical court ruling, even when there had been fraudulent evidence, was unprecedented in British law. Oddly, one example to be ruminated over concerned Augustus's uncle, "mad" Thomas Hervey, pursued for his wife's debts. If the findings of the ecclesiastical court were not respected, Wallace argued, it would be chaos. It sounded a little sparse. Anna Porter wrote that although he was "universally admired" and made the "most of a bad cause," "his manner [was] unpleasing." There was a "heat and vehemence in his manner that rather fatigues than strikes the hearers." The lawyers were reviewed as if they were on stage at Drury Lane.

Elizabeth had adopted the right demeanor on the first day: a balance of humility and dignity. A woman who had triumphed across the courts of Europe—and observed numberless accused in the dock at Bow Street Magistrates' Court—knew how to conduct herself. The London Evening Post reported, "the Duchess behaved with the spirit of a heroine. She was dignified without arrogance, collected without audacity, and humble." Mr. Dunning, for the prosecution, on the other hand had a "manner insufferably bad . . . coughing and spitting at every few words."[19] The voice of Thurlow, the Attorney General, was like "rolling, murmuring thunder." Anna was mesmerized by him—he had "such a tongue! And such sensible eyes! That he may plead any cause to a lady!"*

Elizabeth brought forward a piece of paper, her plea of justification—the sentence of the ecclesiastical court that had ruled her free to marry the Duke of Kingston, Hervey having been unable to prove he had married her. Her lawyer, Wallace, claimed it was "a bar to all indictments to the felony with which the prisoner stood charged." Lots of heads were shaken, possibly the odd snort. Mr. Mansfield spoke, confusing everyone; Dr. Calvert followed, speaking for two long and winding hours in her favor. And then Dr. Wynne, with more cases in which the judgment of the ecclesiastical court had prevailed. Anna Porter said Calvert's voice drawled on like "opiates." Wynne, at least, was "spirited."

The more precisely Elizabeth's lawyers argued in favor of the spiritual court, the more the society crowd wilted. The spectacle was "awful, and splendid beyond imagination," but it had not dawned on most of them that, having traveled for hours to London in shaking carriages, had hair dressed at great expense, and put their diamonds on by candlelight, they would be sitting through byzantine argument about legal precedent. There was one recap—a flicker of hope, some mention of carnal knowledge in Conduit Street—but pickings of saucy patrician gossip were skeletal on day one. Those in the Duke of Newcastle's gallery, including Hannah More, fell on the "very fine cold collation of all sorts of meats and wines, with tea, etc" and, as More noticed, some, such as Lady Derby and the Duchess of Devonshire,[20] displayed "villainous appetites of eating and drinking."[21]

At six, Lord Gower, politician, Kingston's cousin, asked for an adjournment. Elizabeth left the hall, attended by Molyneux.

Mrs. Delany's friends arrived for dinner three and a half hours late, and they devoured muttonchops, lamb pie, lobster, and apple puffs, alongside the day's events. The only drama had involved

---

* Thurlow, Tory, vehement opponent to the American cause (and anti-abolitionist), had at least three illegitimate children. He had made his name in another ducal battle, between the 7th Duke of Hamilton (son of Elizabeth's admirer and Elizabeth Gunning) and Archibald Douglas over the estate of the 1st Duke of Douglas, a dramatic, long-drawn-out case that split public opinion in the 1760s.

Mrs. Barrington, "so fatigued by standing" that she was "seized with violent hysterics, and continued indisposed for a considerable time."[22] All agreed that Elizabeth had acquitted herself well.

Diarists and newspapers were in accord that at the end of day one, the crowd was on the side of the accused. The *Morning Post* reported that Elizabeth "commanded general admiration, strongly indicating that conscious innocence which she avowed to be her state."[23] D'Archenholz wrote to Frederick the Great that Elizabeth's "calm and noble countenance gained her all hearts although the law was not in her favor."[24] Beilby Porteus observed her "great composure and decency."[25]

Even Horace Walpole was won over, writing:

> The doubly noble prisoner went through her part with unusual admiration . . . instead of her usual ostentatious folly and clumsy pretensions to cunning, all her conduct was decent, even seemed natural. Her dress was entirely black and plain, her attendants not too numerous, her dismay at first perfectly unaffected. A few tears balanced cheerfulness, and the presence of mind and attention never deserted her. This and the pleadings of her counsel carried her triumphantly through the first day and turned the stream very much in her favor.[26]

The only thing he queried was her age: she was claiming to be fifty, when his recollections of her in Chelsea meant he knew she must be at least fifty-five. (He was right. She had deducted five years; perhaps because it made her first wedding underage.) What rotten luck to have a childhood playmate become London's most persnickety diarist.

Elizabeth was always a divisive character. Even though she was vilified by the sharpest end of society, she had public support and great loyalty from some of those who knew her. Even when her story was out—mostly thanks to Samuel Foote—newspaper readers were sophisticated enough to realize that he was a scurrilous, opportunist blackmailer. In this case she was, like America's rebels, the plucky underdog. If a deceitful duchess attracted hostility, the sight of the entire aristocracy gathered against one aging, ailing widow was just as repellent. People were urging her on, particularly as she presented herself with such quiet decorum on the first day, in contrast to the condemnatory, talkative, unassailable characters so used to getting their way—in the courtroom, in America. There was a whiff of hypocrisy about them, too: moral opining from men with mistresses and hereditary positions.

Most of the audience were now in the prisoner's favor. But not all. There were several peeresses who wanted nothing good for their "sister." Lady Harrington—Lady Caroline FitzRoy of the Leicester House set who had once set her cap at the Duke of Kingston—wrote: "The Devil confound her! How brazen the wretch looks!"[27] Her husband, however, sent Elizabeth flowers and a supportive letter. All those years ago, she had written his father a letter from Leicester House at the bidding of Frederick, Prince of Wales, asking to be made secretary of war.

A fashion feast weighed down by a few speeches was how the *General Evening Post* summed up day one: "The ladies seemed to outvie each other in the richness of their dresses and the brilliancy of their ornaments; among whom none was more distinguished than the Duchess of Cumberland[28] . . . The trial of a Peer is certainly one of the most splendid spectacles which can be formed by the human imagination; but it is one of the dullest also." Most of the audience could not hear much, so that "when the eye has been satiated by the magnificence of the scene, the spirits immediately flag, curiosity gives way to languor, and in a little time people discover that the fatigue is by much too high a price for the gratification."[29] No wonder the *St. James's Chronicle* focused on the visual impact: "Imagination can hardly picture a more solemn, august, and at the same time brilliant appearance, than the court in Westminster Hall cut yesterday."[30]

However perplexing some of the arguments were, London concurred that it was the only topic worthy of conversation. The *Gentleman's Magazine* admitted that "the importance of the above trial, and our desire to gratify our readers with the substance of it at once, has obliged us to postpone the Account of American Affairs."[31] Walpole wrote to Mann, who had asked him about military matters: "You may think of America, if you please, but we think and talk but of one subject, the solemn comedy that is acting in Westminster Hall."[32]

Elizabeth went back to Knightsbridge, attended by Molyneux. Walpole heard that there was some altercation between the two of them that night and that she "carried him into another room [and] showed him a hole in the ceiling, or wainscot, made by a pistol-ball . . . she used to terrify the Duke of Kingston in that manner with threatening to murder him or herself."[33] Whether that story was true or not, she must have spent the night in a state of miserable agitation; the contrast between her plight and the celebratory behavior of the diamond-decked crowd that evening could not have been more acute.

Day Two: The Case for the Prosecution

On Tuesday, the 16th, some guests, including the queen, had decided that they had seen enough. Tickets were given away, traded, advertised in newspapers. But so keen were the crowds to come in that the hall again filled up noisily to its rafters. At half past nine, Elizabeth was at the Bar once more. It was the prosecution's turn. According to More, Elizabeth scribbled throughout: "She imitated her great predecessor, Mrs. Rudd [a woman who had just sensationally been acquitted of fraud], and affected to write very often, though I plainly perceived she only wrote as they do their love epistles on the stage, without forming a letter."[34]

Thurlow, the Attorney General, professed himself "astonished" at the line the defense had taken. He would, he said, have been ashamed to present such a case for a client. Indeed, it was strange—perhaps they felt it was hopeless—that rather than portray Elizabeth as innocent, the defense rested on the previous judgment of another court which clearly, given the effort and expense undertaken, was not going to be validated. Thurlow argued that in not insisting on Elizabeth's innocence, her lawyers were admitting "every species and color of guilt within the compass of the indictment," and instructed that: "Your Lordships will therefore take the hateful crime to be proved . . . the first marriage solemnly celebrated, perfectly consummated; the second wickedly brought about by concerted fraud." He said that as the first judgment was collusive (i.e., he claimed that Hervey had agreed not to dispute the jactitation clause), the fact that one court had already been deceived only aggravated the crime. The idea that the ecclesiastical court judgment could not be questioned was feeble. Elizabeth's lawyers' arguments were "frivolous" and time-wasting.[35] Anna Porter found him "most entertaining": "his manner, voice, address, command attention . . . his strength of reasoning, justness of argument, propriety to language, demand applause." He maintained "uniform constant superiority."

He was followed by others for the prosecution—the Solicitor General, Alexander Wedderburn, a Dr. Harris, both keen to show the superiority of the civil courts and demonstrate why the defense's key case, which rested on a will dispute, was irrelevant. Ecclesiastical court rulings of jactitation were, in fact, "ludicrous," argued the Solicitor General; what was to stop a man having seventy-five wives if the court could rule marriages in and out so easily? The Earl of Bristol could unmarry and then marry the lady at the Bar again, he said, though that was hardly likely! "What use for this sarcasm?" wrote Anna Porter, sensing misogyny in the air. Horace Walpole noted that it was as much a "trial of the Ecclesiastical Court as of the prisoner" and may, "at least ought to, produce a reform of that Papish tribunal."[36] It was inconceivable that the peers would judge themselves unable to match the ecclesiastical court in wisdom and authority—a court rarely decides its own decision is not the superior one. They eventually agreed the inevitable: that the ecclesiastical court's judgment was not binding to the House of Lords. They had the right to try the case.

Elizabeth visibly buckled under the stress. For the most vitriolic critics, such as More, she was acting and had "performed badly." But Lord Camden* noticed her fragile state and as the Lords also wanted to adjourn, while she was being bled again, they took a vote on whether to give her a couple of days to recover. They voted eighty to fifty-nine not to resume until Friday.

---

* Charles Pratt, 1st Earl Camden, lawyer, judge, Whig, generally opposed to any harsh measures in America, as many Whigs were (Tories tended to favor a harder line).

The *New Daily Advertiser* reported that Elizabeth looked "extremely indisposed."[37] The prosecution had spoken well, and her morale was ebbing away. She was being bled a cup at a time to stay calm. For the overwrought, it could supposedly have a sedative effect.

During the two days' break, in which she was meant to be recovering her health, Elizabeth was with her lawyers.[38] When she was seen in the street, a huge crowd wished her "happy deliverance of her case." However censorious the aristocracy were, the crowd warmed to her—this demonstrative, imperfect antiheroine, with her eccentricity, her courage, the stories that always followed her. The British public could see that, in spite of the splendor and robes, there was no fair play about Elizabeth's trial, with its financial motive and its attempt to put birthright over romantic love. She knew that, too. Secretly, she was making financial arrangements with her solicitor on the presumption she was not going to win.

The hiatus left two days for the resumption of the real business of the era—discussions about how to handle the war in America. It is a peculiar fact that many of those peers most intimately involved in Elizabeth's trial were just as closely connected to the conundrum of independence. Every peer who spoke at the trial—whether they gave evidence, or asked a question—was also emotionally invested in the debate about the American war, put on hold for Elizabeth.

Less than two months earlier, it was Thurlow and Wedderburn who had drafted the strict instructions under which Admiral Howe (brother of a former swain of Elizabeth's, and of a witness to come, the Hon. Sophia Fettiplace) could negotiate with America. The instructions were tempered by Lord Mansfield, but Howe felt they were too restrictive to win peace; the changes he asked for had to wait until after Elizabeth's trial.[39] The Duke of Richmond, who asked the witnesses several questions, was the "radical duke," the field marshal and former Secretary of State who supported the colonists. Lord Lyttelton, a reprobate peer turned moralizer for Elizabeth's trial, felt Britain had not been aggressive early enough. Lord Camden wanted peace, as the British soldiers were suffering from scurvy, frostbite, and lack of food. Lord Denbigh favored an embargo, Lord Grosvenor a standing army over there. Lord Weymouth was Secretary of State for the Southern Department. Lord Hillsborough had been a much-hated (by the Americans) Secretary of State for the Colonies, to whom he opposed all concessions. Lord Barrington—witness to come—had antagonized the Americans when he was Secretary of State for the Colonies, and was now Secretary of State for War. Even the Lord High Steward himself, Lord Bathurst, was implicit in the problem. He had written one of the "Intolerable Acts" that banned trade out of Boston after the tea party and pushed America into war in the first place. Fettiplace's other brother was leading the troops in America alongside Sir Henry Clinton, the latter raised to high command through the efforts of his cousin, Elizabeth's friend the Duke of Newcastle. (The war would also see two younger Meadows brothers, and one younger Hervey, fight too.)

As the *Evening Post* reported on the days that the trial had stalled, money was urgently needed for the fighting; a lottery and a new tax were announced. News from America was slow, circuitous, and invariably baleful. The trial—with its themes of sexual intrigue among courtiers and aristocrats—was more immediately arresting.

DAY THREE: THURLOW'S VERSION OF ELIZABETH'S LIFE, AND THE FIRST WITNESS

Days one and two were about jurisdiction and precedent. Day three, Friday, April 19, contained something far more alarming: Elizabeth's story, as told by the booming figure who had become her antagonist, the Attorney General Thurlow, and the appearance of various witnesses. Elizabeth was brought to the Bar on Friday morning to hear her life narrated back to her through the prism of the prosecution. The thousands of spectators had been refreshed by the halt in the proceedings, and were eager for more.

First of all her lawyers, Wallace and Calvert, had the chance to respond to the prosecutors. They argued at some length that a jactitation was the same as nullity—any first wedding had been canceled—and insisted again that the ecclesiastical court could not be overruled by the Lords. They were wasting words: no amount of quibbling about legalities was going to save Elizabeth, for whom everything was about to fall apart.

The Attorney General Thurlow painted a picture as dark as a hell by Hieronymus Bosch. He thundered through the hall that bigamy corrupted the purity of domestic life, loosened the connections that bound together the moral order, and, worst of all, might create "civil disorder, especially in a country where the title to great honour and high office is hereditary"; in other words, bigamy could confuse and corrupt aristocratic bloodlines and inheritance. He knew his audience: at this sentence, there was a "great uproar behind the bar," and the Serjeant at Arms had to make another proclamation for silence. Anna Porter thought Thurlow "masterly." He "shone" and had an air of infallibility. "No man was ever as wise as Thurlow looks," said Charles James Fox.*

With caustic certainty, Thurlow stated that Elizabeth's marriage to Kingston was all about money, and that her motive aggravated her crime. He allowed no possibility of love from her: "Dry lucre was the whole inducement, cold fraud the only means to perpetrate that crime." He, of course, had not seen all that anguished care on the sickbed, the tender concern, the dreadful loss. He then summed up much of Elizabeth's life in his rumbling voice, from her arrival in London in 1740.

He related some of the history we know in three episodes, all presented in the most unfavorable light. The first was meeting and marrying, at eighteen, the seventeen-year-old "boy" Hervey, at Lainston, and keeping it secret to preserve her salary and because his family would object (in fact, Elizabeth was twenty-three, Hervey twenty). Hervey's sailing to the West Indies, their falling-out, and—a revelation to most in the hall, both distressing and damning—the birth and death of their baby. (How slight could a marriage be if it produced a child?) Then, the second episode, which made her look even more guilty: the retro-creation of the register on the Reverend Thomas Amis's deathbed in Winchester, in February 1759, which Thurlow claimed was because of the then

---

* The Whig statesman, reformer, and later ally of the Prince of Wales was an enemy of Thurlow (who was anti-reform, anti-American, and an ally of George III).

Earl of Bristol's ill health. He recounted what had happened to that register afterwards. Mr. Merrill had inadvertently lent it to the Reverend Stephen Kinchin, Amis's successor, when his aunt Hanmer died in 1764; when Merrill died in 1767, Mr. Bathurst, husband of Merrill's daughter Mary, returned it to Kinchin, who transcribed Merrill's death below Hanmer's, and kept it. Credibility, compassion, and salvation were slipping away from Elizabeth with every word Thurlow spoke. Why would she have asked for a register to be made of a marriage that had not happened? This news surely undermined her case.

The third period consisted of Hervey's request for a divorce via, Thurlow claimed, Ann Craddock in 1768. This was the first, ominous mention of Aunt Hanmer's maid. As for Elizabeth's response to Hervey—the jactitation—"a grosser artifice, I believe, was never fabricated," said Thurlow. Craddock's evidence was never heard, he said, and the story of the marriage moved from Lainston church to Merrill's house in order to make it sound less legitimate. (Here is a clear example of Thurlow's twisting of the facts: as the chapel was on the drive, this was the same thing.) Why did Mr. Craddock, but not his wife, give evidence to the ecclesiastical court, asked Thurlow, concluding that the Duke of Kingston had married Elizabeth because of a faulty verdict, and that her lawyers were as much to blame as she was.

It was later said that Thurlow's treatment of Elizabeth was marked "both by bad taste and cruelty."[40] He seemed to be fighting not against bigamy, but for an overturning of the Duke of Kingston's will. The prosecution lawyers were brazenly hypocritical with their pious speeches about money; honors, pensions, sinecures were all for sale, and all grabbed with enthusiasm by that bench. The prosecution's Dunning, for example, received a peerage and pension for being Solicitor General, even though he only held the role for three months. Nor, incidentally, were Thurlow and Dunning's love lives without blemish, as the tête-à-tête scandal column in the *Town and Country Magazine* illuminated. In 1772 they ran a piece about Thurlow, "the amorous advocate and the Temple Toast": he had three illegitimate daughters by Polly Humphries, owner's daughter and barmaid at Nando's coffeehouse in Fleet Street (and an illegitimate son by the Dean of Canterbury's daughter). In 1774, it was Dunning's turn, with a "Miss Lucy C-n," the headline: "the prostitute and the powerful pleader."[41]

Thurlow's one-sided narrative unfolded, for most for the first time, the startling disclosures of the impetuous late-night wedding, the baby's birth and death, the deathbed register, and the peculiar jactitation suit.* His low voice seemed to crystallize rumor into truth.

But the pivotal moment in the drama that day was the arrival of the first witness, an incongruous figure in the august setting, populated with the noblest families and most exquisite jewels in the land. The "old superannuated waiting woman," sole living witness to the wedding, Ann Craddock—there at Lainston so many years ago, and loyal to Aunt Hanmer for many more—stepped forth in the darkness of the hall and made her way to the Bar.

Elizabeth's Mr. Wallace asked her the first, vital question: was she being paid to testify? She denied it.

Her testimony took the hall back thirty years, to when the disconsolate duchess, now with so many eyes on her, and the Earl of Bristol, rumored to be hiding out somewhere in Paris (whose absence at the trial is read out, along with the other missing peers, every morning), were an astoundingly beautiful young couple—Lieutenant Hervey and Miss Chudleigh—who had just fallen for each other.

Craddock told how she witnessed the wedding conducted "by the Common Prayer Book," and Hervey and Elizabeth "put to bed" until Aunt Hanmer insisted on them getting up again; how she saw them in bed the morning Hervey left at 5 A.M., because she was the one who had to wake him; "they were very sorry to take leave." She knew it was August 1744, because HMS *Victory* was anchored at Portsmouth and, in the Lainston garden, the greengages, of which the pair were "very fond," were ripe. That Elizabeth—"the lady at the Bar"—had told her she would take her to see her child, a boy, "and like Mr. Hervey." That the boy was born at Chelsea because the late Mrs. Chudleigh could not go there as her son and husband were buried there; that Elizabeth had told her "in great grief" that

---

* Jactitation, a reminder: a suit brought by the wounded party against a person falsely asserting marriage to them.

the child had died. As Craddock spoke, a shocked silence stilled the hall, punctuated by gasps and intakes of breath.

A "piqued, vexed"[42] Wallace then took over the questioning: was Craddock *quite* sure she was not being paid? Lord Buckingham reminded her she was under oath, and the Duke of Grafton and Lord Townshend pressed the point before the skilful Lord Hillsborough had a breakthrough. He forced her to admit that John Fozard, the livery keeper, had promised her a "sinecure" in a letter—clearly from Evelyn Meadows—and that she had shown the letter to Augustus Hervey, Elizabeth being abroad. (Presumably she wanted to see if he—or Elizabeth—would be more generous than Evelyn Meadows.) She said showing it to Hervey was as good as showing it to Elizabeth, as they were "man and wife." Just as her motive was becoming apparent, darkness fell, and the court was adjourned.

Lord Denbigh interjected, declaring that if they adjourned yet again he would forget the whole darn lot. Another peer—the only one to do so during the course of the trial—said that he was offended that the business of the whole nation, the American question, should be neglected on account of an individual. He was so discounted his name does not even survive the accounts of the trial, in the way that Denbigh's did.

There was no consensus on Craddock's testimony. Rival camps were briefing rival papers: "Ann Craddock showed no symptoms of prevarication," reported the *Morning Chronicle*; "Ann Craddock gave evasive answers," reported the generally pro-Elizabeth *Morning Post.*

These rival camps were paying them, too. Two years later it emerged that the *Morning Post*'s editor, Mr. Bate, had extorted money out of Elizabeth (and other women) in exchange for favorable coverage.* As the Meadowses certainly nurtured their own "friendly" papers, there was a parallel battle by newspaper. It was

---

* In September 1778, the *General Advertiser and Morning Intelligencer* accused Mr. Bate, editor of the *Morning Post*, of making £800 a year by threatening to expose "women of fashion," including Elizabeth. Bate had been paid, it was claimed, not to run negative articles about Elizabeth during her trial, and he distributed money to other newspapers too for doing the same. In an exchange of letters, the Reverend William Jackson confirmed Bate's guilt.

already a circulation war. Then, as now, readers believed whatever they wanted to believe, supported by the full force of all their unconscious (and conscious) prejudices.

"The plot thickens," Horace Walpole wrote, as "was produced the capital witness [Craddock], the ancient damsel who was present at her first marriage and tucked her up for consumption."[43]

Day Four: Witnesses on the Stand

Just as Ann Craddock was about to continue her testimony on Saturday, April 20, it emerged that Lord Lyttelton had arranged for a burly constable to stand between accused and witness because it was said that Elizabeth had been "making great play with frowns" at her aunt's maid, motioning at her. Lord Derby prompted Craddock to reveal that Elizabeth had offered her a pension if she moved north, to Yorkshire, Derbyshire, or Northumberland, but that she had refused as she would have missed her friends. Asked to recall the timing of the offer, it was obvious this was in response to the duke's death. Lords Coventry, Buckingham, Townshend, Camden, and Lyttelton all questioned Craddock, and old swain the Duke of Ancaster himself spoke, to ask about Fozard's "sinecure" letter. An insight into Craddock's hand-to-mouth, downtrodden life was provided by Lord Fortescue, who asked her how she had lived since her husband's death: "With what I made off my furniture which was in my house, which was all new." Like Elizabeth in extremis, like Mrs. Cornelys, Craddock lived in fear of the breadline, and now the disparity in status between Craddock and Elizabeth was painfully apparent. Everyone could see that she was an eminently bribable witness. But did that mean she was not telling the truth?

Next on the stand was another visitor from the past—the royal physician, Caesar Hawkins.[44] This reserved, professional man provided another variant in the cast to the unfortunate Craddock and the privileged peers themselves. As he was extremely reluctant to speak because of medical confidentiality (as well as a sense of gentlemanly honor), Lord Mansfield intervened to see off another adjournment. The request of a court, declared Mansfield, super-

seded a doctor's necessity to keep confidences.* Hawkins, now
sixty-five, said that both Hervey and Elizabeth had told him they
were married; that he had destroyed his papers and therefore could
not remember when the child was born, but it was on a street near
"Chelsea College." The marriage and birth were secret. He then told
how he became a go-between for the pair. One day he had bumped
into Hervey on a London street, who had asked him to visit him at
home; that Hervey asked him to relay to Elizabeth that he had the
proofs for divorce and did not wish to mix "malice or ill-temper" in
the course of it, but wanted to act "on the line of a man of honour."

Via Hawkins, Elizabeth had replied that she thanked Hervey for
the "polite parts of his message" but did not acknowledge him to be
her legal husband and would be pursuing a jactitation of marriage
instead. Hervey was "affected and struck by it," saying nothing for
two or three minutes, and then that he "did not conceive he should
have his equal freedom by that method." The doctor added that,
in recent weeks, Hervey had expressed his annoyance at the recent
reappearance of Craddock: if she could not remember then, why
now? This reaction, unless artificial on Hervey's part, of course
undermined the collusion theory.

Hawkins recounted what was probably the most accurate version
of Elizabeth's take on her marriage to Hervey: she had told him
once, when she had had to swear on oath that she was unmarried
during the jactitation suit, that "the ceremony as done was such a
scrambling, shabby business and so much incomplete that she should
have been full as unwilling to have taken a positive oath that she
was married as that she was not married." It was for precisely such
uncertainties that the 1753 Marriage Act had been introduced. (As
Pulteney suggested the act, it may have been because of Elizabeth's
situation.)

Nevertheless, Hawkins understood it was a "real marriage": he
had witnessed the birth—though he could not recall who delivered
the baby—and saw the infant later when asked to examine him by
Elizabeth.

Next on the stand was Elizabeth's friend, the Hon. Sophia Char-

---

* Changing British law in the process; legality supersedes the Hippocratic oath.

lotte Fettiplace, from true Hanoverian stock: her grandmother was "the Elephant": the half sister and supposed mistress of George I. Fettiplace said only that she had heard Elizabeth talk—once—of being married to Hervey "in Hampshire, in a summerhouse, in a garden." That was it. From a family of courtiers, her mother had been Augusta's lady of the bedchamber; one brother was naval commander in the American war; another, General William Howe, head of land forces there; their elder brother, killed in war two decades earlier, had been an admirer of Elizabeth's.

Following Fettiplace was the statesman Lord Barrington, secretary of war, hard liner against the American rebels, in ultimate charge of the army there, to whom General Howe answered. As a friend of Elizabeth, he declared that a man of honor could not betray anything told him in confidence.

When she heard that honorable comment, Elizabeth—who had largely been silent throughout the witness testimonies—suddenly intervened and, to the backdrop of a thrilled hush, spoke up. She said:

I do release my Lord Barrington from every obligation of honor. I wish, and earnestly desire, that every witness who may be examined may deliver their opinions in every point justly, whether for me or against me. I came from Rome at the hazard of my life to surrender myself to this court. I bow with submission to every decree, and do not even complain that an ecclesiastical sentence has been deemed of no force, although such a sentence has never been controverted during the space of one thousand four hundred and seventy-five years.

Her words made an impression on everyone. London's antiheroine had the crowd in the palm of her hand again.

Barrington responded jubilantly, "I do solemnly declare to your Lordships that her Grace's generosity is entirely spontaneous, and of her own accord." But, he wavered, should not such generosity of hers make him even more hesitant to speak, he asked? The Duke of Richmond suggested he should not betray private conversations, but stick to facts. Lord Mansfield delayed the issue by hearing other witnesses while Barrington was thinking; prosecuting counsel lost heart and sought to withdraw him. But Lords Lyttelton, Camden, and Radnor did not want to let him off. The court adjourned to discuss what to do about this "honorable" refusal. They decided he must answer.

In the end, all he said was that he had heard of an engagement "of a matrimonial kind" many years ago, "whether it amounted to a legal marriage or not I am not lawyer or civilian enough to judge." Did he know anything of any bond or payment of costs concerning suppression of witnesses? He most certainly did not.

The last important witness raised the specter of the morning at the Blue Boar Inn: a humble woman powered by fury and revenge. It was Judith Phillips, widow of the Reverend Thomas Amis who had performed the service at Lainston. In excruciating detail, she recalled the creation of the register by her husband's bedside in Winchester that February morning seventeen years ago. That Elizabeth had said it might be "a hundred thousand pounds her way"; that she had told her that the baby, a boy, had died. How she herself delivered the register to Mr. Merrill, and Elizabeth had asked her to keep it secret when they subsequently talked in the garden of Chudleigh House; how once, out fishing, Elizabeth had told her Mrs. Bathurst (John Merrill's daughter) had "used her very ill," keeping her papers (the register) from her. That in Arlington Street she had said of herself, "Was it not very good-natured of the Duke to marry an old maid?"

Elizabeth's lawyer Mr. Mansfield would not let Phillips's testimony rest there. Where was Judith Phillips living? In Bristol. Was her second husband fired by the Duke of Kingston, or not? No, His Grace cooled on him and he resigned. It transpired that she was staying at the Turf Coffee House in St. James's with her husband and, though she denied it, the bill was obviously being paid for by Evelyn Meadows, whom she had met through the livery keeper John Fozard. The Turf Coffee House was an establishment for equestrians: the scheme clearly Fozard's. No one could corroborate any of her evidence—with the Reverend Thomas Amis being dead, it was Judith alone who remembered things like "one hundred thousand pounds coming my way." She recalled, curiously, that when she was in Elizabeth's garden with an inflammation in her eye, Elizabeth was "exceedingly kind" and ordered a boiled egg to be laid on it. That, at least, sounded so odd it must have been true.

The prosecution's Mr. Dunning pointed out that they could not talk to the other living witness at the register scene, Mr. Spearing: "He, though Mayor of Winchester, is now found to be amusing himself somewhere or other beyond the sea, God knows where."

Elizabeth's Mr. Wallace had one more question for Mrs. Phillips. Did she recognize her own handwriting? She nodded. A letter was handed to her, part of an exchange between the Phillipses and the Duke and Duchess of Kingston.

> My Lady Duchess,
> ... permit me most humbly to entreat Your Grace's kind
> intercession with my Lord Duke to continue Mr. Phillips his
> steward ... in return the remainder of our lives shall be passed
> in gratitude and duty.

It sounded like—it *was*—a threat. The Attorney General read two more: on November 7, 1771, Mr. Phillips, at Holme Pierrepont, wrote to Kingston at Newmarket: "... am much concerned to lately observe your Grace's displeasure ... permit my delivering up the charge of your Grace's affairs." He wrote that Elizabeth had promised him a "settlement." Did they blame the duchess for the dismissal, or at least the non-reinstatement? Kingston bluntly wrote back, "After what has passed there is no occasion for many words."

The Attorney General believed this proved that Mrs. Phillips's claim—that her husband resigned—was true. But it also demonstrated the resentment they harbored against Elizabeth, whom they imagined was behind the freezing of relations (she was not: it was Phillips's treatment of tenants that was to blame). Judith Phillips had been exposed as one of the Fozard/Meadows' posse of "low mechanics, hackney coachmen and ale-house keepers"[45] who had been bribed to present some artful, impossible-to-disentangle, blend of truth and falsehood. Phillips's motives: revenge and money. Elizabeth's failure to keep Judith on her side showed that she had never been safe. Only death, or payment and goodwill forever could silence the testimony of these inconvenient witnesses. When it came to her secrets, honor and discretion would only come from those who could afford them, survival being, as Elizabeth was fond of writing, the first law of nature.

Even when it was transparent that witnesses had been paid and were embellishing their stories, it still sounded damning for Elizabeth, particularly that register created, Thurlow insisted, as Augustus stood ready to become an earl. It dawned on Elizabeth that the odds were stacking against her by the hour. Fatigue, fear, and shock precipitated a loss of control. Elizabeth had a "hysterical fit," was carried out unconscious, bled, returned to calm, and stayed until the court was finally adjourned at 7 P.M. (In a faint, bleeding is the worst thing to do: the heart slows and blood pressure must be raised, not lowered. But no one knew that then.)

In spite of this (or rather, because its editor had been paid off) on Monday, April 22, the *Public Advertiser* defended her: "The whole splendid circle of nobility and gentry on Saturday last in Westminster Hall, says a correspondent, seemed to admire the conduct and behavior of the Duchess of Kingston. Her Grace was particularly attentive to the pleadings, &c. and showed herself mistress of that fortitude and serenity so peculiar to great minds under affliction." (The latest gossip from Kingston House was that the previous night, Sir Francis Molyneux had woken with a start thinking Elizabeth had scarpered, and charged out of his bedroom, in just a nightshirt, shouting. A housemaid advised him to dress and took him to see Elizabeth to calm him down.)

But one attendee on Friday, although overawed by the "grandest sight I have ever seen, or expect to see" in the "largest room in the kingdom," the "whole court within covered with crimson," so many people of the first rank that the town of Torrington would not be big enough to hold them, the peeresses covered with diamonds and some of the ladies' heads "a yard high," and at the center of it all, the pitiful prisoner, "dressed in deep mourning," finished his report with the words: "I suppose you will, from the progress of the trial, conclude with us that she will be found guilty."[46]

Not everyone could keep such focus. A newspaper reported that an elderly lady, sitting behind the peeresses and their daughters, "fell asleep, owing to fatigue; and it was with some difficulty she was awaked when the august tribunal broke up."[47]

DAY FIVE: ELIZABETH'S SPEECH, AND THE VERDICT

On Monday, April 22, it was Elizabeth's chance to speak. According to Anna Porter, she was clutching "13 sheets of law paper." She was calm, eloquent, and convinced of her own narrative.

She began in the same vein as she had written to Foote: "My words will flow freely from my heart, adorned simply with innocence and truth." She asked for the protection of their lordships in the absence of her husband, appealed to their "logic" for her "fame and honour." She described her family as "ancient, not ignoble," a tribe of virtuous women and men of valor, the last of the line, Sir John Chudleigh, dying at eighteen at Ostend rather than offering his ensign to a French soldier. ("We are all descended from Adam and Eve, what of it?" scribbled Anna Porter in her notebook.)

Was it not cruel that she was being treated as a criminal for an action [her marriage to Kingston] sanctioned by His Majesty the King, her late mistress the Dowager Princess of Wales, and the ecclesiastical court? She quoted Blackstone, the legal tome, "whose works are as entertaining as they are instructive."

And if it was fair to overturn a previous judgment, why was it not done "during the five years your prisoner was received and acknowledged the undoubted and unmolested wife of the late Duke of Kingston?" Bigamy law, she reminded them, was designed for people who ran away abroad, had more children, and pretended they had not been married before; not for those who had won jactitation suits. If she could be prosecuted, how would those peers protect their own "widows and daughters" from oaths such as that of "one superannuated and interested old woman, who declared seven years ago that she was incapable of giving evidence'? In other words, who would protect future Elizabeths from future Craddocks, mistresses from their servants?

She had suffered because of Hervey's reports, unable to sell her estate in Devon because the purchaser believed she did not have "clear title." (No records survive of such a discussion.) Her land ownership was unclear, her income in jeopardy. She had merely followed the jactitation advice of Dr. Collier. Crime required criminal intent; hers was "an authorised and innocent act."

Such cases were normally brought by the injured party. Not here. It was plain from his three wills, all made in her favor, that Kingston did not think himself injured. It was not due, as "industriously and cruelly" circulated, to her influence that the duke's sister's firstborn—Evelyn Meadows, though she did not mention him by name—was disinherited. If she had wanted, she could have had the duke's fortune for her own family forevermore. But the four younger Meadows sons, including the infirm Thomas, and their heirs, remained in the will.

While she was abroad in sorrow and ill health, bills had been brought in Chancery and then in the criminal court in the hope that victory would enable a civil action; that is, the overturning of the duke's will. She was there solely because of the malice of the Meadows family. Their motives were "unjust and dishonourable." Evelyn Meadows was disinherited because he treated a lady "as amiable as she was virtuous and beautiful" with "fatal cruelty" and, to compound his crime, falsely alleged he had broken the engagement for fear of the duke's reaction. The bounder was also cruel to his mother and sister and "quit actual service" in the war.

Anna Porter had already heard of Meadows's dreadful reputation: "I rejoiced at all she said against the vile man . . . the devil has marked him for his own," she wrote.[48]

Elizabeth had had to return home, at risk to her life, or be outlawed; yet her money was blocked to try to prevent her from making it back. But she had come to defend her honor, not her money.

She then moved on to Mrs. Craddock. Surely, they already doubted her? Why would she have been at the ceremony? If she was telling the truth, would not Elizabeth have ensured her silence? Plainly, she stood to benefit from her testimony.

Elizabeth read out her speech. But now she looked up across the hall and said from memory (and who would question the sincerity in her heart, whatever the facts?): "I call upon God Almighty, the searcher of hearts, to witness that at the time of my marriage with the Duke of Kingston I had, myself, the most perfect conviction that it was lawful." It "showed her power in the pathetic: I never saw a better actress," wrote Anna Porter. Elizabeth's final point: she had entirely relied on Dr. Arthur Collier, the lawyer currently indisposed with St. Anthony's fire.* Would they examine him?[49]

After a discussion, it was agreed that they would not, as he could not attend court.

It was a "long and most curious" speech, compelling, moving, and yet somehow out of place. She mostly spoke emotional truth rather than points of law. It was a heartfelt, civilian attempt at self-justification, a speech to the press, playhouse, or country rather than the courtroom.

The evidence being closed, the London Evening Post reported, "The Duchess of Kingston read, in a very audible voice, and with the utmost composure, her defense to the Court."[50] But, again, her nerves failed her: "The Duchess was so exceedingly affected whilst she delivered several parts of this speech, that she was seized with hysterics, and in that condition was carried out of court, whilst the tears of the spectators bespoke the sympathy of their feelings. After an interval, her Grace recovered and re-entered the court."[51] Her panic resurfaced in another fit of hysteria (or pseudo-seizure) that stopped the court.

Anna Porter was profoundly moved by Elizabeth's plight: "The struggle of passion long stifled, every heart-breaking consideration arising, occasioned one of the most shocking fits I ever saw or could conceive . . . I frankly own that I never was more affected." She was also appalled by the callousness of the peeresses: "It shocked me to see that most of the women spectators called her an actress and were entertained with her situation. Tis strange that we are generally the hardest on the errors of our own sex, a narrowness of mind which I hope proceeds only from the too frequent narrowness of education given many women." She had observed that timeless truth: while men lined up to judge unfortunate women, women could be harsher still. In this case, Porter blamed the reaction on a lack of "sensibility." In Porter's eyes, Elizabeth might be amoral and a social climber

---

* St. Anthony's fire, or ergotism, was a disease caused by eating cereals, particularly rye, contaminated by a fungus. Symptoms included a rash, fever, and delirium.

but those who witnessed her torment should be full of fellow feeling, not laughter. At eighteen, her reaction was one of the next, not the current, generation.[52]

The *Morning Chronicle* called Elizabeth "the prisoner," reporting that her tone of voice was "pathetic," and that "she was frequently so agitated and distressed that she could hardly see for her tears."[53] The *Morning Post*'s paid editor was more cordial, referring to Elizabeth as "Her Grace," and saying she had "behaved with uncommon fortitude through the whole of this trying situation." Perhaps both reports were true.[54]

*

Elizabeth's intense performance was followed by Mr. Barkley, Hervey's attorney, who insisted that Mrs. Craddock, all those years before, had told him she remembered not a jot; he could not say why Mr. Craddock had given evidence for the jactitation suit when he was not at the wedding, and his wife, who was, did not.

A burlesque element arrived in the form of Mrs. Mary Pritchard of Mile End, who claimed that Craddock had confided in her that although she had heard nothing in the church, she was about to make her fortune. Pritchard said that Evelyn Meadows had promised Craddock's brother a job in a customhouse, out of which Craddock would be provided for herself. Anna thought this witness perjured herself at every word, and was "as arrant a *femme d'intrigue* as ever lived." A minor hullabaloo ensued when Elizabeth was accused of making "signs" at her.

Mr. James Laroche, the friend who stood bail for Elizabeth, recalled his many visits to Dr. Collier with the duke, who certainly believed his marriage was lawful. During his testimony Elizabeth collapsed and was carried out again; he had to stop until she came back.

With that, the testimonies ended. The Solicitor General had a chance to respond to Elizabeth's speech, but he called it a "mere argumentative defense" that did not, as was customary, need a reply. Devastatingly, after all that, he had nothing to say.

The more sympathetic Anna Porter did not see it like that, writing: "She certainly had some excuse for what she did: she thought the sentence as valid as divorce."

The Lords adjourned to make their decision in their chamber.

They came back into the hall in order. A proclamation for silence. The Lord High Steward asked them for their verdicts, starting with the man most recently elevated to the English peerage—John, Lord Sundridge (the Duke of Argyll in Scotland, second husband of Elizabeth's old rival, Elizabeth Gunning, formerly the Duchess of Hamilton): "What says your Lordship? Is the prisoner guilty of the felony whereof she stands indicted or not guilty?"

Argyll stood up in his place uncovered (meaning with no hat on) and, "laying his right hand upon his breast," answered: "Guilty, by my honour."

In the same fashion, to a rapt crowd, 116 Lords stood and answered identically, one by one, apart from Elizabeth's friend the loyal Duke of Newcastle, who said, "Guilty erroneously, but not intentionally." Four peers, the Duke of Ancaster and the Earls of Pembroke, Exeter and March,[55] retired without giving any verdict.

Black Rod, Molyneux, brought Elizabeth back in. There was a proclamation for silence.

The Lord High Steward said, "Madam, the Lords have considered the charge and evidence brought against you, and have likewise considered of everything which you have alleged in your defense; and, upon the whole matter, their Lordships have found you guilty of the felony whereof you stand indicted. What have you to allege against judgment being pronounced against you?"

Elizabeth sank "lifeless to the ground" and then recovered, forcing herself to find composure. Now the hall saw the mournful figure in black write something on a piece of paper and hand it to the Lord High Steward. She asked for "the benefit of the Peerage": the right of peers to receive a more lenient punishment; in this case, that she should escape being branded on the hand.[56]

The Attorney General launched into a malicious, even sadistic, argument, "where he attempted to prove that Peeresses had not the least title to the same exemption." Her lawyers objected, but Thurlow asserted that letting her walk free would be "a ridiculous disgrace to public justice."

Fortunately for Elizabeth, the rest of the peers, adjourning to consider the question, were quite aware of the depth of her public humiliation, and thought it punishment enough. It was implicit that she could not use her title. In English law, she had lost her name, her identity, and her marriage to her "dear Duke."

The Lord High Steward told her that the feelings of her own conscience would be her punishment and that in the (surely unlikely) event of her committing bigamy again, the punishment would be capital.

With that, the case was over. The white staff handed to the Lord High Steward at the beginning of the trial was now broken in half by him to show his commission was over; the peers returned to their chamber in the same order they had entered, "except that His Royal Highness the Duke of Cumberland walked after the Lord Chancellor."

Exactly as Lord Mansfield had predicted, Elizabeth had been found guilty, but would go unpunished.

That night, Lord Suffolk, Secretary of State for the Northern Department, wrote to George III to tell him the verdict, that the "long and curious speech" the "prisoner" had made was being transcribed for him, and that she had recovered from her subsequent "hysteric fit." The king, we can presume, had asked to be kept informed. Some of the more judgmental society women rejoiced in the drama of the result. The flamboyant unconventionality of Elizabeth was too disturbing. Hannah More, the evangelical polemicist who, in spite of her writings on morality, could be full of ridicule and spite, wrote to her family, before she went to see Garrick playing Hamlet: "I have the great satisfaction of telling you that Elizabeth, calling herself duchess-dowager of Kingston, was this very afternoon undignified and unduchessed, and very narrowly escaped being burned in the hand. If you have been half as much interested against this unprincipled, artful, licentious woman as I have, you will rejoice at it as I am." She gossiped that some of the Lords had doubts about the non-punishment: "This morning Lord Camden breakfasted with us. He was very entertaining. He is very angry that the Duchess of Kingston was not burned in the hand. He says, as he was once a professional lover of hers, he thought it would have looked ill-natured and ungallant for him to propose it; but that he should have acceded to it most heartily, though he believes he should have recommended a cold iron."[57]

Everyone in the audience aligned themselves with their world view. Beilby Porteus, the clergyman who had praised Elizabeth effusively on day one, had lost sympathy: "The lady seemed to have studied the best manner of behaving. But the whole was to dissemble, and her guilt was so evident, that the Lords could not absolve her, nor the rest of the persons present feel any compassion for her, or attribute her disgrace singly to the natural frailty of a woman."[58] In other words, even for a woman, she had behaved badly.

Horace Walpole concluded his account with his customary hauteur:

> The wisdom of the land has been exerted [for] five days in turning a Duchess into a countess, and does not think it a punishable crime for a Countess to convert herself into a Duchess. After a paltry defense and an oration of fifty pages, which she herself had written and pronounced well, the sages in spite of the Attorney-General, who brandished a hot iron, dismissed her with the simple injunction of paying her fees; all voting guilty, the Duke of Newcastle softening his vote with erroneously, not intentionally. So ends that solemn farce! which may be indifferently bound up with the State Trials and the History of Moll Flanders. If you write to her you must direct to the Countess of Bristol.[59]

The Prussian d'Archenholz, carrying less bias, may have read the crowd more accurately. He thought Elizabeth carried herself with "great nobility and steadiness," concluding that, "All hearts were on her side, even if the law was not."[60]

Through the telescope of history, d'Archenholz's summary is the most convincing. In the patriarchal, legal framework of the day, she could be found guilty. If one accepted the testimony of those corrupt witnesses and the (misled) ecclesiastical court, she had been married before. And yet, as the Hardwicke Marriage Act[61] illustrated, the law itself was perhaps the perpetrator of the crime, with its opaque marriage rules and opportunity for divorce available only to rich men who need not fear for their status. The reputation of Lord Mansfield endured because he could see where others could not: beyond the letter of the contemporary law. In the court of moral justice, of British, Christian, free-flowing mercy, Elizabeth should have been left untried. Law without basic humanity undermined its own legitimacy. Mansfield took the first faltering steps to abolish slavery; he also tried to improve the lot of women.

For Elizabeth, years of stress and legal battle had ended with a whimper: she was free, but no longer the Duchess of Kingston. She was branded by infamy, if not by iron. England was confirmed to her as hostile, mocking territory, where the law would contradict itself and savor the opportunity to humiliate a widow.

While people were being turned away from Westminster Hall thinking the trial was still on, the Meadows family were trying to prevent Elizabeth from leaving the country with a *"ne exeat regno"* (a writ that says, "let him/her not leave the kingdom"). It was said that her loyal—and look-alike—cousin Bell was going around town in Elizabeth's distinctive carriage as a decoy, and that fake invitations were issued to dinner at Kingston House to throw people off the scent.

Elizabeth was already on her way to Dover, in James Laroche's carriage. There her yacht was ready, waiting to sail across the Channel. At noon on Wednesday, April 24,[62] the *Minerva* glided into Calais to the salute of a cannon with the Duchess-Countess, unduchessed but unbowed, on board, heading for a new life on the Continent.

3

DUCHESS COUNTESS

Sixteen Months Later

CHAPTER TWENTY-THREE

COURTING AN EMPRESS

In the late summer of 1777, from the creaking deck of a Russian warship, Elizabeth had her first view of the city Peter the Great had raised out of the mosquito-infested marsh earlier that century. The golden spire of the cathedral of St. Peter and St. Paul flashed above the riverbank behind fortress walls. The river led into embankments of fine-painted stucco, the marble-and-granite palaces built on the bones of the numberless serfs who had died draining the swamps to create the city. Russia's new capital of St. Petersburg was a place of dazzling, barely finished newness and grandeur. The Imperial Winter Palace stood out in the stucco panorama, in its Brobding-nagian scale. "It has the appearance of having been transported to the present spot, like the palace in the Arabian tales," wrote one astonished English visitor.[1]

Elizabeth's response to her conviction for bigamy—her loss of title, status, and dignity—could have been to hide herself away in hermetic humiliation. But that was not her nature. Instead, like a general regrouping after battle, she rebounded onto the Continent on a quest for a new court, and a new protector. She used everything in her armory—connections, courage, riches, imagination—to begin another chapter of her tragicomic life.

At fifty-six, Elizabeth had decided to sail up the River Neva into St. Petersburg to see if the most fascinating reigning monarch on earth, the Empress of all the Russias, Catherine the Great, would accept her.

Elizabeth had first written about the idea of visiting to her friend, Prince Radziwill,[2] in March 1777, the spring following her trial. She had heard about the splendor of St. Petersburg from all quarters. The poet Vasily Petrov had taught her some Russian in Rome;[3] her own chaplain, the Reverend John Forster, had been there thirty years before with a British ambassador;[4] and everyone had read the best-selling stories of the traveler Nathaniel Wraxall, published in 1775.[5] Most decisively, it was her friendship with Count Ivan Chernyshev,[6] former Russian ambassador to Great Britain, and now vice president of the Russian Admiralty College. Chernyshev and his brother Zakhar had long been in Catherine's orbit—Zakhar had been an admirer—and the brothers had helped her win power. There was an inevitability about Elizabeth's voyage north: all routes led to Russia.

In order to make an entrance into St. Petersburg, Elizabeth had commissioned a new private yacht a few months earlier, a replacement for the *Minerva*. The cost was estimated at 5,000 guineas (£5,250). This she could still just about afford, in spite of the fact that she was spending more than she was receiving. (Although the duke's will was being challenged by the Meadows family, estate rents were still being paid to her bank account.) This sea palace would accommodate fifty visitors, as well as crew. In March 1777, when it was almost ready to launch, John Williams at Kingston House ordered wine and beer from Thoresby; the steward there, Stanley, was to watch the items be put on board himself and "order the Captain to take care not to let his people drink the liquor."[7] Williams packed up all manner of things at Knightsbridge, from furniture to knickknacks—china, card tables, damask sofas, flower pots. The expensive elegance of the house she had built was transferred to the new yacht. In May, Thoresby gardener, Henry Mowatt, had been put on notice: he must leave written instructions for others in case she wanted to take him abroad. She planned to present him to Catherine, who was known for her obsession with English gardens.

One visitor who went on board found the yacht "beyond anything of its kind."[8] Weighing 300 tons, there was an organ with "panels of cut mirror"—costing a rumored £1,200 alone—a suite of apartments hung with crimson damask trimmed in gold with chairs to match, and gilt woodwork everywhere. The dining room was 32 feet by 24. Above it was a state room of the same size, in which a ball could be held for twenty pairs of dancers. It was technologically avant-garde, with a stone kitchen, several stoves, a water closet, a bath, and two "Buzaglo" heaters, decoratively fixed into the wall partitions so they warmed four rooms at once and resembled furniture.* All the windows had wooden Venetian blinds.

Elizabeth's floating pleasure palace contained a noisy menagerie, including birds of paradise and two "sanguines," small monkeys who littered young ones on board; and a picture gallery containing works by artists such as Pierre Mignard.

In what would turn out to be a masterstroke of diplomatic bribery, some canvases had been sent ahead to St. Petersburg: Chernyshev had received two paintings from Thoresby to ensure a smooth introduction to the empress. One was a Holy Family, "a Raphael,"† the other a scene of classical tranquility by Claude Lorrain, *Landscape with Figures Dancing*.[9]

A British diplomat in St. Petersburg, Richard Oakes, had heard about Elizabeth's "preparatory steps" to be introduced at court as Duchess of Kingston through Chernyshev, bypassing his own involvement.[10] In applying directly to the sovereign, wheels oiled by those persuasively valuable canvases, Oakes, as he admitted, had been made irrelevant.[11] He did what he could to scupper the visit, by ensuring Catherine's vice chancellor knew Elizabeth's history and, therefore, the illegitimacy of her title. She probably knew anyway—people told her what was in the English press. He comforted himself that Elizabeth was only staying for a fortnight.

Old masters, newborn monkeys, attendants, in-built heaters, had all sailed for Russia out of the port of Calais on August 7, under a

---

* Buzaglo had invented a heating system—wood-burning "warming machines" of cast iron.
† The Claude Lorrain (1669) stayed with Chernyshev until it was bought by the Stroganov family; it made its way into the Hermitage after the Revolution. The "Raphael" has not been identified. *The Battle of Lapiths and Centaurs* by Luca Giordano (c.1688) followed the same path, and now hangs in the museum. As does (among other works) *The Appearance of Christ to St. Martin* (1666) by Claudine Bouzonnet Stella, brought by Elizabeth to Russia but unidentified in the eighteenth century.

French flag. As France would soon enter the War of Independence on America's side, a British flag was more likely to attract pirates or privateers. This had made preparations fraught: Elizabeth's ex–Royal Navy captain of many years, Harden, refused to sail under an enemy flag. When he was replaced by a French captain, le Fèvre, the patriotic English crew revolted. So it was that Elizabeth ended up sailing with a French crew, for whom she had to recruit a Catholic French chaplain, Abbé Sechand, alongside her own clergyman and publicist, the Reverend John Forster. The impoverished "dirty" Abbé Sechand* turned up with just a violin to his name. Elizabeth had two female attendants, a coachman, and a footman, alongside the crew and clergy.

Anyone who assumed Elizabeth would be chastened into contrition by the trial—or even accepted the verdict—was to be disappointed. In a gesture to those peers at Westminster Hall, she named the majestic new yacht that sailed up the Neva, the *Duchess of Kingston.*

The visit to Russia was intended to be a short, showstopping burst onto the imperial scene, a fanfare-accompanied ego boost of an introduction. Since her defeat in Westminster Hall, she had faced two lawsuits: the Meadows family's immediate challenge to the duke's will—their aim being to seize the inheritance off her—and Augustus Hervey's quest to overturn the jactitation suit, his aim being divorce. Relentless legal action prompted thoughts of escape.

Four days after sailing out of Calais, the *Duchess of Kingston* arrived on the Danish coast. The party had seen with "melancholy curiosity" Kronborg Castle, Hamlet's haunted Elsinore, where Caroline Matilda, born at Leicester House after Frederick's death, had been imprisoned. The estranged Queen of Denmark, whom Elizabeth had known since birth, had died of scarlet fever two years earlier.[12] A "favorable wind" blew them towards St. Petersburg—"We outsail everything,"[13] wrote Elizabeth—and on August 20, 1777, they reached Cronstadt, on the island of Kotlin, home of the Russian navy, nineteen miles west of the city. Soon it emerged that the *Duchess of Kingston* was too wide to sail any further than Peterhof, Peter the Great's breezy country palace, his coastal Versailles, a

---

* He was described as coming from "the Order of Necessity."

few miles down the bay from St. Petersburg; hence, Vice Admiral Chernyshev had sent his "equipage" to escort Elizabeth, and she had entered the city on the Russian warship. Chernyshev came to greet her on board himself.

Of course Elizabeth wanted to ingratiate herself with Catherine, the astute politican, empire-builder, and triumphantly self-made woman whose expanding territories and Enlightenment interests were discussed throughout Europe. Catherine the Great was educated, well-read, ruthless, yet sympathetic. When she became empress in 1762, she had written a private note to herself: "Be gentle, humane, accessible, compassionate and open-handed; don't let your grandeur prevent you from mixing kindly with the humble and putting yourself in their shoes."[14]

She had some things in common with Elizabeth: both were fiery women in a male-dominated era, with unconventional romantic lives and limitless enthusiasm for extravagance and collecting. Where Catherine had real, remarkable power alongside her courage, Elizabeth had only her riches and her spirit of adventure.

Neither had had a straightforward past. Catherine was not even Russian. Now forty-eight, she had been born Sophie of Anhalt-Zerbst, a German princess from one of the jigsaw-piece principalities of the Holy Roman Empire. She had been miserably married to Grand Duke Peter, also German, the heir to Russia, at the age of fourteen. Her infantile, deranged husband had been prone to rages, in which he would string up his pet dachshunds. He once hung a rat (on tiny gallows) in his bedroom for disobedience. His happiness in bed came from playing with toy soldiers and dolls on the counterpane. During eighteen years of grotesque, miserable wedlock, Catherine had twice attempted suicide, and then taken control in a *coup d'état* after the death of the Empress Elizabeth. She had a son with a lover—her heir, Grand Duke Paul.

Although painted as nymphomaniacal, Catherine was a passionate but romantic serial monogamist. She had seized power in male uniform—with the help of Grigory Orlov, her then lover and a Guards officer; the Orlovs strangled Peter to protect her right to the throne.

She expanded Russia south and corresponded with Voltaire. Her relationship with Orlov broke down and she found her future (secret) husband, fellow ruler, love of her life: the supremely talented cavalry general Grigory Potemkin. He had a wild brilliance that offset her cool reason. She said they were "twin souls"—and they remained so even after they became tactical partners both with younger lovers (for Potemkin, that included at least three of his nieces). Corulers and best friends, they shared an obsession with building cities, fleets, and art collections. Potemkin was a one-eyed giant who seduced women— one princess by serving plates of diamonds in the place of pudding— and fascinated Europe. "The most extraordinary man I ever met," was the verdict of the Prince de Ligne, "constantly reclining yet never sleeping, trembling for others, brave for himself, bored in the midst of pleasure, unhappy for being too lucky, a profound philosopher, able minister, sublime politician or like a ten-year-old child, embracing the feet of the Virgin, or the alabaster neck of his mistress. What is the secret of his magic? Genius, genius and more genius."* Potemkin discarded convention, wandering around the royal apartments in a sable dressing gown munching on apples or turnips. By the time Elizabeth arrived, he was the most powerful man in Russia.

Luckily for Elizabeth, Potemkin shared Catherine's collecting mania,[15] and the insatiable curiosity for knowledge and experience. He collected people alongside art treasures, in what Catherine liked to punningly call his *"basse-cour"*—his lower court, which also meant farmyard. Most of all, he shared Catherine's Anglophilia.

St. Petersburg had seen the British—merchants, doctors, adventurers, shipbuilders, English clergy, and Scottish Jacobite families known as the "flying geese"—flock to the city in such numbers that the row of houses on Vassili Island was known as the "English Embankment."[16] Sir James Harris, the British envoy, called it "the most beautiful street in all Europe."[17] Another British visitor found that "the banks of the Neva exhibit the most grand and lively scenes I ever beheld," forming "a durable monument of imperial magnificence."[18]

The Russians were besotted in return. They wanted English

---

* The Prince de Ligne was an aristocrat, Austrian courtier, diplomat, field marshal, great wit of Enlightenment Europe whose bons mots were repeated everywhere.

everything: books, gardens, medicine, carriages, maps, cloth, coal, beer, pottery, dogs, horses, grooms, tutors, doctors, history, taste, theater. There were subscription balls, roast beef, and Hogarth prints. "Of all the people who live in our world, the English are, I believe, the happiest and the most envied," wrote one Russian visitor to London in 1772.[19]

So it was that Chernyshev found Catherine and Potemkin both keen to receive the intriguing English duchess. Playful in private, reserved and regal in public, Catherine, like Elizabeth, was earthy, female-friendly, and a glutton for acquisition. Like Elizabeth, she drank Madeira and adored her dogs—in Catherine's case, six English greyhounds given to her by her English doctor, the renowned Baron Dimsdale; she shared her breakfast, often boiled beef and salted cucumber, with them. Like Elizabeth, she enthused about books, coins, china, snuffboxes, jewels, and *objets* such as diamond-encrusted walking sticks.[20] Compared to most courts of the era, women were center stage at hers.[*]

When Elizabeth arrived in St. Petersburg, Catherine was at Tsarskoe Selo, her summer palace twenty miles away. The Reverend John Forster, that hybrid chaplain-publicist-hack so favored by Elizabeth, explained what happened next in a letter published in the *Gentleman's Magazine* in London. The empress being at her "country palace," they thought they would not meet her until she returned, but, as soon as Catherine "was informed of the arrival of the Duchess, she sent her an invitation, fixing the day when she would receive her."[21] An extreme bustle of preparation, shaking out of robes, powdering of hair, applying of rouge, ensued.

Even a seasoned courtier like Elizabeth would have been dumbfounded as her carriage drew up to the summer palace: an unimaginably large "whipped cream" confection, as Catherine called it, designed by the Italian Bartolomeo Rastrelli for Peter's aunt, Empress Elizabeth. And even more so as she stepped up the staircase

---

* When Catherine's friend Princess Dashkoff became director of the Academy of Science, the French tutor at court, Masson, wrote: "One more female reign and we might have seen a woman general of an army or minister of state."

and through the "Golden Enfilade," a suite of rooms of startling opulence—some inlaid with red and green foil—one, a glowing, dusky-orange room lined with amber, a present from Frederick William I of Prussia, that led into a cavernous baroque ballroom shining with mirrors and candlelight. "Like an enchanted palace," wrote one guest, "it dazzles one's eyes."[22] Outside, the English-style gardens with their lawns and gravel walks shaped by her gardener, John Bush, from Hackney, were dotted with arches and obelisks, commemorations of military victories. There was a Chinese village; Siberian, Turkish, and Chinese bridges; and a mausoleum to the English greyhounds. There were fairground games, including a "flying mountain," a kind of wooden roller coaster.

Catherine would rise early and walk her dogs, dressed in a long coat, bonnet, and leather shoes. Her domestic normality stood alongside breathtaking quotidian grandeur. Crowds gathered to watch every time she left the palace, as a cavalcade of 800 horses departed to the blasting of trumpets and the firing of 100 cannons.

Chernyshev, handsome, rich, and solicitous, presented his English duchess to the empress at the summer palace. As Forster wrote, after speaking "for some time . . . her Imperial Majesty went to see a comedy and entered the hall accompanied by the Grand Duchess, her daughter-in-law. She gave the Duchess of Kingston the highest mark of distinction, by placing her on her right." Rumiantsev, Russia's illustrious general, victor over the Turks, was present, as was Catherine's son and heir, the Grand Duke Paul, and his second wife, Maria Feodorovna,[23] who both "showed the utmost attention and politeness to our heroine. Indeed so many honours were never paid in this court to any person whatsoever . . . a crowned head could not have been more honourably treated than the duchess."[24]

One Englishwoman captured what Elizabeth would have seen: "the magnificence and splendor of the dresses beyond anything I ever beheld, a profusion of diamonds, gold, silver and fur, both on the men and women."[25] The dress for the women was "pretty and becoming," visitors were presented in the outward room, the procession was "perfectly magnificent, she is preceded by all her officers of state, most of them tall fine fellows and adorned with ribbons and stars, she walks alone and with infinite dignity. The Great Duke follows her, he is well in his person, and stiff in his deportment."[26]

Russia's scale and ostentation did not seem built for mere mortals. Elizabeth, who had always been too conspicuously opulent and theatrical even for Georgian London, naturally adored it. She complained to Lord Barrington of her journey to Russia, and of how her reception there had soothed her rattled, insulted ego: "My troubled spirit has sought repose even on the watery element, the Baltic sea, nor the more colder northern clime, has not treated me so unkindly as have the cruel Lords, my country, my relations, my companions and many that call themselves my friends."[27]

She was delighted with her treatment, grateful for the status given to her by Catherine. "Her Imperial Majesty is [as] gracious as she is great," she wrote, "she was all gentleness, courtesy and affection." Particularly pleasing was that she had been given "the same honours, apartments [and] attendants" as the King of Sweden, and precedence after the Grand Duke and Duchess. She sensed female empathy for her plight, writing, "her feeling and sympathising heart loves me because I am unfortunate." So began the most important relationship of her next few years. Embraced by the most powerful sovereign in Europe, Elizabeth must have felt a sense of redemption after the denigration at Westminster Hall.

Oakes, the British diplomat, was forced to admit that her plan had worked. "Through Count Chernyshev's good offices Lady Bristol was invited by the empress to Tsarskoe Selo Wednesday last, was received as Duchess of Kingston, and treated with a great deal of distinction," although, he reassured himself, it was "in a less ceremonious manner" than usual.[28]

Loaded with diamonds and presence, even in Russia, a land of giant jewels and ballrooms, Elizabeth made a glorious impression. It was said that she wore a duchess's diamond coronet and that the St. Petersburg aristocracy thought she was royal, believing her to be a sovereign noblewoman. They had heard she was close to the royal family in London. People talked about her wealth and the amazing treasures in her possession. She was sometimes referred to not only as

Her Ladyship, but also as Her Highness. Not by Catherine of course, who was quite aware that she had an adventuress in her midst.

Elizabeth was quickly absorbed into the St. Petersburg social life. Palace entertainments were held on a colossal scale—8,000 people might attend on one evening. Some, such as the Friday or Saturday masquerades, were semi-public. On Sunday, a court would be held; Monday, a French comedy; Thursday, a French tragedy followed by a ballet. In its candlelit splendor, the court was much more convivial and exuberant than that of George III. As Forster told, while Elizabeth was there, the Spanish ambassador gave a dinner, Chernyshev another, on Friday there was a ball at court, the French ambassador was having a dinner with "all the nobility" on the following Thursday. Once acknowledged by the empress, Elizabeth was invited everywhere. She returned the hospitality on board her yacht. She held a magnificent entertainment to which Chernyshev and "several persons of first rank" came: the admiralty yacht and twenty gondolas brought in the guests. "As soon as dinner was served a band of music composed of pipes, drums, clarinets and French horns" played English marches and, after dinner, concertos were played on that expensive organ in the antechamber. "In short," Forster gushed in the English press, as he was paid to do, "everything that is most grand at this court seems to vie with each other in distinguished marks of respect to this illustrious visitor."[29]

Such social triumph was sweet for Elizabeth after the humiliation of her conviction. Not everyone was so enthusiastic about her, of course: the English community were irritated by this peacocking felon[30] from home. The local English reverend, William Tooke, wrote: "The duchess, instead of exhibiting that dignity of behavior and elegance of manners which might have been expected from a person of such exalted rank, seemed at times by ostentatious displays of her wealth, to rival the entertainments of the palace; and at others, armed with such servility and meanness, as to excite universal contempt."[31] This was wishful thinking in a place where excess was embraced. The Russian St. Petersburg *ton* were intrigued, taking their lead from all those well-publicized meetings with the empress and her circle. Elizabeth's yacht was a draw:[32] crowds of nobility "hurried to visit" the "most luxurious and modern one that had ever visited Petersburg," towns-folk crowded to see it in the harbor even from far away.

Elizabeth's behavior in Russia provides an insight into her effective modus operandi: she told everyone who would listen that she had undertaken "such a hazardous and expensive journey with the sole wish to see with her own eyes the greatest of the living monarchs." Alongside flattery, there was power-broking—she traded on other friendships: "such a high opinion of her expressed by a friend of Frederick the Great flattered the power-loving Empress." When she advised her friend Prince Radziwill how to behave at the St. Petersburg court she told him to go with minimal retinue, keep his intentions to himself to avoid jealousy, and take no one with him who might undermine his strategy—in Radziwill's case, his fiery younger brother, who might say something regrettable.[33] Elizabeth certainly had a habit of keeping her plans undisclosed (she had kept secrets for so long, perhaps it was second nature), and she never traveled with an equal who might have their own agenda.

Unarguable soft power, in today's terms, was Elizabeth's favorite weapon. She was the most artful, most charming courtier—a skill honed by years of practice. In some ways she was a very modern figure; she would be described as a networker, a woman who could trade favors and friendships, leverage goodwill, the currency of the court, her weapons against the patriarchy. Alongside her clergyman publicist, she had an instinct for public relations herself, although, as in the Foote affair, she was better at attracting attention than molding it to her advantage.

Elizabeth was convinced she had made herself a new friend. As with Bell Chudleigh and the Electress of Saxony, her female friendships were sentimental in their intensity and their expressions of devotion. But if she thought she had already lined up an empress next to her electress, she was getting ahead of herself. Catherine was extremely astute and publicity conscious herself—she could see through it all. She wrote to her friend, publicist, and agent in Paris, Baron von Grimm,[34] from Tsarskoe Selo shortly after Elizabeth's arrival: "On foolishness: the Duchess of Kingston came here in her own yacht with a French flag . . . She certainly doesn't lack spirit . . . she finds me very friendly, but because she is a little deaf and I cannot raise my voice very high, she can't profit much from it."[35] However, her actions belied her written doubts; and as for not pursuing the friendship, Elizabeth had other ideas.

*

St. Petersburg was the last of Elizabeth's attempts to ingratiate herself into a new court after the trial. The European odyssey had begun seventeen months earlier in Calais, from where she could communicate with friends, stewards, and lawyers in England via its efficient packetboat service without having to set foot on treacherous British soil. This small, neat, stone port, the medieval frontier between England and France, was dominated by its harbor, its citadel, and its colorful British visitors. As Foote wrote in his mischievous play, *A Trip to Calais*, the English here were often those hiding either from the law or from the judgment of England itself—debtors, elopers, runaway wives, mistresses, misfits, *grandes horizontales*—alongside the more nonchalant young aristocrats and their tutors at the beginning or end of a Grand Tour.

Just hours after the Lords' damning verdict, Elizabeth had sailed into Calais, as planned in anticipation of a guilty verdict, and "the principal persons in the town," such as M. Caffieri, the king's land tax agent, were waiting on shore to greet her "with every possible mark of respect and civility."[36] England's loss was Calais' financial gain. Elizabeth's attempt to stay at the most fashionable hostelry, the Hôtel d'Angleterre,* went less respectfully. This inn, owned by M. Pierre Dessein, in which Foote had set the first act of his play, was a place where an English noblewoman would expect the finest suite. But Dessein, more avaricious than shrewd, having heard the verdict, thought Elizabeth did not have any money, and would only give her an insultingly small room. The bigamy case had not even touched on the will as yet, so all her money was still her own. The next morning, he discovered his mistake and offered her the best apartments. Given that Elizabeth had gone into voluntary exile because she could not bear the scorn of the English after her defeat

---

* On Rue Royale, "a spacious mansion with 111 beds," which had gardens, stables, and its own playhouse.

(as well as wanting to escape the Meadows family), Dessein's slight was an ill omen: shame had followed her across the Channel.

Elizabeth's movements were discussed everywhere. It was said that she had an armed sentinel standing to attention in Calais and even, humorously, that she was now going around the port with the Bristol livery on her coach. Of course Elizabeth no more desired to be the Countess of Bristol than Augustus wanted her as his wife; both were mortified to be married. It was noted that, although in exile, she had no intention of living in a lowly fashion. She bought a large, handsome townhouse with a cheerful exterior and a fine view of the port from M. Cocove, a local landowner,[37] who had run short of money, and let his family, whom she befriended, stay across the quadrangle.[38]

But her sights were set higher, to what she knew best and valued most: a royal court—specifically, one that would greet her as the Duchess of Kingston. First, she tried Bavaria. In October 1776, she left Calais to visit the electress, who was in Munich with her brother Maximilian Joseph, the enlightened, musical Elector of Bavaria.[39] However, Bavaria was always under threat from its neighbors, and the elector was keen to maintain his friendship with Britain. When Elizabeth arrived, she discovered that as he did not want to offend his ally George III, he would not receive her as Duchess of Kingston.

With this disappointment, Elizabeth decided to head for Vienna, where she arrived on November 28. For a now notorious bigamist who lived on her quick wit and entertaining conversation, attempting to reestablish a title that had been snatched from her, the court of the Holy Roman Empire was an absurd choice. The prim, pious, widow Empress Maria Theresa was co-regent with her widower son, Emperor Joseph, and in spite of his promotion of music (via Salieri, for example) it was not a glittering or open-minded court. There was the usual round of coffee, cards, and assemblies, but the court was gloomy and competitive: the ailing empress conservative, controlling, and melancholic, the Emperor Joseph argumentative and judgmental. It was the last court in Europe one could imagine welcoming Elizabeth, however amusing she was. She believed that the British ambassador Sir Robert Murray Keith, an army friend of the duke who had been a guest at Kingston House, would introduce her to the pair as Duchess of Kingston, but behind her back, he was scathing.[40] They had an animated conversation about his refusal, supported, on her side, he admitted, "with spirit, address, wit and perseverance."[41] She seemed to be homesick. A Dutch doctor she consulted while she was there walked into her rooms to hear her shouting "old clothes"; she was teaching her pet parrot the street cries of London.[42]

When Elizabeth had fled to the Continent after the trial, two fresh lawsuits had pursued her. Having enjoyed their taste of victory at Westminster Hall, the Meadows family revealed their true, and obvious, aim: to overturn the Duke of Kingston's will "as being obtained under false suggestions." So much was to be expected. But they had now been joined by Augustus Hervey who, having stayed quiet throughout the trial, launched his own legal action. In order to secure a divorce, he first had to persuade the ecclesiastical court to set aside the jactitation suit, which had declared he would be prosecuted if he claimed to be married. Clearly the decision by the House of Lords that Elizabeth was his wife made a mockery of that suit, but in order to proceed with divorce he had to overturn the original judgment in the court in which it had been made. Presumably, he wanted to marry Mary Nesbitt, the widow and former courtesan with whom he was now living in Norwood, St. James's Square, and at Ickworth.* To this end, Augustus's lawyers had taken painstakingly detailed new witness statements from Ann Craddock and Judith Phillips.

In response to the attacks coming from two directions, Elizabeth's lawyers sought delay and prevarication in everything. They were confident that Kingston's money would be hers, so tightly worded was his will; but they were unsure as to whether Hervey—or Bristol, as he now was—would be able to secure a divorce. Elizabeth did not want one. Whatever the recent verdict, and in spite of the fact that it was the Bristol title that had reduced her punishment, she

---

* Nesbitt was said to have been born in a wheelbarrow, the daughter of an oyster vendor. She is the honey-haired beauty clutching a dove, a symbol of innocence, in the Reynolds portrait in the Wallace Collection (1781). It was painted to rehabilitate her reputation; in 1772, her husband had died insane and bankrupt due to her infidelity. Later she became a salon hostess, and possibly a spy during the French Revolution.

did not accept she was married to him. She felt another judgment against her, and a divorce, would make her more vulnerable to the Meadowses' malice.

One sunny afternoon in June 1776, some unwelcome visitors had tracked Elizabeth down at her Calais house, renamed the Hôtel Kingston.[43] Two local notaries and a London-based French wine merchant, Morlet, entered the courtyard and asked her servants to deliver her a letter "concerning a London lawsuit" from Lord Bristol. Elizabeth refused to look at it, passing on the message that she had resolved "to live in peace." After some pleading, they left it on the kitchen table; as they departed, they saw Elizabeth, dressed in black, peering through an upstairs window. (Dr. Bettesworth* of the ecclesiastical court would not agree to Bristol's request to reconsider the jactitation clause unless he had proof that Elizabeth had had notice of it, hence the attempt to deliver the letter.)[44] A few months later, when Elizabeth was in Vienna, John Williams, Kingston House butler, signed a statement saying he forwarded all post in his mistress's absence. Four days after that,[45] Dr. Bettesworth said that Elizabeth's proctor† had to appear before him within two weeks to respond to the Earl of Bristol's bid to overturn the jactitation suit. If it succeeded and the ecclesiastical court disallowed their former judgment as the Lords had done, Elizabeth would legally become the Countess of Bristol, thereby opening the way to divorce.

Elizabeth had to leave Vienna and travel through deep snow to Munich, and from there to Paris to discuss this situation with her lawyers. "They are trying to give me a husband without my consent and judge my case without hearing it," she wrote to Radziwill.[46]

The English press followed every development; for example, the *Morning Post*: "The Meadows family are pursuing the Kingston estate with all imaginable spirit and vigilance."[47] The Earl of Bristol, the report added, was ill; his doctors had pronounced "the air of Great Britain too sharp for him at present." His frailty meant that he was in a hurry. To complicate matters further, the Meadowses aimed their muskets at Bristol, too. It was reported that "the pros-

---

* Chancellor of the Diocese of London.
† Proctor—a lawyer in the ecclesiastical court.

ecutors, or rather persecutors of the Duchess of Kingston, have lately amended their Bill in Chancery; they have made Lord Bristol a party."[48] In other words, the Meadowses were accusing him of collusion.

Things were not going smoothly at Thoresby either. Samuel Sherring, the steward, was attempting to carry on as usual but, using the doubt over her title as their excuse, some tenants were refusing to pay up. In this they were encouraged by the Meadowses, who fed stories to the press about how one could "foresee the doubts which these proceedings must necessarily create in the tenants of the late Duke's estates, and in all other persons as to their safety in paying monies to her,"[49] while she continued to call herself duchess. Newspapers (again, prompted by the Meadows family) suggested that her probate might be revoked, or annihilated, by legal action; her previous marriage, they argued, invalidated the will.

Elizabeth might have been in shock, and under attack, but she had lost none of her fight. When the Duke of Portland asked if a cottage near Thoresby could be made available in her absence, Elizabeth's reply was warm: possibly she was relieved that an English duke would still address her politely, as duchess. From her "voluntary exile," she agreed to his request, before launching into a complaint about shooting on her land. She was planning to spend her "later days at Thoresby," she wrote, as she could shoot "very well," having learned in Bohemia, so she asked Portland to ensure that no one encroached on her land. She softened the complaint by sending some burgundy and offering to buy him some champagne.[50]

Whatever her intentions of returning to Thoresby, in the meantime she made sure nothing was left behind for the Meadowses to loot. Before the trial, the pianoforte had been boxed up; a marble fireplace ripped out; and one of her maids, Eliza Lapp, wrote to Thoresby, asking for the "cartoons," eight large pictures, to be packed up as privately as possible and sent to London in cases, which "must not be made with green wood on any account as the pictures would [become] moldy and entirely spoiled."[51] (These would be sent to St. Petersburg. They may be the ones by Pieter Boel and Abraham van Diepenbeeck that now fill the walls of the Winter

Palace.*⁾ Bricks had to be removed from a window to extricate the vast pictures. Thoresby itself was now deserted. After a visit nearby, Horace Walpole wrote that Sherwood Forest needed some new "outlaws" to liven it up now that "Duchess Robin Hood" had "run her country."[52] Without Elizabeth, it had "little chance of regaining its ancient glory." At Kingston House in London, butler John Williams was surreptitiously sorting out the Thoresby plunder. He wrote in a panic on December 1 trying to trace some pictures taken down from "the Blue Room" that Elizabeth had already "given away."[53] Not only had it rained on the wagon that had brought them down to London, but some of them seemed to have gone missing. (They turned up in time to be sent to Chernyshev.)

It never seemed to dawn on Elizabeth that multiple possessions in multiple countries might cause her trouble. A kerfuffle also broke out in Rome, where she had long meant to return and never quite found the time. The Prelate Monsignor, who had lent her "a whole grand apartment" in his palazzo in the Piazza dei Santi Apostoli, had tired of her delays and ordered her agent to leave with all her belongings. This left the agent in question, Mr. Hendrick, in distress, as he had no instructions and nowhere to store anything.

Elizabeth was resourceful when it came to retaining status. With the electress's help, she persuaded the Elector of Bavaria to give her a new title in 1777—the Countess of Warth[54]—in her own right, as he would not let her use duchess, and she refused to be Countess of Bristol. Now she had a legal title she was happy to use, and which no one could deny her. She also successfully applied for the right to own property in France and leave it to whomever she pleased,[55] a patent that was granted in the name of "the Duchess of Kingston." She was taking every step she could for a secure life in exile: rights to property and an inalienable title of her own, not dependent on any husband, wanted or not.

---

* Probably the Pieter Boel/Abraham van Diepenbeeck series of hunting scenes, cartoons for tapestries (1660s). Two—*Lion Hunting* and *Hunting for a Tiger and a Leopard*—are on display.

As much as Elizabeth was sailing towards a new empire when she went to Russia, she was attempting to sail away from difficulties. Her bitterness towards Augustus Hervey was calcifying. She complained to Lord Barrington of his attempts to "defame" her, his "double-tongue" that "stung" her "to the heart."[56] However far north she traveled, she could not escape the "agonising situation" in her mind. Uncertainty grated on her nerves: how far would Augustus go to achieve divorce, and what would happen if he succeeded? She asked Barrington to be the go-between, to ascertain Hervey's proposals. She claimed to bear her pain with "Christian fortitude," but she was apprehensive about returning across the perilous "Baltic seas" in time for November, when the next legal term began and Augustus Hervey's suit must be dealt with. The Meadowses' attempts to overturn the will in Chancery seemed to have stalled; they were waiting to see, as Elizabeth had worked out, what happened with Hervey.[57]

*

When the brief, triumphant St. Petersburg visit had to come to an end, the divorce suit necessitated a return to Calais, from where she could defend herself against her enemies. As she wrote to Barrington, she was leaving Russia "unwillingly" in order "to be again persecuted in the November term, by Lord Bristol." She asked Barrington to tell Hervey, "I set sail if the wind is favorable on Tuesday the 23 of Sept," instructing him to "be very mild with him" and "amuse him if you can," although she wished Augustus "was in heaven for he wears hard on my breaking heart—I cannot think with patience on the man who puts me to the rack to be revenged on his brother."[58] His desire for divorce, she believed, was motivated by his loathing of his younger brother, the Bishop of Derry, and their bitter succession battle.

The dignified exit from Russia after the short, mighty blast of a visit was not to be, thwarted by a natural catastrophe: the worst storm of the eighteenth century struck St. Petersburg just hours before Elizabeth was due to sail. On Friday, September 19, all her belongings were on board waiting for a "fair wind," but, the next day, a hurricane arose "such as are only known in the West Indies—

the *Duchess of Kingston* lost all her anchors, cables, rudder, all her rigging, masts, long boat etc—she is strained everywhere." The crew and company were safe, "but how to get home with upwards of fifty persons in this season," Elizabeth wrote, "God will I trust in his mercy direct."[59] Long, rolling waves from the ocean, gathering wind, and a violent storm surge drove the water up to unprecedented levels. Hundreds of people drowned; buildings and bridges were overturned; the linden trees and fountains in the Summer Garden were destroyed. The waters rose 14 feet above their usual levels before they quickly slipped back down again, leaving chaos in their wake.

The *Duchess of Kingston* was now a pile of useless, mastless wood and broken furniture stuck on a sandbank like a discarded giant's toy. The British muttered about the French captain. He had lost his head and failed to protect his ship. "The Countess of Bristol's yacht," wrote Oakes back to London, "was driven from four anchors with the loss of her rudder and two of her masts. She now lies in two feet of water and will be got off with great difficulty, if at all practicable before the winter."[60]

Conventions of hospitality meant that Catherine would repair Elizabeth's yacht at her own expense, although this could only be done in fine weather. The *Duchess of Kingston* was raised onto the ice by means of ingenious contraptions and hundreds of people, its contents stored in the admiralty offices. With this assistance, Elizabeth was more enamored with the empress than ever. Catherine was "gracious, compassionate and generous, she has not an equal in the world for nobility of mind," Elizabeth wrote to Radziwill; she was "so deserving of all the praise one can bestow on her."[61]

As Oakes divined, all this attention, all this civility, could only mean one thing—"Lady Bristol," as he called her, would be back. She was so pleased with her reception that she intended to return the following year. Her friend Chernyshev was encouraging her to spend the rest of her days in Russia, but Oakes could not help suspecting that he had "some parasitical view upon her wealth," adding that not only had the empress agreed to refit the yacht next spring, but her vice chancellor had even sent a messenger to England "to prevent [Elizabeth] suffering in her lawsuits from her unforeseen detention here."[62]

Oakes was probably right about Chernyshev—how could a man not be self-interested with such canvases already lining the walls of his St. Petersburg palace?

By November, the seas were rough and Elizabeth had no choice but to return overland. Winter was coming and St. Petersburg was freezing over. Working people carried on as usual, wearing fur and sheepskin, their beards and horses covered with icicles; but sometimes coachmen froze to death waiting for their passengers, as "great fires of whole trees" were kindled in palace courtyards to provide some semblance of warmth.

The storm only served to increase Elizabeth's irritation with Augustus Hervey, who had plunged her into a "world of sorrow" and whose motives she could not understand, as she confided in Barrington. He should have had no reason to resent her. She did not think he was after her money: "I never heard he was covetous when he had less than he has at present." The world would surely believe "it is out of revenge to his brother."[63] In the meantime, letters to her were to be sent care of Chernyshev.

Preparations for the journey were interrupted by the distressing news that the Reverend John Forster had elected to stay put. "She was enraged at my not returning with her," he wrote to a friend in London,[64] though "she knew I had a fit [of] the gout then upon me; and she was to travel by land at the very very worst season of the year." Later, he congratulated himself on his decision: "The difficulties she met upon the road are not to be expressed. Her coach alone weighed three tons, and was obliged frequently to be dug out, when twenty horses could not move it. But vanity and obstinacy are the most shining parts of her character."[65] She was obstinate—it was her strength and her weakness.

Hervey was exasperated, too. He complained to Barrington that he had met with nothing but "chicane, delays and expense." He insisted that, "as to her fortune, as she knew, I had never received a guinea from her . . . no[t] anything but an old gold snuff box, given her by Lord Stair . . . I never would touch anything of hers, which she must be convinced of, from my having refused absolutely when she married her Duke, even the repayment of the many very considerable sums I had formerly paid her creditors for her." All he wanted was his liberty, "were she worth the Indies I would never have a farthing."[66]

Catherine's coruler Prince Potemkin, meanwhile, had also befriended Elizabeth. He flirted with her, seduced by her riches, her aesthetic commissions, her Englishness, and her verve. She was an exotic, flamboyant, notorious addition to his court, that "*basse-cour.*" At Catherine's bidding, he loaned her one of his young officers, Colonel Mikhail Garnovsky, to escort her back across Europe. He was to advise her, but also to spy on her. Elizabeth admired Potemkin, describing him as "a great minister, full of *esprit* . . . in a word, all that can make an honest and gallant man."[67]

Soon she was full of admiration for Garnovsky, too, a clever, entrepreneurial royal favorite who spoke eight or nine languages. Equally, Potemkin would become enamored with the creations of Elizabeth's friend, the inventive London jeweler James Cox, from whom he eventually commissioned the Peacock Clock, the centerpiece of today's Hermitage.*

In November, Elizabeth wrote to Cox, her confidant, that her French crew, sent home on another ship, had mutinied; and, as she was trying to smooth his way into the Russian market, that she had arranged for a Russian general to show some of Cox's diamonds to the empress, in the hope she would order her own. To Barrington, she described the torturous overland trip back to Calais. At "the first hour after midnight" they had set out "on the most horrible night that can be imagined" on the rocky, rainy roads towards Courland.† Describing herself as an "unfortunate wretch," her constitution weakened by "sickness and sorrow," covered in "St. Anthony's

---

* Over 3 meters high and made of gilt bronze, a peacock stands on an oak tree, with an owl in a cage and a cockerel. A dragonfly points out the time on a mushroom at the base of the tree. There are squirrels, frogs, acorns, leaves, and when wound up—once a week, on Wednesdays, when the museum is open—bells ring, the owl moves, the peacock fans his tail feathers, and the cockerel crows. It was thought that Elizabeth brought it to Russia; she most likely introduced Potemkin to Cox's work. From a payment in Catherine's account, the Hermitage now believes that Potemkin bought it himself through a third party.

† Courland was a Baltic duchy, now Latvia.

fire,"[68] Elizabeth feared that Hervey would be "satisfied" (i.e., that she would die). Yet she was resolute, referring to the Stoic philosophy from the Leicester House favorite, Addison's *Cato*, that fortitude would "conquer fortune."

Eleven days later, in Riga,* she wrote bitterly, "I think I am a wanderer on the face of the Earth." She mourned her yacht, "all the little pleasure I proposed in my life, was to be in her." The one compensation was the gentleman she had been given for a courier, in whom the empress had "justly, great confidence":[69] Mikhail Garnovsky. As the only person who had access at all times to Catherine and Potemkin, he must have been particularly captivating. This was the beginning of an enduring relationship that was much speculated upon—were they lovers? It is impossible to say now, but it seems that Elizabeth struck up close platonic friendships with younger men from an overflow of maternal tenderness with no outlet—most of whom happened to be handsome, with a military bearing.

The empress tried to ensure the journey was as smooth as possible, and not just by lending Garnovsky. She ordered boats to cross a river continuously for thirty-six hours to stop it freezing, so they could pass through. Elizabeth could not tell, she confided in Barrington, why Catherine "has taken your unfortunate friend so much under her protection and friendship but she is so good as to say that she will be my advocate, counsel and friend forever." Yet fevers, and thoughts of Augustus Hervey and Evelyn Meadows, intruded. On Christmas Day 1777 she had been stuck for eight days in "the most melancholy place I ever saw,"[70] an alehouse by the River Nogat, she wrote to cousin Bell, who was now ensconced as mistress of Kingston House, receiving weekly hampers of rabbits, fowl, bacon, cheese, and wine from Thoresby. The journey on to Königsberg† was a litany of floods, snow, hail, quicksand, and potholes so deep it took twenty horses to pull the carriage out of them; all so punishing on her worried and weakening frame.

Next stop was Berlin, where she arrived in early January. After meeting with the British envoy, Hugh Elliot, she decided to leave,

---

* Courland/Latvia's capital.
† Now Kaliningrad.

saying she hoped to have the honor of seeing Frederick the Great in the spring instead; it was not the first time she had remembered a date elsewhere having seen the uncooperative English representative. The king had advised his wife—to whom Elizabeth had written—that the English minister must instruct what name she should be presented under, although "the best thing would be not to see her at all."

Inconveniently, Elizabeth now heard that her steward in Rome had "plundered" her palace. She must go there and retrieve what was rightfully hers, or lose it forever.[71] But that would have to wait, because she also received notice that she must be in Calais by February 19, or risk losing the suit with Augustus Hervey merely by her absence. With a detour to visit the electress in Saxony, where she parted with Garnovsky, and snow so deep on the roads it damaged the carriage—she had to spend one night in a filthy inn while it was mended—she did not make it in time.

When she arrived in Brussels a few days late she heard the devastating news: the ecclesiastical court had already decided that it agreed with the House of Lords. Her first marriage was legal; she was the Countess of Bristol. Her last line of defense against divorce—and her first line of moral defense against the Westminster Hall verdict—were both blown. She was overwhelmed with fury. How could they—representatives of the clergy, who had facilitated her marriage to the Duke of Kingston—disagree with their own previous judgment?

CHAPTER TWENTY-FOUR

HERVEY VS HERVEY

In desperation at the unwanted identity of Countess of Bristol being thrust upon her, Elizabeth thrashed around wildly for salvation. Could Lord Barrington investigate whether the Lords might reverse their sentence with the help of her ally, Lord Hillsborough?[1] That way, the ecclesiastical court would have no choice but to follow suit.

Augustus's reaction was just as drastic: the moment he heard the judgment, he sought divorce via Lord Barrington. At fifty-four, and in uncertain health, if he was to have any chance of marrying Nesbitt (who was thirty-four) and having a legal heir, and denying that dreaded brother the Hervey inheritance, he had no time to lose.

Legally, a married woman's property belonged to her husband. For now, he had sought nothing, but, as Elizabeth confided in Barrington, she was concerned about her fortune, because what would happen if they divorced?

Elizabeth felt the "highest indignation" at Hervey's insistence, but decided to delay her answer until the "cool return of reason." At heart, she did not believe he was after her money—he "was ever accounted generous"—but thought that his low-sprung desire to deny his brother title and inheritance might "prompt him to beggar me and disgrace himself." His demands, his tone were both upsetting. There was a nostalgic flicker of those two impulsive young people at Lainston three decades earlier when she wrote, "as a gallant and gay lothario he ought to know that a woman of spirit can only be conquered by soft persuasion, and soothing eloquence; and that

I was not made to receive harsh commands." Augustus's claims that in seeking divorce on account of the consummation of her marriage with the Duke of Kingston, he would give her his "word of honour" he would not seek her fortune, were not enough.[2]

Negotiations rapidly soured. To Barrington, she quoted from his letter: "Lord Bristol will take every legal step in his power to distress the lady, by publicly issuing proper notice to her tenants, agents and receivers, stopping all further payments . . . they will be accountable to the Earl of Bristol." So much for leaving her money alone. She returned threats across the Channel in a private letter to Augustus, because, she wrote to their go-between, "I do not wish anything that may mortify Lord Bristol to appear before the eye of any mortal unless in this cruel circumstance necessity obliges me." (Was she threatening to reveal collusion in the jactitation suit?)

A fortnight later she wrote to Barrington twice in one day, demanding security from Hervey for her money again: "I will not fail in anything I engage . . . I will not acquiesce in any one thing." She had discovered that the younger brother, the bishop, had been snooping around Rome attempting "to discover from my steward and secretary if I would, or would not, oppose a divorce." Bristol must keep his "present transactions" a "profound secret" from his brother. When Elizabeth's possessions were moved while the Palazzo Ruffo was being repaired, the bishop had gone to the comic lengths of taking an apartment in the same lodging house "to be with my secretary" in order to garner intelligence. Paranoia was setting in now. Elizabeth believed, "The Bishop acts in concert with my nephew Evelyn Meadows."[3] Perhaps she had reason to be paranoid. Neither wanted her to divorce—the bishop, in case his brother remarried; Evelyn Meadows, in case Hervey somehow got the money instead of his family. At another turn, she heard a rumor that the Meadowses had hired the same lawyer as Augustus Hervey. And yet they had accused him of collusion. Who was in league with whom?

In May, there was a standoff: Elizabeth would not answer Hervey's proposals without security for her fortune. Hervey, as he made plain to Barrington, would not provide security until she had agreed to the divorce. From Ickworth, he wrote that guarantees could only come afterwards, and "disagreeable consequences may ensue" if

Elizabeth did not proceed. He was unwilling to lose another year. Elizabeth protested: it was the "most unreasonable request on earth," that she should "not be made secure of all I possess on earth but by words." Lord Barrington had just resigned as secretary of war because he detested dealing with the American Revolution, but he would not find much peace as the Bristol go-between.

As well as being stuck in the middle of two inheritance psychodramas, Elizabeth was concerned with the theft of her possessions in Italy; her library was "now dispatched all over Rome," her pictures, wardrobe, plate, "valuable trinkets . . . in a commode"; these things had either already been pawned or might yet be "sold for a trifle."[4] As the temperature there was rising by the day, she must get there as soon as possible.

Elizabeth finally left for her third visit to Rome on July 2, 1778. Mid-month, she was in Lyons in "perfect health." Two weeks later, she boarded a felucca from Marseille to Leghorn in Italy. It was to be a short stay with a trip to St. Petersburg afterwards. Horace Mann kept track of her, writing: "The soi-disant Duchess of Kingston arrived yesterday at Leghorn in seventeen days from Calais. She is going to Rome to fetch the greater treasure in diamonds, plate, etc., which was deposited there under the sanction of the late Pope . . . She is not to pass here now, and perhaps the rebuff that she met with at Vienna will induce her to shun this [Florentine] Court hereafter."[5]

When she arrived in August, she discovered that her belongings were indeed dispersed around the city. She acted quickly,[6] taking valuables out of the Monte di Pietà, the pawnbroker,* and packing them off to Calais in wagons, as Mann reported to Walpole, who dismissively replied: "She is a paltry mountebank. It is too ridiculous to have airs after conviction."[7]

She stayed in a first-floor apartment in the Palazzo Guarnieri, "one of the best houses in Rome,"[8] above the Spanish Steps, near those affable monks at St. Isidore's, but the heat was suffocating, possessions were missing, her health fragile—and, woundingly, she

---

* Run as a charitable enterprise by the Catholic church.

got a very different kind of reception from her previous visits to Rome. There was a palpable change in the atmosphere around her, particularly from the fellow British. One Englishman wrote that although Elizabeth had "worked her way into the great houses"—he saw her at the Duke of Grimaldi's,* the Spanish ambassador—"we cannot visit the scarlet woman stigmatised and burnt in the hand by metaphor."[9] An English admiral's widow wrote to a friend: "the Duchess of Kingston, as she called herself, was here for some weeks; no persons of fashion noticed her; however, she pushed herself into the public conversazioni, but the reception she met with did not admit of her going twice. Her dress (which she told some gentleman was the same as the Empress of Russia wore) was that of a tragedy queen."[10] English vitriol was as high as ever.

William Hendrick, the agent who had been left in charge of the departure from the Palazzo Ruffo in her absence, was blamed by Elizabeth for the theft of silver, various gowns, and expensive fabric, as was made plain in the report filed by her doctor in Rome, Dr. Frey (or Frei).† Frey wrote (originally in French) that Elizabeth had hired Hendrick many years before and, having been put in charge of her belongings between March 1775 and August 8, 1778, he stole:

  40 bolts of turquoise damask
  Some bolts of crimson damask
  One gown of silky fabric, hand-woven with flowers on a
      white background
  A blue gown . . . with exquisite silver flowers
  Another similar lady's gown, pink silk
  (the above-mentioned lady also remembers) some blouses,
      decorated with lace, which she is not able to enumerate at
      the moment
  Other varieties of table-linen, for the use of the cited lady
  Embroidered bolts of white cotton fabric

* Grimaldi, former prime minister of Spain, was now the Spanish ambassador in Rome.
† The Swiss Dr. Frey was particularly popular with the German colony there.

Muslin bolts, both smooth and hand-woven, of the most
    exquisite [quality]
taffeta bolts
46 pairs of bed sheets, some fine silk, some ordinary
Solid silver coffee spoons, with the above-mentioned lady's
    own coat of arms
Silk blue blanket, and other things[11]

The Duchess believed her servant to be guilty, he added, because although the boxes were found closed, they were unnailed from the bottom in order to facilitate the theft. Also while she had been away he had charged expenses that "exceeded his own status." Elizabeth surmised that Hendrick had been part of a theft plot, in which he had deliberately left her boxes open (as well as fiddling his expenses). What she retrieved but could not take with her, she left in the care of the duke's distant relative, Sister Wortley Montagu, at the Ursuline Convent in Via Vittoria.*

Augustus Hervey's younger brother Frederick, the Bishop of Derry, was still in Rome, staying in Castel Gandolfo[12] with his wife Elizabeth, who wrote to her daughter Mrs. Foster that "Lady Bristol, who still calls herself D. of K., is just come to Rome, and they say is busy packing up all her effects."† Of course they referred to Elizabeth by that title: they wanted to reinforce the fact that Augustus was married. What with the unsolved theft and the hateful Herveys, Rome, where she had so recently considered settling, no longer held any allure. That enchanted status now belonged to St. Petersburg.

On the way back to Calais from Rome, Elizabeth was nearly shipwrecked. Ironically, the realization that she wanted to survive restored her spirits. "I was the first that leaped into the boat to save myself from the perils of the sea," she wrote to the Duke of Newcas-

---

* A relative of the duke's aunt, Lady Mary Wortley Montagu. The convent is now the Roman conservatory of music. Prince Charles Edward Stuart's long-suffering wife, Countess D'Albany, ran away and hid here for a year in 1780.
† Mrs. Foster, born Elizabeth Hervey, known as "Bess," later became the Duchess of Devonshire after the death of the first duchess, her friend Georgiana.

tle, offering condolences for the death of his son, Lord Lincoln, at twenty-seven.[13] "Good souls who depart this life are in a far happier state than we poor mortals left on earth and never believe that we are separated forever," she wrote. She herself had lived "five years in perfect happiness," only to be "unfathered, unmothered, no child to comfort me, and bereft of brother, sister and all of kindred obliged to seek for peace and quiet in a foreign land, all united at home to deprive me of my fortune." But she had found the antidote to sorrow—travel: "destroying our health by sorrowing we are guilty of a slow and cruel suicide . . . endeavour to dissipate by changing the scene your present gloomy thoughts."[14] She accompanied this with a second letter. Would he, out of memory to his friend, back Kingston's heir Charles Meadows to take Lord Lincoln's place as one of the Members of Parliament for the county of Nottingham? (The good-natured Newcastle did indeed become his patron, and Meadows took his seat as a Whig MP a month later.)

Evelyn Meadows was another matter. It seemed as if the validity of the duke's will would finally be tested at the Court of the King's Bench in the next legal term, but, she believed, Meadows wanted to put it off "in hope that some of the witnesses in my favor may die."[15] He wrote to his aunt offering a "compromise." An irate letter, dictated from bed while she recovered from the shipwreck, tumbled out in reply: painful as it was to refuse a request from the duke's nephew, she had offered friendship immediately after the will was read, and returned to England to assist Charles and Evelyn enter Parliament and help with their debts. Instead, she had found that letter of prosecution waiting for her at Kingston House. "Self-preservation is the first law in nature. I did not sleep until I set out to return to Calais . . . I trusted myself in a small boat and went on board an Ostend trader . . . your uncle's widow arrived at Calais with only a young lady and not even a change of clothes or linen." She knew his intentions: "You have declared I should not have any peace while on the face of the earth . . . you have deprived me of my name, and would deprive me of my fortune." She reminded him that she had offered him £2,000 a year before the trial, and that he had demanded £10,000. "Remember you are a gentleman," she wrote. "Urge me not beyond what I am able to bear." She asked him to "trust to my generosity," adding that she daily lamented the loss of the duke "more and more."[16]

Elizabeth frequently corresponded with London's most inventive jeweler, James Cox, ordering presents to ingratiate herself at court—such as a book for Potemkin bearing his insignia in diamonds—and pouring her heart out to him in the next sentence.[17] In sympathy with his financial troubles, she helped him secure commissions at the imperial court, advising him to send smaller items that others apart from the empress could afford. She shared her money worries, too, telling him that she had been robbed not only at Rome, but at Calais; M. Dessein of the Hôtel d'Angleterre had taken £800 of her money.[18] Gardener Henry Mowatt, meanwhile, had reached St. Petersburg bearing presents for the empress: "twenty brace of gold pheasants, and such a collection of other devils as I believe was never got together in one place."[19]

Alongside the presents, home comforts were arriving in what was surely becoming permanent exile: Kingston House's John Williams had shipped "two hundred weight of cheese" and chintz furniture to Calais.

But mostly Elizabeth was preoccupied with her fear of Hervey's divorce action. A married woman's property belonged to her husband—and she was anxious about her "landed estate" in Devon and her one from "my father's friend Lord Bath,"[20] who had adopted her as his "'daughter.'"[21] "I have annexed such dark and terrible ideas of divorce that it shattered my whole frame," she wrote to Cox on February 6, 1779, writing to him until 5 A.M., and then awake again at half past eight. (She had a new commission for him too.[22]) She was not opposing divorce because of the Bristol title; she was pleased enough with her new title as Countess of Warth, which mattered to her because "after having lived in strict friendship with the Royal Families of Berlin and Saxony" she did not want to lose friends through loss of rank. One dread followed another in battalions. She still believed that she ran "a greater risk from Mr. Meadows as soon as the divorce takes place." She wrote—as she often did—that her happiness was "not fixed on riches." (A strange line to write in a jewelry commission, but still.) "I had a small fortune once, and was contented, nor was I always Duchess of Kingston." Hervey knew well that "it was not one, but two Dukedoms, was at my option, but I have no regret . . . for neither of the other two would have made me happy."* She believed the best course would be to get the Lords to repeal their decision because there was so much plotting in there, could Hervey even be sure that his divorce would be passed when the Bishop of Derry had his own faction in the Lords? He might persuade them to block it.

The reason for Bristol's haste to divorce became publicly apparent in March 1779, when he appeared in the House of Lords to defend another admiral, Keppel, at a court-martial over a naval battle.[23] As he could no longer walk unaided, Hervey was carried into the chamber in a chair by two of his servants. Leaning on crutches, he said he had been prevented from his parliamentary duty by his health. This gave him great unease because he had intended to set up an inquiry about the state of the navy, and the neglect of duty of the 1st Lord of the Admiralty, for their Lords to consider; he had come to give them notice that he meant to pursue this inquiry after the House's recess.

Feeble, and in excruciating pain, Hervey's oratory retained its power. He addressed the Lords in Keppel's defense again, on April 23, beginning: "Instead of applause and testimonies of approbation for his conduct, the tools and scribblers of power were employed in every quarter of the town to whisper and write away his exalted character."[24] It was a virtuoso appearance in aid of a colleague. But he was a shadow of the "gay and gallant lothario" he once was. The 3rd Earl of Bristol would have to have a very quick divorce if he was going to remarry and procreate in time to thwart his detested brother.

In mid-May, a fleet of Russian warships stopped at Elsinore in Denmark on their way to St. Petersburg. The squadron, ordered by Chernyshev, was escorting Elizabeth back to Russia from Calais as

---

* The Dukes of Hamilton and Ancaster, both dead by now. Hamilton had died in January 1758, at thirty-three, after falling ill while out hunting; Ancaster in August 1778, at sixty-four.

if she were an empress herself. The newspapers recorded her every move.[25] Chernyshev was endlessly solicitous, although Elizabeth was already asking for the return of those paintings she was now insisting he had merely been asked to look after. (It was said she had not realized how valuable they were.)

Unfortunately, Catherine slightly resented such privileges being given to another woman, partly because Chernyshev was falling out of favor. She would rather those ships had been picking up her books from France (she had bought Voltaire's entire library after his death) than the English duchess. She wrote:

> . . . the Duchess of Kingston has come on board my frigates . . . This is what to hope for when promoting a vice-president of the Admiralty; as soon as he rises, I am treated like a fool. I did not even imagine that his vessels could turn left and take this library at Calais; I had to send it by road via Holland. My Vice-President has shipped his Duchess here in vain, she will deceive him like many others, and he will never have more than the paintings that she has deposited with him and the lawsuits that follow them.[26]

Elizabeth, who had recently written to a friend that she was willing to "lay her heart" at Catherine's feet, had no idea how she was viewed by the perspicacious empress.

Summer in St. Petersburg was the luminous outdoor season: an eternal twilight of glowing "white nights" that prompted a brief, intoxicating spell of park revels and insomnia, from the end of May to mid-July. June and July were hot and stormy, with heat that scorched the ground and loud, rumbling thunder. There were boat trips around the clock: one English visitor described how a favorite diversion was to go "upon the water in barges four or five miles out of town" to go fishing, with music and provisions, "and have a fire made in the woods" to cook the catch.[27] Every June, there were masquerades for which Catherine's reign was famous—four or five thousand people a night at Peterhof, the palace further up the Gulf of Finland where Elizabeth had first berthed the *Duchess of*

Kingston. (Casanova went to one that lasted for sixty hours.) The grounds, with their central canal, water jets playing, dotted with statues, sloped down to the Baltic where there was a landing quay.[28] Inside, the gilt-and-mirror ballroom led through lacquered Chinese "cabinets" (rooms) to a central picture hall, from where the empress could observe the garden down to the sea. The Chesme Hall, with its paintings commemorating victory in sea battle against the Turks, had just been completed; at the empress's order, a ship had been set on fire so the artist could copy it. One might come across the empress herself "in a blue domino," playing cards most of the night. There were fireworks and illuminations all the way along the gulf as far as the eye could see; festoons of multicolored lamps, royal yachts on the water. The music, dancing, and "wanton hours" were intoxicating, producing a delirium of "mirth and gallantry"; nothing, wrote one overwhelmed English guest, "could be better calculated to produce that giddy and tumultuous feeling of mingled wonder and delight."[29]

Elizabeth was now firmly ensconced in Russia, taking part in a vigorous social life in one of the few places she would be treated as a duchess. Her repaired yacht had become a visitor attraction.[30] In June, a top general threw a breakfast for the St. Petersburg *ton* in the Summer Gardens to celebrate the Duchess of Courland's birthday, where there was "dancing on the hot sand in the sunshine, fountains playing and a fête like those one has heard one's great-grandmother speak of in other countries."[31] The following Sunday, the British ambassador's sister, Gertrude Harris, "dined at the Duchess of Courland's; visited the Duchess of Kingston . . ." On another Saturday in August, Elizabeth was at Cronstadt alongside Miss Harris at Admiral Greig's, the Scottish-born admiral in the Russian navy,* who had become the governor there.

Occasionally mundane matters intervened: as the duke's will was still unsettled, Elizabeth's finances were stretched. The house-keeper of the Bath property had died, and she did not approve of the suggested replacement, a Mrs. Speake, because her husband "in one drunken fit may set fire to the whole of Bath."[32] After years of delay, she asked Bell to urge Mr. Feild to have the case against

---

* "The father of the Russian navy."

the Meadowses heard at the Court of King's Bench as quickly as possible.

And then, suddenly, thirty-five years after their first meeting—*deus ex machina*—Elizabeth's doomed marriage to Hervey was over as rapidly as it had begun. As his nephew wrote to his son's captain, and the *Public Advertiser* reported, on the morning of Wednesday, December 22, 1779, "At the age of 55, Hervey had died at home in St. James's Square at twenty past two without pain."[33] He was buried at Ickworth. Both the Bishop of Derry and the Duchess of Kingston exhaled at last.

On Christmas Day, Walpole wrote to a friend, "Lord Bristol has outran me; and leaves an Earl-Bishop and a Countess-Duchess."[34] Hervey had left behind him an illegitimate son, Augustus Hervey, now a fourteen-year-old midshipman on board HMS *Queen*; his companion of eight or so years, never to be wife, Mary Nesbitt; and the insufferable bishop brother to whom he bequeathed as little as he could, emptying the estate of cash, furniture, and even the herds of deer.

At last, the threat of divorce was lifted from Elizabeth. The widowed Duchess of Kingston was now, legally, the widowed Countess of Bristol. This just left the Meadows family to contend with.

CHAPTER TWENTY-FIVE

DIAMONDS AND ICE

With the threat of divorce lifted forever, St. Petersburg was a joy for Elizabeth. When winter arrived, the city turned into an ice world. Carriages, sledges, pedestrians crossed the Neva, providing constant entertainment. Townspeople with sledges mounted ladders up the side of ice-hills to glide down the other side, affording a "perpetual fund of amusement to the populace."

Draped in furs, the noblewomen of St. Petersburg looked like glorious marine creatures in their open sledges—according to an English traveler they endeavored "to display their fancy in the form and embellishments of these whimsical carriages." The most elegant had "the appearance of shells, painted with showy colors; so that the ladies and gentlemen who drive in them resemble divinities of the sea."[1]

Snow muffled the noise on the ground, broken by church bells and heavy ships cracking through the ice. The interiors of St. Petersburg's palaces were as ornamental as their inhabitants. In the dark Russian nights, torches and chandeliers glazed and light bounced off marble, looking glasses, and diamonds in imperial ballrooms. The short days meant parties started at 4 P.M.

So far from home, Elizabeth's spirits, spending, and title flourished unchecked, except when it came under the scrutiny of British citizens—most witheringly, Sir James Harris. In January 1780, he wrote to a friend of his disapproval of the two Englishwomen in town: "Duchess of Kingston & Berkeley[2] . . . with the first though here for a long while, I have no connection, and certainly shall not begin one on so dirty a score—she fears me more than she loves me, and I believe no one ever went such lengths as I have ventured with her, without being exposed to her invective and dirt."[3] Lady Elizabeth Berkeley—otherwise known as Lady Craven, the daughter of Elizabeth's fellow maid of honour, Elizabeth Drax—had her own scandal brewing; she had left her husband and children to go traveling.

While Harris froze Elizabeth out, most of St. Petersburg society, including the imperial family, embraced her, as she wrote to Bell back in Knightsbridge: "I am so tired with the pleasures of this week that I can hardly hold my head up to day. We have had four balls running, where there was Her Majesty, the one more magnificent than the other, I think that all the jewels I ever saw in all the Courts of Europe, are not more in number than them here." Her exuberance was unthinkable in the days of legal strife in England:[4] "I supped last night with Her Majesty in a greenhouse that was three hundred foot long, the walls were not only covered with orange and lemon trees but there were walks of the same as likewise natural flowers in the month of February, the same as in summer. The supper was magnificent, you must excuse my dear Bell: my not signing my letter as I am obliged to leave it to Jack to seal, I am going to spend the evening with the Grand Duchess."*

Underneath the frantic social life, Elizabeth had a strong, unsatisfied maternal urge, combined with a desire to have an heir of her own. Around this time she acquired a growing need to form a legacy and tie up loose ends. She asked Bell to send word to her brother-in-law, the Reverend Nathan Haines,† that when she came to England she would "run away" with his son Chudleigh Haines, who was nine, as in she wanted to adopt him and make him her heir. (Haines had remarried, with more children by his second wife.) He was not her only target. The youngest of Potemkin's five orphan nieces, Tatiana Engelhardt, was a particularly sparkling and appealing child

---

* The Grand Duchess, Maria Feodorovna, Catherine's daughter-in-law.
† Haines, widower of cousin Susannah, now had various Nottinghamshire clergy roles given to him by Kingston.

of eleven whom her uncle had brought to court. Perhaps seeing her younger self in the child, Elizabeth offered to adopt her, educate her, and make her the heiress to her fortune. Catherine refused, deciding she could not bear to part with her—indeed both Catherine and Potemkin regarded Tatiana as their own child—and later made her the youngest maid of honour.*

At the end of March she wrote to Bell, the closest family she had, longing to come to England and see her, full of happiness and affection: "I love you more and more each surviving day." Two of her servants—"Mrs. Ann" and Seymour, "a very honest man"†—had married each other. She wanted to settle all outstanding legal business "before Lord Mansfield" and talk through estate matters with Charles Meadows. She was "perfectly well," having lost her shortness of breath, and was sleeping all night.

But the capricious Catherine's diminishing affection for Elizabeth was perhaps beginning to show through. Young naval architect Samuel Bentham—one of Potemkin's English talents—wrote from St. Petersburg in 1780 that according to her ex-employee, the Reverend John Forster: "His Duchess is going to Dresden soon because people don't respect her enough here. She keeps open house but can't prevail upon any but Russian officers who want a dinner to come to see her. The Empress is polite to her in public but she has no private conferences which is what she expected and what she herself had put into the English papers."[5] It seems as likely Elizabeth was talking of Dresden because the electress was ill and she wanted to visit her.

Even if his words concerning Catherine had a grain of truth—the empress was preoccupied by her new young favorite, Alexander Lanskoy, a protégé of Potemkin, who had introduced him to her—Bentham seems to contradict himself in his journal, written on the same day. He had seen Elizabeth at the house of an intimate of the

---

* Tatiana, b. Jan. 1, 1769, was the youngest child of Potemkin's sister. She first married a Potemkin cousin, Count Mikhail Sergeevich Potemkin, and then art collector Prince Nikolai Yusupov in 1793; their descendant Prince Felix Yusupov was one of the assassins of Rasputin in 1916.

† Elizabeth was not always the best judge of character. After her death, Seymour stubbornly drank through her Russian cellar and would not let the executors enter the property in St. Petersburg.

empress who had married a princess of Württemberg: "Friday—In the evening I went to a concert at Count Razumovsky's[6] from an invitation the young Countess gave me the day I dined there. Sir James came there also. The Duchess of Kingston was there." Perhaps it would have been better if she had not been—Harris ignored her as always and, worse than that, she "fell asleep every time the music played piano, and awaked with the forte. She served the company to laugh at."[7]

Elizabeth was in a curious position—included in the social round, mocked by the British, physically exhausted, and yet settled in Russia. Whatever Bentham might think, the city suited her theatrical exile.

A few days later, on April 14, the Court of the King's Bench in London addressed the Meadowses' new action over the Duke of Kingston's will, ten years after he had written it (in an action called a *devisavit vel non*—"did he devise/bequeath it or not?"). The court heard from both sides, Mr. Dunning for the Meadows family and the duke's attorney and apothecary, both witnesses to the will.[8] The attorney testified that when the will was drawn up, a blank was left for the beneficiary of the greatest bequest, and the duke filled in the name with his own hand and kept it private. At this, Dunning and Bearcroft, for the Meadows family, gave up.

In under one hour, the will was settled in Elizabeth's favor. At last, her legal troubles had melted away like the snow sliding off the English Embankment: there was no threat of divorce and, now, no chance that the Meadows family could overturn the will.

When she heard, Elizabeth fired off letters full of her good news, including one to the pope. "Your Holiness! ... you will be very pleased to know that the persecuted Duchess of Kingston has finally triumphed over her enemies, without pride, nor seeking revenge for seven years of almost unconscionable sorrows." There was no doubt she saw it as a war, with her the victor, "my enemies have avowed that they cannot produce a single witness, nor anything to plead against me: I have put all my hopes in God, who by his divine protection has given me strength to support me during so many trials and with so many enemies. I put myself at your feet, and I pray that Your Holiness will continue his good grace and protection over me."[9]

In relief, in excitement, Elizabeth turned hostess in St. Petersburg. Samuel Bentham wrote that the whole world including him had been invited by her to a *bal masqué*. He vacillated because he thought Elizabeth a snob. "I don't know whether I shall go or not. I declined an invitation she gave me to dinner some time ago, by Sir James' advice, on account of her having told our Forster, that, as I was an <u>architect</u> [Bentham's underlining] she could not introduce me into company."[10] Was her snobbery really this intense or did Forster and Harris, always so rude about her, want to discourage their young friend from associating with her? Bentham did go to her ball, as we can imagine most of St. Petersburg did, if they were invited.

For Bentham, like so many others in St. Petersburg, Elizabeth was an object of fascination. He got to hear of everything; he wrote of her property plans. Catherine had given her an estate at Schlüsselburg on the Neva, east of St. Petersburg, but he had heard that she was seeking another. He also mocked Elizabeth's vanity: "She spends five or six hours at her toilette now; when she has a ribband and star, to adjust, she will have no time left for eating and sleeping."[11] If there is truth in the toilette, we can presume she was perfecting her wig and cosmetics; Catherine's court aped Versailles in the use of white face paint, rouge, patches, white powdered wigs, and scents of jasmine and orange blossom. The English usually found the foundations and the fragrance excessive, but Elizabeth wanted to fit in.[12]

Of course, it is true to character that after so many years in the orbit of Princess Augusta and the electress, Elizabeth longed to be in Catherine's inner circle—everyone at court did. There were five ranks in the imperial court,[13] and she was hoping to infiltrate the fourth, as a Statsdame,* which would have seen her addressed as Your High Excellency, wearing a portrait of the empress surrounded by diamonds hanging from a silk ribbon on her right shoulder. She was dismayed to learn that the honor was not open to foreigners.

Yet Russia suited her. Now gardener to her Imperial Majesty, Henry Mowatt sent a buoyant description back to Thoresby,

---

* "Lady of the Suite"; it usually came with the Order of St. Catherine, the empress's order for women, represented by a diamond star.

observing that Elizabeth was in "good spirits and better health, by much, than at any time since the Duke's death, goes to bed about ten, and gets up most mornings about five, seldom later than six, works hard all day and can get upstairs and down nearly as well as I can. Her lungs are strong and good, and gives her cheers as often and as loud as ever!" She was living royal hours, by the habits of Frederick the Great and Catherine herself, who was always up at six and in bed by eleven. Mowatt continued: "Her Grace is upon very social terms with Her Majesty and likes the country very much." He and Elizabeth saw each other every day, as "she is my great friend, and more to me than a mother."[14] And Mowatt, presumably, was a surrogate son.

She was now living in a palace in St. Petersburg built by the Vorontsov family, one of St. Petersburg's grandest families.[15] It was a splendid baroque wonder designed by imperial architect Bartolomeo Rastrelli (who designed both the summer palace and Peterhof), by the Obukhov bridge over the Fontanka river.[16] "Her Grace," wrote Mowatt, had "fitted up [her] very large house here, in the most elegant manner possible (the furniture intended for the great gallery at Thoresby), crimson damask hangings, ditto window curtains, most splendid fine musical lustres!* Grand organ, plate, paintings: and other ornaments displayed to the greatest advantage."

Even such splendor was not enough for the ever-restless Elizabeth. She wrote to her friend Prince Radziwill continuously, promising to come to see him at his territories in the west, but wary of over-promising her influence at court. As she was uncomfortably aware, Radziwill was convinced she was the conduit to the restoration of his estates. Delayed by ill health from leaving St. Petersburg, she had to stop at an estate of Prince Potemkin's at Narva with a fever. But in early July, she was with Radziwill, who had laid on a celebration of extraordinary magnificence for her.

A few years later, a "foreign gentleman" who had been present

---

* As seen by the author in the Hermitage, December 2019, who was just as impressed by the size, sparkle, and ingenuity of the melodic chandelier as Elizabeth's gardener Henry Mowatt had been nearly two and a half centuries ago.

related events.[17] Elizabeth arrived at a village called Berge,* in a duchy that belonged to Radziwill. One of his officers told her the prince would visit her without ceremony the next morning, and took her to a house ten miles away, where she was waited on by his staff. The following day, Radziwill arrived with forty carriages, each with six horses; his nieces, various Polish nobles, "600 horses in a train, a thousand dogs, several boars and a guard of Hussars." This "assemblage" gave an "air of romance" to the episode, heightened by the prince's manner.

He had arranged two feasts. For the first, he led Elizabeth into a village of forty wooden houses "fancifully decorated with leaves and branches," forming a circle, in the middle of which had been built a suite of three rooms, one for the prince, one for his retinue, and one for the "repast." As Elizabeth and the prince entered on foot, the enchanted village appeared to slumber. Fireworks were lit, two vessels engaged in a mock battle on a nearby lake, and they enjoyed a sumptuous feast on gold plate. Elizabeth sang French songs after dinner; and the village houses were "suddenly converted into forty shops," containing the "richest commodities." The prince selected a "variety of articles" for her, including a magnificent topaz. The three rooms became a ballroom, the ball opened by the prince and Elizabeth dancing minuets. As they left, the whole creation was set ablaze and the "villagers" danced around the fire. The night was said to have cost the prince £5,000.

Such largesse, the type of aristocratic splurge that triggered revolutions, was a sign of both his wanton extravagance and his belief in her power at the imperial court.

And that was only the first feast; the second took place at an estate ten miles from Nesvizh,† and was followed by a wild boar hunt in the pitch-black woods at night. With the prince's pack of dogs baying, Elizabeth watched as a regiment of Hussars and huntsmen with flaming torches surrounded a raging wild boar—a gruesome test of

---

* Now Birzai in northern Lithuania, several miles from Riga.
† Now in Belarus, 75 miles southwest of Minsk. It was the Radziwill family estate from the sixteenth century until 1939, when they were expelled by the Red Army.

courage. She spent fourteen days with the prince, dining and sleeping in his houses, traveling between them on specially illuminated roads, greeted by local magistrates and cannon fire at town gates, at which Elizabeth is meant to have said, "He may fire as much as he pleases, but he shall not hit my mark!" Radziwill's friend Count Oginski, a diplomat and composer who had built his own theater,[18] staged a concert for Elizabeth, during which he performed on six different instruments himself.

By the time the party arrived in Warsaw, local nobility were convinced that Prince Radziwill was about to marry the English duchess. This was too entertaining an idea not to reach English ears, who decided she was somehow about to be a princess or even Queen of Poland. The British ambassador in Brussels, Lord Torrington, wrote to the Duke of Portland: "The Duchess of Kingston is married or on the eve of being married to a Prince Radziwill— after having had two husbands and gone through all the degrees and rank in her own country, she means to end her days in Poland in the state of a Sovereign Princess."[19] The House of Radziwill, he claimed, were so much in debt that they were negotiating loans, and saw the duchess as an easier route to money.[20] Mrs. Boscawen, bluestocking relative of the Meadows family by marriage, wrote to Mrs. Delany: "Mademoiselle Chudleigh, Hervey, Kingston, Bristol, Wartz; is now Princesse de Radzivil, and may be Queen of Poland . . . a curious finishing to the edifice of her extraordinary fortune."[21]

A month later, Torrington had to admit that the non-wedding was off: "The Duchess of Kingston has jilted Prince Radziwill and left him after all was settled, the family come to Warsaw from all parts, and fetes been given without end."[22]

In fact, Radziwill was already married. One reason for the sympathy between them might have been their marital complications: his first marriage had been annulled in 1760, his second fared little better, and he and his wife lived separately. Thus, he had two living wives. Boscawen, Torrington, and others were all unaware of the stipulation of the Duke of Kingston's will, put in to protect her from fortune hunters: the money was no longer hers if she remarried.

Back in St. Petersburg, Elizabeth thanked Radziwill for his fantastical efforts. Yet she was wary that such generosity might come with overly high expectations: "all the small credit I have at court will be used for you and it will be a pleasure if I succeed."[23] Ever the courtier, connector, favor trader, she did speak to Potemkin on Radziwill's behalf, in the hope that he would make Catherine listen to the prince's pleas to have his estate returned to him.

This would never happen. Elizabeth's instincts were right: she had no political influence over the empress, although she did have her goodwill, and she intended to make use of it. On the trip with Radziwill, she had thought not only of his salvation but also her own. As they traveled through the scarcely populated far western territories of Estonia, looking over the wide Baltic coast, she had come up with the most unlikely scheme. With Catherine's permission, she decided to spend her inheritance on a vast tract of land from which she could watch the ships sail to St. Petersburg, and establish herself in a manor house surrounded by music, gardens, and farms—just like an English landowner, but with the addition of a vodka distillery—and pass the remainder of her days, she supposed, in rural peace.

But with Elizabeth, nothing was ever that simple.

CHAPTER TWENTY-SIX

CHUDLEIGH ON THE BALTIC

Bizarrely, for the next few years the bigamous duchess in exile could be found with Catherine's blessing in the remotest corner of the Russian empire, in frail health and alone, trying to re-create her Devon homeland on the northern, German-speaking coast of Estonia. At sixty, she was embarking on a frenzy of extravagant property acquisition of which this Baltic manor house and its lands was the first. As she traveled across Europe spending her money she was pursued by every rogue, fraud, and mountebank on the move across the Continent.

The extraordinary thing about flawed, complex, restless, brave Elizabeth was that for all her declining splendor, with her health, fortune, and faculties in decline, she had a timeless, irrepressible exuberance to her: she never gave up on her adventures. She was reckless, unwise, impulsive. But, as Catherine the Great had said after their first meeting, *"ce n'est pas l'esprit qui lui manquait"*—she did not lack spirit.[1] Her inheritance, though legally hers, had not yet arrived in her bank account, but with the help of banker's drafts and credit she started spending and spending like the tsarina herself. It was as if that early displacement from Chelsea, and now from England, those years in rented property, followed by uncertainty of ownership, were all being compensated for in an unhappily frantic outbreak of grandiose, high-risk property development; places she could create, name, and bequeath.

In March 1781, she paid local nobleman Baron Johan von Rosen

85,000 "silver roubles"[2] for the three neighboring estates of Voka, Toila, and Oru. This made sense to her at the time because she felt healthier in Russia than elsewhere: the climate agreed with her.[3] The weight of legal action had lifted, and she believed herself to be financially secure. (Her joy at winning the will dispute had been tempered by the news that the dowager electress had died in Dresden on April 23, 1780, after a few months of illness, at the age of fifty-five; another reason to settle in Russia.)

Elizabeth's new property was over 120 miles from St. Petersburg by road; a difficult journey even now. The estates stood thirty miles long and deep on the edge of the North Estonian Klint, a limestone plateau that ended in an escarpment, below which the waves of the Baltic lapped onto a rocky beach. In a land of fir and tundra, peat bogs and waterfalls, the main estate, Voka, was a simple manor house built of plastered wood. But tireless Elizabeth had elaborate plans. By the time she left, alongside the vodka distillery, there was a brewery, a pharmacy, and a weaving workshop;[4] a mine, a quarry, fishing and pearl-fishing in the Pühajõgi* river, and a pharmacist living on the estate.† Eight cannons symbolically guarded the house on two bastions overlooking the sea.

With the empress's permission, Elizabeth renamed it "Chudleigh." At the trial, her identity, her name, had been stolen, as she saw it: she decided to affirm that of her birth family.

In Elizabeth's busy imagination, "Chudleigh" was to be a country estate with an English-style garden, made profitable by the kind of industrial activities undertaken by the late electress and Prince Potemkin.[5] The fantasy was prompted by homesickness and restless energy: if she could not go to England (she would not go anywhere she could not call herself the Duchess of Kingston), England would come to her. Later prints show a long, low, gracious clifftop house with windows overlooking the sea, the approach to which was described by a visitor a few years later as a "gentle eminence" from

---

* *Pühajõgi* means "Holy River" in Estonian.
† Brandanus Heinrich Mayer/Meyer may have also been hired to design mines, for gold or cobalt, according to Sven Lepa, "The Duchess of Kingston and the Manors of Voka and Toila from 1781 to 1806."

which could be seen "the grey waters of the Gulf of Finland and the small marine hamlet of Chudleigh, formerly the seat of the celebrated Duchess of Kingston."[6] A spot that would appeal to a West Country seafarer.

Elizabeth had entrepreneurial drive, if not financial sense. Vodka kitchens proliferated all over Estonia in the late eighteenth century.[7] Voka had a vodka kitchen, full of intoxicating fumes of barley and rye, a brewery, and a water mill under one roof.[8] To serve the result, there were five taverns nearby on her own land, and an inn built by Elizabeth "for the reception and accommodation of strangers."[9] Included in the purchase were the serfs; according to the "Soul List" of 1782, Voka had 171 peasants, while Toila had 238, meaning that Voka was small and Toila middling in size. In the same inventory, an ironmonger, carpenter, tinsmith, weaver, and stonemason were listed in the Voka workshops; the carpenter from the yacht was put in charge of the distillery. Alongside this hive of production, Elizabeth aimed for Leicester House–style musical entertainment, just as she had at Thoresby, according to an Estonian source: "The Duchess of Kingston brought her organ, sheet music, and many other musical instruments here and created a choir. She hired a Czech choir master for the peasants." Estonian peasants were taught how to play cellos and trumpets, and sing Italian arias at her bidding.

Oru, which had been pasture for wandering cattle herds, would be transformed into a glorious landscape. On this lush wooded promontory with its wide-open coastal backdrop, Elizabeth built seven garden pavilions and a conservatory heated by a tin stove.[10]

As many liquors were meant to have medicinal properties, a pharmacy alongside the distillery and brewery was an irresistible step for infirm Elizabeth. Vodka alone was said to be good for skin ailments, fatigue, digestion, and killing infections. In addition, the woman who had once sent a plow to Frederick the Great aimed to become a pioneering modern farmer. A Russian historian[11] claimed Elizabeth wanted to introduce English-style agricultural management at Chudleigh so that the estate could become "a model for all Russia, and its owner would win great recognition."

"I have got a magnificent estate," Elizabeth proudly wrote to Bell on April 10: "Her Imperial Majesty has given it the name of

Chudleigh and at the next revision of Russia it is to be inserted in all the maps."[12] To the duke's trustee, Richard Heron, she enthused, "I am disposed to spend a great part of my time in this country being tempted by the friendship of the sovereign and the excellency of the climate, which for weak nerves is a sovereign remedy." She wished he and Lady Heron would come to Russia, to "see upon my estate some of the finest romantic prospects in the world, and fifteen miles of the finest coast and a bold sea, every ship that passes from any part of Europe to St. Petersburg pass[es] before my window, it will be a pleasing sail that brings you to an anchor on my small coast."[13] All those passing boats to watch: just like the Thames at Chelsea.

It might have seemed romantic; it was certainly expensive. Apart from the serfs, stone, and sea, there was nothing there: everything had to be transported. In April the first ship, the *Happy Meeting*, arrived from Hull, with a Lincolnshire farmer, Richard Maw, on board; he had been hired to look after the farm for fifty pounds a year.[14] The cargo included plants, Portuguese and Spanish wine, shells (to build a grotto), port, beer, six heifers and a bull, four pointers ("Pero, Moll, Ponto and Juno"), spaniels, turkeys, ducks and turtle doves, five cases of books, a tent, china, furniture, an organ, and some plows. And a box of pineapples. From the volume and complexity of the orders, the sleuthing steward at Holme Pierrepont predicted Elizabeth would never return to England.

Visitors could see the attraction of the place but were not convinced: its charms were weather dependent. In early August, Elizabeth was staying at an inn to the west of Chudleigh on the way back to Calais when she met the famous doctor Baron Dimsdale and his wife;[15] he was on his way to St. Petersburg to inoculate Catherine's grandchildren against smallpox (the process discovered in Turkey by the Duke of Kingston's aunt, Lady Mary Wortley Montagu, see p. 131). Elizabeth Dimsdale wrote in her journal that they met with Elizabeth, who had expressed great joy at seeing the Baron and insisted they have breakfast with her:

> . . . as she had very fine tea, and butter from her country
> house which she had lately purchased and it was a very fine

situation ... in short she pressed us so much, and wanting a good night's rest, we agreed to go. The house stands delightfully pleasant, having a fine view of the Baltic which looked smooth and calm, but when I recollected how dreadful it appeared the morning after travelling from the Haff,* I should be very sorry to live so near it. We went about the grounds. The steward said when the Duchess returns next summer there is to be very great alterations, a new house built and the grounds laid out. She gave sixteen thousand pounds for it [Elizabeth's spending always increased in the retelling], and has only eighty slaves.† The steward said she ought at least to have as many more.[16]

In spite of the bleak spot and the overpayment, the baron and baroness "lay very comfortably in her Ladyship's bed, every part of the bedstead was iron, and the furniture white dimity. We were very well entertained, a good supper and breakfast."

Another Englishman was in agreement about the aspect: "I set off, through a woody morassy country to Chudleigh ... a plaster house whitened, stands upon the summit of a cliff, with a boundless view of the sea, towards Petersburg and Sweden: in a fine climate it would be sweet, but here the sea looked black and dismal, and in such an uninhabited country, that a man can never be very cheerful."[17]

There was another dark cloud on its horizon: money. Elizabeth had been spending money she had not yet received. In this, she was again—from that impulsive marriage, that created register, the promises and then failure to pay witnesses—the architect of her own downfall. In October, she was back in Calais, considering coming back to England to hasten her inheritance. If she did, she asked Bell, would she get a "mob at her heels" for "other people's debts"? (There

---

* The freshwater lagoon.
† Usually referred to as serfs, they were feudal dependants with no rights, but they differed from slaves in that they could only be sold with the land they were attached to (though many ignored this). In 1775 Catherine brought in measures to prosecute those who treated their serfs with cruelty. Serfdom was not properly abolished in Russia until 1861.

were still debts on the duke's estate to be paid—Heron's excuse for the delay.) Ill health and sorting out finances made her focus on her legacy. Chudleigh Haines was on her mind again as possible heir; she was keen that he should be properly educated, possibly in Germany. In the spring, her efforts to see Bell, meeting her in Spa in Belgium, came to nothing, after she wrote to the Prince of Orange in the Netherlands to see if she could travel there in safety, and he advised against it. She was never to see her adored cousin again; Bell died on October 18. No wonder Elizabeth was dwelling on the next generation.

What she had not mentioned to Bell was that she needed money not only for her "perfect paradise" in Estonia but also for another wildly lavish property project: a house in the parish of St. Pierre de Montmartre, in Paris, that she had decided to buy at a cost of 78,000 livres. (She agreed to pay an extra 12,000 livres for its contents, including statues, such as a marble Bacchus; and another 60,000 livres for building work.)[18] The contract for buying 16 Rue Rochechouart from M. Chevalier de la Crosse included a plan to double the house in size. Perhaps a place as distant as Voka prompted the desire for a townhouse. France—now at war with England, since they were on America's side—was the only other place she could call herself the Duchess of Kingston.

Elizabeth was out of control, pouring money she did not have into schemes of impossible luxury and complication. The sheer deranged impracticality of managing two projects 1,700 miles apart did not cloud her enthusiasm; there was no one around her to rein her in. The Thoresby stewards were forwarding any rents coming in as quickly as they could.

In the meantime—perhaps because she was becoming conscious of her legacy—Elizabeth had instigated a rapprochement with the Meadows family. Friendly letters were exchanged with Charles Meadows's wife and, even more remarkably, in 1781, her tormentor Evelyn Meadows, who had been looking for her in Bonn while she was with Radziwill,[19] started receiving £200 every six months from her. It was an extraordinary act of generosity given the persecution to which her nephew had subjected her. Elizabeth was a forgiving character; she had a Christian need to believe in forgiveness and redemption. She could not control her own spending, but she did not stint on passing her money to others.

Unfortunately, Elizabeth could not distinguish between those who deserved her help and those who did not. The late eighteenth century was a fertile breeding ground for fraudsters: as travel routes opened up, titles popped up alongside them and there was no means of checking who anyone was. Maternal instinct, a trusting nature—and, of course, obvious wealth—made her a magnet for mountebanks. It is poignant that she thought the best of people; people usually assumed the worst of her.

She even launched one rascal into Potemkin's train. Her god-daughter Elizabeth Gilbert had married a handsome soldier, James Semple,[20] who claimed to be Lord Lisle, grandson of Lord Semple. The duchess encouraged him to try his luck in Russia, and furnished him with a letter for Ambassador Harris; Harris, who must have been impressed with his "lineage" and war stories, given that he loathed Elizabeth, introduced him to Potemkin. Semple was presented to the empress in Highland dress; the patrons of the English tavern in St. Petersburg welcomed the Scottish lord; Potemkin, who had great respect for the British military, took to him immediately, and asked him to serve as a captain in his own suite of the army. (Potemkin was always recruiting "foreign advisors," i.e., spies. Men with flexible morals suited the task.) This was some progress, given that there was neither peerage nor fortune: Semple was the penniless son of an excise man in Ayrshire.[21]

According to Semple, when he went back to Chudleigh to acquaint the duchess with his startling progress, she had quarreled with Madame de Porquet (she had employed de Porquet, the daughter of Calais' M. Cocove) who would not come out of her room. "The Duchess, in all the native violence of her disposition," he claimed, locked her in her room for several days. Semple claimed he had to effect a reconciliation in that "dreary spot."[22]

Inevitably, Elizabeth and Semple fell out over money. Elizabeth sent Potemkin a letter complaining of his conduct, but the fraudster spent eighteen months in Potemkin's caravan of 200 adjutants in

Kherson,* and, according to Semple, redesigned the Russian army's uniform into one "at once elegant, convenient and well adapted to the severities of the climate."[23] In 1784, the "Northern Imposter" abandoned his wife, children, and Russia altogether. He sold his carriage to four different Russian noblemen, promising to send it to each of them before fleeing St. Petersburg in it himself.† In his memoirs he described his fights with Elizabeth, but even he allowed that she was a "great wit."

Sometimes she was warier. When Stephen Sayre, an American merchant and agent who had been acquitted of a plot to kidnap George III in London and believed himself to be irresistible to women, arrived in St. Petersburg in 1780, he attempted to borrow money off Elizabeth (such was her fame); she dispatched him quickly.[24] Then there was John Worta, three decades her junior, who introduced himself as an Albanian prince. An impeccably mannered writer, poet, and philosopher, he had spent six months living in the chateau of the Prince de Ligne and inveigled his way into friendships with Jean-Jacques Rousseau, Prince Grigory Orlov, and Frederick the Great's heir, Frederick William II of Prussia.

Whenever Elizabeth befriended a man, there were rumors they might marry. One version was that she had met Worta in Rome, where she had "reigned almost like a sovereign." He was "the handsomest man that nature ever produced," glittering with jewels and brilliant conversation. She was still beautiful, she became his slave, they decided to marry.[25] (For all the gossip, letters that survive from Elizabeth to Worta—"Mon Prince"—sound more friendly than passionate.) He left a trail of aliases across Europe: Worta, Prince Castriotto, Count Stefano de Zannowich.[26] He met a grisly end: in April 1785 he was arrested for defrauding a trading house in Amsterdam, and a few days later, slit his wrist open in his prison bunk. In Baroness d'Oberkirch's romantic retelling, he inhaled poison hidden in his signet ring, and confessed his falsehoods to Elizabeth, writing

---

* The city Potemkin was building under Catherine's orders in Ukraine.
† His story became so well known that he inspired Thackeray's picaresque serial *The Luck of Barry Lyndon* (1844).

"to you, whom I have loved, and by whom I have been loved, I will reveal my guilt . . . I admit that I am but a low adventurer, born in the humblest grade of society . . . to you alone, can my unbending spirit bow."[27] His father, he said, had not been an Albanian royal, but a Turkish ass-driver. Elizabeth's friendship with him showed not only that she was a magnet for chancers, but that if they were attractive and articulate, she was lonely, benevolent, or gullible enough to respond.

With her expanding property empire and flotillas of cargo to pay for, Elizabeth urgently needed that inheritance. Plentiful goods were reaching her that spring—cash to pay for them was not. She was living on credit. On board the *Eleanor*, Captain Green brought a nursery's worth of seeds, bulbs, and plants, including herbs, vegetables, flowers such as jasmine, lavender, roses, sweetbriars, daffodils, crocus, narcissus, hyacinths, tulips, and orange and lemon trees, alongside hampers of pigeons and hogsheads of ale.[28] The *Watson*, then the *Galliot* followed carrying 25,000 tiles, with the instructions, "do not forget the green color."

Legally the money was hers, but none of it had been paid to her. In February 1782, she reminded trustee Heron that, although she regarded her "pretty and profitable estate in Estonia" as "a perfect paradise," she had depended upon her money from the duke's trust to pay for it. Could he help her receive it at last? "The loss and expense . . . is beyond all anybody can imagine, the anxiety, care, and sorrow, is what your humane heart can easily conceive."[29]

A year later, her coffers were still empty and in February 1783, realizing that she had overpaid for Chudleigh,* she appealed to the supreme court of Estonia to rescind the contract, but it was impossible without a colossal fine.

Her peculiar response was to spend even more. Catherine wrote to Potemkin: "As for Kingston, she has written to me asking for permission to buy a certain village."[30] This was a well-known tavern (built as a rest stop for Peter the Great; Catherine had visited too)

---

* Baron von Rosen had only paid 28,000 silver roubles for Voka, the jewel of the trio, in 1780.

and its land, "Krasnyi Kabachok," the "Red Pub"[31] on the silver birch–lined, swampy road between Peterhof and St. Petersburg, a fashionable spot for the St. Petersburg nobility to have a house.* Anxious about money (though much of the fault was hers) and furious with Semple, Elizabeth fell ill and asked the empress if she could go to Carlsbad to recover. On August 3, 1783, Catherine wrote to an official: "The Duchess of Kingston wrote to me now, she asked that we don't hinder her on her journey to Karlsbad spa. She promises that she has no debt . . . she has St. Anthony's fire on her legs, so she is in a hurry to get there."[32] For Catherine, the novelty had worn off by now: she referred to her as "Kingstonsha"—that Kingston woman—although she still made sure she had what she wanted.

Elizabeth's troubles were compounded by predictable news from the distant building project at Montmartre. La Crosse and his architects had fallen out with the builders, each blaming the other. She had to explain her version of events at the French consulate in St. Petersburg; pages and pages of legal testimony ensued; it was an unmitigated disaster. La Crosse had hired glaziers, carpenters, pavers, and roofers to build a new courtyard of the house, with a new picture gallery, library, dining room, and salon around it; with parquet flooring, marble fireplaces, and everything in the finest materials. But the wrong wood and stone had been used, the sculpture alcoves were asymmetrical, an octagonal antechamber was irregular, a staircase was askew. Supervising a building project hundreds of miles away had precipitated the last thing Elizabeth wanted after a decade of trying to escape it: a fresh flood of legal action.

In October 1783, Elizabeth was overdrawn at her bank, Drummond's,[33] annoyed at having to borrow money because the trust was still not forthcoming. She was owed over £1,000 for the duke's funeral, more than £3,000 she had paid to creditors, and a balance left over from rents after legacies and legal costs of nearly £10,000. To her complaints, Heron replied that Kingston's debts, funeral costs, and "principals of legacies" had all come to £18,140 13s 2d. The duke's creditors included tradesmen who had waited for their

---

* It still is. Vladimir Putin has one there now: the National Congress (Konstantin) Palace.

money for ten years, some of whom faced prison if they were not paid. He was sure she would understand that their need was greater than hers.[34] Heron suggested she borrow the money as a mortgage from Charles Meadows instead.[35] It seems that Heron was being obstructive in not providing Elizabeth with her money and that he may have covertly agreed with Charles Meadows a strategy for preserving the estate; perhaps he had convinced himself—after hearing of her spending habits—that this was his duty to the late duke.

At the turn of 1784, Samuel Bentham was at Elizabeth's house twice in the first week alone, on Wednesday and Sunday night, suggesting some kind of open house. But a few months later, Catherine collapsed in grief when Lanskoy, her 26-year-old favorite, died after a short illness. She was brokenhearted and howled with Potemkin. For a while, the court carousel stopped turning. "The Duchess of Kingston is sunk into neglect. Nobody thinks of her," wrote a young Englishman in St. Petersburg.[36]

However quiet she had become in St. Petersburg, Estonia was another story: more ships sailed from Hull for Chudleigh in April and May 1785, with their bounty of flora and fauna: the *Vigilant* with trees, shrubs, a hamper of pigeons; the *Young William* with more plants, four dogs, and "sea stock," a mixture of fat and oatmeal to feed them on board.

Back in Nottinghamshire, her agents, William Sanday at Holme Pierrepont and William Pickin at Thoresby, were frenetically gathering rents together to send to Drummond's to pay for it all. Montmartre, meanwhile, had descended into open warfare: Elizabeth refused to pay the balance; La Crosse took her to court.* He lost, but appealed, and the verdict was overturned. Just as with that impetuous marriage to Augustus Hervey, Elizabeth's impulses had led to drama and debacle. To hunt down her own money and settle the case, Elizabeth left St. Petersburg and, in December 1785, arrived in Calais.

Although she did not know it then, she had left Russia forever.

---

* At Châtelet, a Paris court (with prisons and police headquarters) of the *ancien régime*. The stronghold was demolished between 1802 and 1810.

CHAPTER TWENTY-SEVEN

CHUDLEIGH ON THE SEINE

In the restless, reckless energy of her Montmartre house project, Elizabeth, now in her mid-sixties, had caught the mood of the moment in Paris, or it had caught her. The pre-revolutionary decade was a building boom. A flurry of finance poured into new aristocratic houses, churches, the bridge at the Place de la Concorde. The Palais Royal had been turned into a carousel of dizzying entertainment, political debate, and foppish consumerism by the last Duc d'Orléans.[1] There were concerts, operas, plays, and exhibitions; the Montgolfier brothers' hot air balloon, and faux science such as Franz Mesmer's animal magnetism. The Palais arcades, then as now, sold an extravaganza of goods: furs, jewelry, calling cards, medals, toy soldiers, the *accoutrements* of privileged Parisian life.

After an exhausting three-month journey back from Russia, as Montmartre was uninhabitable, Elizabeth had taken up residence at the Hôtel du Parlement d'Angleterre, Rue Coq-Héron, five minutes' walk from the Palais Royal. Her Paris social life took her into all sorts of circles: the salonista Madame de Guimont, the art-loving Fermier-Général[2] Chalut de Vernin. Often more popular outside the judgmental British nobility, she was welcomed into the Polish and Italian Exiles' club. She had become friends with the married portrait painters Richard and Maria Cosway. Devon-born Richard, a libertine with a simian appearance, was a celebrated artist[3] who had come to Paris to paint the current Duc d'Orléans' young children. His beautiful wife Maria, blue-eyed, fair-haired, half-Italian, twenty years his junior, painted miniatures. In their set was Thomas Jefferson, now American envoy in Paris.[4] Maria had met him in Paris and embarked on a love affair, and a lifelong correspondence.[5] As an architect, Jefferson was delighted by the constant construction around him: "Paris is every day enlarging and beautifying," he wrote.

The author of the Declaration of Independence was America's second ambassador to Paris—he had followed Benjamin Franklin in 1785. The declaration had come just weeks after Elizabeth's trial, but after the Howe brothers had failed to broker peace on Staten Island that September, four years of fighting had followed. France had joined America's side against Britain and the peace treaty was eventually signed in Paris in 1783; although the decisive battle had been at Yorktown in 1781, when Charles Cornwallis surrendered to the French/American forces. As the world turned around, in those few short years before the French Revolution, Elizabeth could leave Russia and settle in France—which felt far more like home than rural Estonia, or St. Petersburg—because of the new peace. No one in Paris knew how brief that peace was to be.

Elizabeth and the Cosways had connections: in Florence, Maria had studied under the Kingstons' old friend, Johann Zoffany; Richard was close to the royal family and had become the first and only "Painter to the Prince of Wales."[6] Mrs. Cosway was a sociable polyglot with many friends. In London her Sunday-night concerts—at which she was main performer—were occasions of splendor. Horace Walpole wrote of receiving her "bushels of little Italian notes of invitation."

As Maria wrote to Jefferson in September 1786, they were dining with Elizabeth at St. Cloud, on the outskirts of Paris.[7] Jefferson wrote to "Madame Cosway" around that time at Rue Coq-Héron; it seems she was staying with Elizabeth. Richard Cosway sketched the final portrait of Elizabeth: a soft, ageless face drawn in pastels, tinted with light color, loose white hair, and an assertively modest, buttoned-up dress, drapery in the background, a still penetrating, knowing gaze.[8]

While Richard Cosway was drawing her, Elizabeth was given the chance to frame her own history, too. Elizabeth apparently narrated her life story to Baroness d'Oberkirch, a noblewoman from Alsace, whom Elizabeth met in Paris.[9] At the request of d'Oberkirch, and her friend Bathilde d'Orléans, Duchess of Bourbon,[10] Elizabeth spent the day[11] with the two young aristocrats at Bourbon's neoclassical Château de Petit Bourg at Evry, south of Paris. The baroness recorded that Elizabeth retained traces of "no ordinary beauty," her deportment rivaled only by the queen herself, Marie Antoinette; she was regal, with the grace of a goddess.

Invited back by Elizabeth, the baroness praised her capacity for entertainment. Not only were her suppers "celebrated for their refinement and luxury. She is somewhat of a gourmand, and patronises the gastronomic art," but she found her "a most extraordinary woman . . . her great knowledge of society, her wit, and brilliant imagination, which reflected as a mirror all that passed before it, gave a brilliancy to her conversation that I have seldom seen equalled. She is proud and self-willed, opposed to almost all received wisdoms . . . She is generous and noble."

Elizabeth gave immense sums in charity at Calais, wrote the baroness, who was fond of her company: "Our supper at her house was very pleasant. She . . . would feel anxious to return to her native land, if the injustice she had suffered did not prevent her; besides that, most of her early friends were dead." Elizabeth liked Paris "extremely" and her house became "the rendezvous of everyone distinguished either by talent or rank." She told the baroness, "I shall certainly never return to England; it is a stupid place. The English are ever seeking amusement without finding it, while the French possess it without the fatigue of running after it." She maintained her passion for music—admiring Gluck, whom she had last seen in Vienna (appropriately, the opera *Iphigénie en Tauride* is said to be his finest)—and for jewelry. After supper, Elizabeth showed the baroness her jewels, which were "more valuable than the treasury of St. Mark at Venice." To the baroness's astonishment, Elizabeth had already numbered each piece for their recipients after she died. One diamond, "very valuable, and of the purest water," was for the pope; there was an entire set of ornaments of different jewels ready for Catherine the Great.

While focusing on the afterlife, Elizabeth had also decided to make peace with her enemies. In 1785, told that Evelyn Meadows was about to be arrested for debt at Metz,[12] she assured him she would try to extricate him from his predicament, as his friend. She was casting around for an heir and, luckily for him, he fell into trouble at just the time she was in the frame of mind to help. She obtained an order by which his arrest was prevented,[13] rented a house for her persecutor in Chaillot, now in the 16th arrondissement, but then a village outside Paris, and gave him a pension. She was "much and justly praised for this generosity and clemency."[14] Although when Horace Walpole heard of this extraordinary magnanimity, his verdict was that Elizabeth was "robbing Peter to pay Peter."[15]

Since her return to France, Elizabeth had been chasing her money from executor Heron. His latest reason not to pay her was that her signature as Duchess of Kingston was not legally acceptable, in spite of his view that Her Grace was "in law as much Duchess of Kingston as the wife of any Duke in this Kingdom is his Duchess." If she did not need the money, it was "very safely deposited," he added, disingenuously, given how often she had asked for it.[16]

In January 1786, Charles Meadows, with the third Meadows brother, General (William) Meadows, offered to lend Elizabeth £9,727 as a mortgage against the estate in place of the rent money she was owed. (A plan Heron had suggested when Elizabeth was still in Russia.) Elizabeth wrote to Heron in irritation at the offer, particularly as she would only be able to have half the money because the general was caught up in a legal action of his own—but stating that as "revenge is not the part of a Christian," she had forgiven them and, she hoped, "made happy" her adversaries. "These wounds can never be cured: I never meant, thought or believed I deserved the vehemence and rancour with which I have been treated."[17] Her money—one payment of £5,000, one of just under £10,000, finally came through in August.

Beset by the illnesses that had plagued her for so long, thinking she was not long for the world, Elizabeth formed the first draft of her peculiar, labyrinthine will over many months. On October 7, 1786, she finally signed it; by which time it contained a detailed inventory of possessions, with spaces left for names to be filled in at a later date. There was property in England, Russia, and France; heirlooms in all those places, and in Rome; pictures, jewels, plate, live animals, silver, silks. Some lots were marked by a letter code, the intention being that Elizabeth would decide who was in favor on an accompanying piece of paper. Such was her desire for harmony, or atonement, that she made up not only with the Meadowses, but added in a codicil that she left the pearl earrings and necklace "that I usually wear" to none other than the French mistress Kingston had spurned for her, Madame de la Touche. This remarkable flourish must have been rooted in her need to make amends; she was settling her accounts before God. Kingston too had attempted to do so—he had always been generous with Madame de la Touche.

And then Elizabeth made the final grandiose decision of a life lived on a grandiose scale, the swan song of her rash and acquisitive nature. Perhaps learning through her new friend, the Duchess of Bourbon, that the estate at Seine-Porte outside Paris, which had belonged to the duchess's late father, the Duc d'Orléans, was for sale, she bought the Château de Sainte-Assise in June 1787.[18] It was a wedding-cake chateau with a long lawn that swept down to the Seine where it had moorings, just like those of the Royal Hospital on the Thames at Chelsea. By modern standards it was vast, by Catherine the Great levels, not at all.

It was so expensive—by one account, £58,000[19]—that she had to pawn jewelry and pay in installments. She wrote to a Versailles official,[20] requesting the king's permission to change the name. She described how she had forsaken "profitable" rabbit hunting[21] to create a textiles factory (hemp), which would save money for the government. She expressed love for France, "although I am a foreigner, I am extremely close to this country and to His Majesty, and I have always been so, and wherever I travel I always praise his merits, and this is the reason why I intend to please him and give joy to my own heart by creating schools in Calais for the children of the poor and the rich, teaching them how to read and write." There would be six nuns and six monks teaching 2,000 poor children—which led to the point of the letter. She wanted to change the name of Sainte-Assise to one of a family that had been in England "since the Saxons conquered that island": a family that had built a town, and had their own barony: Chudleigh. The charm offensive worked—on June 30, Louis XVI approved the change of name.

At the same time, that spring and summer she rearranged her financial affairs. In April and June 1787, a notary[22] organized power of attorney in France for Evelyn Meadows because Elizabeth was planning to go back to Russia. She employed a French captain and a boat to take her there.[23] The journey was abandoned because of ill health, and she gave power of attorney in Russia to her steward, Cramp, instead.[24]

In July, she bought an apartment for Evelyn Meadows to live in on Rue de Bondy.[25] In a supreme act of Christian forgiveness, this was the extent to which she had befriended him. She had also increased his allowance to £600 a year. She also bought further lands around the chateau of Sainte-Assise, in October.[26]

What possessed her to take on such a ludicrously ambitious project alone, at her age? In the process of putting her affairs in order, she had bought the one last property she needed to fulfill her dream and secure her legacy, her lasting identity. Calling it Chudleigh was an attempt to set her name in stone, having had her married name (as she saw it) publicly stolen from her. She was, in a sense, writing her own obituary, and balancing her book with charitable gestures, good deeds, and magnanimity.

Her health that summer was in decline, a fall in July so debilitating that she could not return to Russia that winter. Her morale began to sink with her strength. Her loyal Knightsbridge butler John Williams hoped she would never go back to Russia; he thought the journey too much for her. She wrote as much to Garnovsky, now Potemkin's secretary, expressing her regret at not being able to see the prince. Never in good spirits when unwell, she told him she felt "insulted" by all the world. In August, her agent from Thoresby, William Pickin, found her at Calais recovering from a "slight fever."

Before the end of the year, Elizabeth wrote to Heron, whose nephew she had appointed to a clerical living, in the final surviving letter between them; she was still chasing her inheritance, feeling "oppressed," annoyed that her rooms at Bath were not let. Thoresby was under siege from the Meadowses, who were borrowing against the estate, and the neighboring landlord, Lord Chesterfield,[27] who was taking advantage of Elizabeth's absence—hunting, even building, on her land. Her staff attempted to sort things out behind her back so as not to incur her displeasure.

As 1788 began, the estate, island, farm, windmills, feudal rights of "Chudleigh," Seine-Porte, France, were all hers. Peace had been made with Evelyn Meadows. And yet Elizabeth was in low spirits because of ill health and uncertain finances. In February she wrote to her cousin and executor, George Payne,[28] fearful about her money; and to Maria Cosway, regretting her absence from the Hôtel du Parlement d'Angleterre, where she was intending to stay for five weeks before returning to Calais. Her strength had faded to the point that, in April, there was rumor she had died, which she had to deny to friends, staff, and bankers. Although increasingly isolated, she was still something of a tourist attraction to the peripatetic English *ton*: her last visitor was an MP, Temple Luttrell,[29] brother-in-law of King George III's younger brother.

As the royal treasury was running empty, Paris itself was in uproar and, as Elizabeth wrote to Maria Cosway, this had held up her wretched Montmartre lawsuit. She somehow had not foreseen that buying Sainte-Assise when she still had the burden of legal action on Montmartre would cause her immense stress when she was too weak to bear it.

One of Elizabeth's maids in Paris told how Elizabeth had been brought low by buying an estate that was "good for nothing, but to feed rabbits," the Montmartre lawsuit and "her former extravagance in equipage, living and jaunting from place to place." She had spent so much that she now had to pawn most of her jewels just to pay for the "common necessaries of life." Early one morning, a messenger told her long-standing servant Mr. Lilly that the Montmartre suit had gone against her; Lilly went to her apartment and "told her attendant to acquaint her Grace. This sudden news of her loss threw her into a violent passion." This was an indignity too far. She grew so miserable that a doctor was called, who found that her "disorder originated from uneasiness," and advised her to drink small quantities of diluted Madeira.[30]

In the hot and thunderous August of 1788, Paris was simmering on the brink of revolution through want of bread. The royal treasury was destitute and soldiers were being paid with mere promises. Starvation stalked the country. On the 8th, the king summoned the Estates General* for the first time in 150 years. On August 24, the minister of finance resigned, and in desperation the king called back Jacques Necker, the minister dispatched when he made the inglorious figures in the royal treasury public.† Young men gathered in central Paris, lighting bonfires and setting off fireworks. The *ancien régime* was on the precipice. Sparks of revolt were kindling in the crowds.

A few streets away from the fireworks in the Place Dauphine, the furious, once-beautiful Englishwoman of sixty-seven was lodging in defiant exile from the repressive old order of her disapproving homeland, the inhospitable chaos of the Montmartre building site, and the overgrown parkland of her new chateau at Sainte-Assise. In her rented townhouse on Rue Coq-Héron, as the carriages ran relentlessly over the cobbles and the tradesmen shouted out their wares beneath her, she lay sleeping, a few days after she had heard the distressing news about her last lawsuit.

In the early hours of August 26, in the upper stories of her rented apartment in the Hôtel du Parlement d'Angleterre, this gray-haired, notorious woman in a nightgown, with watery blue eyes but a still imperious manner, asked her attendants to help her out of bed. She dressed and staggered across the room, sat in her armchair, stool at her feet, and demanded a glass of Madeira, and then another, and a slice of toast. With a female attendant holding her hand on either side of her at her request, she slipped into sleep and from there onto her final journey, into the place of no return, a fact that they only realized when her hands began to go cold in theirs.

And the moment she died, all hell broke loose.

---

* The Estates General: the *ancien régime*'s representative assembly of the three estates; the first, the clergy; the second, the nobility; the third, the people.
† Swiss-born Necker had been dismissed as finance minister by Louis XVI in 1781.

CHAPTER TWENTY-EIGHT

BATTLE OF WILLS

A maid said that "a great confusion instantly arose" while poor Elizabeth's body was still warm.[1] The apartments were plunged into a heartless frenzy, everyone striving to take as much as they could before officials arrived to seal up the Hôtel du Parlement d'Angleterre. In a grotesque, sorrowful scene, looting began: boxes and wardrobes were flung open, lace, linen, dresses scattered and stuffed into trunks in haste with silver plate, pictures, and furniture assessed around the corpse.

The Hôtel du Parlement d'Angleterre contained only Elizabeth's most portable valuables. The Duchess-Countess had acquired multiple possessions, just as she had titles. She had left a trail across Europe: property, some half-built or half-paid for, in three countries; goods in four. In each place, there were rivals and pretenders to her legacies. The will would prove questionable in its legality and, as her mounting debts became apparent, its feasibility. Into the next century and thousands of miles apart, numerous people became involved in the ignominious hunt for her fortune.

"As boys scramble for the fruit of a shaken tree," reported one newspaper on the instant tussle over her belongings, "so is there a general struggle among the needy for the movables of the late Duchess of Kingston. A fracas has already happened in consequence of a contention who should take charge of the diamonds."[2]

The first predator to pick belongings from around the corpse was the ungrateful villain Evelyn Meadows. Her own nephew by marriage was the final mountebank to deceive her. Despite his aunt being so generous, so forgiving to him, age had only compounded the greed and duplicity of the eldest Kingston nephew, who darted across Paris the moment he heard the news and, within an hour of Elizabeth's death, had packed up all his aunt's diamonds, pearls, silver plate, and "taffeta curtains" into large trunks with the treacherous connivance of her Parisian steward, Mr. Lilly.* Conscience and kindness were suspended by all. The female servants fled wearing Elizabeth's silk gowns, taking the best lace with them. The rooms were stripped bare while her body lay decomposing in the heat, the miserable, toxic stench of death filling the apartments, and cartloads of furniture and goods trundled over the cobbles in a carriage back to the apartment Elizabeth had bought for Evelyn Meadows. A newspaper reported that his one-time mistress, Clara Hayward, "now a Parisian grisette† . . . vows vengeance unless the wardrobe be committed to her care." Callous jokes started while Elizabeth's body was still in situ: "An English wit, now at Paris, proposes a race on the Boulevards for the Holland smocks [plain linen smocks], Clara to start in puris naturabilis" (i.e., naked).[3]

Evelyn Meadows was in no hurry for the news to get back to England; he wanted as much time as possible to hide his aunt's belongings. A servant's word reached decent, loyal John Williams at Kingston House on August 30. Distraught, he wrote to Heron, incoherent with shock, telling him that she had died on August 26 at seven o'clock. He alone seemed to appreciate the dreadful situation: "I am in great trouble. The body. What is to be done? Where is it to be buried?"

Williams was one of the few who seemed to anticipate the unfolding tragedy and horror of Elizabeth's pitiful end, exacerbated by the opportunism, incompetence, and sheer lack of humanity of those around her. Dr. Fergus Macdonnell, embalmer, asked for fifty guineas above his normal rate for a task "more than usually unpleasant, dangerous and embarrassing."[4] The superintendent M. Guyot taped

---

* John Lilly, or Lyly, had been footboy in livery years before and was finally her maître d'hôtel at Paris.
† Grisette: a flirtatious lower-class girl.

up the apartments and blocked access for twenty-four hours—and as Elizabeth had died in the most sweltering summer heat, her body had putrefied in less than twelve, alarming the servants and neighbors. Macdonnell's assistant became so distressed that he refused to proceed without help. What was usually a job for two became one for five, "at no small risk to us all." When Macdonnell cut open the decaying flesh he found her heart and lungs in perfect condition, but she had burst a small blood vessel, the cause of her death.

Five weeks later, in a deplorable, heartbreaking scene, Elizabeth's body still lay in the Hôtel du Parlement d'Angleterre where she had died. The act of removing her seemed too much for her three distinguished English executors: Heron, Sir George Shuckburgh,[5] and George Payne. In early September, Payne had gone to Paris with the two-year-old will, and discovered that there was a second will,[6] in which he had been left £15,000; it had not, however, been signed. As he had forgotten the papers needed to bury her, he returned to England for them, and fell ill on the way. As one paper reported: "So she remained, the master of the hotel still taking full rent at 30 guineas a month for her original apartments although the Garde Robe [wardrobe or armoire] is now large enough for all her greatness."[7] The cruel wit of the era just emphasized that her potential heirs were more concerned about their own interest than about giving her a dignified burial. The tragic truth was laid bare: the "wanderer on the face of the earth" had died alone, in rented accommodation, in a foreign land surrounded by people whose love was not for her, but for their own material gain.

Newspapers shared the same concern, immediately airing the universal speculation: what was going to happen to her money? They also offered ambivalent judgments on her life, the *London Chronicle*, for example, which attempted to describe her complexity: "The late Duchess of Kingston, though by no means distinguished among the train of Diana [goddess of chastity], was not destitute of good qualities . . . Her wit and humor, though rather of a coarse quality, were strong, and derived great advantage from a very extensive knowledge of life. She was of a very capricious temper, and though shrewd and penetrating, was very easily imposed upon."[8]

Evelyn Meadows, in his fifties by now, was not the only vulture already circling in France. M. Cocove, son of the man from whom Elizabeth had bought her house in Calais (brother of Mme de Porquet, the woman whom she had once locked in her bedroom in Estonia), saw gold. He traveled to England to convince various Chudleigh cousins that under French law, if the will was invalid, they stood to inherit far more than had been left to them. Of course, he would require a hefty cut in exchange for his help. Only a distant cousin, Colonel Phillips Glover—once a second violin in the Thoresby orchestra—was desperate or gullible enough to listen to him. Glover set off for Paris in keen pursuit of the money on behalf of the Chudleigh cousins. He was a lethal combination of impoverished and impulsive. Court-martialed from the militia for using "language contrary to good order and discipline," he had once killed an apothecary in a duel in Manchester.*

The will in either version was, indeed, invalid in France, as it was neither in Elizabeth's own handwriting nor witnessed by a notary. Her belongings—those that had not been taken by Evelyn Meadows or the servants—were "taken possession by the King's officers." At one newspaper's estimate, "the Duchess's effects in France, in estates, diamonds and furniture, is said to be about three hundred thousand pounds."[9] But even if that figure was true—which it was not—allowance had not been made for her considerable debts.

Nearly two full months after her death, reading in the press the dreadful news that Elizabeth's embalmed body still lay, unbelievably and tragically, in its apartment, another opportunist arrived at the Hôtel de Parlement d'Angleterre. This was a quack by the name of Dr. Freeman, who had traveled to Paris from London to restore the duchess back to life by means of "animal magnetism," the modish theory that life force could be communicated through living things. When asked why it failed on Elizabeth's corpse, Freeman explained that "the surgeons who embowelled her Grace . . . cut the right ventricle of her heart." He consoled himself with coaxing seven

---

* A fight had broken out in a queue outside a theater, for a reason lost to eighteenth-century Manchester.

drowned kittens back to life in Calais on the way home, for which he was awarded a medal.[10] As Payne had failed in his duties and had left Elizabeth so appallingly unburied, it fell to the speculative distant relation Colonel Glover (neither Heron nor Shuckburgh, in his thirties, crossed the Channel), at his own expense, to pay off the servants, check the body out of the lodgings, and finally, in November, dispatch Elizabeth's corpse to a Protestant vault where it awaited transport to England. Elizabeth had been specific in her burial wishes. If she died in Russia, Catherine was to decide where she should be buried, as "my heart has been with her this long time"; if England, it should either be in the church in Devon[11] "without pomp" and a "handsome" headstone at a cost of up to £500, or with her coffin chained to the duke's in the family vault at Holme Pierrepont. Charles Meadows agreed to advance £1,000 of his new wealth towards the burial, and gave permission for her to lie in the vault.

She might have dreamt of rural Devon or a great ceremony by orders of the tsarina in St. Petersburg, but, poignantly, her body stayed in the anonymous vault in Belleville where, as far as we know, her bones still lie. As the revolution convulsed France the following year, she would never have a tombstone or a proper burial. In spite of Charles Meadows's offer, it seems that no one had the willpower to move her.

Many months later, Whitehead, Kingston's one-time valet, wrote, "I find her desire of being buried by the side of the Duke of Kingston, at Holme Pierrepont in Notts, and that the coffins might be chained together, is not complied with." It never would be.

No one deserved such a fate, certainly not the once-intrepid Elizabeth.

*

Disputes over her belongings spanned many years and many miles, from St. Petersburg to Plymouth. They were never quite untangled. The battle for her inheritance was as perilous as her life. Some of those who staked a claim would end up in debt, others in prison. The will, even if it had been allowed, had been written with so many blanks in it that multiple opportunities lay for contention. The spaces were proof that, wearied by years of legal action, she did not know who to trust. The will was, like its author, an eccentric, imaginative, fanciful work—a mixture of procrastination, social climbing, making amends, name-dropping, wishful thinking, and revenge. No wonder it was printed and reprinted to public delight.

England was more straightforward than most. As the duke would have wished, Elizabeth left most things to the designated heir, Charles Meadows. The respectable second son took the name Pierrepont, and later Viscount Newark as he became, to his elder brother Evelyn's disgust, the rightful owner of his uncle's estates at Thoresby, Holme Pierrepont, and elsewhere. Seven years later, Evelyn Meadows tried to block Charles from also being awarded the title of Earl Manvers and Herries. He failed. Charles finished Thoresby and commissioned the renowned Humphry Repton to landscape the grounds. A hundred years later, his descendant, the 3rd Earl Manvers, knocked it down and Anthony Salvin designed a Victorian pile for him. It is now a hotel. The lake on which the duke's fleet gathered is barred from public access because of subsidence, from coal mining. Charles Meadows's eldest son inherited the Manvers title, which died out in 1955 with the death of the 6th Earl. His daughter Lady Rozelle split the estate between two cousins, the responsibility now with their children: Grigor Pierrepont on the Thoresby estate and Robert and Charlotte Brackenbury at Holme Pierrepont. The title of the Duke of Kingston had died out on that stormy night in Bath, with its second holder.

Elizabeth would have been incensed to discover that the Hall estate in Devon, that "fairy land" of her childhood, was not, the law decided, hers to bequeath. Always loyal to her own impoverished relations, she had chosen the Reverend John Penrose and his descendants to inherit Hall; the condition being that the heir was to take the name and arms of Chudleigh. As shown in Paris and Estonia, she was keen for her own name to live on; her brother, her first cousin, the last baronet, and all her male cousins who bore the name had predeceased her. This was another wistful bid to ensure a succession—Chudleighs at Hall in the style of the Pierreponts at Thoresby.

But that was not to be, either. Both Penrose and Charles Meadows believed Hall to be theirs, and they came to a standoff over, of all things, the local vicar. Both presented a candidate for the vacancy of Harford Church (a living that came with the Hall estate) to the Bishop of Exeter, who refused to endorse either. In 1803, as legal action stirred in Chancery, they settled out of court, and Charles Meadows—Viscount Newark by now—inherited Hall. (Without a valid will, Meadows had argued, Elizabeth's property should become part of the Kingston estate.) He sold it to a stranger in 1803.

He also inherited Kingston House in Knightsbridge and all its land, though Elizabeth intended to leave some of that elsewhere (few belongings reached their allotted destination). The stucco terraces of Ennismore Gardens were built on the paddocks and gardens in the nineteenth century. Later occupants of the house itself included the Duke of Wellington's elder brother, the Marquess Wellesley, an ancestor of the queen,[12] and the first practicing Jewish MP, Lionel de Rothschild. Kingston House was the last aristocratic house in the area to stay standing. It was not demolished until 1937, when the valuable estate made way for blocks of flats overlooking the park: the gargantuan block of Kingston House North lies on the site of the original house.

James Christie held three auctions of Elizabeth's belongings. In May 1789, a four-day sale saw the contents of Kingston House on the block: Smyrna and Wilton carpets, birds of paradise in glass cases, a plaster of a sleeping cupid, a carthorse, a "milch" cow, a copy of Dr. Johnson's dictionary, pictures by Rubens, Brueghel, Cuyp. A twelve-day sale of the contents of Thoresby that June included furniture, tapestries, carriages, linen, and dogs. The jewelry came later, in February 1791, on behalf of Colonel Glover. It made £7,400, for a selection of rings, necklaces, and shoe buckles, consisting of emeralds, rubies, and sapphires (most of the diamonds and pearls had disappeared, courtesy of Evelyn Meadows), and some filigree, such as a box decorated with "a portrait of Voltaire."

In France, there were legacies of one thousand *louis d'or*[13] for a friend of Elizabeth's from Rome, the Abbé Gian Domenico Finateri, now a priest at Versailles; for the son of Cocove of Calais—the man who caused so much trouble by firing up Colonel Glover—and for the sister of M. Caffieri, the customs master at Calais. The Calais house, gardens, stables, and outbuildings were left to be the residence of Calais' commandant, including all the "wines and liquors" in the cellar, which comprised about 40,000 bottles, in excellent condition. During the revolution, its magnificent salons became a depot for confiscated goods. It later became a hotel, a favorite with the English. Paintings by Pierre Mignard in the gallery at Calais were left to the Lord Mayor and Aldermen of the City of London for the Egyptian Hall of the Mansion House: they would never arrive. A strange choice of recipient: its appeal probably that this was the rival basis of power in London to the House of Lords who, as Elizabeth saw it, had so betrayed her.

Far from being grateful, Cocove Jr. not only sought out the cousins but even defrauded Glover, who gave him money to pay interest at the pawnshop that never reached its destination. The colonel was horrified to discover that in French law, the heir was responsible for the deceased's debts. Pursued by Glover through the courts, Evelyn Meadows finally appeared in the dock on December 24, 1788, "strongly suspected of having made a depredation [sic]" on the duchess's effects with "a person nam'd [John] Lilly" as accomplice.[14] Lilly reluctantly admitted his role. Meadows eventually produced a list of items Elizabeth had "sent him" in a great trunk, which he now had to return: the duke's silver plate, for example, onto which—with startling alacrity—he had already substituted his own cypher. He referred to his aunt as the "Countess of Bristol," not the duchess he had addressed so solicitously in life.

By the close of 1788, the executors had turned on each other. Heron felt the case was a "perfect Hydra, and requires a Hercules to combat it." Payne, he wrote, "though a perfect gentleman," was no Hercules.[15] Accused by Heron of having let Evelyn Meadows abscond with Elizabeth's belongings, Payne defended himself. What was he supposed to have done, alone in Paris, without probate, the apartments under seal, and an embalmed body of a Duchess-Countess he had no permission to move?

Evelyn Meadows avowed that Elizabeth had bought the Château de Sainte-Assise for him. His claims were drowned out by the realization that the debts in France—the jewels at the pawnshop, the mortgage on Sainte-Assise, money still owed to La Crosse for Montmartre, embalming costs, staff wages—came to an immense £56,000.

The fight between Glover and Meadows tipped into a press war.

Glover recruited that old journalistic pugilist, the Reverend William Jackson, who had so vigorously fought Elizabeth's cause with his pen against Samuel Foote, and retained his loathing of Foote's accomplice, Evelyn Meadows. Much closer relatives, such as Elizabeth's first cousins, Sir George's daughters, had shown much more sense in staying out of it.

On January 22, 1789, *The Star* reported on the absurd treasure hunt, siding with Meadows:

PARIS, JAN. 17.

Indefatigable has been the industry of the would-be heirs of the late Duchess of Kingston; and all this to enrich the lawyers of this country, and impoverish themselves. For pearls, diamonds, millions, having ransacked all the pawn-brokers of Paris, and all her Grace's chests and cupboards, as well at Calais as here, they are now busy ferreting for hidden treasures in the rabbit-burrows of St. Assise. We were to judge, however, from the saturnine looks of those greedy gold-finders, their success has not been equal to the investigation which they have made.[16]

By 1793, at the best estimate, Colonel Glover was £18,000 out of pocket, his intended sale of Elizabeth's French properties having been wrecked in the maelstrom of the French Revolution.

The Château de Sainte-Assise was sold to an industrialist, and then passed through various hands—including the Beauvau family, Princes of the Holy Roman Empire. In the twentieth century it became the headquarters of a radio company, who sold it to the French navy who tracked nuclear submarines from the site. Though traces of its former grandeur remain, it is now semi-derelict, its garden on the Seine choked with weeds.

By the time executor George Payne arrived in St. Petersburg in 1789, Elizabeth's steward there, "that rascal Seymour" (a "good, honest man" in Elizabeth's unsuspecting view), was giving away cases of wine to anyone of influence and drinking his way through the rest. He would not let Payne into the house. Eventually he was evicted by court order, and an inventory taken. Items without names attached in the will were sold at auction.

From St. Petersburg, Payne wrote to Heron in exasperation, "If I could have foreseen that I could have met with so much trouble and vexation as I have experienced here, and have suffered so long an absence from my family, I should not have been induced for double my legacy to have undertaken the business."[17]

Elizabeth's decision to leave those blanks in the will had made a tortuous process even more so: Colonel Garnovsky, Potemkin's charming officer spy who had escorted Elizabeth across Europe after that first visit to Russia, and Baron von Rosen, from whom she had bought the property, both claimed to be the intended heirs of Chudleigh in Estonia and, in Garnovsky's case, of all her property in Russia. Chudleigh, its contents, and its "forests, mines, quarries" had been left as tantalizing blanks; with 30,000 roubles* to be paid to her apothecary, still living there; a tenth of the value of what the mines produced for whomever Catherine chose; and freedom for her "four musical slaves" after six years, with a pension. The land given to her by the empress, at Schlüsselburg, next to Potemkin's estate, was left blank; the land around the Red Pub or Tavern on the road to Peterhof, blank too; as was the house in St. Petersburg. Various pieces, including those musical lusters (giant, musical chandeliers), an organ, and alabaster tables were left to Potemkin; multiple other belongings were left blank, or to Charles Meadows. Some pictures— the Holy Family supposedly "by Raphael" and the Claude Lorrain painting, both "lent" to Chernyshev—were to be returned to England for Charles Meadows, along with a statue Henry Mowatt had delivered from Rome that was lying in Chernyshev's garden. In these bequests she was either being dutiful—those pictures for Meadows had come from Thoresby in the first place—or showing her adoration; to Elizabeth, the maverick Anglophile general, Potemkin, was irresistible. Few of her wishes, apart from the Potemkin bequest, came about. The Claude Lorrain is in the Hermitage; the Raphael, possibly a misattribution, untraced. Other pictures were to be offered to Catherine for 100,000 roubles and if she "does not

---

* c. £6,000 (Marteau currency converter).

accept them, the King of Spain"[18] should be offered them. Fifty thousand roubles were to be paid to Garnovsky.

Catherine was said to have bellowed with laughter when she saw the will. She, of course, found in favor of her friend Garnovsky against Baron von Rosen. She decreed that the debts should be paid first, then the specific legacies; the remainder would go to Garnovsky. When the property was sold, only 50,000 roubles were offered for Chudleigh (35,000 less than Elizabeth had paid for it); 14,000 for the house in St. Petersburg; clothes, rum, and other goods were auctioned for 3,000 roubles.*

Garnovsky was a calculating fellow. Back in July 1787, he had written to Potemkin's secretary when he heard Elizabeth had bought Sainte-Assise: "Kingstonsha ["that Kingston woman"], indeed, has bought an estate in France worth two million pounds. So, a part of the inheritance that I had been expecting has been sacrificed at the Temple of Venus to some French cupid, my rival."[19]

He was rich for a while. But when Catherine was succeeded by her son Paul III in 1796, the colonel, as part of Potemkin's camp, fell out of favor, as Paul had loathed Potemkin. He was convicted of underpaying the legacies, and thrown into prison.

Pictures, silver, and musical lusters ended up in the Hermitage, where they are to this day. Garnovsky was eventually released. The once-proud star of the *basse-cour* died in extreme poverty.

Chudleigh in Estonia was still inhabited by a Mr. Wilkinson (Elizabeth's steward) in 1806.[20] Neighboring Oru, the parkland, was bought in the nineteenth century by one of Russia's richest men, Grigory Jelissejev. He built an Italianate palace on the site, which became the summer residence of Estonia's prime minister before it was destroyed in the Second World War. There is still an expansive coastal park there.

In an act of gratitude, Elizabeth wanted Dr. Frey, the Swiss doctor who signed the theft report in Rome, and attended her there, to have the belongings she had left with Sister Wortley Montagu.[21] (Such was the lottery fever in the air that even the holy Abbé Finateri tried

---

* Divide by five for pounds sterling.

to claim some Roman goods above his legacy.) The executors sent Andrew Stuart, a wily, blunt-speaking lawyer,[22] to Rome on their behalf to assess the legacy there. Admitted into the convent, he peered into three dust-coated boxes in the dim corner where they had been dropped, under the care of the nun who showed him her fond letters from Elizabeth. One box contained scraps of poetry, accounts, and travel journals "of no value whatsoever"; another, curtains, bed, and table linen, and the last, some "old-fashioned" silver plate, worth no more than its weight. Stuart had a fifteen-minute "tête-à-tête" with a gracious pope, who was willing to receive "a gold snuff box with the Holy Family by Raphael" left to him in "acknowledgement of his gracious protection." Raphael had never knowingly painted a snuffbox, wrote Stuart to Heron.[23]

The jewelry formed the most whimsical bequests. For the "acknowledgement of a heart full of gratitude for the particular friendship with which her Imperial Majesty has always distinguished me," Elizabeth left "a pair of pearl earrings with my aigrette* containing five red pearls" and "one large red pearl suspended from an Imperial crown of brilliants," a pearl that she believed to be the rarest jewel in the world, to Catherine.

The British Museum was left two large pearls and the watchcase Mary, Queen of Scots had given to a "friend on the scaffold in her last moments."[24] The Countess of Salisbury, daughter of Elizabeth's old friend, Lord Hillsborough, was left white pearl pear-drop and diamond earrings that "belonged" to the original Countess of Salisbury, the Catholic martyr executed by Henry VIII.[25]

There were jewels for old friends the Dukes of Newcastle and Portland, and for the Barrington family (Admiral Barrington was to have her frigate), money for executors, cousins, and relations, such as £5,000 for the duke's great-nephew, the son of Frances Campbell (née Meadows); £500 for Maria Egerton, who had stood next to her in white satin at the trial. There were generous legacies to "old and faithful" John Williams, £4,000, and more for his wife; even

---

* An aigrette adorned a headdress or hat—it was a bejeweled ornament holding a spray of feathers (the word comes from the crest of an egret).

his children were to get £3,000 each; legacies for treacherous John Lilly, servants at Calais, Thoresby, and St. Petersburg, including the sybaritic Seymour and the interpreter and coachman there. Loyalty, from rich or poor, was to be rewarded in Elizabeth's mind.

The will was generous to those who did not need it as well as those who did, but there were other altruistic thoughts. Money was left to enable the town of Calais to separate their prisoners of war and debtors from criminals, and for a water mill to provide free corn for the poor when the wind dropped. (These suggestions were thought deranged at the time.) The first idea was said to be Semple's, who had been distressed to be placed alongside proper felons when imprisoned for debt. As someone who had experienced poverty and debt, Elizabeth was ahead of her time in wanting to destigmatize insolvency.

Many of Elizabeth's valuables came into the possession of Prince Potemkin. Some were left to him directly, some, such as tapestries and paintings, were bought from (or given to him by) Garnovsky after her death. So too were silver vases, used as wine fountains, and a wine cooler by the silversmith Philip Rollos—fish soup was served in the latter at a Potemkin ball, and he ate out of it when he went traveling. *The Magnanimity of Alexander the Great* (Or *The Family of Darius Before Alexander the Great*, 1689) by Pierre Mignard, now in the Hermitage, came from Potemkin's Tauride Palace, and had been bought from—or given to him by—Garnovsky.

One guest described the famous masquerade ball Potemkin held to celebrate Russia's victory over the Turks in April 1791, at the Tauride Palace, at which Catherine was guest of honor. Three thousand guests awaited her arrival. Plants had been decorated with glinting diamonds and scarlet fish swam in crystal bowls. The ceiling was hung with "two chandeliers of black crystal hanging above vases of white Carrara marble . . . In them [the chandeliers] were clocks with extremely clever music; they had been bought for 42,000 roubles . . . In one of the halls was a lovely golden elephant." Another guest wrote: "To light this vast portico, they also hung 32 chandeliers, and one of excellent size and quality at each end, each with an organ inside. These used to belong to the

Duchess of Kingston . . . A luxurious clock, that once belonged to the Duchess . . . is in the form of a golden or gilded elephant, which moves its eyes, ears and tail when the clock strikes."[26] This elephant clock traveled from the Hermitage to the Shah of Persia as a present in 1817, but most of the treasures in Russia were bought off Potemkin's estate by the Treasury, and taken to the Hermitage, where they still remain today.

*

After a lifetime of snide commentary on his childhood playmate, Walpole decided he was done. "I have nothing more to say," he wrote to Lady Ossory, "I was weary of her folly and vanity long ago, and now look on her only as a big bubble that is burst."[27]

His resolve lasted less than a week. He then wrote to another friend: "You are probably curious, Madam, about the Duchess-Countess's will; but it certainly is not known yet, being lodged at Paris, and the lawyer, who drew it, being in Ireland. She is supposed to have died much in debt. The Meadowses mourn for her, out of respect to the Duke; but I have not heard whether the Herveys do. They ought out of respect to the Earl, since he did not choose to sue for a divorce."[28]

Walpole could not kill off his lifelong curiosity because, in addition to the jewels, the pictures, and the houses—from Chudleigh on the Baltic coast, to the newly bought princely Chudleigh chateau on the Seine—there was another, vital legacy. By force of personality, scandal, courage, gossip, and circumstance, her story blazed its own trail.

EPILOGUE

While executors, lawyers, nephews, and distant cousins scrambled over Elizabeth's inheritance—prizing boxes open in Rome, selling pointers in Nottinghamshire, and drinking their way through her cellar in St. Petersburg—the first chronicles of Elizabeth's life began to appear. Courtesy of the printing presses of London and Paris, they were told and sold again through a filter of fictional embellishment.

Thackeray made a twisted muse of Elizabeth, to whom so many of his heroines, most particularly coquettish Beatrix Esmond in *The History of Henry Esmond*, who becomes the manipulative widow Baroness Bernstein in *The Virginians*, owe part of their story. Her ability to pick herself up from disaster—and run rampage not only through society, but Europe too, is pure Becky Sharp. Elements of her life inspired Wilkie Collins and Charles Dickens.

No wonder authors and eighteenth-century publishers and penny printers loved her. Everybody had heard of her, and her salacious trial. There was a cast of kings, empresses, popes, statesmen, and naval heroes. She fulfilled a desire for moralizing schadenfreude, a parable on the theme of avarice, ambition, and the evils of the Georgian aristocracy.

Yet Elizabeth still resonates: while society changes, humanity stays the same. The need to judge a woman in the public eye feels as acute as ever. The cruelty of her treatment in Westminster Hall, with those thousands of spectators, so many of whom watched her suffer with relish, would be seen on a bloodier scale soon after her death among the tricoteuses of the French Revolution. It is an instinct found simmering today on social media. The desire to mock and humiliate Elizabeth was quite astounding, from both men and women, some of whom had private lives as questionable as her own.

Of course, Elizabeth was partly to blame. She had sought admiration and fame throughout her life, and used her beauty, wit, and court prowess as weapons for material gain. Take her gauzy Iphigenia costume, a blatant bid for attention: this the press gave her, but she was then horrified to realize that, though she might attempt to manipulate the newspapers, she could never exert control over them. Her mistress, Augusta, Princess of Wales, suffered the same level of spite after her husband's death. Any sign of female hubris was likely to provoke a backlash.

In learning the privileges and the pitfalls of fame, her story is timeless—and yet Elizabeth was also caught on the cusp of change. In this, she was a case study for her era. Her marriages and trial took place during the birth pains of the Enlightenment; born into the rigid world order of the early Georgians, she died in the dawn of the age of reason and revolution, in which America had rebelled, declared independence, and won. That fight for supremacy, the overturning of the oligarchy of the old world, was echoed in the change in marriage from dynastic alliance to romantic freedom. Some—abolitionists, proto-feminists, forward-thinkers—embraced this shift. Others, her more dogmatic peers, recoiled from it.

But she also offended some by challenging the natural order. She wanted to be a free and equal European, a citizen of the world—to go to Russia, say, in a private yacht full of treasures to smooth her path.

While I was writing this book, I learned that (with extraordinary timing) the Hermitage Museum in St. Petersburg was assembling an exhibition about Potemkin. The curators had stumbled across items that once belonged to an English duchess who had inveigled herself into the imperial court. Those possessions that had found their way into Potemkin's collection after Elizabeth's death were about to go on show.

So it was that, a few weeks later, I made my way into the Winter Palace, up the rococo staircase, and through the colossal gilt-and-stucco halls of the Neva enfilade. Here 4,000 people had sometimes dined among palm trees imported from the hothouses at the summer palace; here Nicholas and Alexandra had thrown the last ball, in fancy dress, in 1903. Outside, in Palace Square, a fresh blanket of snow lay on the ground around a twinkling Christmas tree. Inside, in intense heat, workmen mounted the exhibits, hammering nails in the wall. I wandered past the china Catherine commissioned for Potemkin from Sèvres, the most expensive set the factory ever produced, past his pale green woolen field tent, through the rotunda, housing his books, into the former private apartments of the palace.

Here, in what was once the Romanov nursery wing, I came across a glass box. Inside was the most enchanting "musical lustre," as it was described in Elizabeth's will: a giant, delicate crystal chandelier, nearly as wide as it is tall, that turns and plays music when its twenty-four candles are lit. Its branches are connected by fountains of cut glass, chains and balls, and shards of crystal, 1,000 pieces altogether, the thirteen bells of the musical device hidden behind its mirrored center. When Potemkin held his masquerade ball in 1791 in Catherine's honor, this was one of those pieces whose luminous elegance so enchanted the triumphant guests who danced beneath it.

This glittering piece of eighteenth-century mechanical artistry had survived two bloody revolutions, two world wars, including the 900-day Nazi siege of Leningrad, exile in the frozen Urals, and seventy-four years of Communist rule. And now here it was hanging again, every bit as spellbinding as it was when it first looked down on the duchess's St. Petersburg palace ballroom nearly 250 years ago.

This chandelier—along with urns, a silver wine cooler the size of a baby's bath, giant cartoons of hunting scenes, paintings such as that of Alexander the Great by Pierre Mignard that now fills a wall of the Hermitage—forms the imprint of Elizabeth Chudleigh, the girl from the Royal Hospital, Chelsea who had grown up to conquer London and much of Europe before making St. Petersburg her temporary home. There were nefarious motives behind the rapid evacuation of these treasures from England—to keep them from the grasp of her nephew, to bribe her way into a new royal court, and to take revenge on England's patriarchy. Some of these canvases were rolled up in the cover of darkness, and smuggled into Russia on her yacht.

As I wandered through the Hermitage rooms looking at the character in her belongings, their magnificence, excessive scale, and secret history, I was struck by the thought that here, unfiltered by judgment, the dauntless spirit of our roaming antiheroine lives on.

Cast List

Elizabeth Chudleigh, maid of honour to Augusta, Princess of Wales; bigamist, adventuress

Hon. Augustus Hervey, later 3rd Earl of Bristol, naval captain; Elizabeth's first, secret, husband

Evelyn Pierrepont, 2nd Duke of Kingston, owner of vast estates; second—but only acknowledged—husband of Elizabeth

Reverend Thomas Amis, clergyman who conducted the Lainston ceremony

Judith Amis, later Phillips, widow of Rev. Amis; secondly married Thomas Phillips, Kingston's steward at Holme Pierrepont

3rd Duke of Ancaster, Lord Great Chamberlain, court admirer of Elizabeth

Augusta, Princess of Wales, born a princess of Saxe-Gotha, wife of Frederick, Prince of Wales, mother of nine

Lord Barrington, secretary of war during the American War of Independence

Sarah Bate, Elizabeth's companion, soprano at Thoresby, half sister of executor Sir George Shuckburgh

Lord Bathurst (formerly Lord Apsley), lawyer, Tory, author of the "Intolerable Acts," which triggered revolution in America, Lord High Chancellor, 1771–8

Samuel Bentham, inventor, shipbuilder, naval officer, brother of philosopher Jeremy

Lord Bute, tutor to George III; favorite of Augusta; prime minister

Admiral Byng, naval officer, friend of Augustus Hervey; executed by firing squad

Giacomo Casanova, peripatetic Venetian lothario

Catherine II the Great, Empress of Russia 1762–96

Queen Charlotte, born Charlotte of Mecklenburg-Strelitz, married George III in 1761

Vice Admiral Count Ivan Chernyshev, Russian courtier, navy minister

Col. Thomas Chudleigh, father of Elizabeth; lieutenant governor of the Royal Hospital at Chelsea

Harriet Chudleigh, mother of Elizabeth; later housekeeper at Windsor Castle

Isabella "Bell" Chudleigh, Elizabeth's cousin and confidante

Lady Mary Chudleigh, Elizabeth's grandmother; poet, essayist

Sir Thomas Chudleigh, Elizabeth's brother; briefly a baronet before dying in battle

Colley Cibber, actor-manager, playwright, poet laureate

Pope Clement XIV, Anglophile pontiff

M. Cocove, Calais official; sold Elizabeth a house in the town; and later, his acquisitive son of the same name

Lady Mary Coke, envious, journal-writing daughter of the Duke of Argyll

Dr. Arthur Collier, Elizabeth's lawyer, friend of the Fieldings and Samuel Richardson

Teresa Cornelys, Italian impresario who threw subscription balls in Soho

Richard Cosway, fashionable painter of miniatures

Maria Cosway, wife of Richard, also a painter; object of Thomas Jefferson's affections

James Cox, jeweler; creator of the Peacock Clock in the Hermitage, St. Petersburg

Ann Craddock, Aunt Hanmer's lady's maid; key witness at Elizabeth's trial for bigamy

William Craddock, Augustus Hervey's manservant, husband of Ann

Madame de la Touche, married French mistress of the Duke of Kingston

Marchesa de los Balbases, aristocratic widow in Rome

Mme de Porquet, daughter of M. Cocove the Calais official; companion of Elizabeth in Russia

Mary Delany, bluestocking, artist, courtier, letter writer

Prince Edward, Duke of York and Albany, younger brother and childhood companion of George III, naval officer

Electress of Saxony, Maria Antonia, composer, singer, artist, widow

Harriet Fielding, daughter of novelist Henry, cousin and companion to Elizabeth

Samuel Foote, one-legged comic actor/playwright/theater manager inspired by Elizabeth's story and her money

Reverend John Forster, Elizabeth's chaplain and publicist in St. Petersburg

John Fozard, one-time groom to Kingston, with a livery at Hyde Park Stables

Frederick, Prince of Wales, heir to George II, father of George III, but never king himself

Mikhail Garnovsky, spy, secretary, and *homme d'affaires* to Potemkin

George II, German-born King of Great Britain from 1727 to 1760

George III, eldest son of Frederick and Augusta; King of Great Britain 1760–1820

Colonel Glover, first violin at Thoresby, a distant cousin of Elizabeth

Gunning sisters, Irish beauties at court; Elizabeth married the Duke of Hamilton, then the Duke of Argyll; Maria married the Earl of Coventry

6th Duke of Hamilton, Scotland's premier aristocrat, early admirer of Elizabeth

Ann Hanmer, Elizabeth's widowed aunt, guest at Lainston, enabler of the first marriage

Caesar Hawkins, doctor at court

Clara Hayward, mistress of Evelyn Meadows, friend of Foote, courtesan, and actress

Sir Richard Heron, Notts grandee and politician; Thoresby estate trustee and executor

George Hervey, 2nd Earl of Bristol, diplomat, elder brother of Augustus Hervey

Lord Hillsborough, Secretary of State for the Colonies, then for the Southern Department

Lord Howe, eldest of the Howe brothers, military hero, suitor of Elizabeth; killed in battle in 1758

Reverend William Jackson, Irish clergyman, journalist, and publicist for Elizabeth

James Laroche, Bristol slave trader, friend of Kingston and Elizabeth

John Lilly, long-standing servant of Elizabeth, first horn in Thoresby orchestra; in Paris when she died

Horace Mann, childhood neighbor of Elizabeth, envoy in Florence

Lord Mansfield, Lord Chief Justice, reformer; the century's most influential lawyer

Lord Masham, Frederick's auditor-general, son of Queen Anne's "favorite," Abigail Hill

Lady Masham, wife of the above; as Charlotte Dives, a maid of honour with Elizabeth

Lady Frances Meadows, only sister of the Duke of Kingston, heir to the family fortune until her brother's marriage to Elizabeth

Philip Meadows, Frances's manipulative, mercenary husband; deputy ranger, Richmond Park

Evelyn Meadows, their eldest son, a debauched inheritance hunter

Charles Meadows, upright second son, naval officer, MP; eventual heir to the Kingston estate

John Merrill, Elizabeth's cousin, widower; owner of Lainston House in Hampshire—scene of the first marriage

Sir Francis Molyneux, courtier, 6th Baronet, Notts aristocrat, Black Rod

Hannah More, poet, playwright, moralist, abolitionist

Lord Mount Stuart, son of Lord Bute, later 1st Marquess of Bute, Tory MP, diplomat

Mary Nesbitt, courtesan, mistress to Augustus Hervey, salon hostess

2nd Duke of Newcastle, friend and Notts neighbor of Elizabeth and Kingston

Friar O'Kelly, Irish brother from St. Isidore's, Rome

Mary Penrose, cousin and companion to Elizabeth

Anna Porter, diarist, married John Larpent, inspector of plays

Prince Grigory Potemkin, Catherine the Great's secret husband, coruler, military leader

William Pulteney, Earl of Bath, Elizabeth's mentor, Whig politician; Britain's shortest-appointed prime minister

Prince Karol Stanislaw Radziwill, turbulent Polish prince

Sir Joshua Reynolds, "grand style" English portrait painter, first president of the Royal Academy

Samuel Richardson, the celebrated novelist, frequenter of spa towns

Stephen Sayre, American rebel/spy who left London for Russia

Sir Charles Sedley, school friend of Hervey, Notts friend of Kingston

James Semple, "prince of swindlers," married to Elizabeth's god-daughter

Lord Thurlow, Tory MP, lawyer; Attorney General during Elizabeth's trial; writer of the instructions for the Howe brothers' negotiations for peace in America

Horace Walpole, childhood neighbor of Elizabeth, son of the prime minister, prolific man of letters, aesthete

Thomas Whitehead, Kingston's valet, Elizabeth's enemy

John Williams, Elizabeth's faithful butler at Kingston House

John Worta, articulate fraudster who claimed to be an Albanian prince

Lady Mary Wortley Montagu, Kingston's aunt; writer who brought smallpox inoculation to London

NOTES

To access the author's endnotes, which include
detailed information about this book's
sources and additional content, please visit
**https://www.simonandschuster.com/p
/materials-for-the-duchess-countess.**

For additional information about *The Duchess
Countess* or other works by Catherine Ostler,
please visit www.catherineostler.com.

SELECT BIBLIOGRAPHY

PRIMARY SOURCES

Abbé le Blanc, *Letters on the English and French Nations* (1747)

A Catalogue of the Rarities to be seen at Don Saltero's Coffee-House in Chelsea (1729)

Almon, J., *The Parliamentary Register; or, History of the Proceedings and Debates of the House of Lords*, vol. 5 (1775)

Anon., *The Fair Concubine: Or the Secret History of the Beautiful Vanella* (1732)

Austen, Jane, *Persuasion* (1818)

Autobiography and Correspondence of Mary Granville, Mrs. Delany, ed. Augusta Hall (1861)

Beckford, William, *Italy; with Sketches of Spain and Portugal* (1834)

Bentham, Jeremy, *The Collected Works of Jeremy Bentham*, ed. Timothy L. S. Sprigge (1968)

Boscawen, the Hon. Frances, *Admiral's Wife: Being the Life and Letters of the Hon. Mrs. Edward Boscawen 1719–61*, ed. C. F. Aspinall-Oslander (1940)

Boswell, James, *Private Papers of James Boswell*, vol. 2, ed. Geoffrey Scott and Frederick A. Pottle (1928–34)

Bubb Dodington, George, *The Diary of the Late George Bubb Dodington, Baron of Melcombe Regis* (1784)

Burney, Dr. Charles, *The Present State of Music in Germany, the Netherlands and the United Provinces* (1775)

—, *Memoirs of Dr. Charles Burney, 1726–1769*, ed. S. Klima, G. Bowers, and K. S. Grant (1988)

Byng, John, *The Torrington Diaries: Containing the Tours through England and Wales . . . 1781–1794*, vol. II (1934)

Calendar of Home Office Papers of the Reign of George III, various volumes, ed. Richard Arthur Roberts (1881)

Carteggio di Pietro e Alessandro Verri, vol. 7: luglio 1774–dicembre 1775, a cura di Emanuele Greppi e di Alessandro Giulini (1931)

Casanova di Seinglat, Giacomo, *History of My Life*, trans. 1970 W. R. Trask, vol. X (1765)

Chudleigh, Lady Mary, *The Poems and Prose of Mary, Lady Chudleigh*, ed. Margaret J. M. Ezell (1993)

Churchill, John, *The Letters and Dispatches of John Churchill, first Duke of Marlborough*, ed. George Murray, vol. 4 (1845)

Coke, Lady Jane, *Letters from Lady Jane Coke to Her Friend Mrs. Eyre at Derby, 1747–1758*, ed. Mrs. Ambrose Rathbone (1899)

Coke, Lady Mary, *The Letters and Journals of Lady Mary Coke*, ed. J. A. Home (1889–96)

Colman, George, *Posthumous Letters, from various Celebrated Men, addressed to Francis Colman, and George Colman the Elder* (1820)

Coxe, William, *Travels into Poland, Russia, Sweden and Denmark*, vol. II (1792)

Defoe, Daniel, *A Tour Through the Whole Island of Great Britain*, vols. 1, 2 (1724, 1725)

Dimsdale, Elizabeth, *An English Lady at the Court of Catherine the Great, the Journal of Baroness Elizabeth Dimsdale 1781*, ed. Anthony Cross (1989)

D'Oberkirch, Baroness, *Memoirs of the Baroness d'Oberkirch*, ed. Count de Montbrison, vol. 3 (1852)

Dobrée, Bonamy, ed., *The Letters of Philip Dormer Stanhope, 4th Earl of Chesterfield*, vol. VI (1932)

Eton College Lists 1678–1790, ed. R. A. Austen Leigh (1907)

Fielding, John, *The New London Spy, Or, A Modern Twenty-Four Hours Ramble Through The Great Metropolis* (1794)

Frederick the Great, *Œuvres de Frédéric le Grand*, Tome XXIV, ed. Johann D. E. Preuss (1846–57)

Gowland, John, *Epitome of a Manuscript Essay on Cutaneous Diseases* (1794)

Granville, A. B., *St. Petersburgh: A Journal of Travels to and from that Capital*, vol. I (1828)

Green, George, *An Original Journey from London to St. Petersburg* (1813)

Grenville Papers, *The Grenville Papers: being the correspondence of Richard Grenville Earl Temple, K.G., The Right Hon. George Grenville, their friends and contemporaries*, ed. William James Smith, vol. IV (1853)

Harris, James, ed., *A Series of Letters of the First Earl of Malmesbury*, vol. 1 (1870)

Herbert, Sidney, *Letters and Diaries of Henry, Tenth Earl of Pembroke and his Circle* (1939)

Hervey, Augustus, *Augustus Hervey's Journal*, ed. David Erskine (1953)

Hervey, John, *Memoirs of the Reign of George II: From His Accession to the Death of Queen Caroline*, vol. I (1848)

—, *Letter-books of John Hervey, First Earl of Bristol*, ed. Sydenham H. A. Hervey (1894)

—, *Some Materials Towards Memoirs of the Reign of George II* (1970)

Hervey, Mary Lepel, *Letters of Mary Lepel, Lady Hervey* (1821)

House of Lords Journal, vol. 34 (1775–6)

Jefferson, Thomas, *The Jefferson Papers* (1743–1826)

Johnson, Samuel, *Letters to and from the late Samuel Johnson*, vol. 1 (1709–1784)

—, *The Vanity of Human Wishes: The Tenth Satire of Juvenal Imitated* (1749)

Justice, Elizabeth, *A Voyage to Russia* (1739)

Keats, John, *The Complete Works of John Keats*, vol. 5 (1820)

Kielmansegge, Count Frederick, *Diary of a Journey to England in the Years 1761–1762* (1902)

Kinservik, Matthew J., ed., *The Production of a Female Pen: Anna Larpent's Account of the Duchess of Kingston's Bigamy Trial of 1776* (2004)

Knight, Lady, *Lady Knight's Letters from France and Italy 1776–1795*, ed. Lady Elliot Drake (1905)

Kurakin, Prince Alexander, *Arkhiv kniazia F. A. Kurakina* (1894)

Letters to and from Henrietta, Countess of Suffolk and her second husband the Hon George Berkeley (1824)

Lord North's Correspondence, 1766–83, ed. Edward Hughes, *English Historical Review*, LXI/243 (April 1947), pp. 218–38

Macdonald, John, *Memoirs of an Eighteenth-century Footman: Travels 1745–1779* (1927)

Manuscripts and Correspondence of James, First Earl of Charlemont, vol. 1 (1891)

Melville, Lewis, ed., *The Trial of the Duchess of Kingston* (1927)

Memoirs and Correspondence of Sir Robert Murray Keith, ed. Mrs. G. Smith, vol. 2 (1849)

Montagu, Elizabeth, *The Letters of Mrs. E. Montagu, with some of the Letters of her Correspondence* (1813)

—, *Queen of the Blue-stockings: Her Correspondence 1720–1761*, ed. Emily J. Climenson (1906)

—, *"Queen of the Blues," Her letters and friendships from 1762 to 1800*, ed. R. Blunt (1923)

More, Hannah, *The Letters of Hannah More*, ed. R. Brimley Johnson (1925)

Noel, Emilia, ed., *Some Letters and Records of the Noel Family* (1910)

Papers of Empress Catherine II from the State Archives of the Foreign Ministry Collected and Published with the Royal Permission on the Instructions of His Majesty Sovereign the Heir Prince Grand Duke Alexander Alexandrovich

Penrose, John, *Letters from Bath 1766–1767* (1983)

Pope, Alexander, *The Works of Alexander Pope* (1753)

Potemkin, Prince, *Memoirs of the Life of Prince Potemkin; Field-Marshal and Commander-in-Chief of the Russian Army* (1812)

Richardson, Samuel, *Correspondence of Samuel Richardson*, ed. A. L. Barbauld (1804)

Richardson, William, *Anecdotes of the Russian Empire in a Series of Letters, written, a few years ago, from St. Petersburg* (1784, new edn 1968)

Roberts, William, *Memoirs of the Life and Correspondence of Mrs. Hannah More*, vol. 1 (1835)

Rochefoucauld, Alexandre de La, *To the Highlands* (1786)

Saussure, César de, *A Foreign View of England in the Reigns of George I & George II: The Letters of Monsieur César de Saussure to his family*, ed. Mme van Muyden (1902)

Selwyn, George, *George Selwyn and his Contemporaries*, ed. John Heneage Jesse, vol. I (1843)

Semple, James, *The Life of Major J. G. Semple Lisle, written by himself* (1799)

—, *Memoirs of the Northern Imposter or Prince of Swindlers: Being a Faithful Narrative of the Adventures, and Deceptions of James George Semple, commonly called Major Semple* (1786)

Sherlock, Martin, *Letters from an English Traveler* (1780)

Smollett, Tobias, *Travels Through France and Italy* (1766)

Sprange, Jasper, *The Tunbridge Wells Guide* (1786)

Swift, Jonathan, *Gulliver's Travels* (1726)

—, "Remarks on the Characters of the Court of Queen Anne," *Swiftiana* (1804)

—, *The Poetical Works of Jonathan Swift* (1879)

Swinburne, Henry, *The Courts of Europe at the Close of the Last Century*, vol. 1 (1841)

Thackeray, William Makepeace, *The History of Henry Esmond* (1852)

—, *The Luck of Barry Lyndon* (1853)

—, *Vanity Fair* (1848)

The Collection of Autograph Letters and Historical Documents formed by Alfred Morrison, The Hamilton and Nelson papers, vol. 1 (1897)

The Private Correspondence of Sarah, Duchess of Marlborough, vol. 2 (1838)

Walpole, Horace, Various volumes of letters (all letters listed by date); *Memoirs of the Reign of King George II*; *Memoirs of the Reign of King George III*; *Complete Works* (of all these, there are numerous editions)

Whitehead, Thomas, *Original Anecdotes of the Late Duke of Kingston and Miss Chudleigh* (1792)

Wollstonecraft, Mary, *The Female Reader*, preface (1789)

Wortley Montagu, Mary, *The Complete Letters of Lady Mary Wortley Montagu*, ed. Robert Halsband, 3 volumes (1965–7)

Wraxall, Nathaniel, *A Tour Through some of the Northern Parts of Europe, particularly Copenhagen, Stockholm and Petersburgh* (1776)

—, *Memoirs of the Courts of Berlin, Dresden, Warsaw and Vienna* (1799)

HISTORICAL MANUSCRIPTS COMMISSION

HMC Carlisle, The Manuscripts of the Earl of Carlisle preserved at Castle Howard (HMSO, 1897); HMC Dartmouth, The Manuscripts of the Earl of Dartmouth, vol. III (HMSO, 1896); HMC Egmont, Manuscripts of the Earl of Egmont: Diary of Viscount Percival afterwards First Earl of Egmont, vol. I, 1730–1733 (HMSO, 1920); HMC Hastings, Report on the Manuscripts of the late Reginald Rawdon Hastings, Esq., of the Manor House, Ashby de la Zouch, vol. III (HMSO, 1934); HMC Rutland, The Manuscripts of His Grace the Duke of Rutland, K.G. preserved at Belvoir Castle, vol. III (HMSO, 1894); HMC Townshend, The Manuscripts of the Corporations of Southampton and King's Lynn (HMSO, 1887) [pp. 370, 369: Hamilton ill; Hervey in Lisbon]; HMC Various, Report on Manuscripts in Various Collections, vol. VIII: The Manuscripts of The Hon. Frederick Lindley Wood; M. L. S. Clements, Esq.; S. Philip Unwin, Esq. (HMSO, 1913)

ARCHIVES (UNPRINTED MATERIAL)

References to specific manuscript numbers are in the notes. I consulted the following collections:

Bedfordshire Archives

Wrest Park (Lucas) Papers: Letters between Beilby Porteus and 2nd Lord Grantham

British Library

Barrington Papers; Diary/Letter-book of Samuel Bentham;
    Egerton family papers; Forrest's Tours; Hardwicke Papers;
    Portland Papers; Chudleigh, Elizabeth, Duchess of Kingston,
    letters written in various secretarial hands to her jeweler, Cox

Durham University Library

Letters of Rev. Robert Wharton

Hampshire Record Office

Letters of the 1st Earl of Malmesbury

House of Lords Record Office: The Trial

HL/PO/JO/10/7/479B; HL/PO/JO/10/7/503A

Kent History and Library Center

Norman letters

Lincolnshire Archives

FL Glover 4/2/2, 5, 7, 25, 44, 45, 49

London Metropolitan Archives (LMA)

DL/C/0277—microfilm X/019/143: Consistory Court Deposition
    Book; DL/C/0280—microfilm X079/110: Consistory Court
    Deposition Book 1776–1780; DL/C/0558—cause papers,
    matrimonial and testamentary; DL/C/0558/012–013—Hervey
    (Augustus) Including affidavit in French and translation:
    jactitation of marriage; DL/C/0558/052–055—Hervey
    (Duchess of Kingston v Earl of Bristol) Including inhibition,
    Court of Arches: office copy indictment [Middlesex Sessions],
    for bigamy: office copy verdict, House of Lords: appeal;
    DL/C/0559/001—Chudleigh v Hervey, divorce for adultery

National Library of Scotland

EC's letter to electress before her trial; Letters of the Elliot family
    of Minto

National Library of Wales: Manuscript Collection

Peniarth 418, f. 80: gifts for EC from the electress; ff. 83–3a: gratitude from EC re. lawyers for ecclesiastical court case; f. 84: EC and Kingston visiting Alice Yeo nr Plymouth; f. 113: Christmas at Pierrepont

Norfolk Record Office

Walsingham (Merton) Collection, WLS XLVIII/1, 425X9: EC and Kingston in West Country

Royal Bank of Scotland Archives: Drummond's

DR/427/73, f. 1253: Captain refuses to sail *Duchess of Kingston*; DR/427/94, f. 1022: EC payments to Meadows; DR/427/102, f. 1022 and 1026: EC's finances in 1784
DR/427/110, f. 1437: £5,000 added to EC account; DR/427/114, f. 1021: EC paying Evelyn an allowance; and others

Royal Collection Trust

Georgian Papers Programme, https://gpp.rct.uk

Surrey History Center

Manorial Records of Frensham Beale; sale of Pierrepont Lodge

The National Archives (TNA)

C 12/1051/2, ff. 1–3: Meadows revive their case; C 24/2450: Ann Craddock eyewitness; C 33/442, f. 160: Chancery stop EC receiving money; C 33/444, ff. 48 and 606–7: contents of Kingston's estate; Chancery rule in favor of EC over Kingston's estate; C 33/446, f. 501: Meadows revive their case; C 33/448, f. 484: delay in EC, Hervey, and Meadows Chancery case; C 193/133B: the trial
FO 65/11: taxes in Estonia [in 1783 the head (or soul tax) introduced by Peter I for Russia's interior was extended to the Baltic region]; FO 68/1: illness of electress
LC 5/23 f. 221: Mrs. Chudleigh becomes housekeeper at Windsor Castle

PRO 30/43/11, Gertrude Harris's travel journal, ff. 84, 85, 93:
   St. Petersburg society; PRO 30/43/19, f. 2: Semple
SP 80/218: British ambassador refuses to receive EC in Vienna; SP
   81/112: Elector of Bavaria refused to receive EC as duchess; EC
   applied to be made a countess in Bavaria
SP 88/115: EC reunited with electress 1778; illness of electress; SP 91/101
   ff. 161, 164, 182, 190, 201: EC arrives St. Petersburg 1777; EC
   wants to present herself at court in St. Petersburg; EC's yacht; SP
   93/29, ff. 97–8: report on EC wanting to remain Protestant
SP 98/79, f. 68: Villa Negroni; SP 98/80, ff. 37–8: EC's belongings
   under pope's protection
WORK 11/24/5: Duchess of Kingston trial prob. 11/715/415, will of
   Sir Thomas Chudleigh.

University of Nottingham Manuscripts and Special Collections

Manvers Papers (Ma); Newcastle (Clumber) Collection (Ne C);
   Portland (Welbeck) Collection (Pl, Pw)

West Sussex Record Office

Arundell MSS (letters of Father John Thorpe), 2667/20/22
Royal Collection Trust Georgian Papers Programme, www.gpp.rct.uk

Archives Nationales de France

Z/1J/1132: Elizabeth's house in Montmartre; O/1/201, f. 52: EC
   applies to change name of her estate to Chudleigh; MC/ET/
   LXXI/76, 78, 79, 81, 84, 85, 87

Beinecke Rare Book and Manuscript Library, Yale University

EC's letters to Cox (also BL) Nov. 13, 1778; Feb. 6, Mar. 3, Apr. 29,
   1779
MSS 3211, Feb. 29, Mar. 24/Apr. 3, 1780, Apr. 10, 1781, Oct. 5,
   Nov. 21, 1781, Apr. 11, 1788: letters from EC to Bell re. Russia;
   MSS 17662, Sep. 19, 1782: letter to Meadows; MSS 17934,
   May 27, 1782: letter from EC to Mrs. Meadows; Osborn MSS
   17935, Feb. 6, 1779: EC and Duke of Hamilton; Osborn MSS
   (letters of Sir James Harris to Batt), f. 3: Sir James Harris on EC

Houghton Library University of Harvard

58M-110, Mrs. Elizabeth Montagu to her sister, May 8, 1749

National Historical Archive of Belarus

Fond. 694, op.1, d.336, ff. 7–30 Letters between Elizabeth and Prince
    Radziwill

Sächsische Haupstaatsarchiv Dresden

Nachlass Maria Antonia, Nr. 62, Bl. 155–94 Letters from EC to
    Electress of Saxony

Italy

ASV, Segr. Stato, Particolari (Secret Vatican Archive, Secretaryship of
    State, Personalities)

Russia

SIRIO, XXIII (1878), Russian archives

Secondary Sources

Akhamatova, E. N., "A Few Words about Mikhail Antonovich
    Garnovsky," *Russkaya Starina*, XCIV/5 (1898), pp. 401–6
Anon., *An Authentic Detail of particulars relative to the late
    Duchess of Kingston* (1788)
—, *The Northern Hero: Being a Faithful Narrative of the Life,
    Adventures, and Deceptions of James George Semple,
    commonly called Major Semple*, G. Kearsley (1786)
—, *A plain state of the case of Her Grace the Duchess of Kingston
    with considerations calling upon the interference of the high
    powers to stop a prosecution illegally commenced* (1776)
—, *Histoire de la Vie et les Aventures de la Duchesse de Kingston*
    (1789)
—, *The Life and Memoirs of Elizabeth Chudleigh* (1788)
—, *The Life and Memoirs of Elizabeth Chudleigh, afterwards
    Mrs. Hervey and Countess of Bristol, commonly called
    Duchess of Kingston* (1789)

Ashdown, Dulcie M., *Ladies-in-Waiting* (1976)

Ashelford, Jane, *The Art of Dress* (1996)

Baring-Gould, Sabine, *Historic Oddities and Strange Events* (1889)

Barnett, Gerald, *Richard and Maria Cosway* (1995)

Batchelor, Jennie, *The Literary Encyclopedia* (2008)

Black, Jeremy, *The English Press: A History* (2019)

Blanning, T. C. W., *The Eighteenth Century: Europe 1688–1815* (2000)

Bleackley, Horace, *Ladies Fair and Frail: Sketches of the Demimonde during the Eighteenth Century* (1909)

Borman, Tracy, *Henrietta Howard: King's Mistress, Queen's Servant* (2007)

Boyer, Abel, *The History of the Life and Reign of Queen Anne* (1722)

Bucholz, R. O., *The Augustan Court: Queen Anne and the Decline of Court Culture* (1993)

Buck, Anne, *Dress in Eighteenth Century England* (1979)

Cannon, Richard, *Historical Record of the 34th, or Cumberland Regiment of Foot* (1844)

—, *Historical Record of the Fourteenth, or the King's Regiment of Light Dragoons* (1847)

Chadwick, Owen, *The Popes and European Revolution* (1981)

Childe-Pemberton, William S., *The Earl-Bishop: The Life of Frederick Hervey, Bishop of Derry, Earl of Bristol* (1925)

Churchill, Winston S., *A History of the English-Speaking Peoples*, vol. 3: *The Age of Revolution*, ch. 5 (1957)

—, *Marlborough: His Life and Times* (1934)

Cobbett, William, *Parliamentary History of England: 1779*, vol. 20 (1814)

Colley, Linda, *In Defiance of Oligarchy: The Tory Party 1714–1760* (1982)

Cross, Anthony, *By the Banks of the Neva: Chapters from the Lives and Careers of the British in Eighteenth-century Russia* (1997)

Cruickshank, Dan, *The Royal Hospital Chelsea: The Place and the People* (2004)

Curtis Brown, Beatrice, *Elizabeth Chudleigh, Duchess of Kingston* (1927)

Davis, Henry George, *The Memorials of the Hamlet of Knightsbridge* (1859)

Dean, C. G. T., *The Royal Hospital Chelsea* (1950)

Dickens, Charles, ed., *Household Words*, VII (1853)

Elwin, Malcolm, ed., *The Noels and the Milbankes: Their Letters for Twenty-five Years, 1767–1792* (1967)

Felkersam, A., "Gertsoginya Kingston I eyo prebyvanie v Rossii," *Starye Gody* (June 1913), pp. 3–35

Field, Ophelia, *The Favourite* (2002)

Fleming, J., *Robert Adam and his Circle in Edinburgh and Rome* (1962)

Fletcher, Ronald, *The Parkers of Saltram, 1769–89* (1970)

Foote, Samuel, *A Trip to Calais* (1778)

Galt, John, *George the Third: His Court and Family* (1820)

Gervat, Claire, *Elizabeth: The Scandalous Life of an 18th Century Duchess* (2004)

Golden, Janet, *A Social History of Wet Nursing in America: From Breast to Bottle* (1996)

Greig, Hannah, *The Beau Monde: Fashionable Society in Georgian London* (2013)

Grundy, Isobel, *Lady Mary Wortley Montagu: Comet of the Enlightenment* (1999)

Hodson, J. H., "The Building and Alteration of the Second Thoresby House 1767–1804," in *A Nottinghamshire Miscellany*, ed. J. H. Hodson et al. (1962)

Johnson, C. P. C., "Philips Glover and the Duchess of Kingston's French Estates," *Lincolnshire History and Archaeology*, vol. II (1976), pp. 29–34

Karnovich, Evgeny, "The Duchess of Kingston and the Case about her Assets in Russia (1777–1798)," *Russkaya Starina*, XVIII/8 (1877)

Kelly, Ian, *Mr. Foote's Other Leg* (2012)

Lepa, Sven, "The Duchess of Kingston and the Manors of Voka and Toila from 1781 to 1806," from *Õpetatud Eesti Seltsi Aastaraamat: Annales litterarum societatis Esthonicae* (2008)

Livingstone, Natalie, *The Mistresses of Cliveden* (2015)

Martin, Morag, *Selling Beauty: Cosmetics, Commerce, and French Society, 1750–1830* (2009)

Mavor, Elizabeth, *The Virgin Mistress: A Study in Survival; the Life of the Duchess of Kingston* (1964)

Melville, Lewis, ed., *Society at Tunbridge Wells in the Eighteenth Century and After* (1912)

Mingay, G. E., *English Landed Society in the Eighteenth Century* (1963)

Moffat, R. Burnham, *Pierrepont Genealogies from Norman Times to 1913* (1913)

Moody, Henry, *Our Country; or Hampshire in the Reign of Charles II* (1863)

Northcote, James, *The Life of Sir Joshua Reynolds* (1818)

Olsen, Kirstin, *Daily Life in 18th-century England* (1999)

O'Sullivan, Suzanne, *It's All in Your Head: Stories from the Frontline of Psychosomatic Illness* (2015)

Oulton, Walley Chamberlain, *Authentic and Impartial Memoirs of Her Late Majesty Charlotte, Queen of Great Britain and Ireland . . . including various interesting and original particulars never before published* (1819)

Pearce, Charles E., *The Amazing Duchess: being the romantic history of Elizabeth Chudleigh, maid of honour, the Hon. Mrs. Hervey, Duchess of Kingston, and Countess of Bristol* (1911)

Pennant, Thomas, *Some Account of London* (1790)

Porter, Roy, *English Society in the Eighteenth Century* (1982)

Pyatnitsky, Yuri, "The Story of the Peacock Clock," *Nashe Nasledie*, 117 (2016)

Radcliffe, S. M., *Sir Joshua's Nephew* (1930)

Rimbault, E. F., *Soho and its Associations* (1895)

Rodger, N. A. M., *The Command of the Ocean: A Naval History of Britain 1649–1815* (2004)

Roger, Jacques, *Buffon: A Life in Natural History* (1997)

Schama, Simon, *A History of Britain: The British Wars 1603–1776* (2009)

Sebag Montefiore, Simon, *Catherine the Great and Potemkin: The Imperial Love Affair* (2010)

Somerset, Anne, *Ladies-in-Waiting* (2005)

Stainton, L., "Hayward's List: British Visitors to Rome, 1753–1775," *Walpole Society*, 49 (1983)

Stone, Lawrence, *Family, Sex and Marriage in England, 1500–1800* (1979)

—, *Road to Divorce: England, 1530–1987* (1990)

—, *Uncertain Unions: Marriage in England, 1660–1753* (1992)

—, *Broken Lives: Separation and Divorce in England, 1660–1857* (1993)

Summerson, John, *Georgian London* (1945)

Sutton, John Frost, *The Date-Book of Remarkable and Memorable Events Connected with Nottingham and its Neighbourhood 1750–1850* (1852)

Tooke, William, *Life of Catharine II, Empress of Russia*, 5th edn (1800)

Turgenev, Alexander, "Mikhailovich Memoir," *Russkaya Starina*, T.47, No. 9 (1885)

Vickery, Amanda, *The Gentleman's Daughter: Women's Lives in Georgian England* (2003)

—, *Behind Closed Doors: At Home in Georgian England* (2009)

Vorontsov Papers, Arkhiv kniazia Vorontsova (40 vols. 1870–1895), vol. 32.

Walters, John, *The Royal Griffin: Frederick Prince of Wales 1707–51* (1972)

Woolf, Virginia, *The Death of the Moth and Other Essays* (1942)

Worsley, Lucy, *Courtiers: The Secret History of the Georgian Court* (2010)

Wright, Thomas, *England Under the House of Hanover*, vol. I (1848)

LIST OF ILLUSTRATIONS

Family trees by Kiri Marshall

Lainston's twelfth-century chapel of St. Peter, 2017, by the author; Augustus Hervey, a detail from a conversation piece by H. Gravelot, Liotard, and others, 1750, now at Ickworth, National Trust; the 2nd Duke of Kingston, circle of Jean-Baptiste van Loo, 1741, by courtesy of Grigor Pierrepont.

Page 4:
The family of Frederick, Prince of Wales, by George Knapton, 1751, now in the State Dining Room, Windsor Castle; two etchings of Elizabeth as Iphigenia by an unknown artist, c.1749.

Page 5:
Elizabeth Duchess Dowager of Kingston taken at the Bar of the House of Lords engraved for the *Lady's Magazine* and *The representation of the Trial of the Duchess of Kingston at Westminster Hall*, anonymous engraving, 1776; Elizabeth in pastels by Francis Cotes, 1763; a ticket for the trial, courtesy of the British Museum.

Page 6:
Augustus Hervey by Thomas Gainsborough, 1767–8, now at Ickworth, National Trust; Lady Frances Meadows, eighteenth-century school of Nathaniel Hone, photograph by Patrick Langton, courtesy of Robert and Charlotte Brackenbury; the Bishop of Derry, 4th Earl of Bristol by Élisabeth Louise Vigée Le Brun, 1790, painted in Naples, now at Ickworth; Horace Walpole by John Giles Eccardt, 1754, and Lady Mary Coke by Allan Ramsay, 1762.

Page 7:
Catherine the Great by Fyodor Rokotov, 1780, in the State Hermitage Museum; Prince Grigory Potemkin by Johann Baptist von Lampi the Elder, c.1790, in the Hermitage; Pope Clement XIV by Giovanni Domenico Porta, 1770s, and the Electress of Saxony, self-portrait, c.1772.

Page 8:
Kingston House, Knightsbridge, 1854, watercolor by Thomas Hosmer Shepherd in the British Museum; engraving of Chudleigh in

Estonia, *Chudleigh in Estland*, 1859, by Wilhelm Siegfried Stavenhagen; Thoresby Park, 1818, drawn by J. P. Neale, engraved by H. Hobson; photographs of Château de Sainte-Assise, 2019, and Holme Pierrepont, 2019, by the author.

Inside cover:
St. James's Park and the Mall, British School, *c*.1745, the Royal Collection Trust / © Her Majesty Queen Elizabeth II 2021
A View of the Fire-workes and Illuminations at his Grace the Duke of Richmond's at White-Hall and on the River Thames, on Monday May 15, 1749, Perform'd by the direction of Charles Frederick Esq. Etching by an unknown artist © akg-images: Fireworks/London/1749/Copper Engrav.

ACKNOWLEDGMENTS

The genesis of this book was the startling appearance of Elizabeth Chudleigh in the masterful *Catherine the Great and Potemkin*, written by Simon Sebag Montefiore. With his advice, encouragement, and wisdom, curiosity became obsession, which in turn became this book.

Across thousands of miles and over many months I traced Elizabeth's thoughts and footsteps, from the luminous ballrooms of Catherine the Great to the Tudor hallways of the home of the Duke of Kingston's family. Some of the locations in this book survive as if untouched by time, others swept away as if they never were; but either way, archivists, curators, family, friends, and historians all made this project joyous and fruitful.

In England, I owe thanks to Charlotte and Robert Brackenbury at Holme Pierrepont Hall; Gregor Pierrepont at Thoresby; John Howell at Lukesland; Victoria Slater at Lainston House Hotel; David Lyall and Emma Crunden at the Royal Hospital Chelsea; and Jane Branfield and the Duke of Wellington at Stratfield Saye. I am also indebted to Dr. James Arkell of the Nightingale Hospital, who dauntlessly applied some of his expertise to a cold case from a quarter of a millennium ago.

For my Russian research, thanks are due to the historian and archivist Lyuba Vinogradova; the inimitable and good-humored Geraldine Norman and Janice Sacher of the Hermitage Foundation UK; Dr. Mikhail Piotrovsky, director of the State Hermitage Museum; the Hermitage's Natalia Yuryevna Bakhareva, the late Marina Nikolayevna Lopato, and the art historian Catherine

Phillips. All so generously opened my eyes to the wonders and mysteries of Elizabeth's life in St. Petersburg. In Rome, much gratitude to the ingenious historian Giampiero Brunelli.

Of course, there would be no book without the assistance of insightful archivists here and abroad. Here, notably the Historical Manuscripts Commission; Kirsty McGill at Bedfordshire Archives; the British Library; Rhianna Watson at Durham University Library; Adam Jones at Hampshire Record Office; the House of Lords Record Office; Lara Joffe at Kent History and Library Center; Jan Dann at Lincolnshire Archives; London Metropolitan Archives; Iona Murphy at the National Library of Scotland; Linda Davies at the National Library of Wales; Elizabeth Chaplin at Norfolk Record Office; Plymouth and West Devon Record Office; Lyn Crawford at the Royal Bank of Scotland Archives; Joanna Murtagh at Surrey History Center; The National Archives; University of Nottingham Manuscripts and Special Collections; and the Georgian Papers Programme at the Royal Collection. Abroad, Isabelle Geoffroy and Sophie Olive at the Archives Nationales de France; Sara Powell at the Beinecke Rare Book and Manuscript Library at Yale; Mary Haegert and Will Gregg at the Houghton Library at Harvard; the National Historical Archive of Belarus, the National Archives of Estonia, and Dr. Jörg Ludwig at Sächsisches Staatsarchiv—Hauptstaatsarchiv, Dresden.

For general writerly and other support, in no particular order, my thanks and love go to Richard Dennen (Nostradamus to some), Frances Osborne, Plum Sykes, Jackie Higgins, Joanne Cash, Aurora Dunluce, Angela Lynch, Luke and Liza Johnson, Alain and Charlotte de Botton, Luke and Liza Johnson, Helen James, Emma Walmsley, Katharine Macdonald, Kate Morley, Ed and Alice Heathcoat Amory, Ian Livingstone, Genevieve Davies, and Sasha Slater.

I have endless gratitude to and admiration for my agent Georgina Capel and her team, Rachel Conway and Irene Baldoni. Heartfelt thanks too to the clear- and far-sighted Ian Marshall at Simon & Schuster, who did a wonderful job of overseeing and directing the project; as did Louise Davies who cast her sensitive eye over everything. Thanks also to Rebecca McCarthy, Sophia Akhtar, and Kiri Marshall. For this American edition, I am indebted to the marvelous and wise Peter Borland at Atria, his assistant Sean

Delone, and Samantha Hoback. All have been such a pleasure to work with.

I am indebted to the resourcefulness and advice of Dr. Rebecca Coll; to the inspiring historians who read the manuscript: my glorious ally Natalie Livingstone; the barnstorming Andrew Roberts; the astute Amanda Foreman; and the pioneering Hallie Rubenhold. Other sharp readers in my wonderful family to whom I am indebted in so many ways: my ever-encouraging mother Patricia Ostler, my sister Jane Ostler, my parents-in-law Piers Paul Read and Emily Read.

To my children, Clemmie, Nathaniel, and Angelica, thank you for being so game when I made you break into the derelict parklands of the Château de Sainte-Assise, or diverted you all to the car park of the University of Nottingham archives when you were supposed to be on holiday. And to my husband, Albert Read, for reading and rereading countless drafts; I am in awe of your judgment.

INDEX

EC indicates Elizabeth Chudleigh.